Guide to Netscape Navigator Gold

Guide to Netscape Navigator Gold

Neil Randall

Ziff-Davis Press
an imprint of Macmillan Computer Publishing USA
Emeryville, California

Development Editor	Kelly Green
Copy Editors	Dave Hepler and Margo Hill
Technical Reviewer	Mark Hall
Project Coordinators	Barbara Dahl and Ami Knox
Cover Illustration	Regan Honda
Book Design	Paper Crane Graphics, Berkeley
Word Processing	Howard Blechman
Page Layout	Janet Piercy
Indexer	Anne Leach

Ziff-Davis Press imprint books are produced on a Macintosh computer system with the following applications: FrameMaker®, Microsoft® Word, QuarkXPress®, Adobe Illustrator®, Adobe Photoshop®, Adobe Streamline™, MacLink®*Plus*, Aldus® FreeHand™, Collage Plus™.

If you have comments or questions or would like to receive a free catalog, call or write:
Ziff-Davis Press, an imprint of
Macmillan Computer Publishing USA
5903 Christie Avenue
Emeryville, CA 94608
510-601-2000

ISBN 1-56276-396-2

Manufactured in the United States of America
10 9 8 7 6 5 4 3 2 1

For Catherine and Michelle

Contents at a Glance

Table of Contents

Part 2 Solid Gold: The Fastest Way to Create Web Pages

Part 3 Pure Gold: Advanced HTML

Acknowledgments

I have a feeling that writing this book was probably a bit like pulling teeth, but since I've never actually pulled teeth I really can't say. What I do know is that the delays in the Netscape Gold software itself caused me, my team, and my editors all sorts of fascinating moments. For actual users of the software, there's no question that the delays were a good idea, but for those of us writing about it they made things a tad difficult. But then, it's only the users that matter, especially those users who are now holding this book. I mention all this as a prelude to thanking the people who helped me get this book finished.

First, my team. Stephanie Wunder was, as always, excellent from start to finish, shifting topics and direction with nary a word of complaint (well...not to me at least), and turning in material on time and fully complete. Celine Latulipe similarly came through with her usual flair, style, and reliability, and provided a last-minute addition that I couldn't have done without. Marcia Italiano delivered strong contributions in several chapters, and helped me greatly with the project's organization. Keith McGowan gave me some crucial behind-the-scenes help, despite the fact that he had no time to do so. I thank all of these people, without whom this book simply wouldn't have happened.

Next, the people at Z-D Press. Suzanne Anthony, Kelly Green, Barbara Dahl, Ami Knox, and Steve DeLacy had the unpleasant task of continually trying to pry chapters out of me, and they did so with considerably more humor than I myself managed at times. For their patience and support, my thanks. They understood better than I the problems of writing a book about a continually moving target, and they kept me going even when I thought the software itself had let me down.

From Netscape Communications itself, thanks to Chris Holten for putting up with my endless early requests for the software, and Len Feldman for helping me get started by explaining what the program would look like and what it would let me do. And of course to the entire Gold design team, without whom there wouldn't be a whole lot of point to this book at all.

And once again, my thanks to Heather, for enduring yet another impossible project. If anybody is standing in a book store and reading this paragraph, wondering whether or not to buy this book, I promise you that the proceeds will be spent on a lovely vacation for this amazingly deserving woman. There—if that doesn't do it, I don't know what will.

PART

1

The Golden Age: Netscape, the One-Stop Browser

- *What's a Web Browser, Anyway?*
- *What Do Web Browsers Do?*
- *How Does Netscape Navigator Gold Fit In?*
- *Everybody Must Think Netscape's the Best Thing in the Whole Wide World, Right?*
- *So I Should Feel Bad about Designing for Netscape?*

CHAPTER 1

The Most Important Browser of All

THE UNIVERSE IS HARDLY LACKING IN WORLD WIDE WEB BROWSERS. If you're seriously into navigating the Web, you have several at your disposal, whether your operating system of choice is UNIX, the Macintosh, or Microsoft Windows. For Windows users in particular, browsers are practically crawling out of the webwork, and you could easily spend a full day of your life installing the lot of them and trying them out. You'd even have to *pay* for some of them, and on the Internet that's pretty unusual. Most software on the Net is available for free, at least for nonprofit uses and at least for a limited period of time.

What's a Web Browser, Anyway?

What exactly is a Web browser? Actually, *browser* isn't the "official" word for it. The technical name is World Wide Web *client*. The Internet is designed according to a *client-server* model of computing, where the software that feeds programs and files to the network is called the *server,* and the software with which users gain access is called the *client*. The client-server model applies to electronic mail (e-mail), file transfer (FTP), newsgroups (Usenet), and every other Internet activity, including the World Wide Web.

All these applications work essentially the same. In e-mail, a mail server (or two) controls the sending and receiving of the mail, and your e-mail program—technically a mail client—allows you to read your mail and compose messages to other networked users. Similarly, you use an FTP *client* program to retrieve files from a computer that has been established as an FTP *server*. And while news servers are far less common than FTP or mail servers, you still need a news client to get newsgroup messages off the news server on which they're stored.

The same holds true for the World Wide Web. Your computer contains a program called a Web *client*—better known as a browser—and what it accesses is a computer that's been set up as a Web *server*. If nobody had Web pages on a server, your browser would be useless, except to look at whatever Web pages you had stored on your own hard drive. A Web server does exactly what its name suggests—it serves Web pages—and your browser is programmed to retrieve and display them.

What Do Web Browsers Do?

When originally designed back in the very early 1990s, the Web browser's only function was to retrieve and display documents written in *Hypertext Markup Language*, better known as HTML. HTML is a coding language, in which all special formats and functions have specific codes. When a Web browser retrieves an HTML file, it interprets these codes and displays them as the author of the file meant them to be displayed.

So what? Good question. The important thing about HTML is that it's exactly the same no matter what operating system you're working with or which Web browser your readers use. In other words, HTML is platform-independent and client-independent. That means—and here's the important part—that the World Wide Web can be used by anyone with access to a Web browser, and that everybody who accesses a Web page sees exactly the same thing. It's true compatibility, something the computer world has only been able to *dream* about.

The compatibility dream is slipping, but we'll get to that in a minute.

The World Wide Web is made possible by a protocol called *Hypertext Transport Protocol*, or HTTP. (A *protocol* is simply a technical standard that allows computers to exchange information.) Through HTTP, Web browsers can retrieve HTML pages. But one of the most powerful features of the Web is that it isn't restricted to one protocol only. The Web was designed to incorporate the Internet's other leading protocols as well, including FTP, gopher, Telnet, newsgroups, and e-mail.

What this means is that your Web browser can accomplish all your most common Internet tasks. You can cruise the Web, you can navigate gopher menus, you can retrieve and download files via FTP, you can log into another system through Telnet, and you can even interact with newsgroup and e-mail users. That's the ideal, but until recently it wasn't completely implemented.

How Does Netscape Navigator Gold Fit In?

Netscape Navigator Gold (we'll just call it Gold) offers the most complete one-stop Internet package to date. In fact, there isn't much you can do on the Internet that you *can't* do through Gold. As you'll discover over the next several chapters, Gold gives you the most advanced view of the World Wide Web, offers a thoroughly functional FTP package, and lets you enter and traverse the Net's many remaining gopher sites. (Gopher sites are rapidly becoming obsolete, their functions taken over by the Web itself.)

But that's not all. Gold also gives you a full newsgroup program that lets you read *and* post to newsgroups, and an e-mail package that lets you not only compose e-mail messages but read incoming news as well. Most browsers give you a window for composing mail, but until now none has offered e-mail reading capabilities. The closest has been Wollongong's excellent Emissary package (http://www.twg.com/), but there e-mail is effectively separate from the browser itself. In Gold, e-mail and news are separate windows within the main browser window, and all three windows are closely linked.

For the regular Internet tasks of communicating and collecting information, then, Gold is a one-stop resource. It is first of all the most advanced Web browser of all, and therefore offers the best possible means of viewing the World Wide Web, by far the Internet's most popular information resource. With the inclusion of full e-mail and newsgroup support, Gold becomes a program you never have to close at all. The Web, e-mail, newsgroups, and FTP are the Internet's popular functions, and Gold incorporates the lot. The only things you don't get are some of the specialized HTML capabilities found in programs like Microsoft's Internet Explorer (http://www.microsoft.com/windows/ie/ie.htm) and Simon Fraser University's NCompass (http://www.excite.sfu.ca/NCompass/), but if you need those capabilities you can easily download and install them, write HTML code for them, and copy it into Gold. For the most part, though, there's very little Gold can't handle that you're likely to want to do.

Gold's capabilities extend to one other extremely popular task: creating your own Web pages. Until very recently, writing Web pages was a two-step process: write the HTML code, then load the page into a browser and see what it looks like. Programs like Microsoft's Internet Assistant (http://www.microsoft.com/msoffice/freestuf/msword/download/ia/default.htm), NaviSoft's NaviPress (http://www.navisoft.com/), and Vermeer's Front Page, (http://www.vermeer.com/) introduced the idea of editing a page directly inside a Web browser, but all of them have significant limitations in HTML features. Netscape Gold raises the ante to much higher stakes by allowing users to create a full-featured HTML page, complete with all Netscape enhancements, right inside Netscape Navigator itself. The result? An ability to use the best browser on the planet to design pages for that browser, without ever leaving the browser to do so. This is extremely powerful, and it's what this book is all about.

Everybody Must Think Netscape's the Best Thing in the Whole Wide World, Right?

Uh, no. I do, but I'm obviously biased (after all, I want people to buy this book). Still, to judge from the market share Netscape appears to have achieved (anywhere from 55 to 80 percent of the browser market, depending on whom you listen to), the majority of the online world thinks very highly of it. But a sizable contingent of Netscape haters, or at least Netscape mistrusters, remains. Simply put, they think Netscape has betrayed the initial concept of the World Wide Web.

The problem lies in those HTML items called *Netscape extensions.* Basically, what happened was this. When Netscape Communications formed to create a new browser, they decided that they would distinguish Netscape from other browsers, specifically the famous and ubiquitous NCSA Mosaic (http://www.ncsa.uiuc.edu/SDG/Software/Mosaic/). There were a number of ways to do so, but one of the most dramatic would be to support and incorporate elements of HTML that hadn't yet been officially approved. By whom, you ask? The Internet Engineering Task Force (IETF) cooperatively decides what will ultimately stand as official HTML features, and many that Netscape wanted to include were proposed but not yet adopted. So Netscape adopted them for their browser anyway.

(Actually, there's a bit of irony in the relationship between Mosaic and Netscape. The developers who joined to form Netscape Communications were originally the developers of Mosaic at NCSA—the National Center for

Supercomputing Applications at the University of Illinois. When they formed their new company, they called it Mosaic Communications, and the browser was simply called Netscape. The Netscape name became so popular, however, that they changed the company name to Netscape Communications, and renamed the browser Netscape Navigator.)

The result was a powerful browser that offered Web designers significantly greater control over how their pages would appear. This would seem to be a good thing, but it also meant that browsers other than Netscape couldn't display them the way they were intended. This meant that the Web community's dream of full compatibility no longer existed, as the danger of proprietary code raised its ugly head. The serious Internet community wanted an HTML standard; and Netscape's new tags, however useful and attractive, deviated from that standard. The community began to howl.

Netscape listened, but not completely. Each release of Netscape has seen an increasing number of special HTML elements added, and Navigator Gold is no exception. Among the most controversial is the use of frames, which you'll see throughout this book. Frames are certain to become a huge success in Web design, yet Netscape put them in place without really telling anyone. The result is an IETF scrambling to figure out what to do with frames as HTML standards, a number of software firms trying to get their browsers to support frames, and any number of Web designers remaking their pages to incorporate them. But since only Netscape Navigator and NCompass currently support them, they're anything but platform-independent and browser-independent.

Netscape has helped build the Web beyond anyone's wildest expectations. But through its insistence on unsupported HTML features, in many ways it has undermined the Web as well. The company's greatest competition right now is no longer NCSA, a research institution, but rather Microsoft, the greatest software heavyweight of all time. Both companies believe in giving their users whatever they want, and ultimately the two could split the Web and its dream of perfect compatibility asunder. That's the fear among the Web's long-time researchers, and as a Web designer it's your responsibility to know what's going on.

So I Should Feel Bad about Designing for Netscape?

Not at all. Netscape Navigator is the most popular browser in the world. You owe it to yourself to learn how to tailor-make your pages for its capabilities, because your readers will expect it. In fact, you owe it to yourself to master the browser's strengths, and to adopt new Netscape enhancements as they become available. But you might consider offering your pages in a more standard format as well, simply as a means of increasing your readership. By all means shoot for the stars, but keep in mind there are people on the Web with airplanes rather than spaceships.

Just remember this: When you design for Netscape Navigator, you're designing for the Internet itself. With Netscape Navigator Gold, your design work just became much easier.

Caveat Downloader

Caveat emptor is Latin for "let the buyer beware." But since it's permissable for all users to simply download Gold before deciding whether or not to buy it, I decided on the distinctly non-Latin "downloader" instead.

Here's the "beware" part —Netscape Navigator Gold 2.01, the first official release of the product and the one on which this book is based, lacks many important Web design capabilities. Among these are forms, tables, imagemaps, frames, and Java, and there are more. These were promised in the initial announcements, but as the program slipped deadline after deadline the company decided to add them later. Gold remains an excellent program, but as of right now it won't solve all your Web authoring needs.

As a result, Part 3 of this book discusses raw HTML coding only, which is much less nice to look at than Gold's dialog boxes. Later editions will incorporate Gold's new capabilities as they appear. If you wish, you can experiment with other HTML editors, many of which *do* incorporate tables, forms, and so on, and extract the code you create into your Gold documents.

- *The Golden Screen*
- *Home Sweet Standard Home*
- *What's All the Fuss About?*
- *The Joy of Frames*
- *Electronic Mail*
- *Newsgroups*
- *A Sip of Java*

- *Plug-In—to the Future*

CHAPTER

2

Take the Golden Tour

NOW THAT YOU HAVE NETSCAPE NAVIGATOR GOLD INSTALLED and running, it's time for a quick tour. A tour of what? Good question. Normally you think of Gold as software for touring and writing for the Web, and that's partly what we'll do here. Mostly, though, in this chapter you'll be touring Gold itself; you'll be learning the software by doing what it does best, making its way through the World Wide Web.

The World Wide Web's a cool place. It has been since it first hit the news back in 1993, and it shows no signs of lessening in coolness. To view the Web you need a browser, but to view the Web in its full unexpurgated glory you need the best browser on the market. Fortunately for us, that means Netscape Navigator Gold. (Which is fortunate, because if the best browser was something else you'd feel ripped off about buying this book, and we'd have wished we'd written a different one.) Surfing the Net no longer means choosing between browsers that offer essentially the same functions and data presentation; it means downloading Gold and seeing the Web again through new eyes.

In this tour, you'll visit several sites. Each site demonstrates one of Netscape's basic or enhanced features while simultaneously displaying the visual effects produced by the software design itself. Sit back and relax, put your feet up on your keyboard, and sip away at a good, relaxing something or other. Or, if you prefer, fire up Gold and follow along for the full electronic effect. It's your choice.

The Golden Screen

Not surprisingly, the first thing you'll notice when you load Netscape Gold is the display itself. There are several major components, and we'll run through them all here. We'll move, in a Western cultural fashion, from left to right and top to bottom. Figure 2.1 shows the entire display; just keep referring back to it as you nip through the brief explanations.

The Menu Bar

Located along the fashionable top of the screen, you'll find Gold's *sine qua non*, the menu bar. What's in the menus is covered in detail in Chapter 3, so there's no point spending much time on them here. Table 2.1 lists the functions of these menus.

The Toolbar

As software designers have discovered, there are basically three kinds of people in the world—users who prefer menus, users who prefer keyboard shortcuts, and users who prefer toolbar icons. So far, this tour accommodated the first group; here, it accommodates the third. (If you're really dedicated to keyboard shortcuts, even to the exclusion of all else, head straight for Chapter 3).

Here they are, button by button, in Table 2.2.

Get used to the button bar; you'll use it often. Clicking the Back icon is faster than selecting Go/Back, for example, and Reload is a frequently used button as well. The most useful of all, though, is Stop, which you'll find yourself clicking whenever a page is taking forever to download. And, of course,

Figure 2.1

The Netscape screen as seen from Windows 95

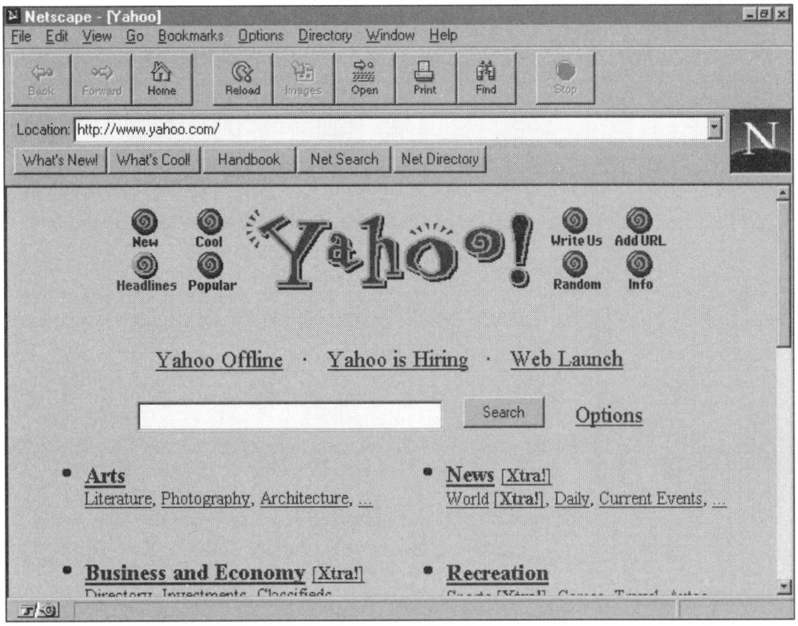

as a Web author in the making, you'll be hitting the Edit button so often you'll wear it out.

The Location Box

The Location box has two related functions. First, it offers a place to type URLs (see the Introduction), so that you can go directly to a specific site and page on the Web. In this way, it is identical to clicking the Open button or selecting Open Location from the File menu (which, by all rights, should be in the Go menu for precisely this reason).

When you're typing in the URL, the name of this box changes to Go To. Once the page is loaded, it goes back to Location.

The second function of the Location box, available for Windows users only, is to let you revisit sites you've recently visited. Netscape's handbook says it stores the most recent ten sites you've visited. As I'm writing this, it has 15 sites stored. Who knows what the limit truly might be?

The Directory Buttons

The directory buttons take you directly to some of the sites also featured in the Directory and Help menus. Table 2.3 tells you where they take you.

Table 2.1

Golden Menus

MENU	FUNCTION
File	Start the HTML editing function, go to a specific Web location, open a local HTML file, start a new browser window, save the files showing on the screen, send e-mail messages, print documents, and—perish the thought—exit Gold entirely.
Edit	Undo, Cut, Copy, Paste, and Find—the usual.
View	Reload a document from the source server, reload an individual frame cell, load unloaded images, refresh the screen, obtain document information, see a document's HTML source code.
Go	Go back or forward one location, load the home page, stop loading a page, access pages viewed during the current session.
Bookmarks	Add the current page as a bookmark for future reference, view and work with saved bookmarks, go directly to bookmarked sites.
Options	Set preferences for appearance, helper applications, e-mail and news servers, security issues, memory and disk cache; toggle toolbar, location, directory buttons, and Java console on or off; specify document encoding.
Directory	Go directly to Netscape's home page, What's New page, What's Cool page, Galleria, Search sites, Internet directory, and White pages.
Window	Open or access Mail and News windows, address book, and bookmarks window, as well as any currently open windows.
Help	Get help on a variety of topics, access Netscape handbook and other useful guides.

The Directory buttons can be toggled on and off. If you want to see more of the actual documents on the screen, these buttons should be the first to go.

Content Area

The big window that contains the Web page itself is called the *content area*. Here you'll find the actual HTML formatting, complete with graphics, animations, Java programs, colors, image maps, frames, and everything else that makes the Web look great. Since most of this book is about the content area, however, there is no point dealing with it now. You'll work with it throughout most of the remaining chapters.

Table 2.2

Golden Buttons

TOOLBAR ICON BUTTON	FUNCTION
Back	Go back to the previously loaded page.
Forward	Go forward to the next (already loaded) page.
Home	Load the home page, as specified in General Preferences.
Reload	Retrieve a fresh copy of the currently loaded page from the original server.
Images	Load the images on the page (only available if Auto Load Images is toggled off).
Open	Access a Web site by typing in the URL manually.
Print	Print the current document.
Find	Find a text string in the current document.
Stop	Stop loading the current document (only available while Gold is in the process of retrieving a file over the Web).
Edit	Open the Edit window with current document loaded and ready for editing.

Table 2.3

Golden Directories

DIRECTORY BUTTON ICON	FUNCTION
What's New	Takes you directly to Netscape's What's New page (same as Directory/What's New).
What's Cool	Takes you directly to Netscape's What's Cool page (same as Directory/What's Cool).
Handbook	Takes you directly to the handbook for your particular version of Gold (same as Help/Handbook).
Net Search	Takes you directly to Netscape page with links to search engines (same as Directory/Internet Search).
Net Directory	Takes you directly to Netscape page with links to Internet subject directories (same as Directory/Internet Directory).
Software	Takes you directly to the Netscape page for upgrading or subscribing to software upgrades (same as Help/Software).

Home Sweet Standard Home

Everybody likes to start off with a bang, but most Web authors introduce themselves to the art of World Wide Web design by constructing a standard, fairly boring home page involving basic hypertext links and graphics. It's not that these people aren't creative; it's just that they don't have the time to develop anything more elaborate. The result, however, is an almost infinite number of personal home pages that do little more than offer a few links to more interesting places.

If you've browsed the Web at all you have undoubtedly come across such personal home pages and are familiar with their almost regulated format and design. Most include a boldface title, hard rule, graphics, and directory of favorite links. As an example, fire up Gold, type **http://randall.uwaterloo.ca/** in the Location box, and check out my own dull, boring, and stale home page. You should now be looking at a screen that looks like Figure 2.2.

Figure 2.2

Neil Randall's home page viewed with Netscape Gold. Notice the sparkling use of elaborate design features. So how'd he get the gig writing this book, anyway?

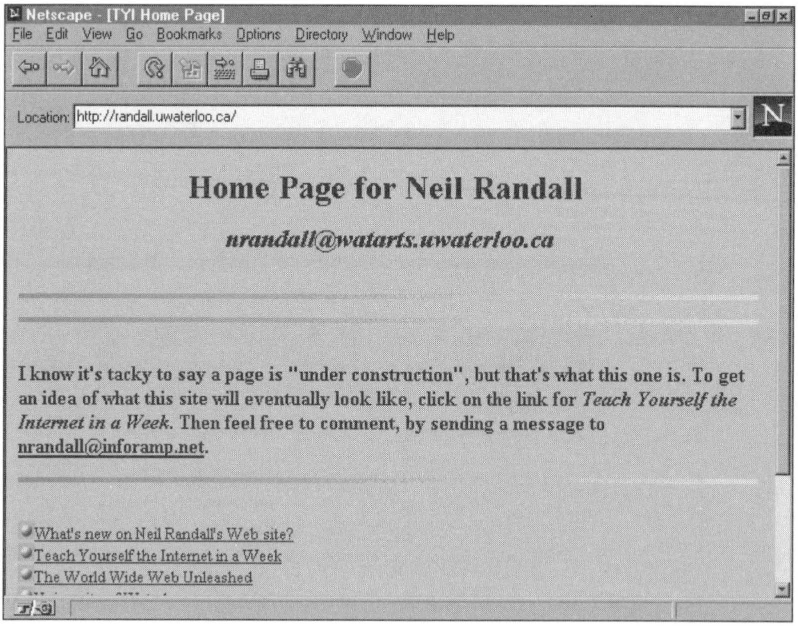

As you'll discover while you wend your way through the Web, the basic simple home page display remains pretty much the same no matter where you go. Perhaps you will notice some insignificant alterations in background color or font style, but the standard appearance and functioning of simple pages are quite similar. You can create pages like this with Netscape Gold almost immediately, as you'll discover when you get to Chapter 13. Only when you tackle more advanced Internet applications will Netscape Gold's superior capabilities be revealed.

But just so you know I'm not a complete dud, click on the link for this book from my home page and see a site awash with color, interactivity, and just plain coolness.

What's All the Fuss About?

So what can the Netscape Gold browser provide that other Web browsers can't? Lots, really. Gold's enhanced capabilities feature faster loading of JPEG images (meaning the pictures will get to you faster than before), HTML integration for e-mail and newsgroups (meaning that Web addresses will appear as hyperlinks in messages), secure document transactions (meaning you can jam your credit card to the limit buying stuff without worrying that someone's about to rip off your card number), and a large variety of additional visual bonuses.

As Web pages develop and grow, Netscape Gold allows them to reach aesthetic heights that were previously impossible. For example, check out the physical design and advanced applications offered by Toronto's James Gang advertising and marketing firm in their Nerdheaven site. Pay special attention to the loading time of complex text and graphic images. The site is at http://www.nerdheaven.com, and the opening page is shown in Figure 2.3

The Joy of Frames

One of the hottest features that Netscape has introduced to Gold users involves dividing pages into separate functioning frames. Frames allow users to view different pages in a site on a single screen—a bit like opening multiple browsers at once. Infi.Net's Cool Site of the Day archive (http://cool.infi.net) uses frames to coordinate directories and sort pages by date (see Figure 2.4). Users may select an archive by month and year, view the contents, and link to the desired site, all on the same Web screen. (Yet another strong use of Netscape's frames feature is the Atlantic Records site at http://www.atlantic-records.com.)

Each frame has its own distinct URL that can point to and be targeted by other active URLs. Developers can now incorporate banners, ledgers, tables of contents, and display panels into their designs. The implications are endless—scroll through multiple sites simultaneously, conduct a database search in one frame and receive results in another, or freeze regions of the screen in place while scrolling through site information. Frames open up a whole new, economical world for Web exploration and promise to become one of the best applications that Gold offers. (For much more on frames, see Chapter 21.)

Figure 2.3

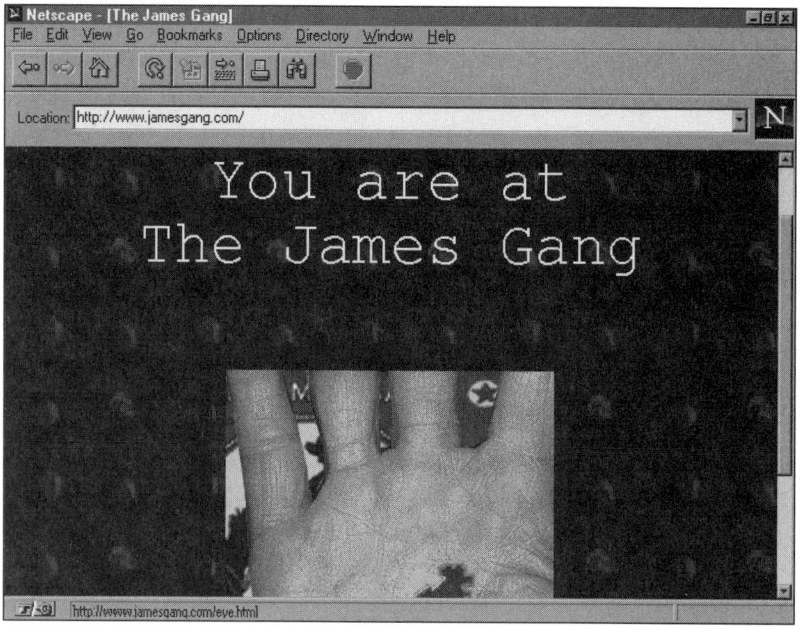

Netscape Gold's manipulation of the James Gang archive. Don't stop here—the whole James Gang site, along with their Web creation called Nerdheaven, is Netscape enhanced.

Figure 2.4

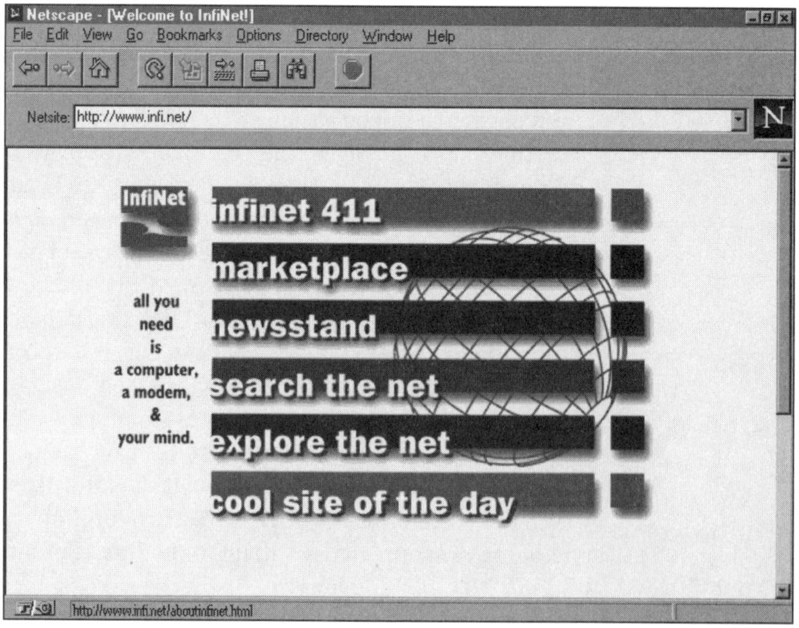

InfiNet uses Netscape Gold frame support to provide users with a single page of functional data.

Electronic Mail

Research personnel and military officials have been sending e-mail over phone lines for a quarter of a century, but only in the past six years or so has electronic mail become the staple of communication that it is today in business and educational fields around the world. Today e-mail has become so common that the power and convenience it offers is largely taken for granted.

So much so, in fact, that Netscape's complete incorporation of e-mail activities into its overall design renders it the most powerful browser on the market. Most browsers have mechanisms for *sending* e-mail, but Gold lets you *receive* e-mail as well. It's not the richest e-mail system on the planet, but it's more than good enough for most users.

Figure 2.5 shows the Netscape Gold mail window. You can display messages in subject threads, and you can organize your mail into folders with ease.

Figure 2.5

Netscape Gold organizes folders and messages and displays all URL addresses as active hyperlinks within e-mail documents.

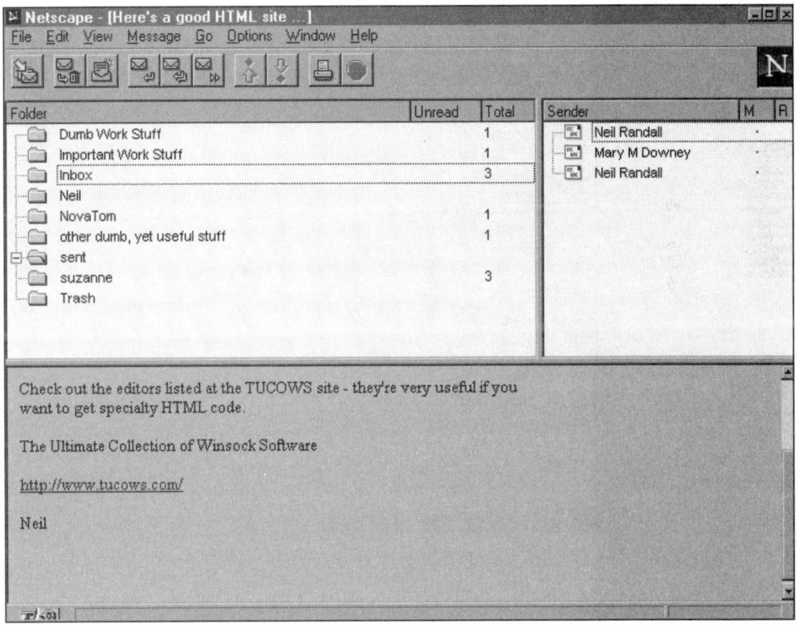

Newsgroups

Netscape's unflinching effort to create the ultimate, one-stop, all-purpose Internet tool led the company to include a fully functional newsgroup package among the browsing, editing, and e-mailing tools. The Netscape Gold News system organizes messages and groups in a framed environment much like the interface found in newsreaders like Agent, WinVN, and others. It also closely resembles Gold's own e-mail system.

Rather than closing your browser and firing up another piece of software, Netscape Gold supplies its own advanced newsreader mechanism, complete with full threading and MIME-compliant news reading and posting—you can even embed live objects, URLs, images, or HTML pages in your postings (see Figure 2.6).

For more on Netscape's news capabilities, see Chapters 9 and 10.

Figure 2.6

Gold's news window gives you easy access to newsgroups and all the fun and frolic therein.

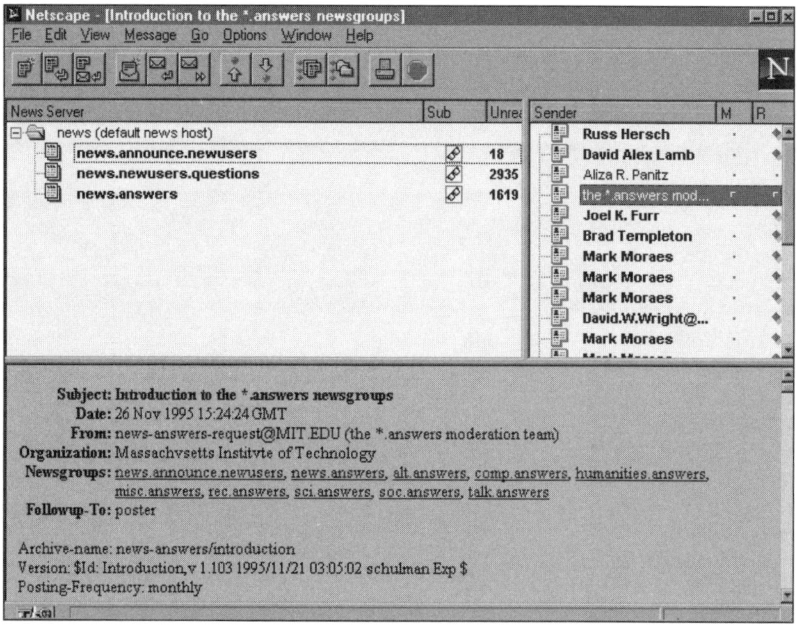

■ A Sip of Java

Just when you thought you had it all figured out and were finally comfortable with your browsing and editing tools, Sun Microsystems introduced an HTML comet—the Java programming language. Originally, Sun's HotJava browser (http://java.sun.com/) was the only program capable of Java display, a restriction that forced users to download HotJava or be content with slight visual impairment. Fortunately, Netscape Gold offers support for Java, allowing Web authors to create custom miniapplications called *applets* that can be downloaded from any server and run safely on all platforms.

Java applets (shown in Figures 2.7–2.10) open up a whole new world for Internet sites, making animation, live updating, and expert graphics rendering easier while providing real time interaction with users and maximum security on public servers. Currently, HTML programmers around the globe are testing Java, mastering its idiosyncrasies and developing pages unlike anything we've seen before. Java pages have already established a substantial presence on the World Wide Web and promise to become a common component in the broader Web community.

Figure 2.7

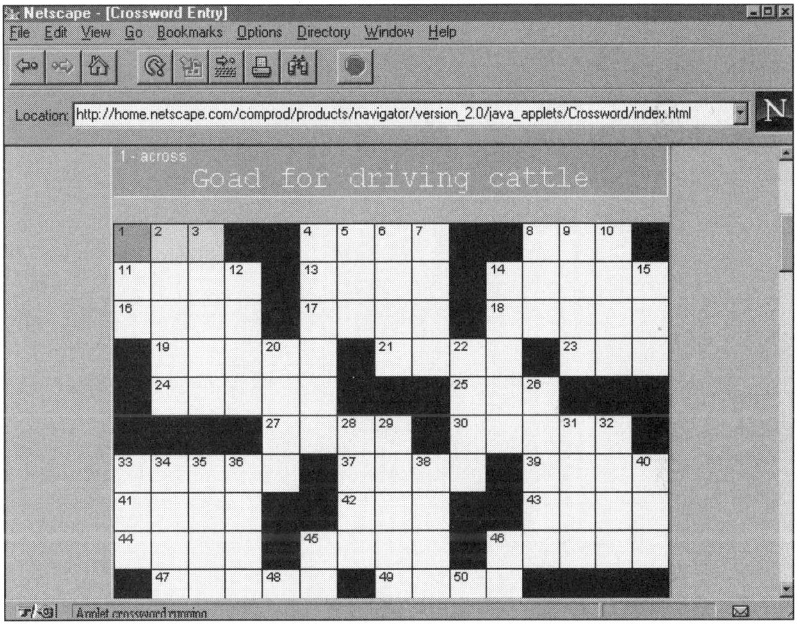

Netscape's Java applets allow Web authors to integrate functional crossword puzzles like this one directly into their personal Web pages.

There *is* some bad news with the Java onslaught. Unlike HTML, which is a formatting language, Java is a programming language and thus significantly more difficult to master. Java's popularity will almost certainly mean that writing appealing Web sites will become more and more difficult. In a way, it's a technological extension that could do more than any other extension to destroy the sense on the Web that *anybody* can be a publisher.

■ Plug-In—to the Future

Up to this point in our World Wide Web tour, we have visited some standard and enhanced sites, and focused on Netscape Gold's impressive capabilities.

Figure 2.8

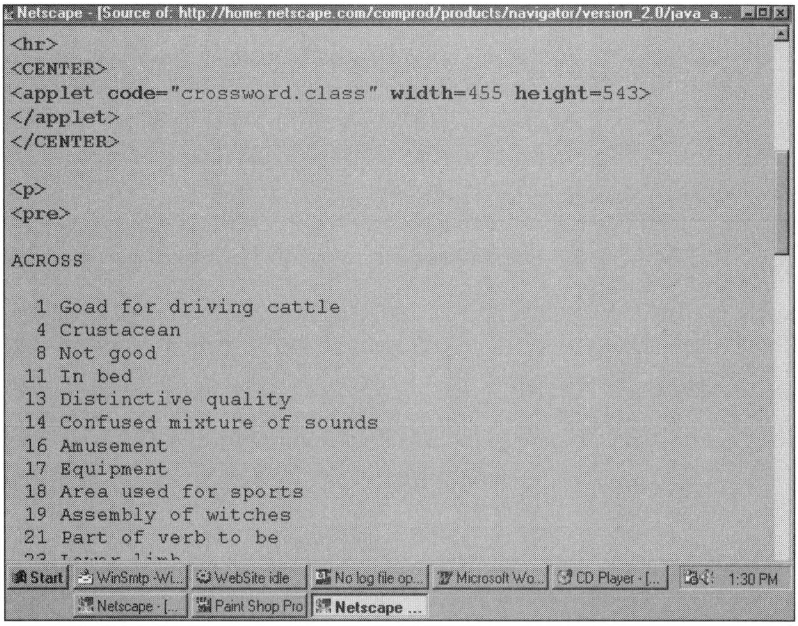

Here's the source code for the Java crossword applet.

Figure 2.9

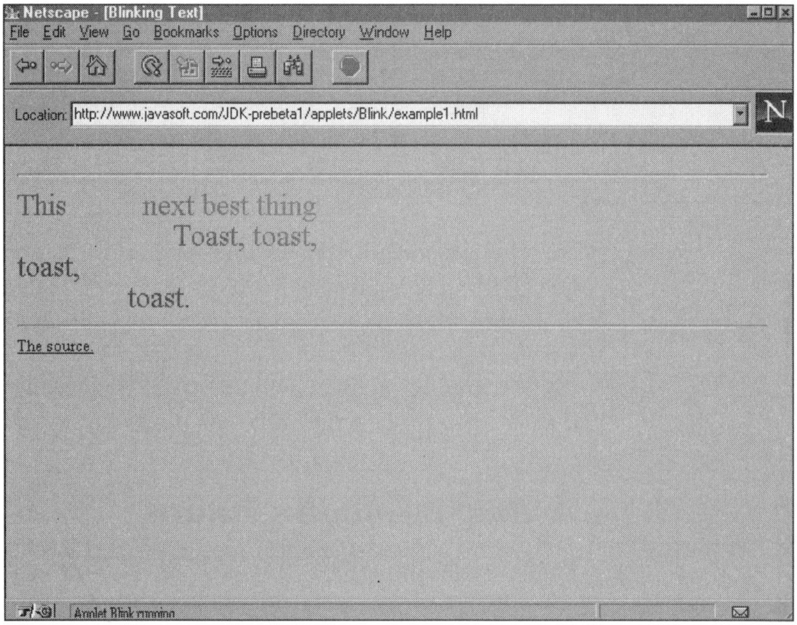

Java applets suggest unique artistic additions for Web pages, including this wildly blinking text.

Figure 2.10

Here's the source code for the Java blinking text applet.

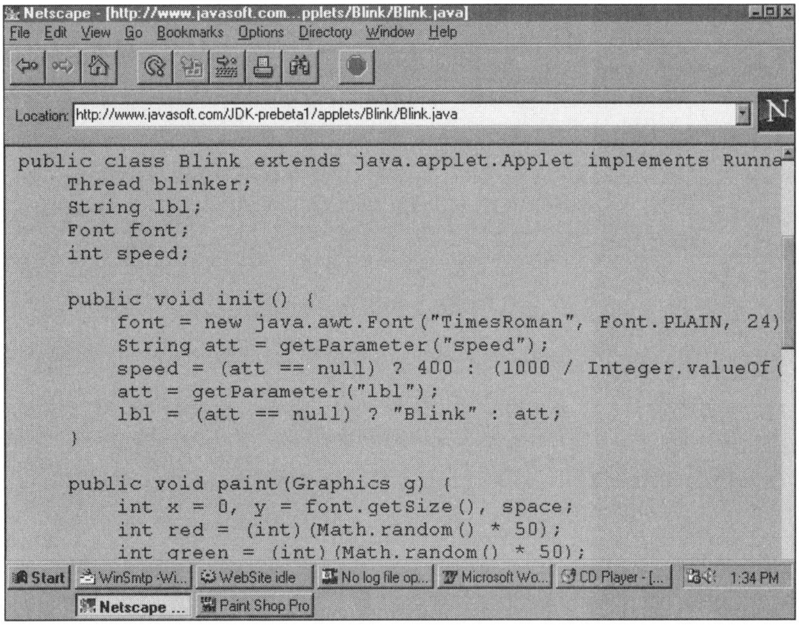
Netscape - [http://www.javasoft.com...pplets/Blink/Blink.java]
File Edit View Go Bookmarks Options Directory Window Help
Location: http://www.javasoft.com/JDK-prebeta1/applets/Blink/Blink.java
public class Blink extends java.applet.Applet implements Runna
Thread blinker;
String lbl;
Font font;
int speed;
public void init() {
font = new java.awt.Font("TimesRoman", Font.PLAIN, 24)
String att = getParameter("speed");
speed = (att == null) ? 400 : (1000 / Integer.valueOf(
att = getParameter("lbl");
lbl = (att == null) ? "Blink" : att;
}
public void paint(Graphics g) {
int x = 0, y = font.getSize(), space;
int red = (int)(Math.random() * 50);
int green = (int)(Math.random() * 50);
Start
WinSmtp -Wi...
WebSite idle
No log file op...
Microsoft Wo...
CD Player - [...
1:34 PM
Netscape ...
Paint Shop Pro

Now let's take a virtual tour of the first VRML (Virtual Reality Modeling Language) viewer to operate as a *plug-in* for Netscape Gold—WebFX. WebFX can be downloaded from the Netscape home page and offers viewers an entirely new look at their world on the Web.

VRML, like Java, is a hot new means of programming the Web. The principle behind VRML is that users will get three-dimensional displays that they'll be able to move through, walk around, see from different angles, and so on. VRML displays require fairly fast Net access to be fully useful, but their potential in the area of simulations, games, and interactive communication is enormous.

WebFX, which has recently been purchased by Netscape and renamed Live3D, plugs right into Netscape Gold. It allows viewers to navigate VRML objects with a variety of simple click-and-drag mouse commands, creating self-propelled virtual reality right on your Web page. Accessing the WebFX program will automatically initiate Netscape Gold and transport you to a virtual start-up screen that offers step-by-step instructions for immediate navigation. Browsing the "What's Cool" section in WebFX reveals some pretty amazing feats that, with a little programming knowledge, could incorporate directly into your Web pages.

Figure 2.11 shows the MTV "cube" through WebFX, while Figure 2.12 features the colorful Crayola site.

Figure 2.11

This virtual MTV "cube" displays the animation used in a popular television commercial.

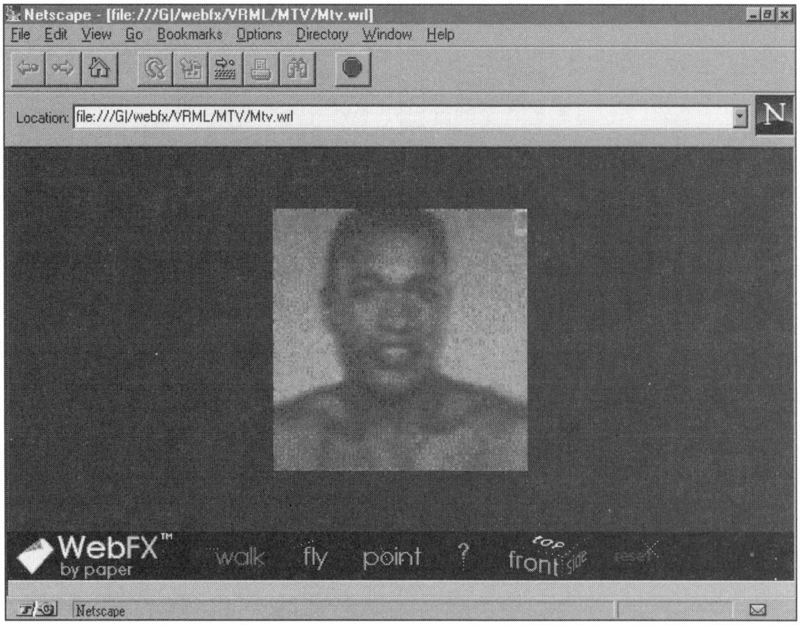

Figure 2.12

Try flying with this Crayola-with-a-twist VRML site—it's an experience to remember!

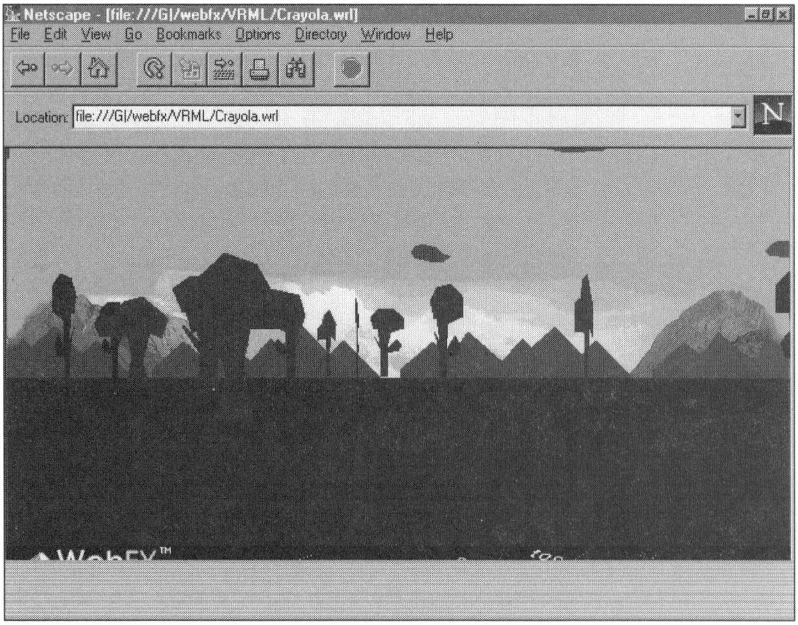

WebFX plans for VRML advancement don't stop at simple navigational plug-in effects. In the very near future, WebFX will incorporate full Java compatibility through a series of procedures which a Java programmer can use to build or edit 3-D worlds and to enhance these worlds with sophisticated behavior. WebFX also intends to support downloading of Java appelets embedded within VRML sites.

Now that you have embarked upon this brief introductory tour using Netscape Gold, it's time to take an up-close and highly personal look at Gold's functions, features, and capabilities. The rest of Part 1 is devoted to doing just that.

- *The File Menu*
- *The Edit Menu*
- *The View Menu*
- *The Go Menu*
- *The Bookmark Menu*
- *The Options Menu*
- *The Directory Menu*

- *The Window Menu*
- *The Help Menu*

CHAPTER

3

Netscape Basics

IF YOU'VE USED ANY VERSION OF NETSCAPE NAVIGATOR, LEARNING the basics of Gold will be the proverbial piece of cake. Gold is nothing more—and nothing less—than the famous Netscape browser with HTML editing capabilities built in. It maintains the same basic structure as Netscape 2.0 (in fact, it *is* this program), so Navigator veterans will feel right at home. Moreover, it's easy enough to use that novices can get going extremely quickly.

This chapter is designed in part for newcomers to the Netscape browsing game. Even if you're a Navigator veteran, this is a very good opportunity to dig into the program fully and see what you might have been missing. Practically all software programs have more to offer than is initially apparent; often in our day-to-day efforts at just getting stuff done we forget to try out all the software's features.

So, to learn the browser and all its new commands and features, we've designed this chapter for novices and veterans alike. By the time you've completed it, you'll know Gold's full capabilities, and that will be helpful when it comes to designing your own Web pages.

Several possible organizational approaches presented themselves, but we chose the fairly standard menu-by-menu approach because that's the way most of us work with software.

The File Menu

Like most software programs, Netscape Gold's File menu carries the standard file management options and browser control commands, allowing you to open or close and save or print a file or Web page. The interesting part is that Netscape Gold also provides users with an electronic mail system, including New Mail Message and Mail Document options, within its revamped File menu. The File menu also contains the entrance to Gold's editing capabilities.

New Web Browser

If you've ever worked on a very slow system, or if you're tired of continually backtracking in your Web sessions, you'll appreciate Netscape Gold's New Web Browser command. Clicking on this option from the File menu simply creates a new Netscape window. The new window has the same history items as the previous window while bringing the oldest page in the history (usually the home page) to screen. You can open as many new windows as you want with your history transferred to each.

Let's say you've just spent what seems like days downloading a large graphics site that you know you will have to return to throughout your Web session, but you would also like to view some other links listed on the previous Web page. Instead of sacrificing your time and reaccessing the graphics page each time you need it, the New Web Browser command lets you open a new browser window and thus have multiple browsers operating at the same time. It also transfers your browser history so that you can easily locate the sites you want (see Figure 3.1). Call up the graphics site on the new screen, then use it from there. If you want, you can have multiple Web sessions going at the same time, all of them linked via the document history.

Figure 3.1

Netscape Gold's New Web Browser command opens a new Netscape window and transfers the browsing history from the previous window.

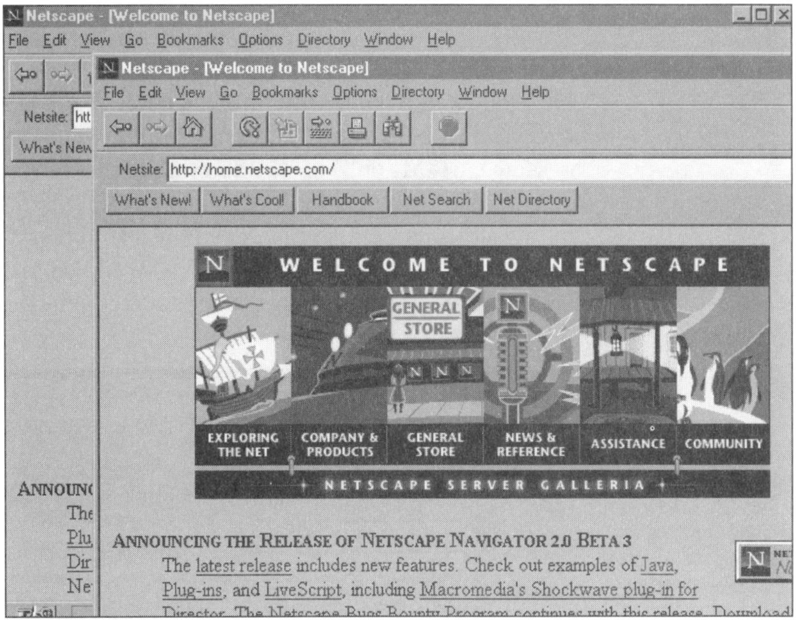

New Mail Message

Gold has a full e-mail system, and the File menu offers an easy way to get at it. By clicking on the New Message Window command during a Web session or by pressing Ctrl+N, you will receive the e-mail message screen shown in Figure 3.2.

Figure 3.2

Netscape's New Message Window command opens this e-mail screen at any point throughout your Web browsing or editing.

For more information on Netscape Gold's e-mail service and message composition, please see Chapters 7and 8.

Mail Document

The Mail Document feature in Gold's File menu is a common item in most of today's Web browsers. Accessing Mail Document with your mouse (or pressing Ctrl+M) pulls up Gold's e-mail screen, with the URL of the site you are currently browsing in the message area. Gold fills in the Subject box with the site's title as well. This is extremely useful if you want to share what you've found with someone you know would be interested. As an example, e-mailing the Netscape home page to a recipient would look like Figure 3.3.

Figure 3.3

Netscape's Mail Document command transmits the URL of the site you are currently browsing to the recipient within the browser window.

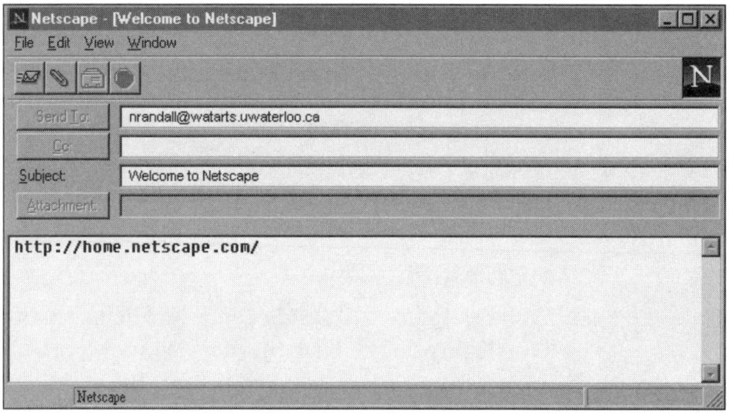

If you have not specified the name of your mail (SMTP) server and your own e-mail address in the appropriate fields of the Mail and News options dialog (see Chapter 5), you'll receive a warning box telling you that you must do so for mail or news postings to be sent.

Open Location

With the Open Location command, you send Netscape Gold out onto the Web to retrieve a document across the Net. Clicking on this menu item or pressing Ctrl+L instructs Gold to display an Open dialog box where users may insert a specific site's address. After you have pressed OK or Enter, Gold will contact the specified page and display it in the browser window. As an example, opening the Yahoo site using Gold's Open Location dialog looks like Figure 3.4.

Figure 3.4

Typing a World Wide Web address into the Location box at the top of Netscape Gold's window performs the same function as the Open Location dialog command in the File menu.

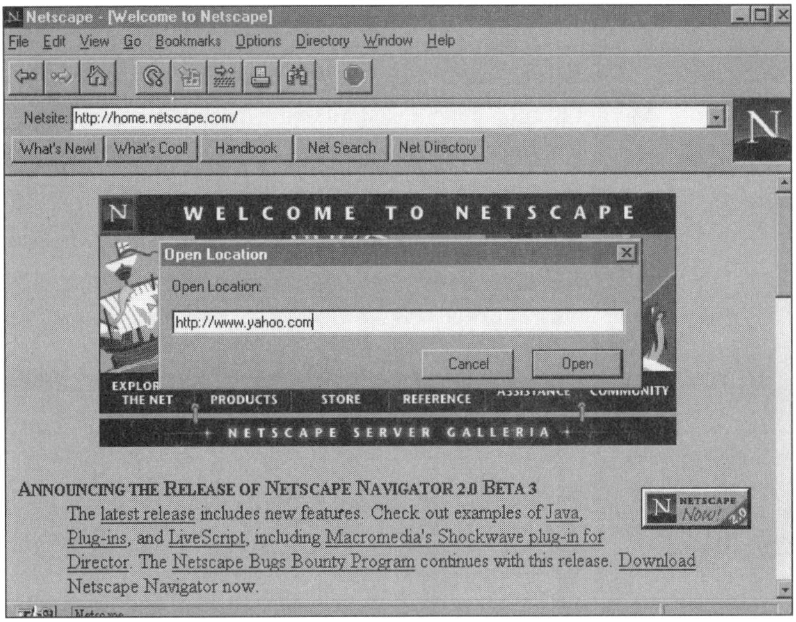

Open File in Browser

Immediately below the Open Location command in Gold's File menu, you'll find the Open File option. This command simply lets you open any file on your local system with a simple dialog box. The Open File option is especially useful for previewing a document's appearance in the Netscape environment prior to publishing it on the Web. Clicking on this element or typing Ctrl+O produces the image shown in Figure 3.5.

Figure 3.5

Netscape Gold's Open File command allows users to call up any file currently saved on their system for viewing in the Netscape environment.

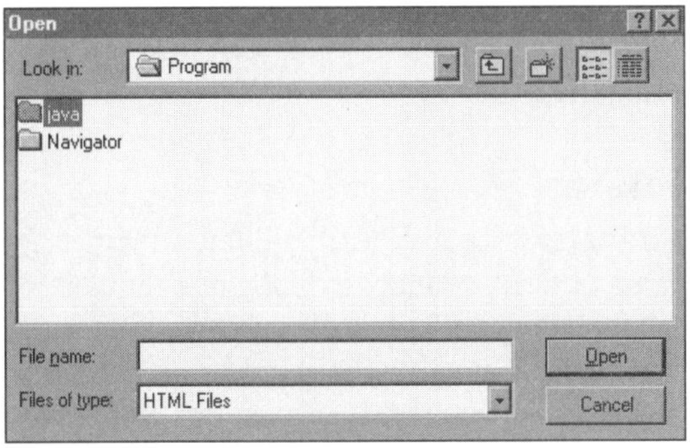

Open File in Editor

Using this command, you can open an HTML file directly into an Editor window.

Save As

Experience in any standard word processing program has probably made you fairly familiar with your Save commands. The Save As option in Netscape Gold produces a dialog box that allows you to create a file containing the content area of the current Netscape page. Sites may be saved in plain text format or in source HTML format. On UNIX, pressing Ctrl+S lets you save the WWW page's content in plain text, HTML, or Postscript format. The Save As dialog box is shown in Figure 3.6.

Figure 3.6

Netscape Gold's Save As command saves the content of your current Web page in the specified location.

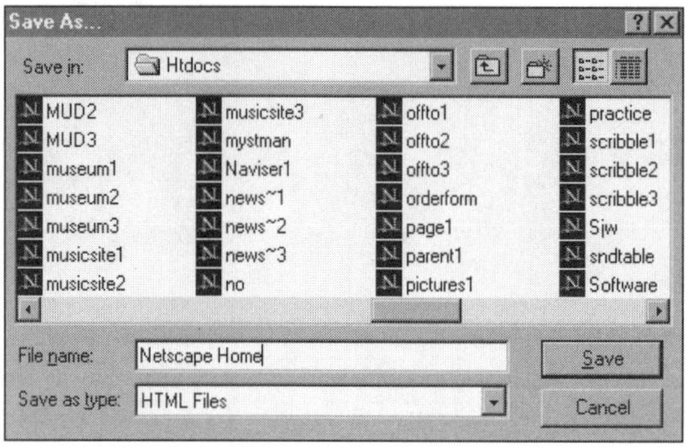

Edit Document

Here's the feature Netscape Navigator users have been waiting for. Edit Document opens an HTML edit window in which you can create or alter Web documents. This command turns Gold into a one-stop World Wide Web authoring and browsing tool, and is pretty much the reason this book exists. Since you'll be seeing the Edit screens throughout this book, there's no point belaboring the issue.

Page Setup

Like most software packages, Gold lets you print the current document. The *Page Setup* option produces a dialog box that lets you specify printing characteristics associated with the current page. You can control precisely how the page prints (see Figure 3.7), and unlike earlier versions of Netscape the printing feature actually works. However, this command is not available for UNIX users.

Figure 3.7

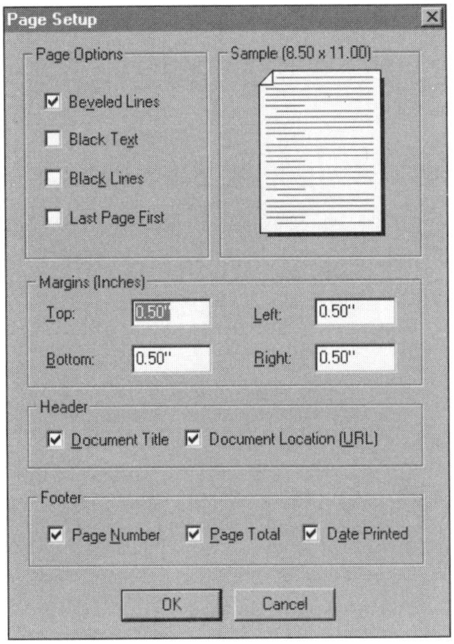

The Page Setup command in Netscape Gold's File menu gives you control over the contents of your header, footer, margins, and layout options while displaying the effects on a sample page.

Upload File

If you've used Gold to launch an FTP session, you can upload a file into the remote directory.

Print and Print Preview

Netscape Gold's Print option prints the content area of your current Netscape document (which might be several print pages in length). A dialog box lets you select printing characteristics, including page number and range. In addition to Print, the Windows platform offers a Print Preview menu item that displays the layout of a printed page on screen. Print Preview is shown in Figure 3.8.

Close and Exit

As with all previous versions of the Netscape browser, the Close command (Ctrl+W for UNIX) closes the current Netscape window; this applies to newsgroup and e-mail windows as well. If you are operating on a Windows platform, Close exits the entire Netscape application when you close the last page. Gold's Exit command closes the current Netscape page and exits the Netscape application. On Macintosh machines the exit function is controlled by Quit instead.

Figure 3.8

Clicking on Print Preview displays a printed version of the Web page you are currently viewing, allowing you to zoom in or out and print the final copy directly from the Print Preview screen.

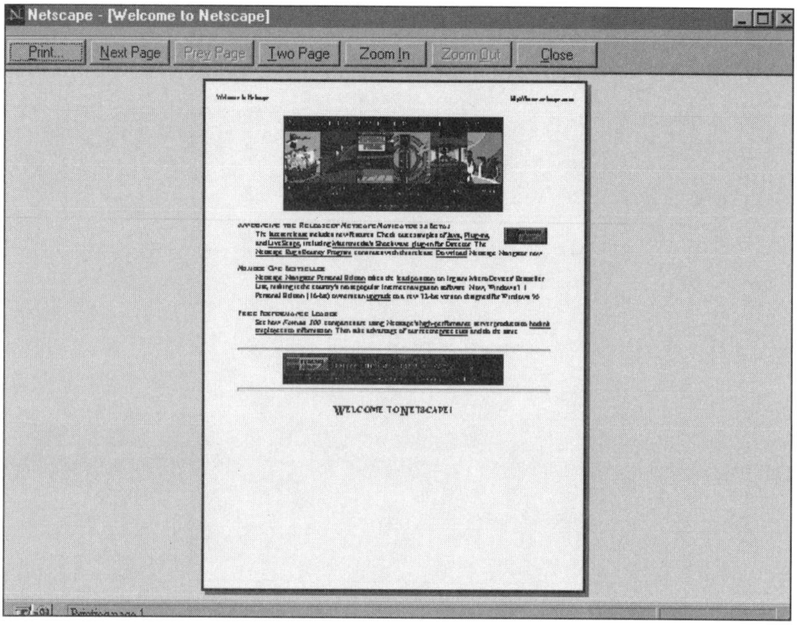

The Edit Menu

Gold's Edit menu contains most of the standard alteration commands that control the movement and location of material on a page. Whether you use these commands in a Web editor, browser, or word processing program, their essential functioning remains the same. Here's a brief overview of the Edit menu to introduce you to the main uses of Undo, Cut, Copy, Paste, Select, and Find throughout your Web browsing activities.

Undo

Netscape Gold's Undo command simply reverses the last action you performed—if possible. Gold reveals its Undo option only when the action you have completed may be reversed. For example, if you have clicked on a site that you don't really want to see, pressing the Stop or Back buttons will undo the operation for you. Similarly, if you are mailing a document or posting to a newsgroup, the individual mail and news dialogs contain internal menus with their own Undo listings. For UNIX users the Undo option is activated by pressing Ctrl+Z.

On the other hand, Undo is extremely useful when you're in Gold's editor, for the same reason Undo is a useful tool in a word processor or spreadsheet.

We often execute a command that we've since decided we didn't want to execute, and Undo lets us step back in time and do it right in the first place. Gold's Undo is hardly exemplary, allowing you to back up only one step, but it's better than nothing.

Cut, Copy, Paste, and Select All

You can select text in Gold through your operating system's normal means, by highlighting with a mouse or with the shift and arrow keys. Netscape Gold's Cut or Ctrl+X command removes the text you have selected and places a copy of the selection in the Clipboard. The Copy or Ctrl+C option places a copy of the selected text in the Clipboard without removing it from its original location. Paste or Ctrl+V places a copy of the Clipboard's contents into the location currently specified by your cursor or selection marker. The Select All listing in the Edit menu highlights all text on the active page for cutting, copying, or pasting. In the browser, the only place into which you can paste text is the Location box. This is useful when you find a URL in another document; you can copy it from that document and paste it into the Location box to go to the site immediately.

Since Netscape Gold lets you highlight and copy material directly from online Web documents, the Cut, Copy, and Paste commands come in very handy when you're using the Edit Document feature. You can, quite easily, borrow whatever ideas you feel like. Just call up another Web page, copy the elements you want, and paste them into your own. It's probably the fastest way to learn your way around HTML.

Find and Find Again

The general rule of thumb in Web design is to keep pages short and light on text, but sometimes it isn't done, and sometimes it's just not possible. There are complete books on the Web, after all, not to mention newspaper and magazine articles, corporate and research reports, and all kinds of other long, text-oriented pages. Gold provides users with Find and Find Again commands for locating words and phrases. Clicking on Find or typing Ctrl+F produces a dialog box (Figure 3.9) that lets you specify a word or phrase to locate within the current Netscape page. Pressing the Find Next button within the dialog initiates the search and continues the find process after Netscape has located the first instance of your entry. If a match is found, Netscape selects the text and scrolls it to a visible position in the content area. The Find Again command in the Edit menu (Ctrl+G) locates another instance of the text specified in the Find dialog.

Figure 3.9

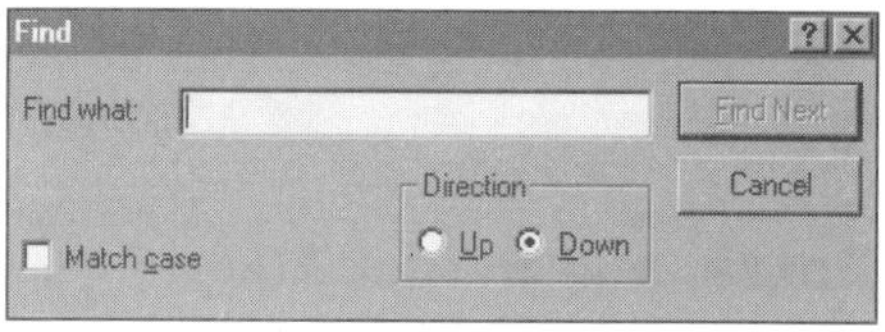

Netscape Gold's Find command allows you to limit your search to items in the same case, in an area higher or lower than your present cursor position on the page. On UNIX and Mac machines, Find Backwards initiates a search from your selection bar toward the beginning of the page.

The View Menu

The View menu offers important controls for the accurate and aesthetic presentation of the Web pages you visit. The View menu has been significantly altered from earlier versions of Netscape Navigator, and now offers more detailed information with the Document Information option and frame support with the Reload Cell option. You won't generally need these commands all the time, but it's important to understand what they do.

Reload, Reload Cell, and Refresh

You've no doubt already discovered the usefulness of the Reload icon on the toolbar throughout your Web explorations. Clicking on the Reload button is the same as selecting View/Reload (or pressing Ctrl+R); it instructs Netscape Gold to produce a fresh copy of the current Netscape page, replacing the original screen with the newest version of that page found on the Web. It's needed because Gold stores Web pages in memory or disk cache (see Chapter 5 for more on caching), and if you call up the same page in the same session, you get the cached page only, which might not be up to date. Reloading the page tells Gold to go to the Web site and download it anew, thereby displaying any changes made to the source page from the time of original loading. Reloading is also extremely useful in Web authoring sessions; it allows you to preview, over and over again, the changes you make to your documents.

The Reload Cell option (Figure 3.10) found in the View menu is new to Netscape Gold and, when selected, loads an updated copy of a page within a frame. Frames, as you'll discover in Chapter 21, let designers offer several windows on a browser screen. Frames are great for all kinds of reasons, but they play havoc on Gold's Back and Forward commands, as well as Reload. Reload Cell replaces the frame currently selected with a copy brought directly from that URL's source location. Again, the reloaded frame displays any changes made to the page from the time of original loading.

Figure 3.10

Clicking on the largest section of this framed Netscape page and selecting the Reload cell option clears the original frame and replaces it with an updated version.

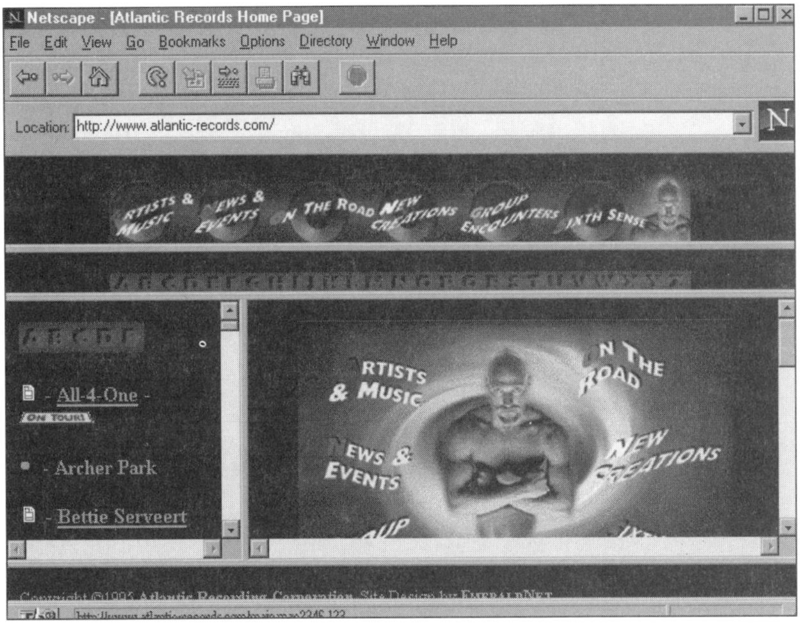

The Refresh command in the View menu brings a fresh copy of the current Netscape page from local memory to replace the one originally loaded. The refreshed page does not display changes made to the source page from the time of the original loading. It's primarily useful when a page's formatting has gone somewhat awry.

Load Images

The Load Images option in the View menu is used only when the Options/AutoLoad Images menu item has been turned off. If it has been, images do not load and are replaced by small icons that occupy the position normally held by each image (Figure 3.11). Clicking on the Load Images command substitutes all of these small icons with their corresponding images, retrieved from their source location (Figure 3.12).

Document Source and Document Information

The Document Source command is one of the most popular selections among World Wide Web artists. When you access it, Gold produces a View Source window showing the current page in all its HTML splendor, both content and coding tags. From this new Netscape window, HTML source code may be copied to your personal applications using the Cut, Copy, and Paste

Figure 3.11

This screen shot displays the Netscape Store page as it appears with the AutoLoad Images preference unchecked.

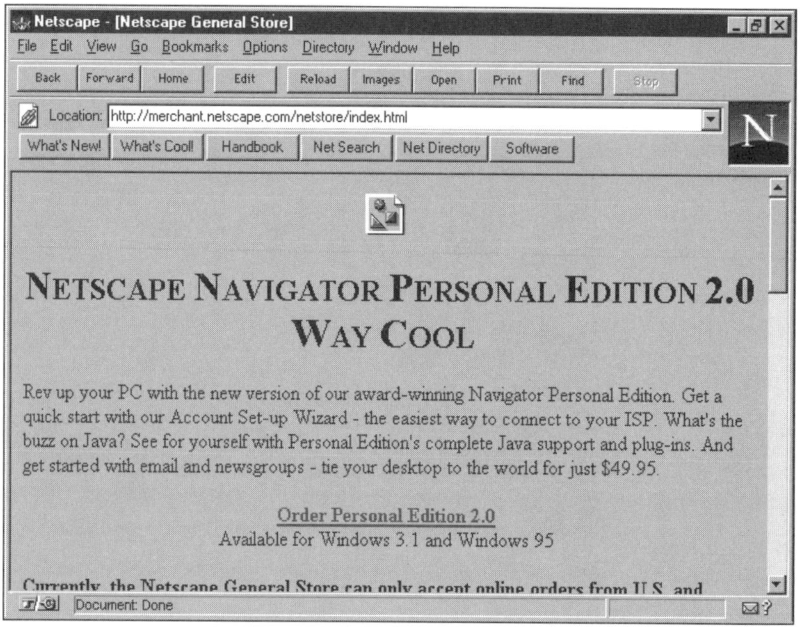

Figure 3.12

Here is the same page displayed after selecting Load Images. Loading the images does not reload the entire page from the source files, and therefore links and text remain the same in both versions.

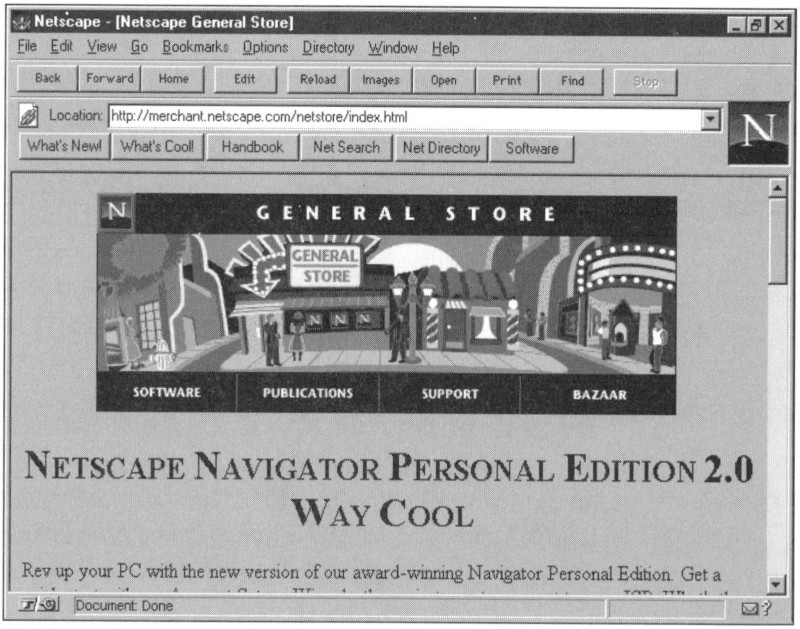

commands listed in Gold's Edit menu, or you can just study how a Web author constructed a page you admire a great deal. The code itself is presented with a color scheme designed to make it surprisingly easy to read (Figure 3.13).

Unaccountably, the Windows version of Gold displays the source text in a dialog box without offering users the option to save it. Macs store the text in a temporary file and display the coded information using a generic text application capable of saving. UNIX systems display the HTML code along with the document title and URL in a dialog that offers a Save button. Despite these differences, all platforms let you specify the application you want to view the source code with by choosing the Options/General/Helpers listings in the Netscape Gold browser and locating the View Source field—click the Browse button to specify the default viewer.

If you ever used WordPerfect for DOS, you'll be familiar with the Document Source idea. It's effectively the same as WordPerfect's famous Reveal Codes command. It bypasses the nice appearance the program gives to the document and shows the code in all its ugliness. For HTML authors, copying portions of code from existing documents to their own documents can save a great deal of authoring time.

Figure 3.13

The source code for the Yahoo home page

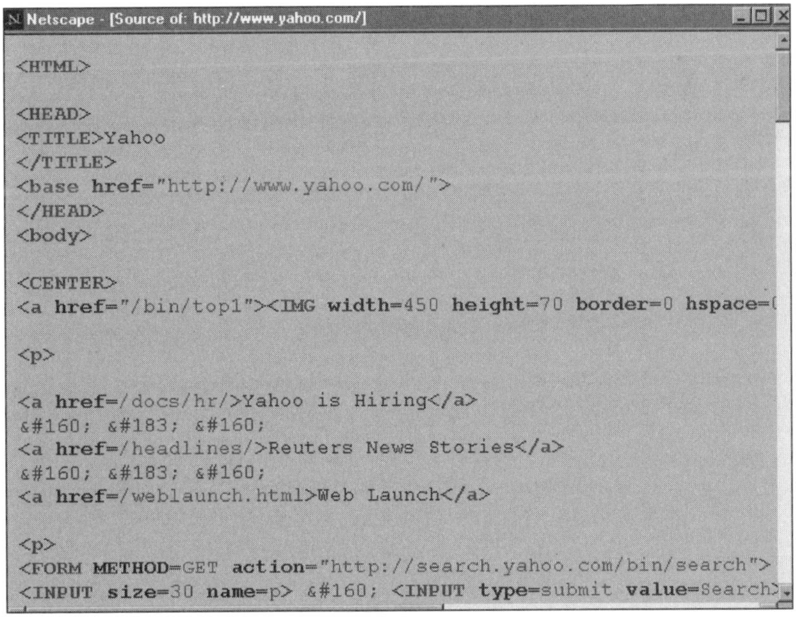

Netscape Gold's Document Information element functions in much the same way as the Document Information command present in most HTML editors. Clicking on the Document Information option in the View menu instructs Gold to display a new Netscape window that details the structure, type, and composition of your current Web page. The Document Information includes title, location, URL, date of last modification, character set encoding, and security status. Figure 3.14 shows the document information for the Yahoo home page.

Figure 3.14

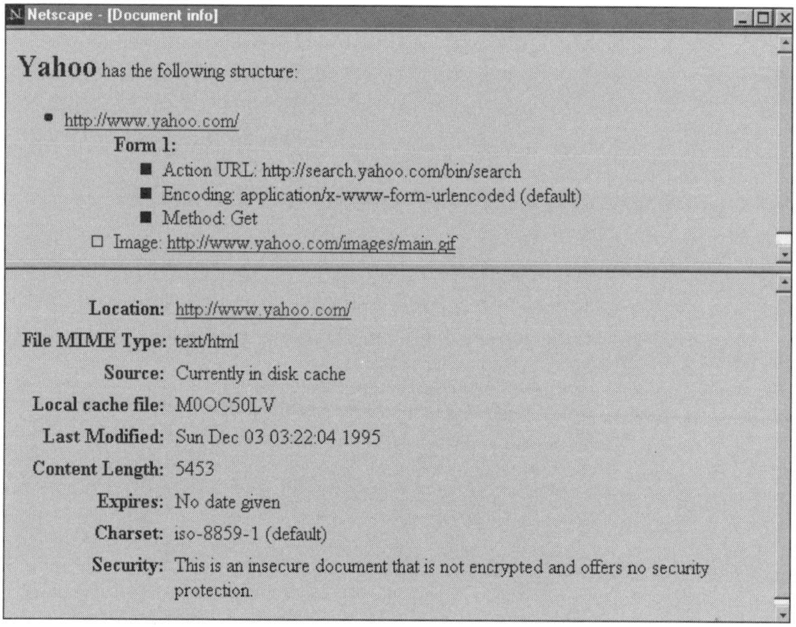

Clicking on the image links displayed in the first portion of this page produces detailed information about the graphic itself at the bottom of the Document Information window.

The Go Menu

The Go menu keeps things fairly simple. Back or Alt+← takes you back one screen, and is identical to the Back icon on the toolbar. Home, like the Home button, loads or reloads the page you've set up as Gold's home page (default is the Netscape home page)—Forward or Alt+→ (like the Forward button) takes you forward one screen, while Stop Loading or <Esc> (or clicking the Stop icon) stops loading the current Web page.

Easy, right? Things become a little more complex once we get to the bottom portion of the menu listings—Netscape Gold's account of your browsing history.

History List

Below the Back, Home, Forward, and Stop Loading menu items, Netscape's Go menu appends the title of each page you visit to a history list. The names contained in the history menu are active links that correspond to the names saved in the History command listed under Netscape's Window menu; they allow you to quickly return to a site that you previously visited. The layout of the history list follows this basic format:

- History item 0 lists the page you are currently viewing.
- History item 1 calls up the first page in the history list.
- History item 2 calls up the second page in the history list.

Here comes the hitch. Netscape Gold only displays the names of the pages you visited as you most recently descended from your home page. For example, if you go from page A to page B to page C, and then return to page A and traverse the path A to D to E, your history maintains only the most recent A-D-E lineage, and it has no remaining knowledge of B and C. Figure 3.15 shows a typical history.

Figure 3.15

Here's my history after a day of surfing the Web.

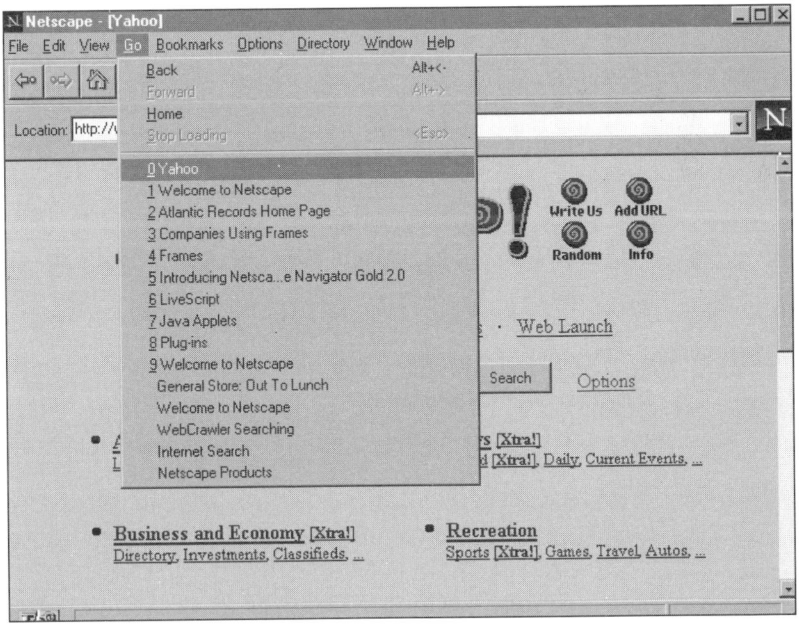

Netscape's history feature has never been satisfactory to many users. Most people like to know *everywhere* they've been, not the current line of browsing descent. In fact, Gold's history feature calls into question the whole purpose of the Web, which for many users is to browse in a largely nonlinear fashion. It assumes that you'll move in an orderly fashion from one site to the next, never returning to the first. The experience of many is that this is not so. I, for one, find the history feature almost useless.

■ The Bookmark Menu

As one of the most popular and important features of the Web, bookmarks have been incorporated into every browser on the market. Although bookmarks themselves are not new, the little extras that Netscape Gold adds to their Bookmark menu make it a fairly practical and organized sorting mechanism. The Bookmark menu provides fast and easy access to your favorite pages, initially displaying two items that help you add and modify bookmarks.

You'll find much more on bookmarks in Chapter 4, including a look at SmartMarks, Netscape's add-on to Gold that takes bookmarking several steps further toward perfection.

Add Bookmark

The Add Bookmark command in the Bookmark menu adds the title of the Netscape page that you are currently viewing to the list of pages in the bookmark file. As you add a page to a bookmark list by clicking on the command or pressing Ctrl+A, the title of the page (or any other name you wish to supply as a bookmark title) is appended to the menu. Selecting the title brings the page to your screen.

Bookmarks become more complex when you learn to set options and regulate folders, aliases, and separators. For more information on adding and organizing bookmarks, see Chapter 4.

Go to Bookmarks

The Go to Bookmarks option in the Bookmark menu performs the same function as the Bookmarks item in the Window menu. Both commands produce an HTML page that lists the bookmarks in the current bookmark file. Clicking on the Go to Bookmarks command or pressing Ctrl+B will produce the screen shown in Figure 3.16.

From the Go to Bookmarks screen, you can open, import, save, edit, and modify your bookmark page using the commands provided in the menus at the top of the page.

Figure 3.16

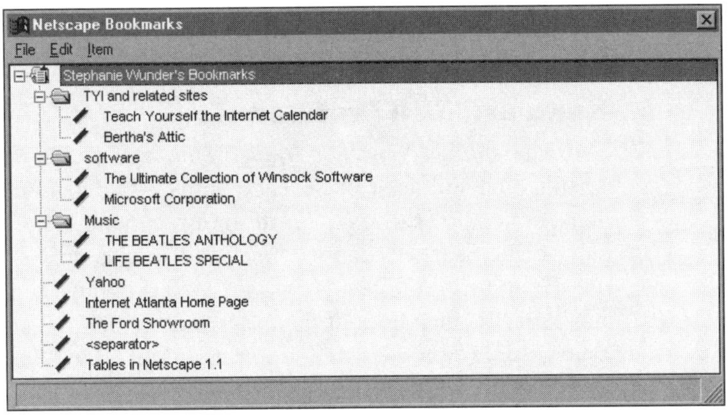

I have modified my personal bookmarks list using the properties menu item and by inserting folders and separators.

The Options Menu

The Options menu is one of the first you should enter when you fire up Netscape Gold for the first time. It is here that you can set your general preferences; mail, network, and security properties; and screen appearance. The Options menu leads to dozens of settings that modify the functioning of the browser according to your wants and needs. The easiest way to investigate all of your options is to click on the various commands and browse their contents, setting applications as you go. For more information on the options discussed throughout this section, see Chapter 5.

General Preferences

General Preferences includes options for selecting characteristics that define Netscape's operation. Clicking on the General Preferences item in the Options menu instructs Gold to produce a dialog box containing tab buttons (Windows) or pop-up menus (Mac and UNIX). Each tab or menu in turn produces a dialog box containing one or more panels of modifiable options.

Most dialog boxes have OK, Apply, Cancel, Defaults, and Help buttons. Click the OK button to close the dialog box while accepting any changes you have made to the panel settings. Click Apply to accept changes without closing the dialog. Click Cancel to close the dialog box without accepting any changes. Click Default to reset panel items to the initial Netscape settings. Click Help, if available, for online help information about each panel.

All preferences are discussed in detail in Chapter 5.

Editor Preferences

Editor preferences are covered in Chapter 12. They allow you to establish the appearance and remote file locations of your documents.

News and Mail Preferences

Netscape Gold's *News and Mail Preferences* dialog presents the panels for setting mail and news preference items. As an example of its increased versatility, Gold allows users the option of receiving e-mail using Netscape Gold itself or Microsoft Exchange, the e-mail service provided with Windows 95.

Before your Golden News and Mail programs can function properly, you must specify the names of the users and servers that will send and receive messages. This option is located under the Identity and Server tabs in the News and Mail Preferences dialog. The Organization tab coordinates mail sorting and news threading while the Composition tab allows control over more specific aspects of mailing and news reading to satisfy individual user's desires.

All preferences are discussed in detail in Chapter 5.

Network Preferences

Clicking on Gold's Netswork Preferences option presents a panel dialog for setting preference items regarding cache, network connections, and proxy configurations.

A cache tab allows you to control the size and location of Netscape Gold's memory cache or reserve and also provides a cache dumping button. These options can become very important if you return to sites repeatedly throughout your browsing sessions.

The Connections tab provides only two modifiable options—the number of network connections you desire and the buffer size. Remember that the more connections you have, the slower your individual connections may seem, and the larger the buffer size, the more saturated your computer becomes. Weigh the pros and cons before extending the default limits.

The Proxy tab is not applicable for users with direct Internet connections but allows remote users to access the Net through a firewall.

All preferences are discussed in detail in Chapter 5.

Security Preferences

Gold's Security Preferences option presents a panel that is designed for setting preference items for security features. The General tab regulates when alarms should sound to indicate an error in your applications and allows you to disable Java support. The Password tab allows you to create and change your password and controls how often Netscape will produce the password dialog. The Site Certificate and Personal Certificate tabs allow you to regulate the accepted digitally signed certificates that Netscape requires in order to function securely.

All preferences are discussed in detail in Chapter 5.

The Show Commands

The middle portion of Gold's Option menu regulates the appearance of your Netscape screen, producing or removing additional options and toolbars as you access them. These are shown in Table 3.1.

Table 3.1

Gold's Show Commands

COMMAND	WHAT IT DOES
Show Toolbar	Produces or removes a toolbar below the Location box on Gold's screen that contains Back, Forward, Home, Reload, Images, Open, Print, Find, and Stop options.
Show Location	Toggles the visibility of the Location box on Gold's screen.
Show Directory Buttons	Produces or removes a button bar leading to Netscape directory locations such as What's New, What's Cool, Handbook, Net Search, and Net Directory.
Show Java Console	Generates a new browser window that displays the Java output for the current site.

The first time you start up Netscape Gold, the toolbar, location, and directory options will be turned on. You may regulate the appearance of your personal browsing screen directly from the Options menu.

Auto Load Images

Gold's Auto Load Images command toggles the presentation of inline images as a page is brought to screen. If the option is checked, images embedded in any page you access are automatically loaded with the text. If unchecked, images are not loaded and are represented instead by small icons that can be loaded later by choosing the View/Load Images menu item or Images from the toolbar. Unchecking this item increases the speed for bringing the text portion of a page to your screen at the expense of aesthetics. Loading Netscape's home page with the Auto Load Images command unchecked produces Figure 3.17.

Figure 3.17

Images are a huge element in the World Wide Web but often consume large amounts of downloading time—especially for slower machines. Unchecking Auto Load Images reduces downloading time by loading text only onto your screen.

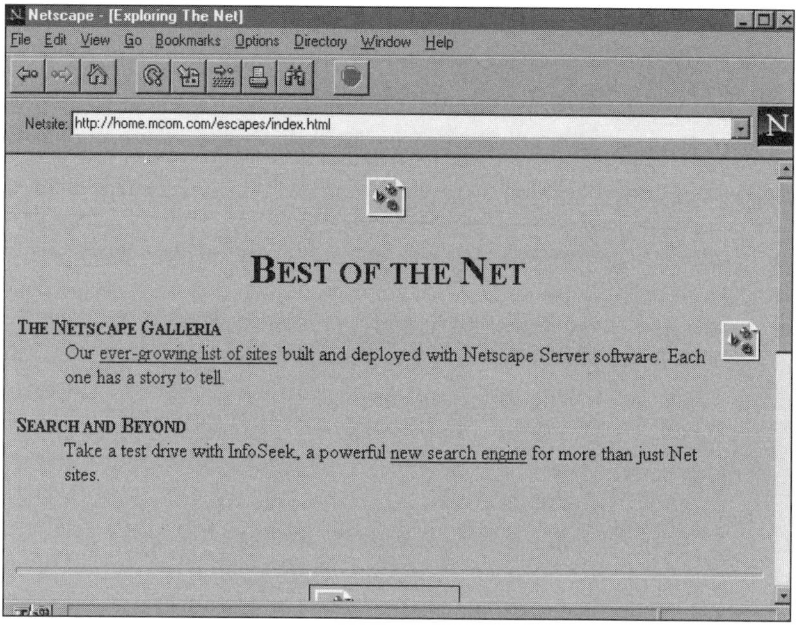

Document Encoding

Don't let the word *encoding* turn you away—an encoding simply represents a translation of glyphs (such as character symbols) to computer codes (such as hexadecimal digits).

In easier terms, Document Encoding specifies the default encoding that a document uses when the document does not specify a character set encoding or when the document specification is not available. You may designate the proportional and fixed fonts associated with the default encoding using the Font panel items located in General Preferences. Gold's Document Encoding menu is shown in Figure 3.18.

Save Options

After you have adjusted Gold's options to suit your viewing needs, you can save the changes you have made by clicking on the Save Options command at the end of the Option menu. This operation saves any changes made to the settings of the Options menu but does not include the preference panel adjustments, which are saved locally by pressing OK. Changes remain in effect for all subsequent Netscape sessions.

Figure 3.18

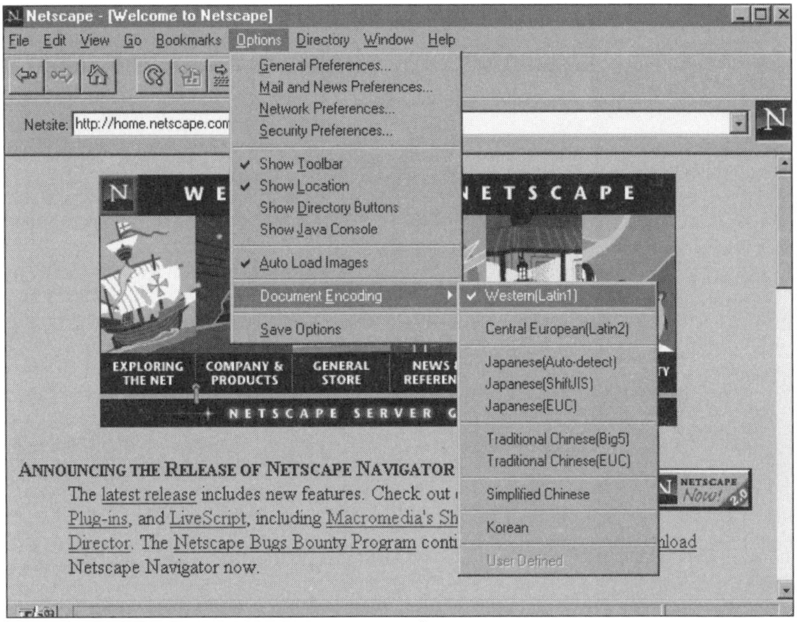

Netscape lets you choose a character set encoding's font display and specify a document's character set encoding. I have chosen Western (Latin 1) from the Font panel as my default encoding.

The Directory Menu

To assist in your orientation and navigation across the World Wide Web, Netscape Gold has compiled a list of starting points and information archives. These sites will help you get started and allow easy location of the sites you are most likely to visit again and again. Think of these links as a set of Gold's permanent bookmarks. Table 3.2 lists them.

Search sites are among the most important directories contained in the Directory menu. From the search site pages, you can locate almost any site on the Web with a few key words and a little sorting power. My favorite is Webcrawler, but try them all and find the ones that best suit your searching needs.

The Window Menu

Like the Window menus contained in all other Windows programs, Gold's Window menu keeps track of the number and content of each Netscape Window you open, while providing links to Gold's complete Mail and News windows. Since you've already been introduced to Gold's News and Mail systems and will participate in a thorough Mail and News exploration in

Table 3.2

Directory Menu Web Pages

PAGE	DESCRIPTION
Netscape's Home	Links users to information on Netscape services, products, new features, and links to the best directories and most popular sites on the Web.
What's New!	Provides a list of direct links to the Web's newest additions and requests submissions. Also presented as a toolbar button.
What's Cool!	Transports users to a frequently updated site of hyperlinks. Netscape provides direct links to a series of cool sites with summary descriptions. Also presented as a toolbar button.
Netscape's Galleria	Provides a list of Netscape customers who have built Net sites using Netscape Server software.
Internet Directory	Links to a series of Web directories that organize the millions of Net sites currently in cyberspace. Also presented as a toolbar button.
Internet Search	Click here for links to the Internet's most popular and effective search mechanisms. Also on Netscape's button bar.
Internet White Pages	Provides links to the best sites on the Net for finding people, places, and addresses.
About the Internet	Learn how to connect to the Net, use e-mail, master Netiquette, and access the most frequently asked, frequently asked questions.

Chapters 7–10, we'll begin with the Address Book and move on to Bookmarks and History.

Address Book

Clicking on the Address Book feature in Gold's Window menu opens an address menu where you may store your most frequently used e-mail addresses under alias names for easy retrieval and message creation. To create the first entry in your address book, select the Add User command from the Item menu and insert the nickname and corresponding e-mail address of the recipient. The next time you wish to compose a message to this same individual, simply double-click on the entry in the Address Book and Gold will produce an e-mail screen with the recipient's address already inserted. Netscape Gold's Address Book also imports aliases from previous e-mail packages and allows the creation of recipient lists. Adding a new user to your Address Book produces the dialog shown in Figure 3.19.

Figure 3.19

To add a new recipient to Gold's address book, create an alias, fill in the recipient's name and e-mail address, and click OK. The recipient's name will appear among the addresses listed in the opening Address Book screen.

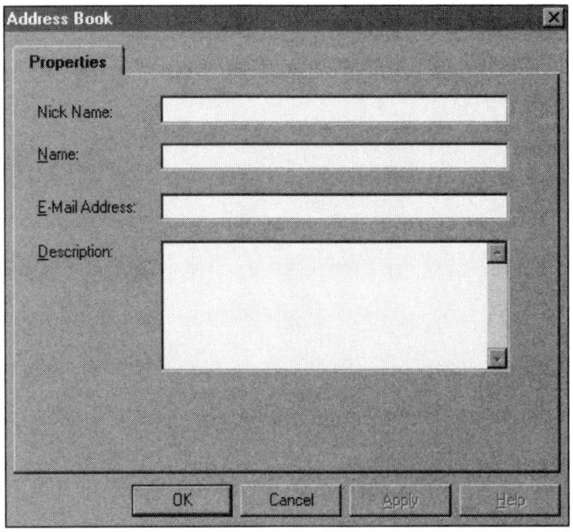

Bookmarks

Are you experiencing a sense of déjà vu? That's because you have already explored Netscape Gold's Bookmark command in the Bookmark menu. To recap, this command opens up a new Netscape Window that displays your personal bookmark file in HTML format. Click on the Bookmarks command or press Ctrl+B to view your collection of hotlinks and make any adjustments.

History

Unlike the Bookmark command, found in the Window menu, Gold's History option differs from the tracking operations that appear below the Go menu. This History command produces a new window that lists, in two columns, the title and URL of each page you have seen as you "most recently" descended from the home page. Pressing the Go to button at the bottom of the window or double-clicking on the selection itself brings the selected page to the screen. Gold also allows users to append the link to the bottom of their bookmark list directly from the history list by selecting the Create Bookmark button. My History dialog accessed from the Window menu is shown in Figure 3.20.

Open Named Window

Below the History command, Gold lists the names of the windows that you have opened in your Net explorations. Each open window is listed as a menu item; the menu item name is derived from the window's type and title. The

Figure 3.20

The History window displays your browsing history in the order most recently descended from the home page.

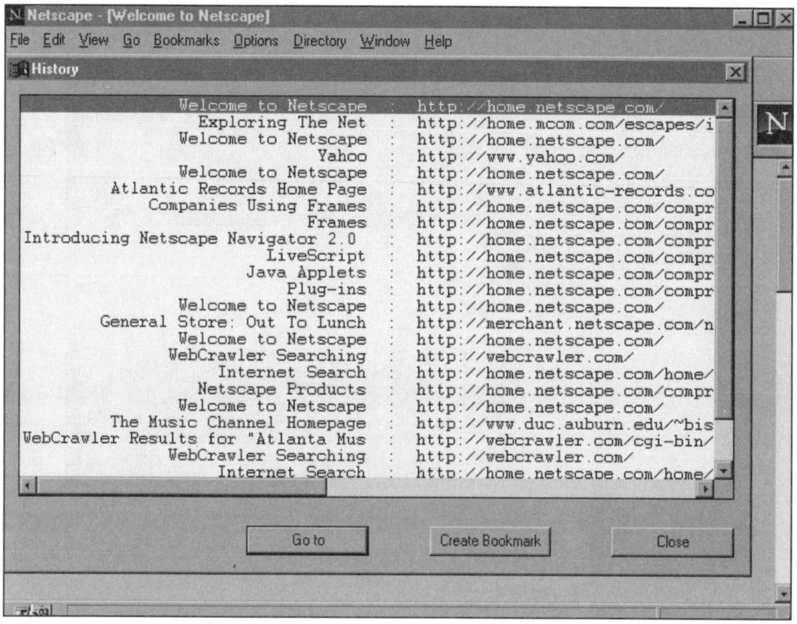

current Netscape window is designated with a check mark. This list allows quick and easy movement from window to window that can also be performed by pressing Alt and Tab.

The Help Menu

Gold's Help menu differs from those of most other browsers because it draws on the World Wide Web for tutorial and information pages while at the same time providing built-in assistance like that of most word processing assistance programs. Gold's built-in assistance allows users to access the help program at any stage in their Internet activities. For Macintosh users, Gold's help appears in pop-up balloon format.

About Netscape

Clicking on the first option in the Netscape Gold Help directory calls up a World Wide Web document dealing with version, copyright, and license information about Netscape software. The single-screen document provides a direct and concise summary of Gold software while linking to an online feedback form and the Netscape home page.

About Plug-ins

A number of companies are developing plug-ins for Netscape Gold. *Plug-ins* are, essentially, programs that become part of Gold, enhancing its capabilities. *About Plug-ins* tells you which plug-ins you've installed, and gives brief information about the company and version.

Registration Information

The Registration Information command in Netscape Gold's Help menu calls up a single WWW screen that provides a 3½-minute registration session. Access the User Identification form and fill in the user id to receive the latest notices for upcoming product releases and updates. In addition, this will make you eligible for the monthly T-shirt drawing. Registration is for Netscape's internal use only.

Software

Netscape Gold's Software command performs the same function as the Software button on the toolbar. Clicking on Software produces a screen that deals with subscription details and upgrades. The online site provides specific how-to instructions for upgrading your current version of Netscape software, and for subscribing to Netscape for one year of membership—complete with answers to Netscape's most frequently asked questions.

Handbook

Do you ever wish that your version of Netscape came with a reference manual? Well, it does, in a way. To locate the online help manual complete with tutorials and additional reference URLs, click on Gold's Handbook command from the Help menu. Here you will find links to basic introductions, instructional lessons, questions and answers, and an alphabetical index for keyword searches. The Handbook command provides notices and summaries for new Netscape software features including on-screen fundamentals. Gold's Handbook covers information for new users and veterans alike, extending from elementary Internet concepts to in-depth discussions of advanced topics.

Release Notes

Netscape Gold's Release Notes provide you with detailed information on the Gold browser, editor, mailer, and newsreader in comparison with other competitive software packages. After browsing the Release Notes site, you will discover that nothing is like Netscape Gold. This summary page reveals Gold's advantages by displaying the actual HTML commands necessary to allow full functioning of certain features. The site provides links that list Gold users' system requirements, new features, security notes, and any known problems or bugs. Hypertext links provide easy access to the information that is most important to you and make learning Gold an easy task.

Frequently Asked Questions

Netscape defines their FAQs as "an invaluable compilation of questions gleaned from previous support conversations." What's most important about the FAQs is that they come from people just like you—people who have many of the same concerns and inquiries as you have or will have in the future. The FAQ page is ordered according to subject and software use, allowing you to quickly scan the available sessions for an answer to your particular question. Netscape also provides a link to their support pages—just in case you require additional information.

On Security

Since Netscape Navigator and the Netscape Commerce Server are the first services to offer a nonproprietary technology called SSL (short for *Secure Sockets Layer* protocol), the Net is flooded with users, like yourself, who want and need more information on the security system maintained by their browser. Gold's Security site begins at the beginning, addressing basic issues of security and then progressing to more complex security applications. This WWW page provides links to other security sites while teaching you about secure transactions, digitally signed certificates, and the limitations that some security systems may impose on users. Even if you don't plan to require security throughout your Net explorations, you should read the information in this site and learn what security could do for you.

How to Give Feedback

One of the most important items for Netscape management is the feedback page contained in Gold's Help menu. Clicking on the How to Give Feedback command produces an online user feedback form that allows you to report any problems or bugs you have found in your Netscape applications. Netscape receives tons of feedback submissions daily, so don't expect a reply or thank you message, but rest assured your complaint will be addressed and the problem solved as soon as possible. The feedback page also lists Netscape e-mail addresses for direct communication and links to the support pages.

How to Get Support

Netscape Gold's online support pages provide information about your Netscape software and how to overcome any problems you might encounter with it, either on your own or with the help of the Netscape technical support team. Gold's support page has three main sections—the Client Support page, the Server Support page, and the Hot Topics directory. The Client Support page provides a directory of helpful information on Netscape Navigator, Netscape Navigator Personal Edition, Netscape Chat, and Netscape SmartMarks. The Server Support page focuses on Netscape Commerce Server, Netscape Communications Server, Netscape Proxy Server, and Netscape News Server software. Hot Topics supplies users with a direct link to the most talked about software sites on the Net. Together, these sections provide a thorough and concise software assistance package.

How to Create Web Services

Now that you have had the grand tour of this Golden browser, it's time to take a more serious look at the other aspects of Netscape Gold use. The last command in Gold's Help menu centers on the Netscape Gold Web editor and its functionality on the Net. If you are finally ready to start contributing to the vast archives of information on the Web and plan to use Gold as your primary Web editor, this site should be your first stop. The How to Create Web Services page is a hand-holding site that takes you from the first stages in HTML construction to implementation and advanced interactive Web applications. The page provides direct links to the best software available for your individual purposes and even directs you to newsgroups that may be of some assistance.

And there you have it! That is your browser in a nutshell; although there's still a great deal to learn about Netscape Gold, you now have an extremely solid basis for locating and retrieving information. But the fun doesn't stop here—nearly all of the elements discussed in this chapter will be examined in greater detail throughout the remaining chapters, so read on and discover what else Gold can do for you.

- *Where Bookmarks Are Stored*
- *The 1-2-3s of Creating Bookmarks*
- *Organizing Your Bookmarks*
- *Creating Folders*
- *Moving Bookmarks*
- *Adding Separators*
- *Sorting Bookmarks and Folders*

- *Changing Your Default Bookmarks Folder*
- *Changing the Folder That Appears in the Bookmarks Menu*
- *Automatically Updating Bookmarks That Have Changed*
- *A Final Note*

CHAPTER

4

Bookmarking Important Sites

THE WORLD WIDE WEB IS A VERY BIG PLACE, AND IT HAS HUNDREDS of thousands—maybe millions—of pages to visit. You can't possibly keep track of all the great stuff you find, or even simply the most useful sites. You need help, and in Gold that help comes in the form of bookmarks.

The trick to any bookmark system is a combination of simplicity and flexibility. Earlier versions of Netscape Navigator offered lots of flexibility, but not much along the lines of simplicity. Gold has streamlined the bookmarking system considerably, to the point where it seems less full-featured than it really is. Netscape also offers a supplemental bookmarking system called SmartMarks, which you can download from their Web site (http://home.netscape.com/comprod/mirror/index.html), but which we won't cover here. Still, if your bookmarks become a fundamental part of your workday, you might want to consider using it. Which isn't to suggest that there's anything wrong with the Bookmarks feature you get with Gold itself. Far from it.

Where Bookmarks Are Stored

Before knowing how to create bookmarks, it's useful to know where and how they're stored. Gold's bookmarks are nothing more than HTML files, stored in whatever directory you prefer, but right in the Gold program directory by default. You can load the bookmark file into your browser just as you can load any HTML file, but using the Open File command in the File menu. Figure 4.1 shows my own bookmark file loaded as a Web document.

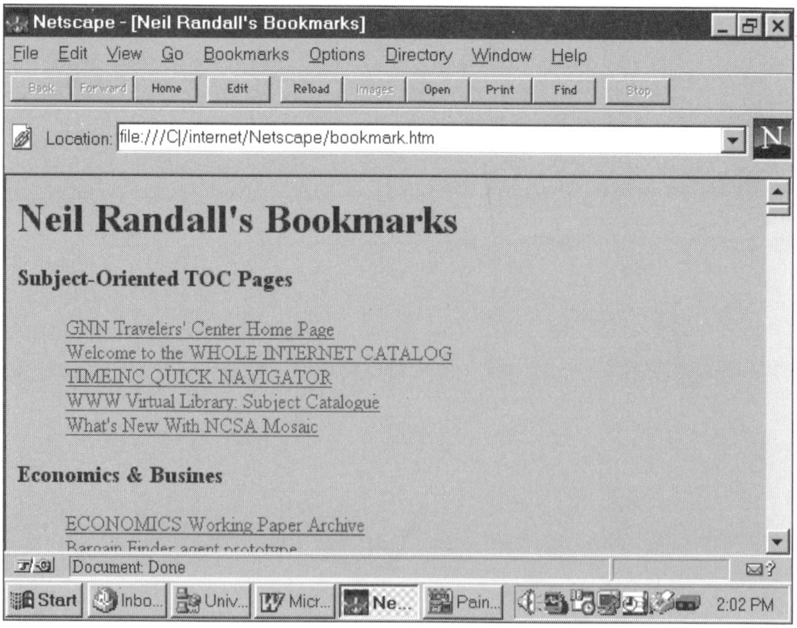

Figure 4.1

Gold's bookmark file appears as a well-sorted HTML page.

In fact, loading your bookmark file into Gold as a standard HTML page is a very good way of using your bookmarks file as a launching pad for your Web. Load it as your first document, or set it as your default document. Then you can use this as a launching window to which you return constantly. See "Setting General Preferences" in Chapter 5 for how to set your default document.

The 1-2-3s of Creating Bookmarks

There are four ways to make bookmarks in Gold. One is fast and easy, one is complex but full-featured, and the third is the one you'll probably use most of the time. The fast and easy way is to simply add the bookmark to the current bookmarks folder; the complex, full-featured method is to insert a bookmark, complete with title and your own comments, in any folder you wish. The third, and best, way is to drag and drop the bookmark to the folder of your choice. If you already have an HTML document with URLs that you wish to incorporate into Gold's bookmarking system, the fourth way lets you import them.

To add a bookmark as you browse the Web, go to the site you wish to bookmark and select Add Bookmark from the Bookmarks menu (or press Ctrl+D). The bookmark will be stored in your bookmark file, inside the bookmark folder you've set as accepting new bookmarks (see "The Bookmarks Window," below). The title of the bookmarked site will then appear in the bottom portion of the Bookmarks menu within that folder, and you can access it from there any time you wish. Figure 4.2 shows the bottom portion of my own Bookmarks menu. This is the easiest way to create bookmarks.

The most complex means of adding a bookmark is from within the Bookmarks window itself. Choose Go to Bookmarks from the Bookmarks menu. Click on the folder in which you wish to store the bookmark (there's only one folder when you first install Gold), then choose Insert Bookmark from the Item menu. This yields the Bookmarks Properties dialog shown in Figure 4.3.

Adding a bookmark this way is simply a matter of typing the name of the site and its URL. You can also type a description if you wish, to help guide you when it comes to revisiting your sites. Unfortunately, Gold does not automatically fill in the title and URL of the site currently showing the browser window, which would obviously be useful.

The third means of creating bookmarks is through Gold's extremely useful drag-and-drop procedure. Basically, you drag a hyperlink from the browser page into the Bookmarks window. To do so, open the Bookmarks window (choose Bookmarks/Go to Bookmarks), and place the browser and Bookmarks window side by side (see Figure 4.4). Next, in the browser window, click-and-hold on the hyperlink you want to turn into a bookmark (click but don't let go of the button), then, still holding the button, drag the

Figure 4.2

All bookmarked sites are accessible via the Bookmarks menu, except those covered under More Bookmarks.

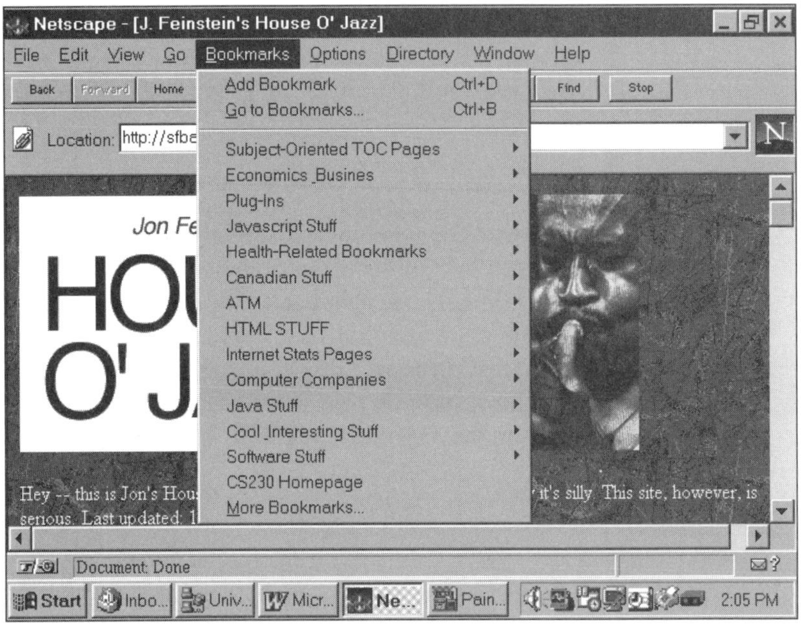

Figure 4.3

The Bookmarks dialog box gives you a place to type the name and URL of the bookmark.

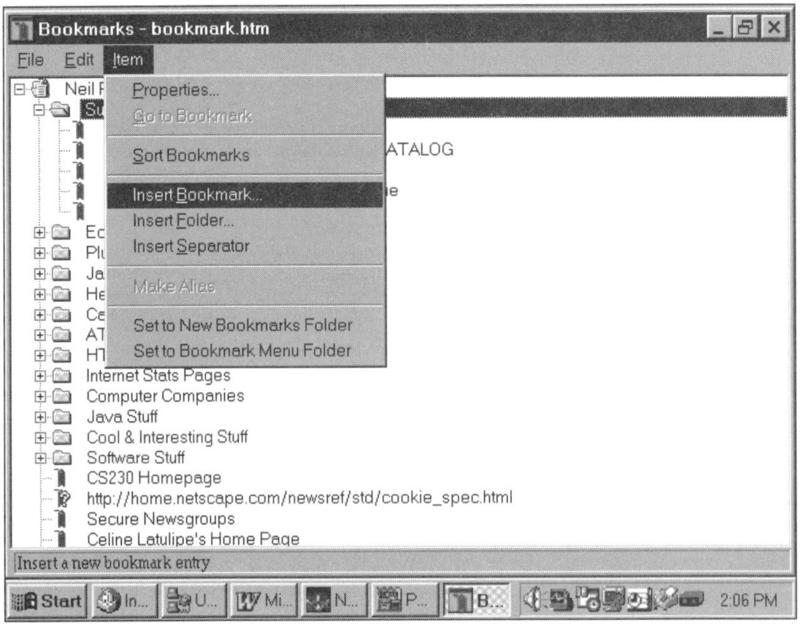

hyperlink to the Bookmarks window. You can drag it to whichever folder you wish. To drag the currently displayed URL in this way, click on the link button beside the Location box under the icon bar. This creates a bookmark for the current page. Again, you can drag the URL to any folder in your Bookmarks window. Because this method lets you organize as you bookmark, it's the most flexible and purely useful bookmarking system of the three.

Figure 4.4

With the Bookmarks and browser windows side by side, you can drag a hyperlink from one to the other.

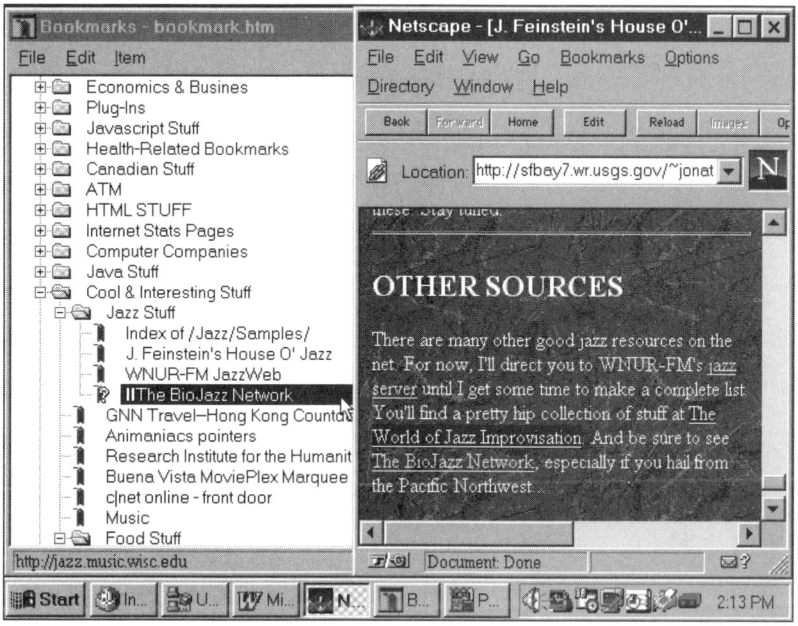

The final way of creating Gold bookmarks lets you do so in bulk, by importing URLs from an HTML document already on your hard disk. When you import such a file, Gold captures all the URLs and places them in your Bookmarks window. To do so, click in the folder (in the Bookmarks window) where you want the URLs to reside, then select File/Import, and browse to find the HTML file on your drive. Click OK, and you've got a pile of additional bookmarks.

Organizing Your Bookmarks

If the Web didn't offer so many sites worth revisiting, you could do nothing but add a bunch of bookmarks and forget about them until you need to go to that page again. But after adding a couple dozen of them, a list of bookmarks starts to become unwieldy. Add a couple hundred, as you'll almost certainly do within the first couple months of Web browsing, and you have what is pretty much a useless list. They're in no order whatsoever beyond when you actually found the site, and they need some careful massaging.

Fortunately, Gold's bookmarking system lets you organize them quite easily and effectively. You can create folders for bookmarks of favorite topics, then move bookmarks into these folders and even copy or clone them into additional folders. And you can have Gold sort your bookmarks and folders alphabetically to make them even more useful. All of these functions are handled through the Bookmarks window.

Creating Folders

When you first install Gold and start using it, all bookmarks you save are placed in a single folder. Eventually, as you find sites on different topics, you'll want to create additional folders named for these topics. For example, you might have a folder called Business, another for Art, another for Software Archives, another for Sports, and so on. The actual topics are entirely up to you.

Creating a folder is quite easy. Click on the area in which you would like the new folder to appear, and it will show up underneath the bookmark highlighted. Go to the Item menu and you will see Insert Folder. You will then see the window for Bookmark Properties (Figure 4.5).

You can name your new folder and enter a short description. Once you click on Okay, your new folder will appear in your bookmarks. You can have as many or as few folders as you like. Once you have them in place, you can start putting your bookmarks in them. The fastest and easiest way to do this is to drag and drop your chosen bookmark into the folder you desire, although you can create bookmarks from scratch as well. If you would like to put the same bookmark into two different folders, you can duplicate it by clicking on the bookmark, and choosing Make Alias from the Item menu. A second exact copy of the original bookmark will appear beneath the original, and it can be moved (by dragging it) to an entirely separate folder. This option is very useful when you want a bookmarked hyperlink referenced in two or more folders, because it crosses topic boundaries.

Moving Bookmarks

Once you start accumulating large quantities of bookmarks and a growing number of folders, you'll want to start moving bookmarks from folder to folder. This is especially true if you bookmark using the simple Add Bookmark system, which places all your additions into the same folder.

Figure 4.5

Bookmark Properties window

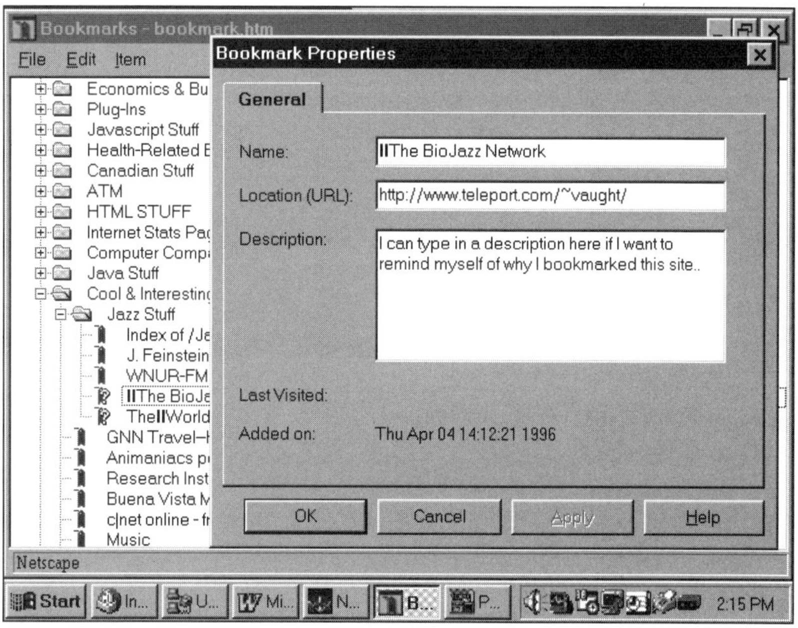

To move bookmarks between folders, open the Bookmarks window, click on the desired bookmark, and drag it to the desired folder. You can select one bookmark at a time, or you can move multiple bookmarks by selecting them through the Ctrl-click or Shift-click combinations standard to Windows selection procedures. You can delete bookmarks by selecting them and then pressing the Delete key.

Adding Separators

Separators are horizontal lines that appear in the bottom section of the Bookmarks menu. Their purpose is to offer a visual separation between long lists of bookmarks and folders, as shown in Figure 4.6. You can place separators wherever you wish in your bookmark listings.

To add a separator in your Bookmarks window, click on the bookmark or folder above the position at which you would like to place the separator. Select Item/Insert Separator. The separator line will appear below the folder or bookmark you had highlighted as <separator>, but in your browser's Bookmarks menu it will appear as a chiseled horizontal line.

Figure 4.6

The separato bar helps you find the bookmarks you want by preventing clutter

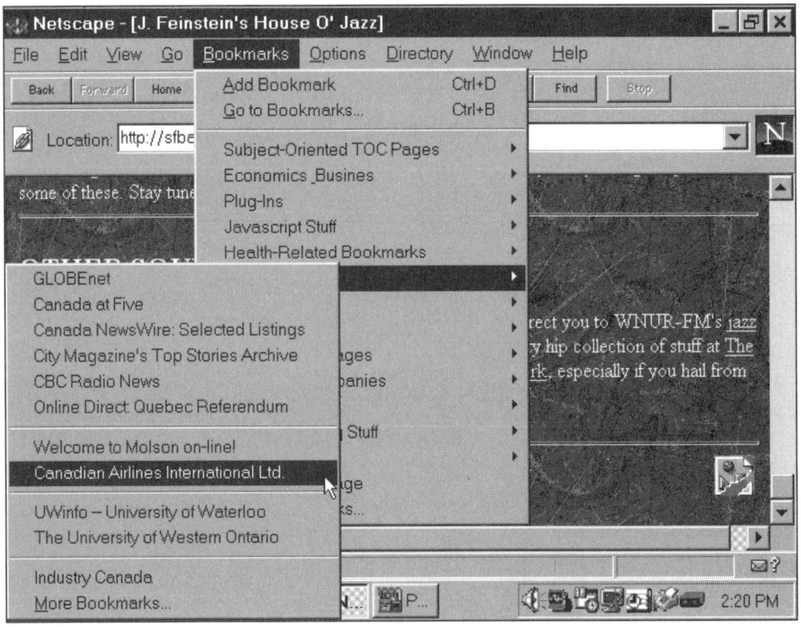

Sorting Bookmarks and Folders

One thing that might help you to organize your bookmarks is to have them sorted in alphabetical order. To alphabetize all folders and bookmarks in them, select Item/Sort Bookmarks. This sorts all folders alphabetically, all folders inside other folders alphabetically, and all bookmarks within folders alphabetically as well. Unfortunately, you can't sort only one or two folders (or even a couple bookmarks); you sort them all, no matter how many you have. Still, it's a useful organizational feature.

Changing Your Default Bookmarks Folder

When you create a bookmark using the Add Bookmarks command from the Bookmarks menu, the new bookmark is placed inside the folder currently specified as the New Bookmarks folder. By default, this is your main folder, but you can change it whenever you like. To do so, open the Bookmarks window, click on the folder in which you want your new bookmarks stored, and select Set to New Bookmarks Folder from the Item menu. This is particularly useful if you're navigating the Web looking for sites of a specific kind, and you decide to bookmark them in a separate category. Simply create a new folder, set that folder to store new bookmarks, then click Bookmarks/Add Bookmark whenever you come across a site worth bookmarking.

Changing the Folder That Appears in the Bookmarks Menu

You can alter the bookmarks that appear in the bottom portion of your bookmarks menu. By default, Gold shows all your bookmarks, albeit separated into folders. But you can select a specific folder to show here instead, in which case Gold will display that folder and all subfolders within that folder. The thing to keep in mind is that Gold shows a folder in that menu, and you can tell it which folder to show. Note that if you select a folder that is inside a larger folder, only the selected folder (and its own subfolders) will be displayed.

To change the currently displayed folder, open the Bookmarks window, click on the desired folder, and select Set to Bookmark Menu Folder from the Item menu. Now check your Bookmarks menu, and you'll see the new folder.

Automatically Updating Bookmarks That Have Changed

Let's face it: Things change on the Web. And you don't have time to check for changes all the time. So why not have Gold do it for you? The File menu contains a command called What's New, and it's immensely useful to your Web navigation. Select one or more bookmarks, then click on the What's New command, and a dialog box appears asking if you want to check for the selected bookmarks or everything on your bookmark list. Gold will go onto the Web, find the URLs and check for changes, showing you its progress via a progress box. You'll be informed of the changes it found, and updated URLs are marked by a slightly changed icon (a "shimmering" bookmark). It's impossible to understand how helpful this feature can be until you give it a try. Essentially, it acts as your assistant, and on the Web that's something we all need.

A Final Note

It takes roughly two hours of being on the World Wide Web to realize the importance of bookmarking. Without them, you'd spend most of your time finding the sites you've already visited, and nobody really has time for that. Netscape Navigator Gold's bookmarks help you keep firm track of your Web activities, help you keep those activities organized, and even tell you which of your sites have been updated since your last visit. The only caveat is this: Too many bookmarks quickly become ineffective. Spend some time with your Bookmarks window, organizing your bookmarks and deleting the ones you no longer need, and this feature will likely become a very major ally.

- *Setting the General Preferences*
- *Setting Mail and News Preferences*
- *Setting Network Preferences*
- *Security Options*
- *Editor Options*
- *The Importance of Setting Options*

CHAPTER

5

Setting Netscape's Options

THE FIRST TIME YOU RUN NETSCAPE NAVIGATOR GOLD, IT WILL retrieve the Netscape Communications home page, and you'll be able to click your way around the Web. But if you're interested in using the package to its fullest extent, you'll have to get your hands a bit dirty and do some configuring. It's not difficult, but some of the options aren't exactly intuitive.

Setting the General Preferences

The General Preferences setup dialog in Gold lets you alter the following seven categories:

- Appearance
- Fonts
- Colors
- Images
- Apps
- Helpers
- Language

This is the most complex and complete set of categories among Gold's various options. Once you've completed setting these categories, Gold will run exactly the way you want, complete with font and color choices, helper applications, and image transfers.

The General Preferences dialog is shown in Figure 5.1.

Figure 5.1

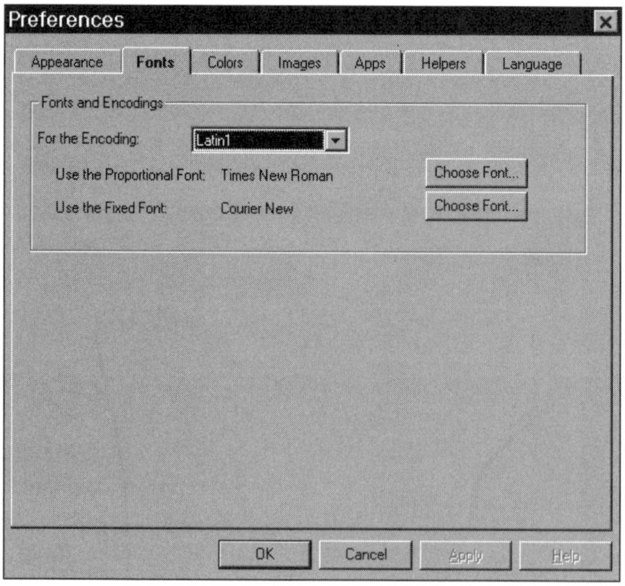

All options can be set from the General Preferences dialog. Just click on the appropriate tab.

Appearance Options

The Appearance dialog lets you set options for toolbar appearance, startup instructions, and the styles of Gold's hyperlinks.

Toolbars

You can display the toolbar icons as pictures only, text only, or pictures and text together. Figure 5.2 shows the three styles in this order.

Figure 5.2

Gold's three toolbar types

Startup

The Startup section of the Appearance dialog has two parts.

The first, On Startup Launch, lets you tell Netscape to open with the browser window, the e-mail window, or the newsgroup window displayed. You should select whichever activity you will need most when accessing the Net. Click in the appropriate box.

The second, Start With, lets you open the browser with no Web page loaded at all, or with a specified home page location. The benefit to starting with a blank document is that Gold doesn't access the Web immediately after loading. The benefit to starting with a home page location, obviously, is that you're exactly where you want to be on the Web whenever you load the program. Click the appropriate radio button.

If you want to start at a specific page all the time, such as the famous Yahoo site (http://www.yahoo.com/), consider saving the page to your hard drive, using the File/Save As feature. You can then specify this file as your home page. Let's say that, using the Windows version of Netscape, you've saved the file as c:\netscape\yahoo.htm—for example in the netscape directory on drive C. You can then tell this file to load with Netscape by typing the following in the Location box.

```
file://localhost/c:/netscape/yahoo.htm
```

Now when you load Netscape, it starts with a file from your hard drive rather than one out there on the Web. You should edit the file to get rid of graphics references (Part 2 of this book is all about editing files), or else it will still have to search the Web. As soon as it's purely a local HTML file, loading Netscape becomes much faster.

Link Styles

"Styles" is probably the wrong word for what you can do from this part of the Appearance dialog, but since it's there we might as well deal with it.

First, you can specify whether or not Gold's links are underlined. This is clearly a momentous decision. Try both and figure out which one you like.

More significantly, you can tell Gold at what point you wish followed links to expire. When you click on a hyperlink in Gold, you access a new document on the Web (you already know that, of course). From that time forward, that same link is shown in Gold with a different color than the normal hyperlink (which is blue by default). These differently colored links, whose related pages you've already referenced, are called followed links.

If you select Never Expire, Gold will show your followed links in the new color every time you load the program, for as long as it's on the same computer. More likely, you want the followed links to expire after a certain period of time (it's 30 days by default) so that Gold won't have to keep track of everything you've ever done on the Web, if for no other reason. If you want to eliminate the followed link colors immediately (in order to start over), click on the Expire Now button. This is particularly useful if other people will be using your copy of Gold and you don't want them to see where you've been.

Fonts Options

One of Gold's more curious design decisions lies in its Fonts options. With many browsers, you can specify exactly which fonts appear for every piece of text in your browser window. Gold is much more restrictive in this way, and also much more difficult to understand.

Figure 5.3 shows the Fonts dialog. The only box here is called Fonts and Encodings. Several encodings are available, ranging from Latin 1 through Japanese, Chinese (Big 5), and Korean. These encodings allow Netscape to display pages written in alphabets or symbols other than the Roman alphabet. The default for the U.S. version of Gold is Latin 1.

For each encoding, you can select a proportional font and a fixed font. Normally, HTML pages use *proportional fonts*, which are fonts in which different letters and characters use proportionately more or less space—a *w*, for

Figure 5.3

The Fonts dialog from Netscape Gold for Windows

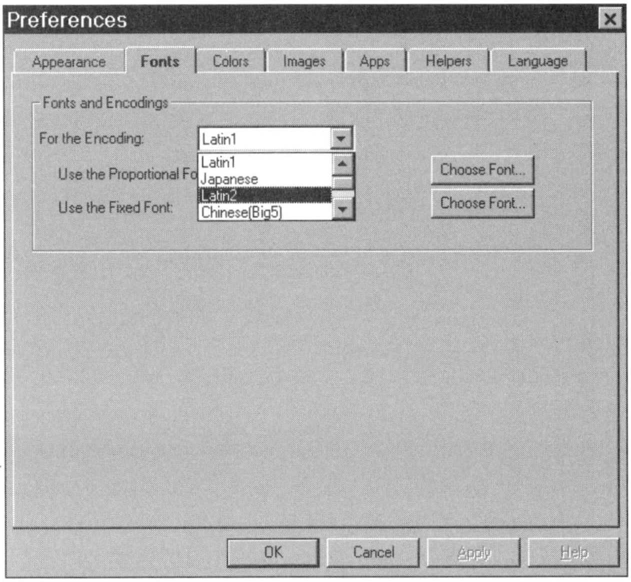

example, uses more space than an *i*. *Fixed fonts*, by contrast, are those in which each character or number uses exactly the same amount of space on the screen.

The default proportional font for Latin 1, the default encoding, is Times Roman (or Times New Roman), 12 point. If you want a different standard proportional font, click the top Choose Font button and select your choice from the dialog. To change the default fixed font from Courier New 8 to something else, click the bottom Choose Font button.

Colors Options

The Colors dialog is extremely important from the standpoint of how documents appear in Gold's main window. From here you can change the color of normal text, normal hyperlinks, followed hyperlinks, and the window background. You can also opt to have a graphic file appear as the background for documents that do not come through the Web with their own. The Colors dialog is shown in Figure 5.4.

Links, Followed Links, and Text Colors

By default, hyperlinks display in a bright blue. To change this, click the Choose Color button to the right of the Links: heading and select whatever color you wish. Netscape will automatically fill in the small checkbox with a checkmark.

Figure 5.4

You can change your browser's appearance by changing the default colors and backgrounds.

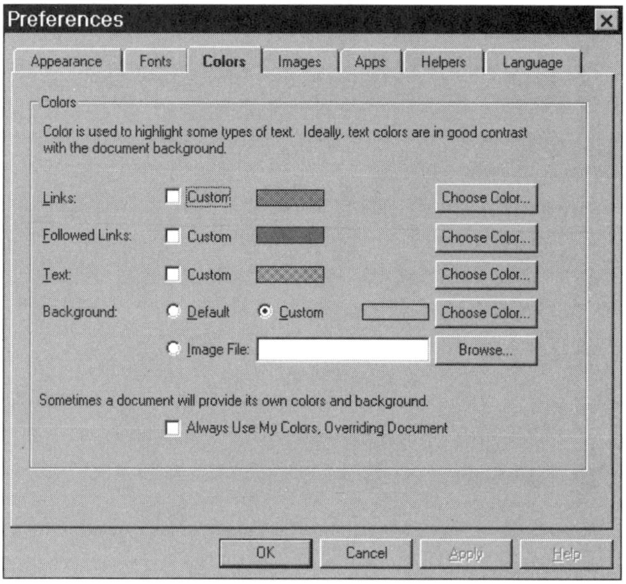

You can change the followed links color and the default text colors in exactly corresponding ways. If you want to change them back to the defaults, click on the checkmarks to deselect the custom colors. You'll be back to normal.

Background Color and Image

One of the most dramatic changes in Web pages over the past year has been the introduction of background colors and images. Until then, Web browsers offered either a white or, more typically, a gray document color. Designers designed for gray documents, and while everything certainly worked, everything also looked largely the same. With Netscape Navigator 1.1, designers could start to specify background colors to spruce up their designs, and they could even offer graphics files that would appear as background images, better known just as plain backgrounds.

But you don't have to rely on Web authors to give your browser an attractive background. Gold's Colors dialog lets you specify a custom background color or a custom background image. To select a custom color, click on the appropriate Choose Color button—as you did for links and text—and select the color you want. If you prefer a specific graphics file to appear as a background image with all documents, click the Image File radio button and either type a path and file name, or click the Browse button and choose the file you want displayed.

There are a couple points to keep in mind about background colors and images, however. If you select black as your default background color, be sure to change the default text color or you won't see any text in your window. Keep in mind that not everybody likes blood red on lime green. For images, you'll want either a faint image or a patterned image. A photograph of your spouse and child might look nice, but as a background it will render the rest of the document practically unreadable.

Overriding Document Colors

One final choice remains from the Colors dialog. By clicking on the last selection box on the dialog, you can tell Gold to use your colors and background image at all times, even if the incoming document specifies different colors and background. In other words, if you like your own choices, you can do away with those provided by other Web authors. Of course, this completely obliterates the enjoyment of seeing what other designers have to offer, but if that's what you want, go ahead.

Images Options

From the Images tab on the General Preferences dialog, you can configure the way Gold displays images contained in Web pages. Two elements are controlled here—image colors and the time at which Gold actually displays them.

The three choices for image colors (not available in the Macintosh version) are Automatic, Dither, and Substitute. If you select Substitute, Gold will use the closest match between your system's colors and the colors on the downloading image. Selecting Dither tells Gold to match the colors even more closely (through the graphical process of dithering). If you choose Automatic, Gold will make the choice itself, selecting Dither when it's practical and Substitute if dithering will take too long.

The Display Images portion of the dialog lets you specify whether Gold is to display the images while they're being downloaded, or to wait until the downloading is complete and display them at that time. In some local area network systems, the latter choice is faster, but most of us will want to choose While Loading. One advantage of the While Loading option is that, if you decide you don't want to see the whole image, you can click the Stop button and get on with your browsing. Figure 5.5 shows a graphic in the process of loading.

Apps Options

One of the confusing parts about setting up Gold is figuring out why there's an Apps and a Helpers tab on the same dialog box. *Apps* are defined as

Figure 5.5

The graphic on this page is fuzzy because it hasn't completed downloading yet.

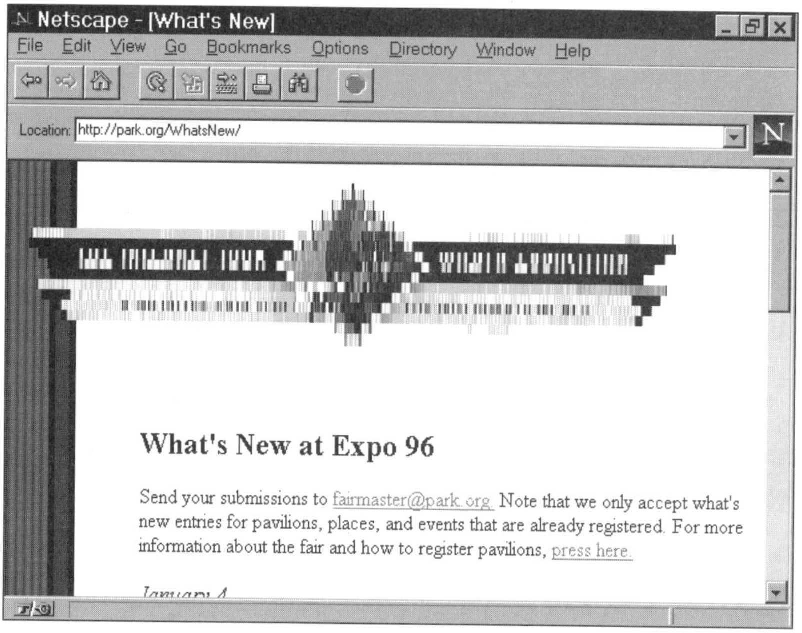

"supporting applications," and they extend Gold's capabilities by calling on other applications to perform duties Gold itself isn't capable of (well, in two cases at least). *Helpers* are usually called "helper applications," and their job is to extend Gold's capabilities by calling on other applications to perform duties Gold itself isn't capable of. See the confusion?

The distinction is this. Helper applications—explained next—are configured to launch whenever a file is downloaded that requires that helper for viewing or playing. Supporting applications, by contrast, don't act on files at all. Instead, there are only three of them, and the first two are launched when you click on a specific hyperlink type. The third offers a replacement for Gold's own View Document Source feature.

In the Apps option area (shown in Figure 5.6) you can specify four items. We'll get the fourth out of the way first since it isn't an application at all. Gold wants to know the name of your "temporary" directory—this is where applications place files on a temporary basis, erasing them automatically as they are no longer needed. For Windows users, the directory is typically c:\temp or c:\windows\temp.

The first item in Apps lets you specify a Telnet application. This program will launch when you click on a hyperlink whose URL begins with *telnet://*. If you have one of these on your hard drive, click on the Browse button and select the appropriate program file. If you don't have one, you'll have to

Figure 5.6

You can change the supporting applications from this dialog.

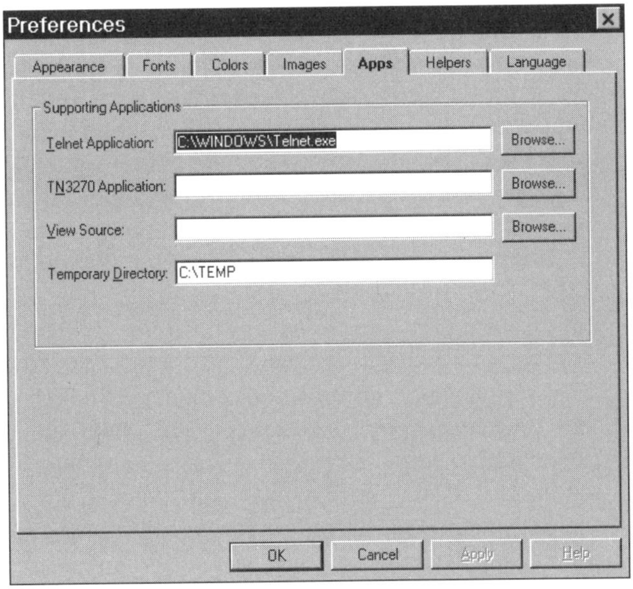

download one from the Net. Chapter 6 contains several sites where you can find Internet applications. Windows 95 users have a built-in Telnet application in their Windows directory.

Apps's second item is a TN3270 application. This is a type of Telnet application, designed for specific mainframe computers. Again, if you have one, click Browse and specify the appropriate program file. If not, find one on the Net in a site given in Chapter 6.

The final item in the Apps dialog allows you to specify a program to launch when you select the Document Source item from Gold's View menu. Selecting this item lets you see the HTML code that makes up the document showing in Gold's main window. Gold already contains a perfectly good source viewer, but if you want to specify your favorite text editor or word processor, or even another HTML editor, as the viewer, you can do so here.

Note that you don't have to fill in any of these items. If you don't intend to Telnet anywhere, or you don't even know what a TN3270 session would be used for, don't bother with either of these. Since Gold contains its own source viewer, the third item can be left blank as well.

Helpers Options

Netscape Gold is a very capable product, but it can't do everything. It doesn't do Telnet, as you've already learned, and more significantly, it can't read every type of file available on the Internet. In all likelihood, it never will. To compensate, it lets you specify external programs that will do the things it cannot.

Most of the files Gold retrieves from the World Wide Web are HTML documents, which have the extension *.html* or *.htm* (for Windows 3.*x* Web authors). That pretty much goes without saying. But there's a seemingly infinite number of other file formats out there that people want to share, and a hyperlink can point to any type of file the author wishes. It might be a graphics file in .pcx format, a sound file in the old Sound Blaster .voc format, a spreadsheet file in Excel's .xls format, or a postscript file in the standard .ps format.

Gold can't display (or play) these files directly. In fact, it can only handle HTML files, GIF and JPEG graphics files, and AU (Sun audio) sound files. But by configuring the Helpers options, you can tell Gold to launch a particular program whenever it encounters other types of files.

As an example, let's say you come across a Web site—http://www.tucows.com/ is a good example—with hyperlinks that point to files in the well-known ZIP format (.zip extension). These are files that contain one or more compressed files, and to expand them you need a program that allows you to unzip them. One such program for Windows users is WinZip; we'll assume you already have this on your machine. When you click on a hyperlink that points to a ZIP file, Gold will retrieve the file, then launch WinZip with the downloaded file loaded and ready for unzipping.

Helper apps are particularly useful when it comes to multimedia files. If you encounter a QuickTime video file or a WAV sound file, you'll need a helper application to see or hear them. By configuring Gold's helper apps, you can have these files play automatically, as soon as the download is complete. Helper apps make Gold—and thus the Web itself—appear as a complete and seamless system.

How to Set Up Helper Applications

Figure 5.7 shows the Helpers dialog from General Preferences. A wide number of helpers are established by default, but most show *Ask User* in the Action column. This means that when Gold encounters a document of that type, you'll be presented with the Unknown File Type dialog shown in Figure 5.8. The purpose of setting up Helpers is to see this dialog as seldom as possible.

You can set any file type to launch whatever application can handle it. Ironically, you can even set HTML files to launch a browser other than Gold. In other words, you could click on a standard HTML hyperlink from Gold and have the program launch, say, NCSA Mosaic to display the page. It was nice of the Netscape people to make this choice available, but it's hard to imagine anyone actually using it. It seems a tad counterproductive.

Figure 5.7

You can set up any number of external applications through the Helpers tab.

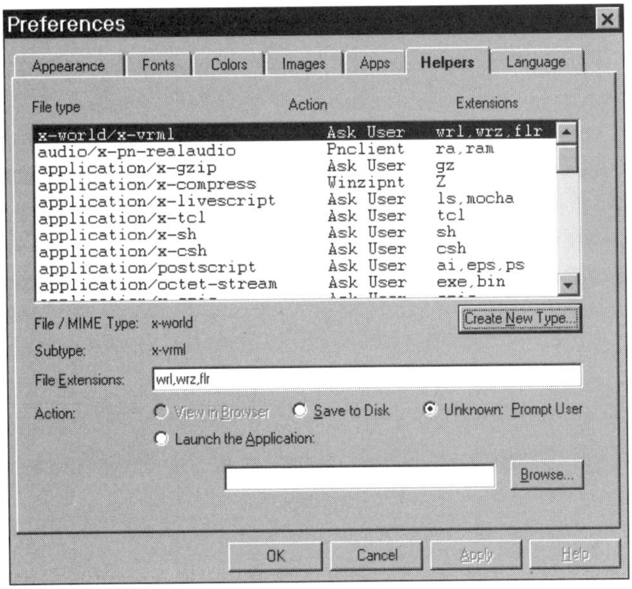

Figure 5.8

When you click on a hyperlink leading to a file with no associated helper, the Unknown File Type dialog appears.

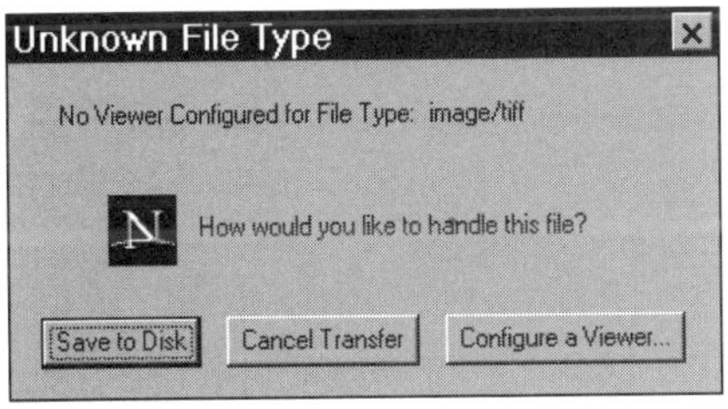

Setting Up Helper Apps from the Unknown File Type Dialog

The Unknown File Type dialog (Figure 5.8) does more than just inform you that the file type isn't set up yet. It provides far and away the easiest way to do the actual setup.

When you encounter this dialog, and you want to set up future files of the type shown at the top of the dialog to launch a specific application in the future, click the Configure a Viewer button. This will yield a Configure External Viewer dialog, in which you can type the path and file name of the program you wish to launch. Or you can click the Browse button and find the program by clicking around your hard drive. When you've filled in the file name and clicked OK, all future encounters with this file type will launch the chosen application.

Setting Up Helper Apps from the Helpers Tab

To set up an existing file or MIME (Multipurpose Internet Multimedia Extensions) type (in other words, those already inside the File Type window), click on the file type, then on the appropriate radio button in the Action area of the dialog.

Most existing file types are set to *Unknown: Prompt User*. This tells Gold to show the Unknown File Type dialog when you click on that file type. If you select Save to Disk, Gold will automatically save that type to disk, and will ask you for a directory in which to store it. If you want Gold itself to display the file, click on View in Browser. This option is available only if Gold is indeed capable of displaying it. Finally, if you want to launch a specific application for that file, click the Launch the Application radio button, then type in the path and file name or click Browse and select the file name that way.

Setting Mail and News Preferences

Gold comes complete with full-featured e-mail and newsgroup applications. You can send and receive e-mail without leaving Gold, and you can read and post newsgroup messages as well. However, until you configure your mail and news preferences, you can't work with either of them.

The Mail and News Preferences dialog (shown in Figure 5.9) is available from the Options menu. It contains five tabs:

- Appearance
- Composition
- Servers
- Identity
- Organization

Each tab lets you configure specific items; you should go through all of them to make sure your services are set up correctly. Setup is relatively straightforward if you've used other e-mail and newsgroup programs, but if Gold is your first such package then it's entirely possible that some of this will be confusing. If it is, don't despair. There isn't an Internet user out there—novice and expert alike—who hasn't torn out large chunks of hair trying to get mail and news configured. Consider it part of the charm.

Appearance Options

Three options are available from the Appearance menu, shown in Figure 5.10. First, you can specify whether you want to display your e-mail messages using a fixed width (nonproportional) font or a variable width (proportional)

Figure 5.9

This dialog lets you set Gold's mail and news servers and information.

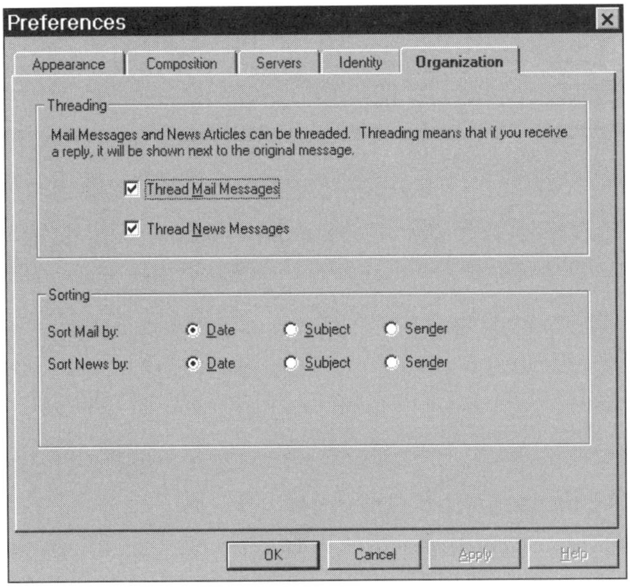

Figure 5.10

The Mail and News Appearances dialog with choices for fonts

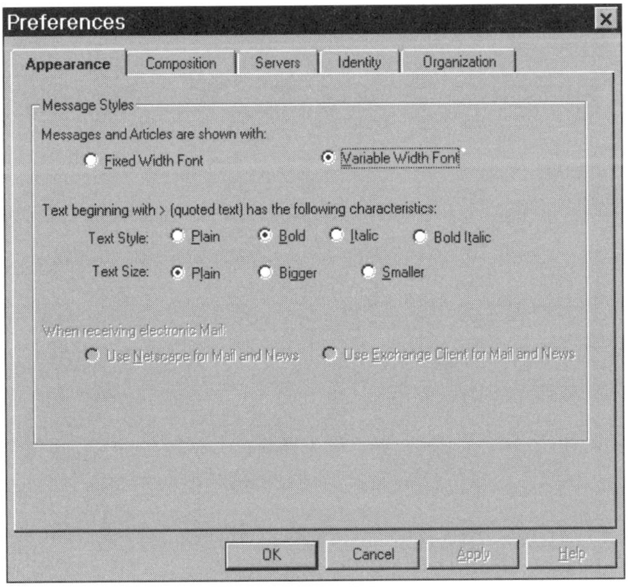

font. The actual fonts used will be those you specified in the Fonts tab from the General Preferences dialog.

Next, you have several options available for the display of quoted text. When you receive a message, you have the option of replying. If you do, the text from the original message can be included in your reply as quoted text. Quoted text is distinguished by the fact that each line is prefixed with a right angle bracket (>).

You can tell Gold to distinguish quoted text even further by selecting a Text Style radio button and a Text Size radio button from the Appearance dialog. Any combination of the two is applicable. Figure 5.10 shows quoted text displayed in italic bold type and a smaller size.

Finally, Windows users can tell Gold whether or not they want to use Netscape for their e-mail or news (the default), or use Windows's built-in Microsoft Exchange client. At least for the sake of learning the package, keep Netscape selected here.

Composition Options

The composition options (Figure 5.11) are extremely important for determining what happens to your e-mail messages and, to a degree, what they contain. From this dialog you select options for sending and posting your e-mail and newsgroup messages, where you want them stored on your hard disk, and whether or not you want them automatically forwarded to an e-mail address.

Figure 5.11

Composition options determine how and when messages get sent out to the Net.

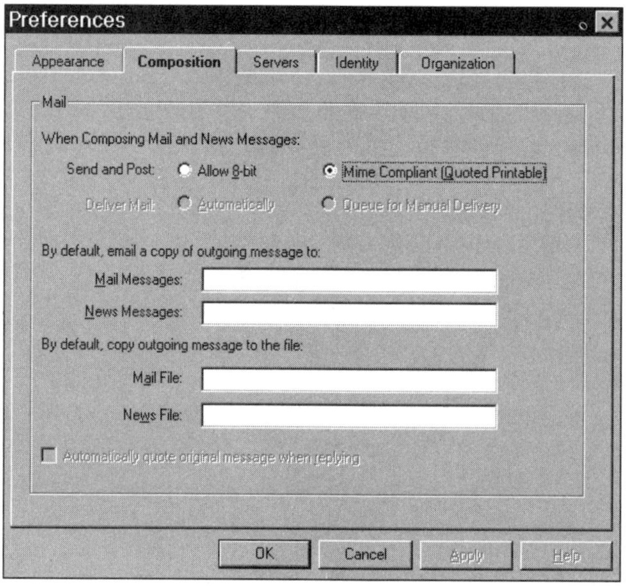

The top of the dialog shows the options available when composing mail and news messages.

The first option, Send and Post, is a bit esoteric. Allow 8-bit is the default, and it gives Netscape's e-mail program compatibility with the greatest number of e-mail server types around the world. Unless you have a reason to change this, leave it at the default. If you discover that your e-mail is coming through with garbled characters, it means that your system's mail package is partially noncompliant with the MIME standard. Choosing Mime Compliant in this case should do away with those display problems.

The next option, Deliver Mail, is a standard feature in most e-mail packages. Selecting Automatically tells Gold to send your e-mail messages out to the Net as soon as you've completed them and hit the Send button. If you choose Queue for Manual Delivery, your completed messages will be stored in a queue until you select the Deliver Mail Now item from the File menu.

The next two sections let you specify what happens to your messages and postings when you deliver them. If you wish, you can automatically e-mail a copy of the messages to a specific e-mail address. This is one way to keep track of everything you've sent, especially if you have a second e-mail address. You can then go into that account and keep or delete whichever messages you wish. Note that you can specify an e-mail address that will appear in the mail and news messages you compose.

You can save a copy of all your outgoing messages to your hard disk by entering the appropriate file in the Copy Outgoing Message boxes. Gold will then keep adding outgoing messages to this file. Unlike many e-mail programs, Gold doesn't offer an out-box in which messages are automatically stored. This preferences choice—considerably more awkward than an out-box—replaces that more typical option.

Finally, you can choose whether or not you want Gold to quote the original message when you're composing a reply. If yes, the original message will appear in the composition window, distinguished by angle brackets (>) at the beginning of each line.

Servers Options

Gold's e-mail system works well, but it won't work at all if you don't adjust the options under the Servers tab of the Mail and News Preferences dialog. Gold must be told where to go to check for mail and news, where to direct delivered mail, where to find newsgroup listings, and so forth. This dialog (shown in Figure 5.12) is an extremely important one, and should be one of the first you alter.

Figure 5.12

Setting your mail and news servers is the only way to get them to actually work.

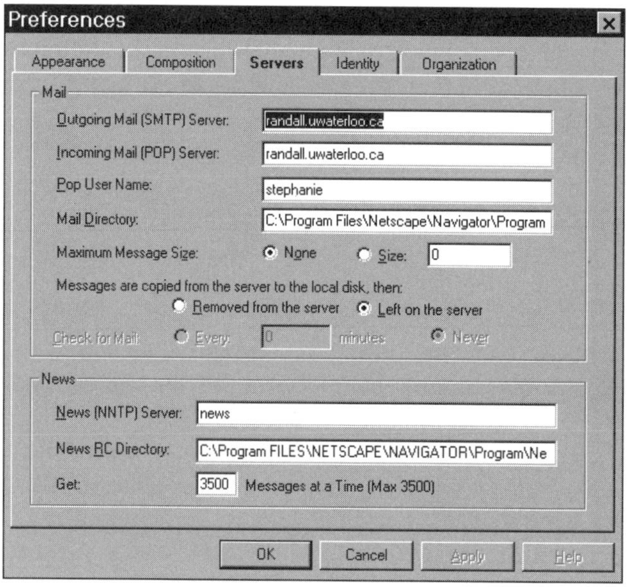

Mail and News Servers

First, you must specify the outgoing and incoming mail servers. Like everything else on the Internet, your e-mail must be "served"—it must be sent from, and brought into, a machine that has been configured to perform those tasks. The outgoing server will be an SMTP (Simple Mail Transport Protocol) server, while the incoming server *must* be a POP (Post Office Protocol) server. If your server is not capable of the POP protocol, you won't be able to use Gold's news for receiving mail.

So how do you find out? If you've configured any other e-mail program, you probably already know. Most servers today offer both SMTP and POP capabilities, so that's rarely a problem. Check with your systems administrators or your Internet service provider just to be sure. They'll also be able to tell you the name of the server, which you must type in the incoming and outgoing server boxes in the dialog.

For many users, the SMTP and POP servers will be the same. Also, for most users the server names will likely be present in the e-mail addresses. If your address is honcho@bigbiz.com, your SMTP and POP servers are probably bigbiz.com. If you're at a university and your address is jstudent@learning.university.edu, your server names are probably learning.university.com. In the latter case, in fact, you can probably get away with just showing your servers as *learning*, without the rest of the address.

But these are just guidelines. Since nothing works properly without the proper mail servers listed, take a few minutes to find out the correct name. It will save hours of frustration.

You'll also need to find out the name of your news server. Again, it will probably have something to do with your e-mail address. If you're connected through a service provider called provider.net, for example, the news server will probably be either exactly the same, or the slightly revised news.provider.net. In large organizations, it might be entirely different. Once again, contact your provider or your systems people to find out. Enter the name in the News (NNTP) Server box near the bottom of the dialog.

Other Options

- **Pop User Name.** Your POP user name is almost certainly the first part of your e-mail address. For example, my address is *nrandall@watarts.uwaterloo.ca* and my POP user name is *nrandall.* You might need the entire address in this box, but try both.

- **Mail Directory.** By default, your e-mail will be downloaded to the directory shown in this box. You can change it to save your mail in any other directory on your hard drive.

- **Maximum Message Size.** You select None, all e-mail messages will be downloaded to your hard disk, no matter how large they are. If you want to tell Gold to retrieve only messages up to a certain size, you can specify this by selecting Size and entering the number in lines. A typical cut-off point might be 50 lines. You'll receive the first 50, and the rest will remain on the server for you to retrieve with a different e-mail program, or after reconfiguring Gold.

- **Messages are copied from the server to the local disk.** After messages are copied from the server, if you select Removed from the Server, Gold will delete the message from the mail server. If you want the messages left on the server, click the other option. You will want to leave messages on the server if you check your e-mail from more than one machine and you want all messages collected on only one of those machines. Your main machine will be configured to erase the messages from the server, while your secondary machine will be told to leave them on.

- **Check for Mail.** If you're connected to the Net full-time via a LAN connection, or if you know you're going to be on the modem for a long time, you might want Gold to check the server for mail periodically (it saves you having to press the New Mail button, truly an onerous task). Clicking Never tells Gold not to check at all. If you want automatic checking, click on Every and then enter the interval. Depending on your e-mail load, you might want to check every ten minutes or once every three hours.

- **News RC Directory.** Information about available newsgroups and your subscriptions is stored in a file called a News RC file. This file lets you access your server's newsgroups without going through the lengthy task of downloading the full list every time you want to read your news. Gold provides a default, but if you already have a News RC file on your drive, you can specify that instead.
- **Get.** You can specify how many messages Gold downloads at any one time. If you have a slow connection, you might want to keep the number low. The maximum is 3,500, and if you have that many messages coming in you might want to consider establishing a new life.

Identity Options

Happily, you'll no longer have any difficulty with your identity. Gold has solved the problem completely. Amazing what the Internet can do, isn't it?

Seriously, the Identity options in the Mail and News dialog (Figure 5.13) let you specify how you want to be known in your messages. Everything here is pretty self-evident, except that *Name* refers to your real name, or whatever you want to call yourself, not your user name—that's reserved for the E-mail box on the next line. Now, you might be wondering why there's a distinction between your e-mail address and your reply-to address. Usually, there will be no difference. You can specify a different address for each, however, which is useful if you have two e-mail addresses and you want to use one for sending and the other for receiving.

The Signature File box lets you specify a text or HTML file to be included as the signature in all your messages. To select it, click on the Browse button or type in the path and file name.

The options in the Identification section of this dialog let you determine how much information to give to the servers on the Internet with whom you communicate. Selecting Nothing: Anonymous User lets you post messages that give no information about yourself. Choosing Your E-mail Address attaches your e-mail address to each message you send. If the server has given you an ID number, you can select Unique ID Number and send your posts that way. These Identification options are primarily useful for newsgroup postings, where you might not want your identity displayed.

Organization Options

Three choices are available from the Organization tab of the Mail and Help preferences dialog. Select Remember Mail Password if you don't want to type in your password every time you access your e-mail (but remember that other users of your system will be able to read your mail if you do so). Thread Messages (there's one for both mail and news) lists messages according

Figure 5.13

Gold's Identity options can be changed if you want to preserve anonymity.

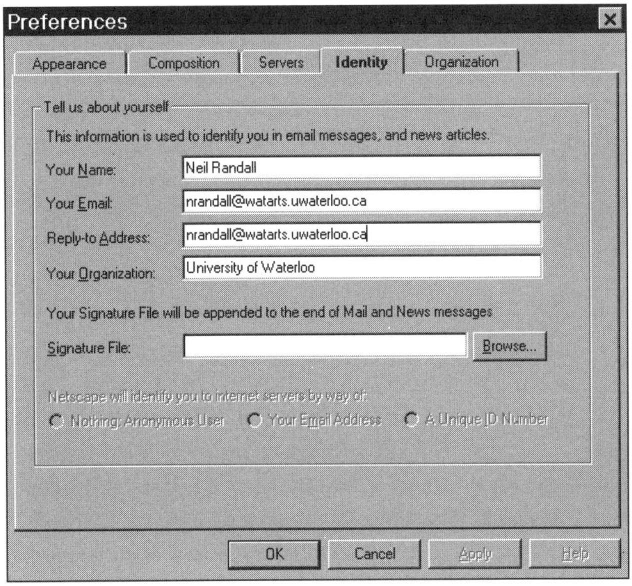

to subject rather than order received, and replies are attached to the original message in the thread. Finally, you can sort your mail and news messages by date, subject, or sender's name.

Setting Network Preferences

Although it might not seem like it at first glance, the Network preferences (Figure 5.14) have a significant impact on how quickly and effectively Gold operates. Through this dialog you can specify information about your memory and disk cache, and you can tell Gold how often to verify that a Web-loaded document is up to date.

Cache Options

Caching is one of the most powerful performance activities for any Web browser. Caching maintains a copy of a visited Web page in your local computer, so that when you visit it again it won't take nearly as long to appear. Instead of going out onto the Web, the browser will take the cached page from your own machine so it doesn't have to go through the often lengthy process of downloading (but see Other Options in the Cache dialog setup, below). This is especially important for modem users, particularly those with lower-speed connections.

Figure 5.14

To make Gold work to its maximum potential, set the Network options carefully.

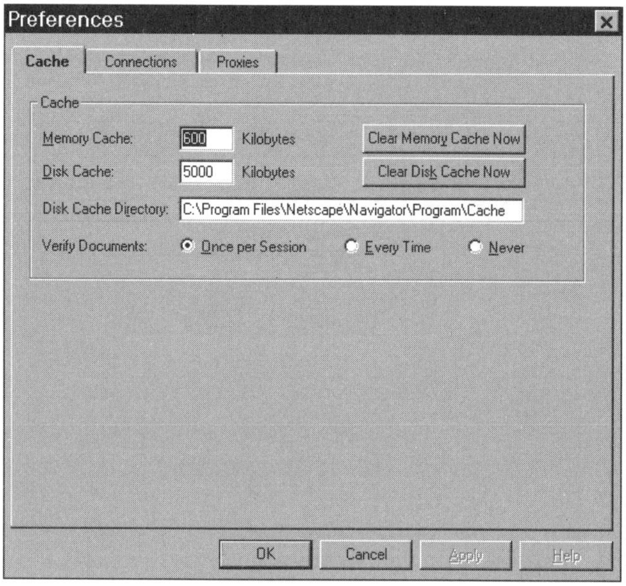

There are two kinds of cache: memory cache and disk cache. The memory cache stores documents in your system's RAM, while the disk cache stores them on your hard drive. Documents cached in memory reload much faster than those cached in disk, but as soon as you close Netscape these documents will no longer be available. Documents stored in disk cache remain available from session to session, as long as your cache doesn't completely fill up.

You can set the size of each cache type in Gold. When cache fills up, Gold will dump the oldest document from cache in favor of a new one. In general, you want as large a cache as you can afford, but the default values provide more than reasonable caching. The Cache dialog offers the following choices:

- **Memory Cache.** Here you set the amount of RAM available for cache by typing in the number of kilobytes (K) you want to allocate. If you have 8MB RAM, you should keep this figure well under 1000K. If you have 64MB, a cache of up to 4MB might be useful. The higher the cache, however, the longer it takes Gold to shut down. This is no problem, of course, for those who never shut it down anyway.To clear memory cache immediately, click the Clear Memory Cache Now button.
- **Disk Cache.** Here you set the amount of disk space available for Gold to store cached documents. If you have lots of disk space available, giving Gold a good solid chunk—10–15MB, say—will improve overall performance. Gold will check disk cache for these documents the next time you start the program and click on a hyperlink, and will replace

the oldest visited document with the most recent should the cache fill up. To clear disk cache immediately, click the Clear Disk Cache Now button.

- **Other Options.** Two other options from this dialog remain. First, you can specify the disk cache directory. Gold creates a default directory, but you can choose otherwise. This is especially useful if you have more than one hard drive and you want to keep your caches on a drive distinct from where Gold itself resides. Second, you can tell Gold to verify documents once per session, always, or never. When Gold stores a document in cache, and later you reselect that document's URL, Gold takes the document from cache, not from the Web. This is much faster, but the actual document might have changed between visits. Verifying the document means sending Gold onto the Web both to see if the document has changed and, if it has, to load the updated document instead of the one stored in cache (the one in cache will be replaced by the updated version). If you select Never, Gold won't do this at all, and you'll only be able to get updated documents by clicking the Reload button when that document is displayed. Clicking Always guarantees continually updated documents, but it slows down your browsing because Gold never relies exclusively on the cached document. Selecting Once Per Session (the default) tells Gold to check for updates the first time in any browsing session you access that URL. After that, it will go to the cached document only.

A browsing session, by the way, consists of the time between loading and exiting Gold. If you leave Gold running at all times, it won't ever think it's in a new session.

Connections and Proxies Options

Most users won't need to change the defaults provided by Connections and Proxies preferences dialogs. You have no choice but to set proxies, however, if you are running Gold from an internal network that puts you behind a firewall. A *firewall* is a technology used by (usually) large organizations to keep the machines of individual users secure from the would-be snooping and tampering of Internet users outside the organization. Essentially, your machine is kept behind locked doors, and information you request comes through a kind of protected gateway to your computer. That gateway, more or less, is called a proxy.

The following elements are configurable:

- **Connections.** By setting the number of connections, you tell Gold how many streams of information it can download simultaneously. Simultaneous connects let Gold retrieve text and graphics at the same time, and it would seem that the more connections the better. But every new simultaneous connection slows the speed of the others, so the default of 4 seems appropriate.

- **Network Buffer Size.** This figure tells Gold how much data to receive in its buffer in one transmission. Again, it would seem the bigger the better, but if you make the buffer too big you can clog up your machine's memory and slow down everything you might be working on. Unless you have a good reason, just accept the default.
- **Proxies.** If you're not accessing the Web through a firewall, the No Proxies option is the one you want. If you are, then you have two choices. You can specify Automatic Proxy Configuration by typing in the URL your organization provides to make this configuration possible (get it from your systems administrators). Or you can set your proxies manually by selecting Manual Proxy Configuration. Click the View button, then enter the proxy information for FTP, Gopher, HTTP, Security, WAIS, and SOCKS. Again, get this information from your systems administrators. This screen is shown in Figure 5.15.

Figure 5.15

If you know your proxy information, enter it in this dialog.

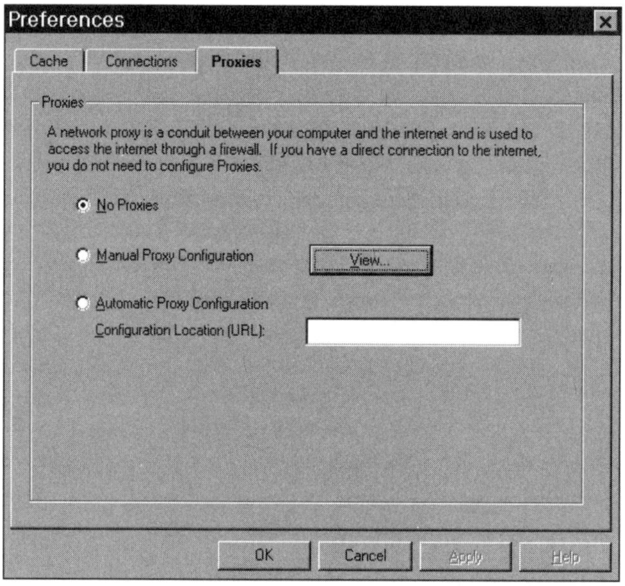

Security Options

Security has become an increasing concern on the Web. Almost from its beginnings, Netscape Navigator has incorporated the use and access of secure documents. In Gold, this has advanced to the point where a separated security options dialog lets you establish when you wish to be alerted for security issues, and also lets you set up new security types. The dialog is shown in Figure 5.16.

Figure 5.16

The Security Options dialog lets you determine how and when you're warned about nonsecure pages.

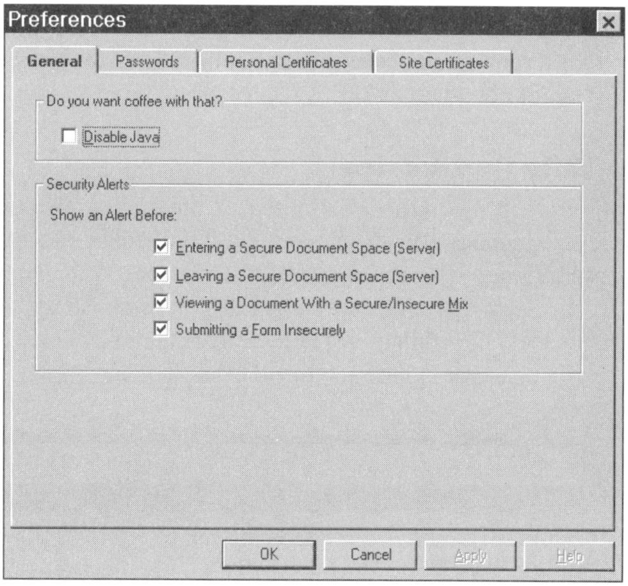

Disable Java

This has nothing to do with security, really, and you'll probably see it moved to a new dialog in the future. For now, clicking here disables Gold's ability to display and run Java programs. See Chapter 22 for more details on Java.

Show an Alert Before

By default, Gold displays a warning panel whenever you encounter a secure document. You can select whether or not you want this panel to appear when you're entering a secure document space (a document on a secure Web server), when you're leaving a secure document space, or when you're viewing a document with a secure/insecure mix (the document has both secure and nonsecure information).

In addition, and perhaps more importantly, Gold warns you when you're about to submit a form to a nonsecure server. In the case of searches and other standard activities, this isn't a problem. But if you're submitting information about yourself, including your home address or your credit card information, pay strict attention to the warning. Nonsecure means nonsecure; there's no protection from meddlers who might want to intercept the information.

It's not actually necessary to display this panel at all. At the far left of the status bar, Gold displays a security key—literally, an icon that looks like a key. If the key is broken with a gray background, the document is nonsecure.

If the key is unbroken and on a blue background, the document is secure. Furthermore, documents with a URL beginning with *https://* come from a secure server. URLs beginning with *snews://* indicate secure news servers. As different kinds of security appear on the Web, however, these indications might not always work.

Site Certificates

As security on the Web increases, the number of possible types of security also increases. In the future, you'll find yourself acquiring "certificates" that guarantee security on specific sites on the Web. The Sites Certificates tab on the Security preferences box lets you establish and edit these certificates (Figure 5.17). Highlight a specific certificate and click Edit to change the information, or click Delete to get rid of it.

Figure 5.17

From the Sites Certificate dialog you can manage and edit your security information.

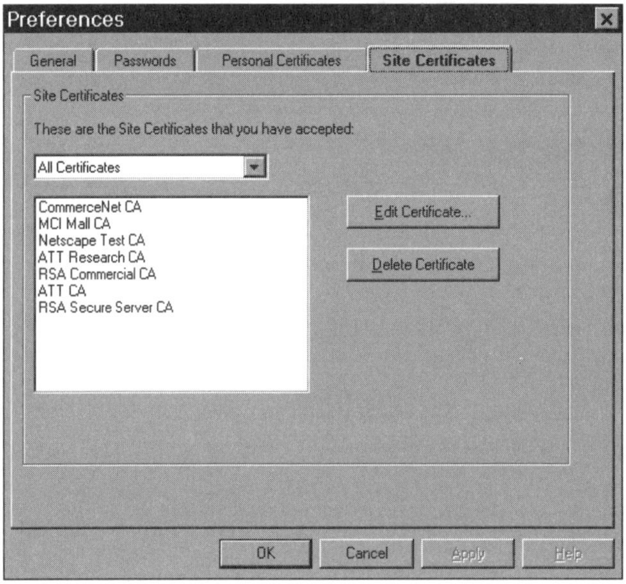

Editor Options

Gold's Editor is where you'll be spending most of your time as you create your Web documents. Setting the Editor's preferences can help keep your work consistent, and can save you time in a number of ways. To set them, select Editor Preferences from the Options menu. This will yield the dialog shown in Figure 5.18. It contains three tabs — General, Appearance, and Publish — each of which contains several possible settings.

Figure 5.18

The Editor Preferences dialog helps make your uploading and publishing work easier.

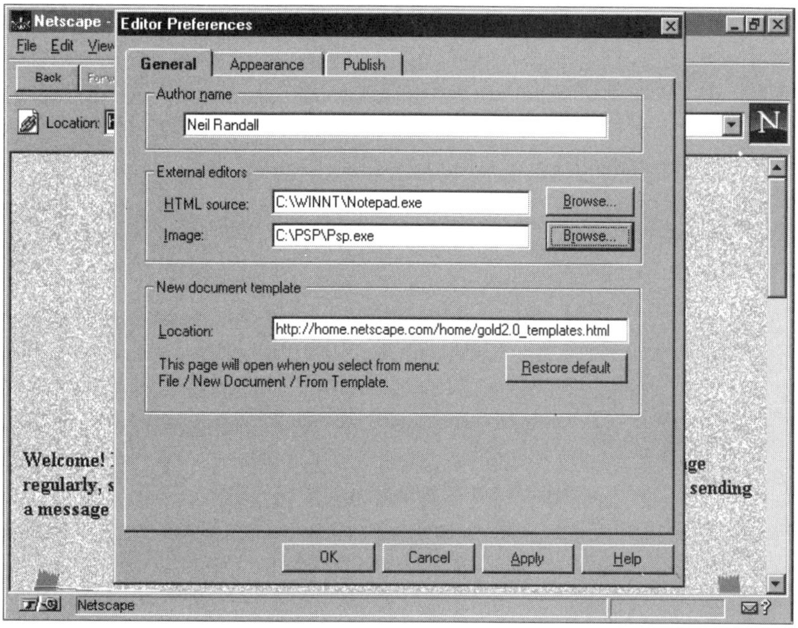

General Options

Through the General options dialog, you can set the programs and fields that will occur as you create all your HTML documents.

Author Name

If you're having difficulty with this one, consider turning your computer off and getting some fresh air. Seriously, though, this is the author name that will appear by default in your documents. Some search engines will look for this information and catalog your documents accordingly.

External Editors

The designers of Gold have been nice enough to realize that the program won't do everything, and that we need other programs to help us get our work done. Here you can select an editor in which you can compose your HTML source code (i.e., the raw HTML that Gold doesn't cover), and another program that will let you edit your graphics. The HTML editor will appear when you select View/Document Source, and the graphics editor will appear when you click Edit Image from the Image Properties dialog.

New Document Template

In the Location box of the New Document Template area, you can specify the page that will open when you choose File/New Document/From Template in order to begin a new document. By default, choosing this menu command will take you to Netscape's site, specifically to the page that includes templates. Other pages will undoubtedly begin to appear on the Web as Gold takes hold, and you may wish to change this.

Appearance Options

The Appearance Options dialog allows you to specify the colors and backgrounds you want all your *new* documents to begin with. It works identically to the Appearance options in the Document Properties box, covered in Chapter 13. Keep in mind that changing options here won't change the current document, just any new ones you begin working on later.

Publish Options

The Publish options dialog is shown in Figure 5.19. From here you can establish how you want your HTML documents to be uploaded (published) when you're ready to place them on your Web server. Typically, the machine on which you author your pages will be different from the machine on which they'll reside (i.e., the machine with the Web server software), and setting these options will help you put them in the right directory on the right machine.

Links and Images

From this dialog you can establish how Gold will handle the changing of hyperlinks and the uploading of associated images.

Maintain Links: When you create your Web, you often create internal hyperlinks (see Chapter 14) that refer to other document files within the same Web. The problem is that moving your HTML files to another computer means that the directory references won't likely be the same, and the links won't work. Gold can change the links when it uploads the file, to make them relative to the directory where they are now stored. Unless you have a reason for *not* wanting these links changed, you should leave this box checked. Note, however, that the links only change for references to documents within the directory to which you're uploading the document. If you want to link to other directories, make sure the links are specific.

Keep Images With: If you have images within your document (and you probably will), you'll need to transfer these to the Web server as well. Gold saves you considerable time by listing the images you've included in your

Figure 5.19

Setting your Publish options saves you time when uploading your documents.

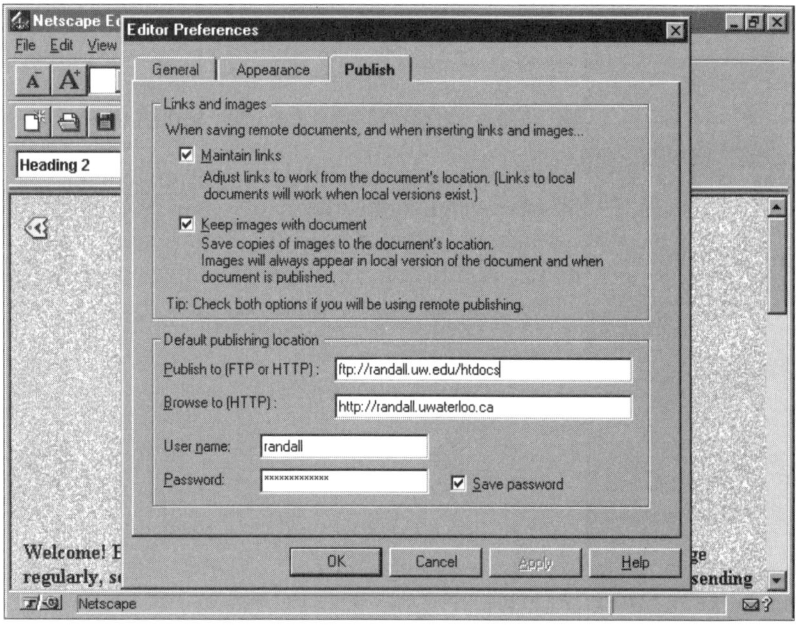

document, and offering to upload them along with the HTML document itself. The only time you wouldn't do this would be if the images are already on the server; this would happen, for instance, if you're editing an existing document from that server.

Default Publishing Location

By selecting Publish from the Editor's File menu, you can upload your documents to your Web server. At that time you can specify where to upload them, but you can set a default location through the Publish options of the Editor Preferences dialog.

Publish To: This is the location where you want your files to be stored. You can upload through File Transfer Protocol (FTP), or, if your server allows it, through Hypertext Transport Protocol (HTTP). Check with your systems administrator about which one to use, although FTP will be the case most of the time. Write the location as a URL, so that an FTP transfer begins with *ftp://*.

Browse To: When you select Default Publish Location from the Go menu of the Gold browser, Gold will retrieve the document specified here. Usually this will be the home page of your Web site, and it's purely a convenience.

User name and Password: To upload your documents, you'll need to specify the user name and password that correspond to the file location. Whatever you use to do an FTP to that site is what you'll type here.

■ The Importance of Setting Options

Netscape Navigator Gold is an easy program to use, but its huge potential makes proper configuration essential. Some features will not work at all without being configured from the Preferences dialog, while others will work more smoothly once you set them appropriately. Visit these dialogs often to make Gold do exactly what you want it to do.

- *Downloading Files through FTP*
- *Downloading Files through HTTP*
- *The Importance of Downloading*

CHAPTER

6

Downloading Files: Multimedia and Helper Applications

ONCE UPON A TIME, DOWNLOADING A FILE FROM THE INTERNET TO your computer demanded a graduate degree in computer science or electrical engineering. With the advent of the Web, these requirements were reduced considerably. With a browser as capable as Netscape Navigator Gold, retrieving files has become easier still. It's still not merely a matter of point and click, but it's not too far from that ideal.

The secret behind downloading through Gold is simple: Whenever you click on a hyperlink, you're telling the browser to go out onto the Web and bring that file back to your hard disk. There's nothing esoteric or mystical about the Web; it's a file retrieval and format display system that works across a large network. The point is that any file that is made available on anyone's Web server and given a hyperlink can be accessed by anyone using Gold; many Web authors take advantage of this fact by posting files of many types on their sites. Most files you encounter will be HTML files, but they certainly don't have to be.

For example, Figure 6.1 shows a Web page with several different types of files. Most are links to HTML files, but there are graphics files and even program (executable) files as well. Clicking on any of these files tells Gold to start the download process. You'll be asked to save it to your hard disk or, if you've configured Gold's Helpers dialog (see Chapter 5), the download will launch an external application. In a few cases, Gold can display the file by itself.

Figure 6.1

This Web page offers links to several different file types, ranging from HTML files to programs.

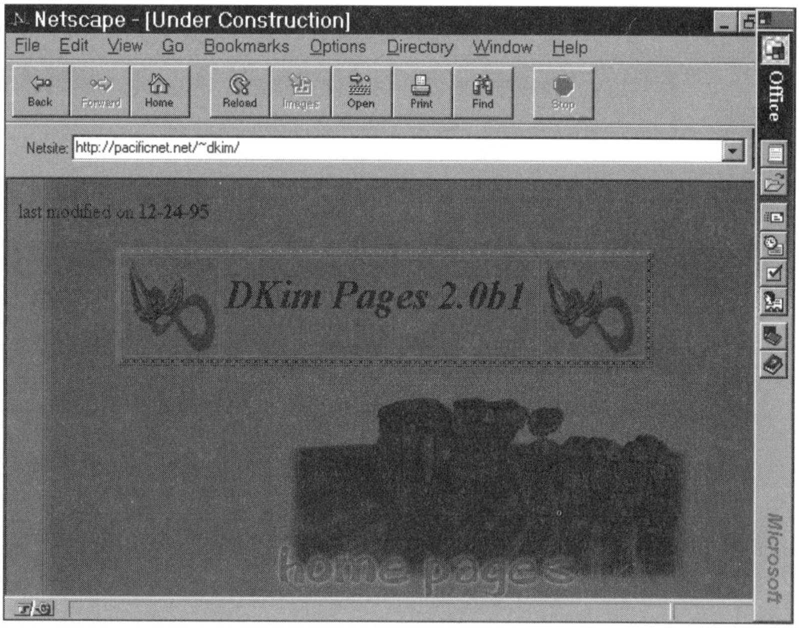

Downloading Files through FTP

File Transfer Protocol (FTP) is one of the oldest protocols on the Internet. In fact, it's been around even longer than e-mail. One of the initial reasons for the development of the Net was to allow researchers to send files back and forth, and FTP became the protocol of choice. It's simple, and over the years it's become extremely effective.

It's also easy to build into Web browsers, which have supported FTP for quite a while. Gold is no different. When you click a hyperlink that begins with *ftp://*, Gold will launch an "anonymous FTP" session and go get the file.

What is anonymous FTP? The FTP procedure demands a log-in name and a password, just like an e-mail session or a Telnet session. To get into the files of your own Internet account, you would FTP to your address, log in with your username (log-in name), and then type your password. This is fine, but if you want everyone on the Net to be able to download files, they'll all have to know your username and password, and that would be—to say the least—not very good.

As a result, FTP offers a means of letting anyone into specific directories where public files are stored. These directories are configured so that everyone using the log-in name *anonymous* can get in, as long as they provide their e-mail address as their password (sometimes the password *guest* works, but this trend is diminishing). Once you do this, you typically have access to all the files in that directory. You won't be allowed to go anywhere else on the destination machine, but you're after the public files anyway.

Gold handles anonymous FTP only. You can't use the browser to access private directories, even if those directories are your own machine. For that, you need a separate FTP program, and many of these are available on the Net. For UNIX users, good ol' FTP itself works great. Mac users will almost certainly prefer the graphical FTP program Fetch (complete with an amazingly cute animated dog), while Windows users have such programs as Winsock FTP at their disposal (Windows 95 also contains a rudimentary command line FTP program).

There are two ways of retrieving files through Gold using FTP. The first way is to click on a link to an FTP *site*. This link will appear as something like ftp://ftp.borland.com/, with no file name showing. In fact, set Gold right now for http://www.borland.com/TechInfo/TechInfo.html. At the bottom of the page, you'll see a link to Borland's FTP tech information archive. Click on it (or enter **ftp://ftp.borland.com/pub/techinfo/** directly into the Location box), and you'll see the FTP directory displayed in Figure 6.2.

What Figure 6.2 shows is the FTP site established by Borland, the software company. They want Web users who are also Borland customers to download documents and files from that site, so they've established one

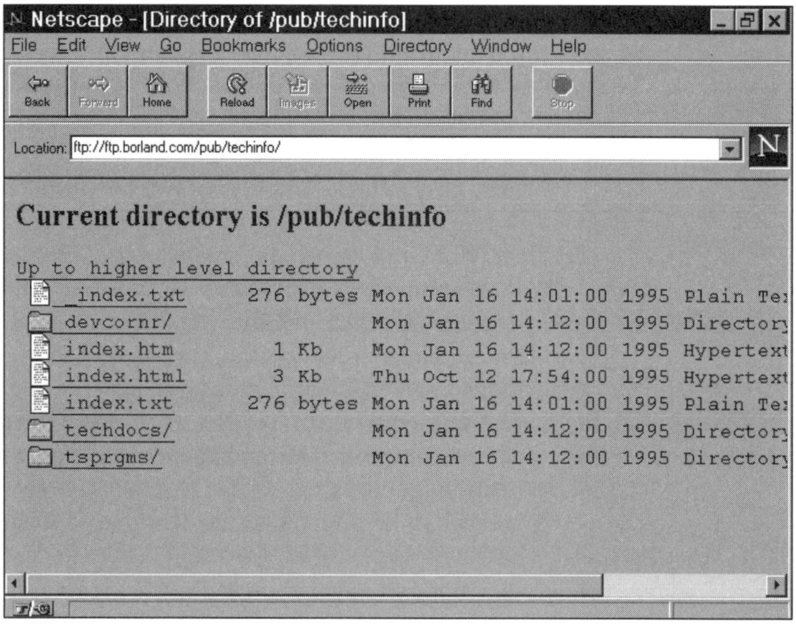

Figure 6.2

Borland's technical information archive is an FTP directory with files and subdirectories.

directory on their host computer as a public FTP area. Anyone who uses *anonymous* as a username and their e-mail address as a password can get into the directory, click in the subdirectories to see what's there, and then click on a file name to retrieve the file. Note that there's one file called index.html—if you select this one, you download an HTML file, which means of course that Gold will display it in HTML format. In fact, that's what I've done for Figure 6.3.

So how does Gold know what username and password to send? First, it's programmed to send the username *anonymous* whenever it encounters an ftp:// hyperlink. As for the password, that's simply your e-mail address, and it takes that information from the Mail and News Preferences dialog (which you set in Chapter 5). Actually, while Gold handles anonymous FTP well, other browsers let you specify other usernames and passwords so that you can log in to private FTP sites as well.

The other way to conduct an FTP download from Gold is to click on a hyperlink that begins with ftp:// but ends, this time, with a complete file name. For example, Figure 6.4 shows the Web page (http://www.qualcomm.com/ProdTech/quest/freeware.html) for acquiring a copy of Eudora Light, a popular e-mail package. (Yes, Gold gives you e-mail already, but lots of people like to try alternatives.) Under the *Click to Download* heading, and in the Macintosh area, each of the hyperlinks is a direct FTP link.

Figure 6.3

The index.html file from Borland's FTP site appears as a fully formatted Web page.

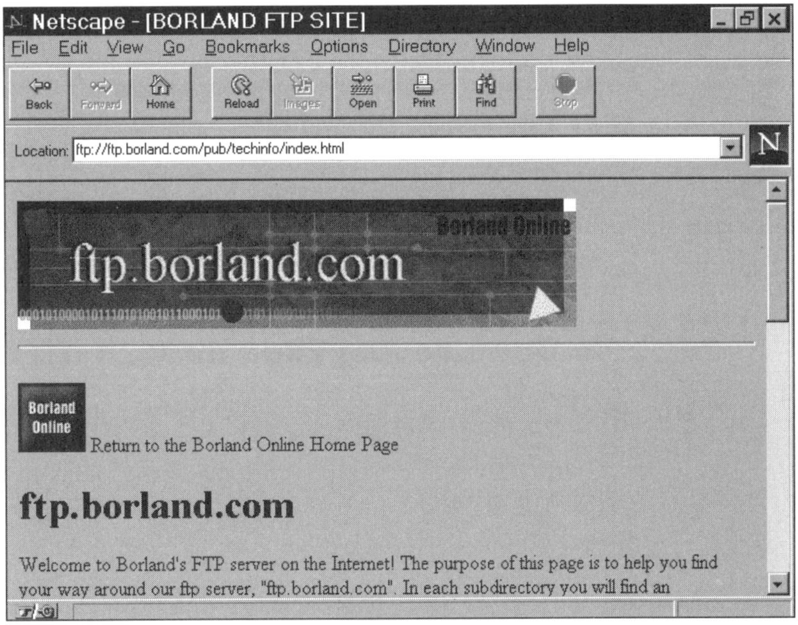

Figure 6.4

Through Qualcomm's Web site, you can retrieve a copy of Eudora Light.

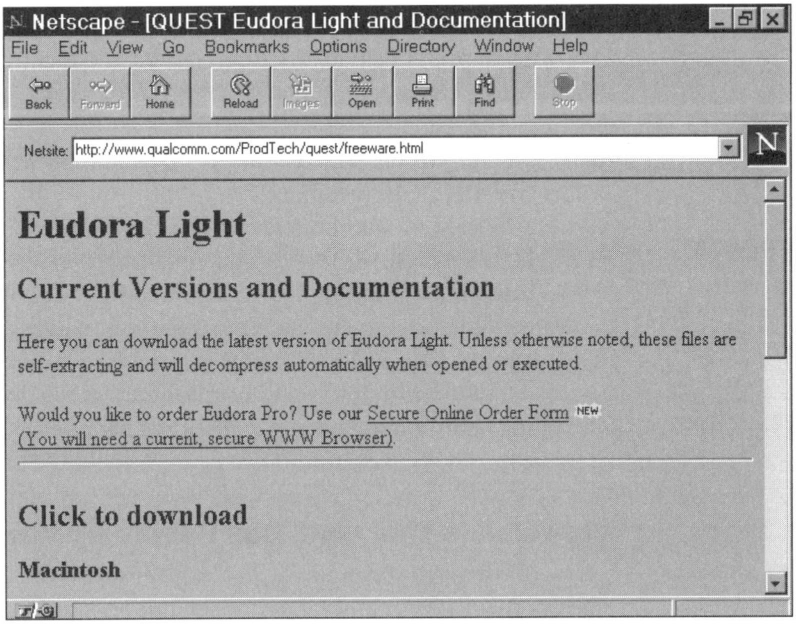

When you move the cursor to the link entitled Version 1.5.3, for example, Gold's status bar shows the URL as ftp://ftp.qualcomm.com/quest/mac/eudora/1.5/eudora153.hqx. This means that clicking on the link will take you directly to the file on the FTP site and start the download process. There's no need to click through subdirectories in search of the file; one click does it all.

Files downloaded through FTP can be configured to load directly into helper applications, through the Helper Options discussed in Chapter 5. For example, a .ZIP file can go directly to your zip program, while MIDI files can automatically launch a MIDI player. Files you get through FTP are no different from files you get in any other manner through Gold.

Downloading Files through HTTP

HTTP is the major protocol of the World Wide Web. It's the opening four letters of the URL of almost every hyperlink on the Web, and if you watch Gold's status bar as you pass the cursor over links you'll see it many, many times during the course of a Web session. HTTP stands for *Hypertext Transport Protocol*, and through it most Web files you select will be retrieved to your computer.

In most cases, URLs beginning with *http://* end with *.html* or *.htm*. A typical example is a link from Apple Computer's home page (at http://www.apple.com/), which leads to information about the company and its history. The link is called About Apple, and its URL is http://www.apple.com/documents/aboutapple.html. Clicking on this link tells Gold to head out onto the Web, using the HTTP protocol, to the Web site on the computer named *www.apple.com* (it's probably an alias, but Gold doesn't care). It then finds the directory called *documents* and retrieves the file called *aboutapple.html.* This is an HTML file (the extension tells you this), and Gold will display it as a formatted HTML document.

But HTML documents aren't the only files HTTP can handle. In fact, it can handle whatever type of file you wish to throw at it. As long as the hyperlink points to the right directory and the right file name, HTTP will download it to your computer. For example, if you click on a hyperlink whose URL is http://204.255.154.100:12345/rawin100.exe—as you can from the RealAudio Web site (http://www2.realaudio.com/release/download.html)—you'll be telling Gold to download a copy of the file named rawin100.exe, which happens to be the RealAudio player for Microsoft Windows.

Downloads That Gold Can Handle by Itself

A more common use of file downloads through HTTP is with multimedia files, particularly graphics files. In fact, not only does Gold download two types of graphics files directly—JPEG and GIF formats—it also displays them in the browser window. As an example, Figure 6.5 shows part of the Paul Cézanne exhibit on display in the WebLouvre (http://sunsite.unc.edu/wm/paint/auth/cezanne/works.html).

Figure 6.5

Paul Cézanne on the Web at the virtual Louvre

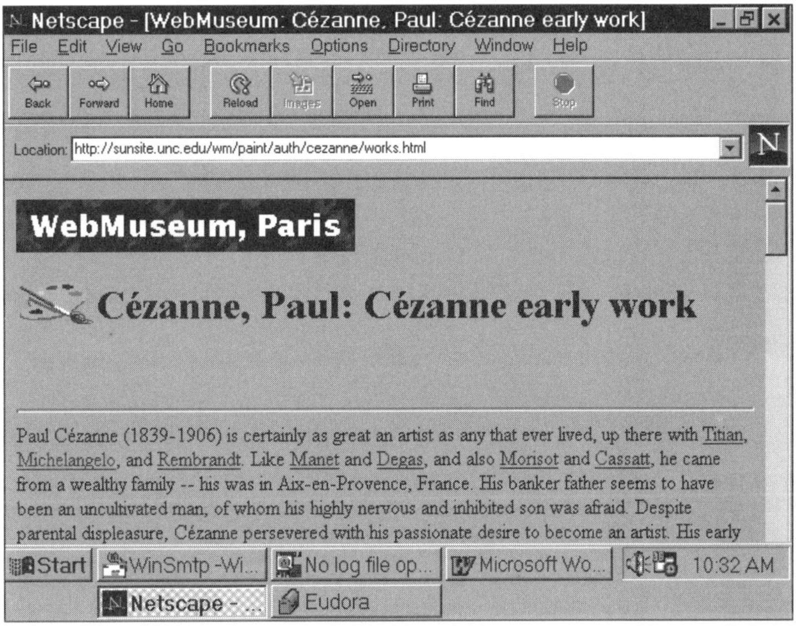

This page shows a number of hyperlinks, one of which is the small graphic entitled "Portrait of the Artist's Father." Clicking on the graphic downloads and displays a larger version of the same picture. It's shown in Figure 6.6.

The file is now on your computer. To save it permanently, you need only right-click on it and select Save This Image As…, or choose Save As from the File menu. Then you'll have it for keeps.

Another type of file that Netscape can play without special configuration is the Sun audio sound file (.AU extension). An example of this type of file is shown in Figure 6.7 at the Star Trek Voyager home page (http://www.paramount.com/VoyagerIntro.html). Next to the text "A Message from Kate Mulgrew" (who plays the Captain of the *Voyager*), you can see two small hyperlinks, one labeled *au 8kHz* and the other *11kHz 68k*; the URL for the first link is http://www.paramount.com/sounds/VOYS08KM.au, and that for the second is http://www.paramount.com/sounds/VOYS11KM.au. Clicking on either downloads a Sun audio file with Mulgrew's voice, and Gold will play it automatically through the Netscape Audio Player (naplayer) program that

Figure 6.6

The large version of "Portrait of the Artist's Father" from the Cézanne exhibit

Figure 6.7

The Star Trek Voyager welcome page, with sound files available for download

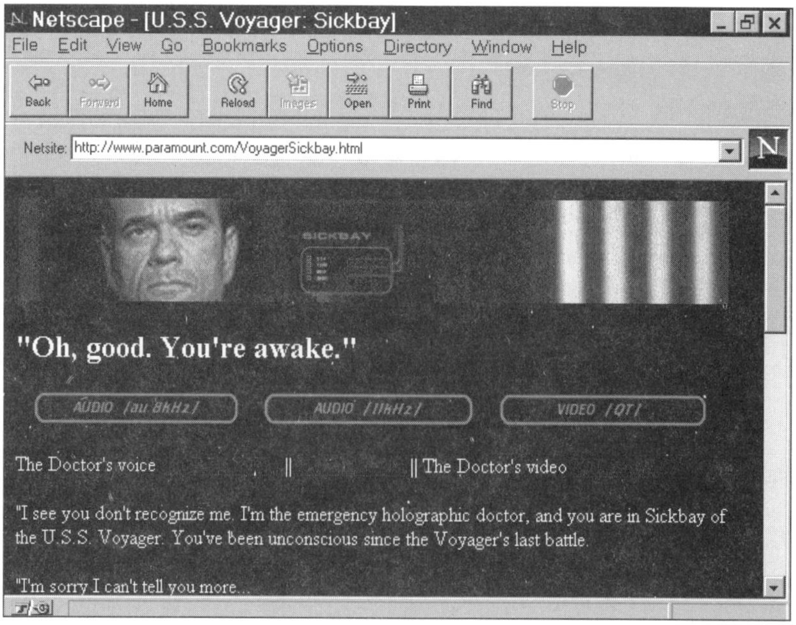

comes with the browser. The difference between the files is one of sound quality. Sound recorded at 8 kHz (kilohertz) is of a lower quality than sound recorded at 11 kHz or higher.

Gold can display two other types of files—standard text (or ASCII) files and XBM graphics files. ASCII files look dull, and XBM files aren't all that plentiful, although they are displayable without a separate application.

Downloads That Gold Needs Help With

Apart from HTML, JPEG, GIF, XBM, AU, and text files, Gold can't do much by itself. Fortunately, the first three represent the most common Web files available, and AU remains a very common sound file. But if you want to explore the full range of downloads available on the Web, you'll need to install some helper applications or Netscape *plug-ins*, programs that install directly into Netscape, thereby changing its capabilities.

Plug-ins are covered in Chapter 10. For now, we'll concentrate on helper apps alone.

Before you can actually install helper applications, you have to find some. Several are included on the CD-ROM accompanying this book. They're listed by platform and category, and you can install them and use them as you wish. Several are shareware, however, and must be paid for and registered after a specifically stated trial period. Shareware isn't free; it's just borrowable for a while.

An excellent place to start locating helper apps is the Netscape helpers index at http://home.netscape.com/assist/helper_apps/index.html. Here you'll find a good selection of available files for all three Gold platforms—UNIX, Macintosh, and Windows. Figure 6.8 shows the main page for the helper apps available at the Netscape site.

In Figure 6.8, you can see links to archive sites for each of the different platforms. Clicking on the UNIX link, for example, takes you to the screen shown in Figure 6.9, UNIX Helper Applications. At the top of this page you can find links to archive sites with a host of UNIX programs. If you know what you're looking for, by all means click on one and start searching.

As you scroll down the page, you'll see links to specific helper apps for specific purposes. Figure 6.10, for instance, shows the audio and graphics choices for UNIX users. It's hardly an exhaustive list, and it might not even be up to date, but it's an excellent starting point. These links will take you either to another HTML page or into an FTP site, where you can download the software.

Installing Helper Applications

Chapter 5 dealt with the details behind configuring Gold to work with the helper applications you have on your hard drive. Before you do the configuring,

Figure 6.8

From this set of pages you can download most of the helper applications you'll need.

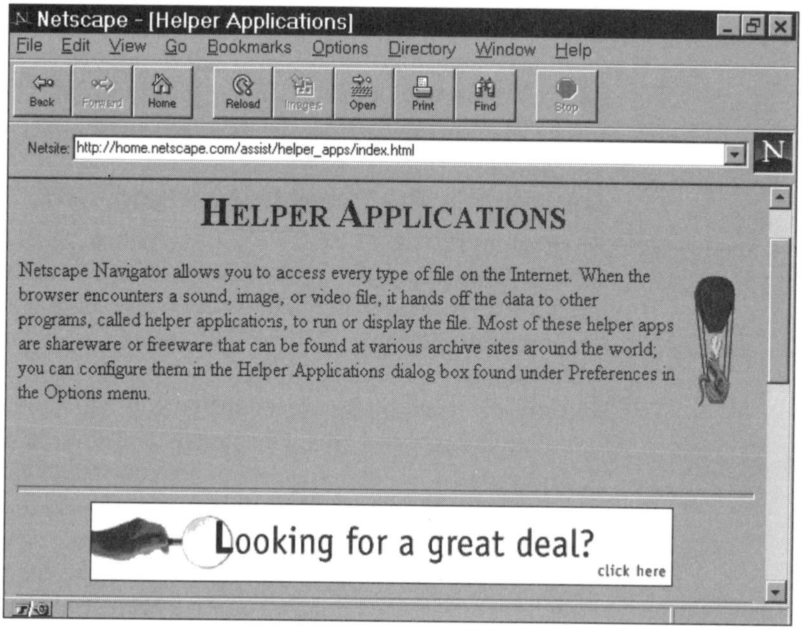

Figure 6.9

The top of each Helper Applications page shows links to FTP archives for that platform.

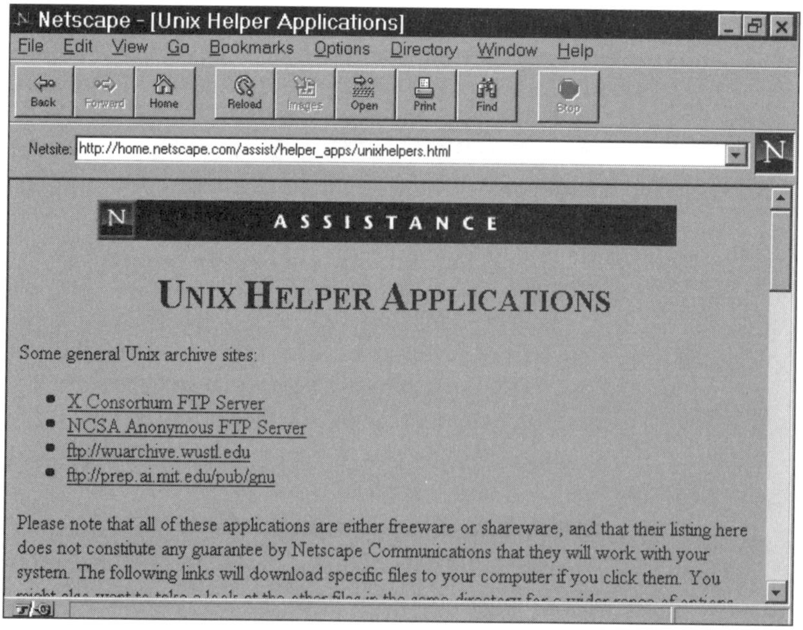

Figure 6.10

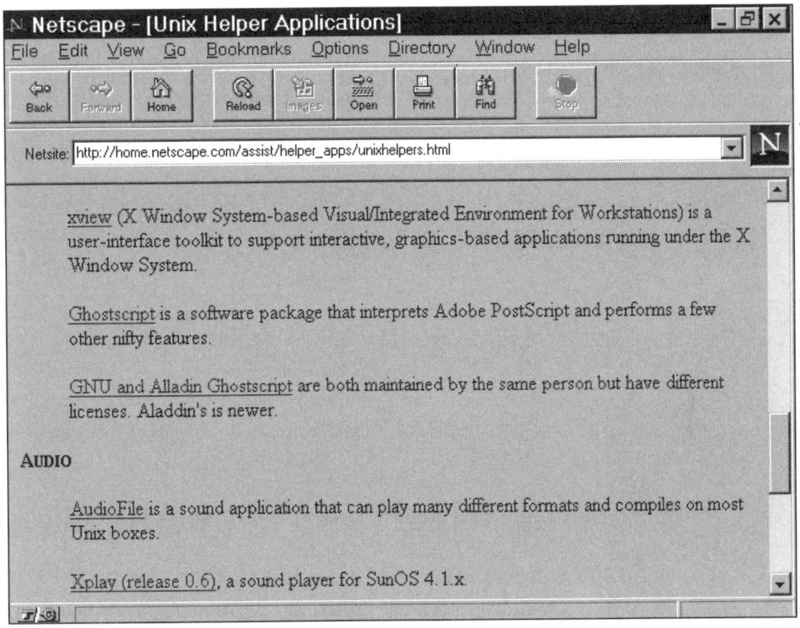

Helper apps for the UNIX version of Gold are linked from this Netscape Corporation page.

however, you have to get the helper apps and install them on your machine. Doing so isn't difficult, but it does demand that you know some of the ins and outs of installing software.

Installing software downloaded from the Net typically involves two steps:

1. Decompressing the software
2. Installing the program

To keep files to a size that people would have any interest in downloading, and to keep all files for a particular program together, FTP archivists usually bundle them together in one large *compressed* file. File compression shrinks the files according to some fascinating and arcane compression techniques, and more than one file can be compressed into one new file. Depending on the type of files, compression can shrink sizes to as little as 20 percent of the original size. For modem users this is especially crucial.

You have to know how to decompress these files if you want them to work. Each operating system has its own file compression types, and you'll need a separate program that will allow the decompression to take place. This book isn't the place to introduce all of them, but you can find them on the Web in the software archives.

Once you've decompressed the files on your hard drive, it's time to install the software so that it's usable. Installation procedures are usually included with the software in a text or word processing document. Load the document into your word processor, print it out, and follow the procedures step by step.

Generally speaking, Macintosh users have the easiest job installing software. Windows users are next. UNIX users have to know exactly what they're doing to get it right. But even a partially experienced UNIX user can often get their software up and running and personally configured before Windows and Mac users, because the UNIX operating system demands a greater familiarity with procedures to get anything done in the first place. Moreover, there are UNIX users all over the Net who apparently truly enjoy helping other UNIX users get things working.

Once the software is installed, you can configure Gold to use it whenever it encounters a file of that specific type. This is handled through the Helpers tab on the General Preferences dialog (see Chapter 5).

The Importance of Downloading

Although it might not seem like it when you first get Gold up and running, downloading files to your hard drive will become an important part of your Web activities. New helper apps are constantly appearing, as are upgrades to the ones you already have. Gold itself is upgraded regularly; you'll need to download it from the Netscape home page and then install it on your machine.

Furthermore, as a Web author, you'll want to start collecting documents, graphics files, video files, audio files, and anything else you need to make your Web pages top-quality offerings. And you might just want to start that art collection for your own satisfaction, or that archive of MIDI files in case you ever get back to that music hobby.

But there's a potential danger to downloading: viruses. Although viruses haven't been a major issue on the Internet, they could easily become so. One of your first purchases should be a good antivirus package, one that offers frequent updates to catch new viruses. There are some fine folks out there just dying to get you infected, and they keep inventing new viruses to make that happen. Go to your software store and buy a good, recent virus package, then install it on your machine and check *every* file you download. Virus packages are also available for download via FTP in various archives across the Web.

- *Read This First*
- *Getting Started*
- *Components of the Mail Window*
- *The Message Content Pane*
- *The Menus*
- *The Toolbar*
- *Options for Your Messages*

CHAPTER

7

Reading Your Electronic Mail

LET'S FACE IT: E-MAIL IS HARDLY AT THE TOP OF THE NEWS THESE days. CNN hasn't featured it in one of their "Wow, is the Net ever special!" segments. Neither the *New York Times* nor Neil Postman has launched into a diatribe about its dehumanizing tendencies. It wasn't even a sharp focus of the Communications Decency Act, that piece of stultifying legislation introduced into U.S. Congress in 1995. E-mail is just e-mail—you do it more or less every day, and getting an e-mail address is just about as newsworthy as getting a telephone number.

But Netscape Gold's e-mail is a horse of a significantly different color. No matter which Web browser you've used until now, you've almost certainly been able to send e-mail messages by calling up a special e-mail utility. If you're seriously into e-mail, however, having a means of just sending mail, no matter how sophisticated the application might be, is considerably less than half the battle. You need to be able to manipulate the messages you send, to create address books and group e-mail addresses, and, most importantly, to *read* messages you get from others. You need, in other words, a complete e-mail package.

Netscape Gold isn't the first browser package to include e-mail. Products such as Quarterdeck's Internet Suite and America Online's GNN Works (formerly Internet Works) have long offered a browser with a button to take you to a separate e-mail program. Wollongong's Emissary came out with a fully integrated package late last year, and it offers a browser, an FTP program, and a full e-mail and newsgroup package, all accessible from the same window. But Web users know that Netscape Navigator is the browser of choice, and nothing else quite fills the bill.

Happily, Netscape solved the problem by adding their e-mail package. Now, in fact, Gold offers the fullest integration of e-mail, newsgroups, and Web browsing of any Internet package. In this chapter we'll take a look at the e-mail *reading* portion of Gold, while in Chapter 8 we'll examine the e-mail *sending* capabilities.

Read This First

Before you can start using Gold's e-mail system, you have to configure it properly. If you followed the Mail and News configuration section in Chapter 5, you'll already have this completed, but if not, you might want to turn back there now. The trick is to establish your mail server, your e-mail identity, and whatever other options you wish to configure by choosing Mail and News Preferences from the Options menu. Once you have these completed, you're ready to start using Gold's e-mail components.

Getting Started

The first thing you probably want to know is how to get to your e-mail window from Netscape. No problem: Go to the Window menu and click on Netscape Mail. This will give you a completely new window to work with; in other words, two of them are open now. Figure 7.1 shows the Mail window overlaid onto the browser window.

Assuming Gold can find your mail server, the next thing you will be asked to do is to type in your password (the Password dialog is shown in Figure 7.2).

Figure 7.1

You can cascade your Gold windows to make both visible and easy to reach.

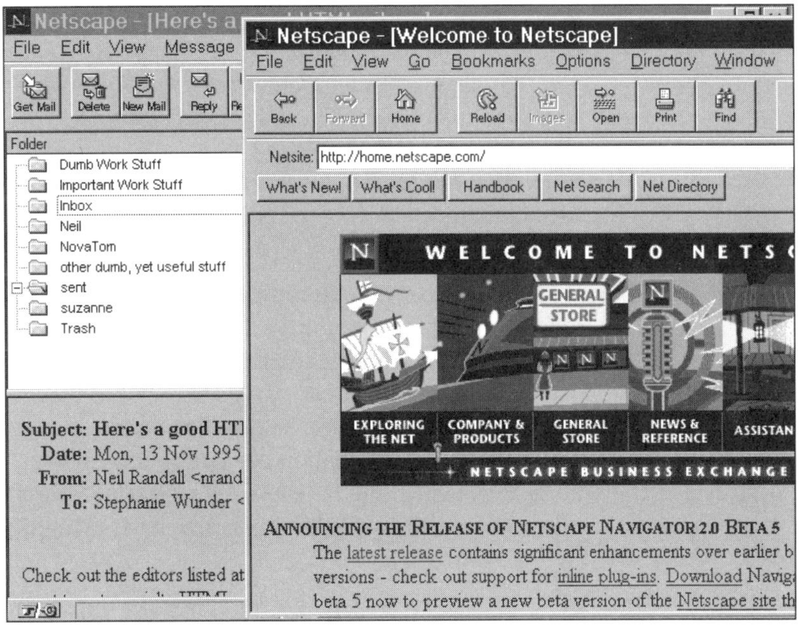

As with all useful passwords, you can't do anything unless you get it right. If it's not working, but you know it's right, make sure that Gold shows the right username. This won't be necessary if you're the only person using Netscape for mail, but if more than one person uses it and changes the configuration, your password obviously won't work. And face it, you could spend hours trying to get into somebody else's mail with your password and not succeeding.

Figure 7.2

Gold's password dialog, hardly a thing of overwhelming complexity

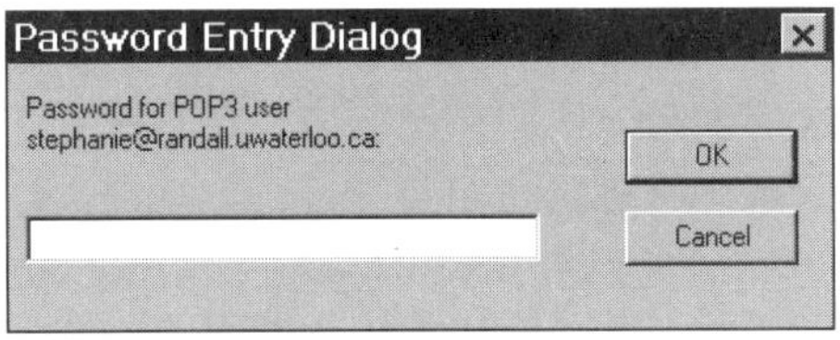

NOTE. *Actually, this bit about passwords brings up a point about Gold's mail system that really should be addressed in future versions, although it's certainly no different from other e-mail packages in this respect (except for ConnectSoft's E-Mail Connection). After you've gone through the process of getting all your e-mail folders set up, it would be nice if every possible user of Gold could get a different window with unique folders and other options.*

Right now, if you set everything up the way you want it, the next person in gets access to all the e-mail messages you'd saved, and can effectively see what you've been doing on e-mail all along. That just can't be good. One method, of course, is to install a separate version of Netscape for each person who uses your computer. This would work, except that it would take up additional disk space and still wouldn't really solve the problem of security (anybody could still get into your mail folders). But again, this is standard in most e-mail programs. You need a password to read new mail, but not to read older mail saved in folders.

It might not be necessary to type your password. If you've configured the Mail and News preferences to Remember Password, Gold will simply take you right into your mail. Obviously, you won't want to do this if you're concerned about others reading your incoming messages.

Once you've typed your password, Gold accesses your mailbox on your e-mail server and proceeds to download the new messages. If you don't have any new messages, a notification box will so inform you. If you're like most people, this is the most common response to entering your e-mail folder, especially since you probably check for messages every 9 minutes or so. Who doesn't?

Components of the Mail Window

You've clicked on OK, and you're ready to go. You now have a fully functional e-mail system, one that's available whenever you're doing a Web session. Even so, it probably doesn't look like any other e-mail package you've ever used—the popular Eudora, for instance—so let's walk around the screen and find out what there is to look at. The e-mail window is shown in Figure 7.3.

First there's the menu and toolbar, but we'll cover these after looking at the more crucial components—the Folder, Message Header, and Message Content panes.

The Folder Pane

In the top left corner is the Folder pane (Figure 7.4). Here you'll find all of the folders that are available to you. At first, you'll have only the Inbox, Sent, and Trash folders to work with, but you can add as many as you need as you go along. Your new incoming mail appears in your Inbox folder, messages you sent appear in your Sent folder, and messages you delete appear in your Trash folder, just like your office, more of less. In fact, it's so much like your office that the messages remain in the Trash until you get rid of it manually. In Gold's case, that means selecting Empty Trash Folder from the File menu of the Mail window.

Figure 7.3

Gold's e-mail window, divided into three separate panes

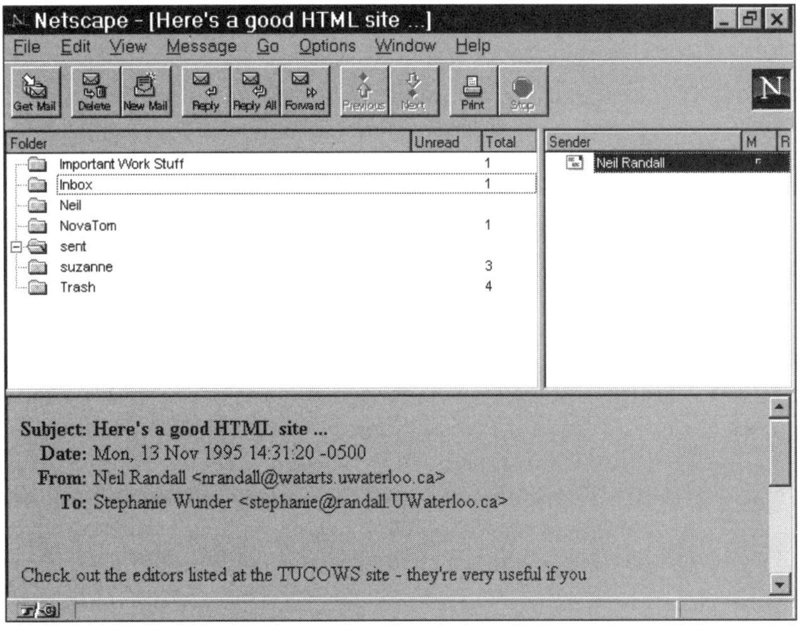

Figure 7.4

A close-up of Gold's Folder pane showing column headings

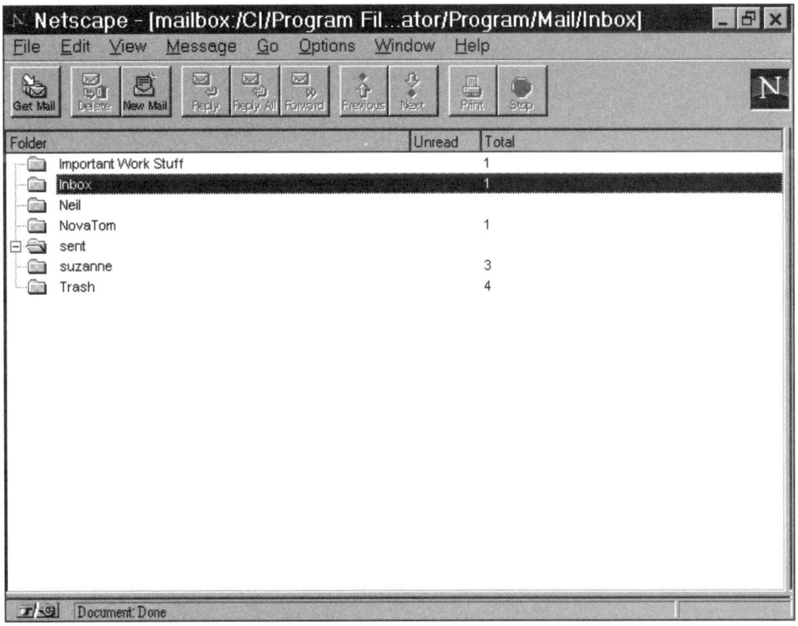

If you look at the top of the box, you will see that there are three columns. The first shows you the names of the folders. The middle column tells you how many messages in each folder remain unread. To its right is a column showing you how many total messages are in each folder (that is, unread messages plus those you've already read).

Technically, you never need any folder other than the Inbox, in which you can store all your messages. However, if you need to store any significant number of messages, you'll want to create a variety of folders. You might have one for future projects, another for correspondence with the boss, and another for information you've picked up from a mailing list; or you might just have folders named after the people who send you messages, especially if these people continually send you messages worth keeping.

To add a new folder, select File/New Folder. A dialog box will appear, asking you to type in the name of the folder. Click OK, and the folder will appear in the Folder pane in its proper alphabetical place. Unfortunately, you can't nest folders within folders, something that in advanced e-mail programs is extremely useful. Perhaps in another Gold incarnation this feature will be modified.

You can change the size of the columns in the Folder pane by positioning the cursor on the lines between the columns until it appears as two arrows pointing in opposite directions. Then you simply drag the column in whichever direction you prefer. This is particularly useful if you want to resize the panes themselves so that, for example, the Message Header pane is larger than the Folder pane (and you can therefore see more information about the messages in the folders). If you want, you can even move columns completely out of the way by dragging them beneath the border of the adjacent pane.

The Message Header Pane

To get to the mail in any individual folder, click on the folder's name. The headers of all the messages in that folder will appear in the Message Header pane at the top right of the Mail window (Figure 7.5).

Headers, in this case, consist of five elements. Sender (Author on the Macintosh) gives the name of the person who sent the message. Subject shows the subject of the message, as the sender typed it in. Date tells you when the message was received in your Inbox. The two single-letter columns, M and R, show (respectively) whether the message has been flagged and whether it has been read.

Messages that have not been read appear in bold, while those you've read appear in normal type. You can't change this, although you can alter the font through the Mail and News Preferences dialog. See Chapter 5 for details.

Figure 7.5

A close-up of the Message Header pane, showing threaded messages

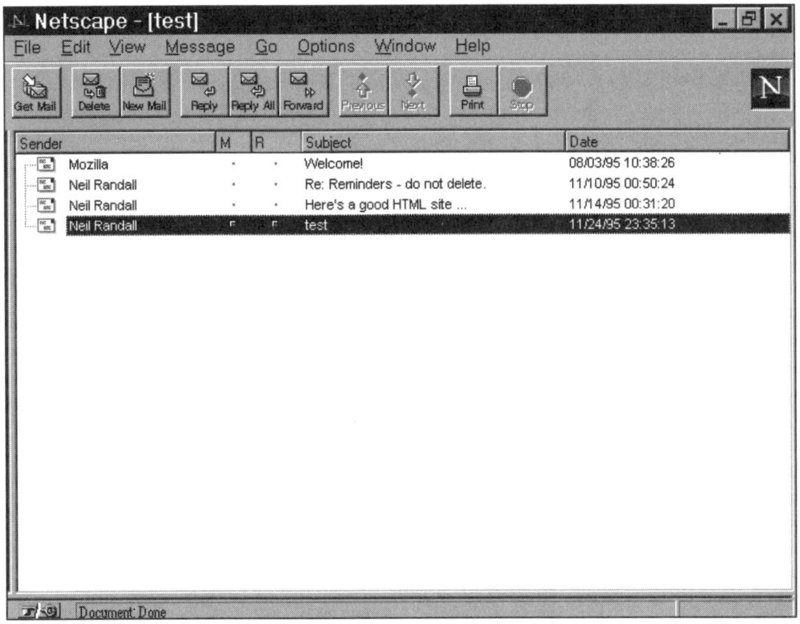

If you've selected Threaded Messages in the Mail and News preferences menu (see Chapter 5), some messages might be indented (as shown in Figure 7.5). The indentations tell you that the messages have been "threaded" according to subject. This means that future messages with the same subject line will also be threaded together, a very nice touch when it comes to keeping track of long, involved threads, especially those that occur in mailing lists.

By default, the messages are arranged according to date. You can change this to sort them by subject or by sender instead. To do so, select View/Sort, and in the cascading menu select Subject or Sender. You can accomplish the same task by clicking the Sender, Subject, or Date title above the Message Header pane.

Once again, you can change the column sizes by dragging. This is highly useful for giving more room to the Subject column, because the message subject is usually the longest single element.

You can also change the sizes of the three panes themselves, once again by simply dragging the borders. In this case, you can drag sideways or up and down. If you make the boxes smaller than the room the folders or messages actually take up, you will still be able to scroll them down as you need them. Among other things, this gives you the freedom not to be distracted with the lists at the top of the screen. This is especially useful if you have so many messages it scares or depresses you.

The Message Content Pane

Folders and headers are all very nice, but the whole purpose of getting e-mail is actually reading it. For this reason, Gold's largest pane, the one that stretches right across the Gold window, is devoted to the content of the messages themselves. This pane is called the Message Content pane, and is shown in Figure 7.6.

Figure 7.6

The main e-mail tool, the Message Content pane

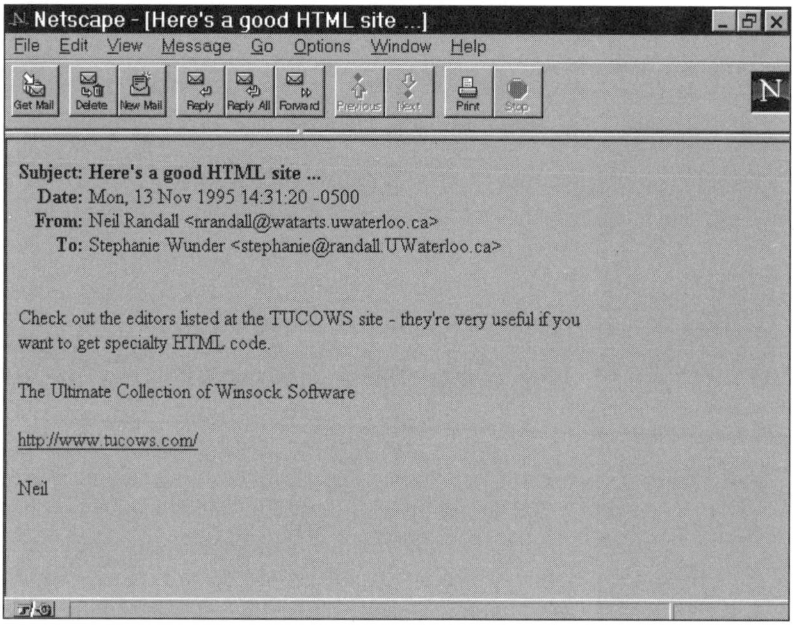

Whenever your fire up Gold's e-mail window, you'll want to know if you have any new mail waiting for you. At first through sheer excitement and later through necessity, checking your e-mail is quite addictive, and you'll probably check more often that you strictly need to. To check for new mail—assuming all your preferences are set correctly—go to the toolbar and click on the Check Mail icon. If new messages are on the server, Gold will download them now. The other way of doing this is to click on the File menu and choose Get New Mail.

The name of the Check Mail icon represents a somewhat questionable decision by Gold's designers. There is no problem with Check Mail, except that there's another icon called *New* Mail. To anyone with more than 8 minutes of Internet experience, "new mail" means there are new messages to read. In

Gold, New Mail means you want to *compose* new mail. Why they didn't just call it Compose Mail is probably one of those unsolvable mysteries.

To read a message, click on its header in the Header pane. As soon as you do that, the message will be retrieved from the mail server to your machine and will be displayed in the Content pane. You cannot view two messages at once in the Message Content pane.

The Header of an E-Mail Message

When a message first appears, you'll see a number of information elements. Here's an example, from a self-generated message (I sent it to myself):

```
Subject: Final test for Gold's mailer
        Date: Sat, 02 Dec 1995 13:58:29 -0500
        From: Neil Randall <nrandall@watarts.uwaterloo.ca>
Organization: University of Waterloo
          To: nrandall@watarts.uwaterloo.ca
```

The *Subject* line, as you'd expect, will match the subject line as it appears in the Message Header pane. This will give you some idea how important good subject lines are, by the way. They're crucial for strong, useful communication.

Date gives you the precise date your mail server received the message (not when it was originally sent). The time is shown as your local time, and the designation on the end of the line tells you your time zone by showing you how your local time compares with Greenwich Mean Time. In this case (Eastern Standard Time), the time comparison is –0500, meaning five hours *behind* GMT. Pacific Standard Time would be –0800, and so on.

Obviously, the *From* line refers to the sender of the message. The difference between this line and the Sender column of the Message Header screen is that this line includes the sender's full e-mail address.

On the *Organization* line, you'll see the information supplied by the senders in their configuration menus. If they've included an organization name, Gold will capture it and display it here.

On the *To* line you'll see your e-mail address and the address of any other recipients of the message. This is the line from which the addresses are taken if you choose to send a Reply (which is covered in Chapter 8).

The Message of an E-Mail Message

Finally, we get to the real point of e-mail: the message itself. The rest really doesn't matter in the long run. Gold's message area is different from that of most e-mail programs, so it's worth taking a complete look at it.

The message content in Gold appears in one of two formats. Most messages will appear as text formatted partly as you specified in Mail and News Preferences (see Chapter 5), with roman type for new text and italics for quoted text (text that's been left in from the original message). This is the most common form of message content because e-mail is predominantly a system where users type back and forth to one another. Figure 7.7 shows an example.

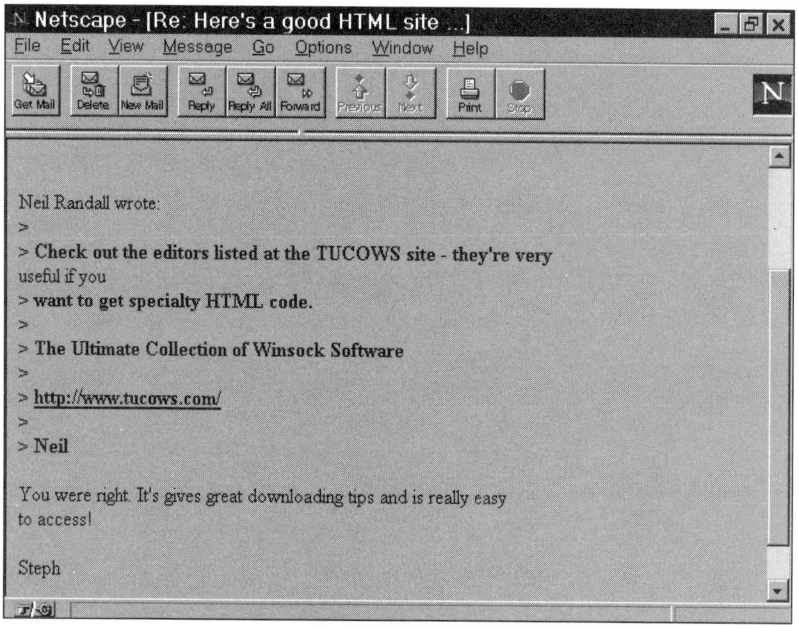

Figure 7.7

The typical e-mail message displays text in a combination of type styles.

Gold has one other message format, however, and it could prove to be immensely significant. If somebody sends you a message with an HTML message attached (see Chapter 8 for attachments), the HTML file will appear with full HTML formatting (as a Web page) in the Message Content area. One of these is shown in Figure 7.8.

In other words, you can now fancy up your messages significantly, as long as you know that the recipient is using Gold. You and another Gold user can start sending fully formatted e-mail back and forth, complete with graphics, video, and everything else HTML can handle. Used in conjunction with the Gold editor, where HTML documents are created, e-mail might finally be able to shed its rather bland text-only image.

Figure 7.8

Gold will display attached HTML files as full HTML documents.

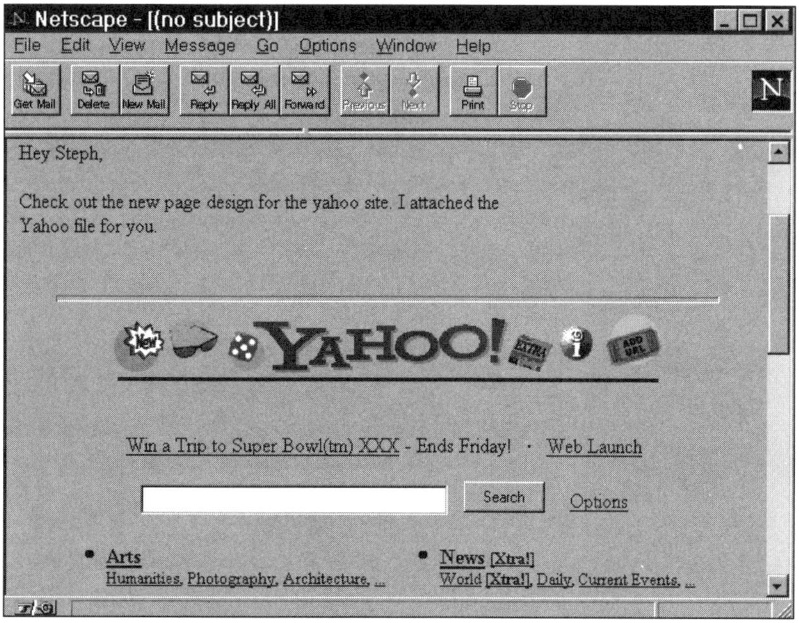

■ The Menus

The menus in Netscape Mail perform the following functions:

File menu	New Web Browser	Open a new Gold browser window
	New Mail Message	Start composing an e-mail message
	Open Folder	Open the currently selected folder
	Save As	Save the currently selected message to the hard disk
	Get New Mail	Retrieve new mail messages from the mail server
	Deliver Mail Now	Send all messages queued for delivery
	Empty Trash Folder	Delete all messages in the Trash folder
	New Folder	Create a new folder for message storage

	Compress This Folder	Compress the contents of the currently selected folder to save disk space
	Compress All Folders	Compress the contents of all folders in the Folders pane to save disk space
	Page Setup	Set up the page for printing
	Print Messages	Print the selected messages
	Close	Close the Mail window (and Gold if Close is the only open window)
	Exit	Exit Gold
Edit menu	Undo	Undo the last action
	Redo	Redo the last undone action
	Cut	Cut the selected text to the Clipboard
	Copy	Copy the selected text to the Clipboard
	Paste	Paste the contents of the Clipboard to the current cursor location
	Delete Message	Delete the selected message
	Delete Folder	Delete the selected folder
	Select Thread	Show all the messages in the current thread
	Select Flagged Messages	Highlight all the messages that have been marked as flagged
	Select All Messages	Select all the messages in the currently open folder
	Find	Find a text string in the current message
	Find Again	Find the previously specified text string again
View menu	Sort	Sort the message in the current folder according to Date, Subject, or Sender. Also thread the message in the folder, re-sort them, or sort them in ascending order.

	Unscramble (ROT 13)	Unscramble messages sent in ROT 13 format
Message menu	Reply	Reply to the current message, using only the sender as the new recipient
	Reply to All	Reply to the current message, with all original recipients copied
	Forward	Forward the current message to a new recipient
	Forward Quoted	Forward the current message with original text in quoted format
	Mark as Read	Mark the current message as having been read
	Mark as Unread	Mark the current message as having been unread
	Flag Message	Flag the current message for later selection
	Unflag Message	Unflag the current message
	Add to Address Book	Add the sender of the message to the Address book
	Move	Move the current message to a folder
	Copy	Copy the current message to a folder
Go menu	Next Message	Read the next message in the mailbox
	Previous Message	Read the previous message in the mailbox
	First Unread	Go to the first message marked as not having been read
	Next Unread	Go to the next message marked as not having been read
	First Flagged	Go to the first message you have flagged
	Next Flagged	Go to the next message you have flagged

	Previous Flagged	Go to the previous message you have flagged
	Stop Loading	Stop messages from loading into the Message Header pane
Options menu	Show All Messages	Show all messages in the current folder
	Show Only Unread Messages	Show only messages marked as not having been read
	Show All Headers	Show full Internet header information for each message
	Save Options	Save the options you have selected
Window menu	Address Book	Open the address book

The Toolbar

The items on Netscape Mail's toolbar perform the following functions:

Get Mail	Retrieve new e-mail messages from the mail server
Delete	Delete the currently selected message
New Mail	Open the Message Composition window with no recipient specified
Reply	Open the Message Composition window with the sender of the currently selected message specified as recipient of the new message
Reply All	Open the Message Composition window with the sender and all recipients of the currently selected message specified as recipients of the new message
Forward	Forward the current message to other e-mail addresses
Previous	Move to the previous message in the Message Header pane
Next	Move to the next message in the Message Header pane
Print	Print the current message
Stop	Stop the retrieval of messages

Options for Your Messages

So what do you do with all those messages you inevitably start getting once you've read them all? One option is to leave them in your Inbox folder, but that hardly seems a long-term solution. Unless you lead an especially inactive e-mail life, you'll eventually end up with an Inbox of truly astounding size.

You have three main options. You can trash the message, move it into a folder, or reply to it a number of different ways. Chapter 8 will handle the reply options; here let's look at the Trash and Move options.

Trash It

This will be one of your most valuable options. You will come to love the freedom of trashing your messages before you even read them. It's even better than an answering machine because you don't even have to hear the messages. Truly a wonderful experience.

How, though? On the toolbar, next to the Check Mail icon, you will see a Delete icon. Click on it, and the currently highlighted message is deleted (you can also just press the Delete key on your keyboard). You can delete a message either before you open it or after you have read it. When you delete a message, it will just go to the trash folder, so don't panic if you delete something by mistake—just click on the Trash folder and there it is. Actually, you can even close Gold completely and the thing will still be there, until you select Empty Trash Folder from the File menu.

The other way to trash a message is to click on it to highlight it, and then click on the Message menu title. Bring the cursor down to the Message/Move, then slide across to select the Trash folder. This is a bit cumbersome, but it works.

When you have more trash than you can shake a stick at, and you're sure that the stuff in the Trash can definitely be discarded, get rid of it. It only takes up room on your hard disk, and it may pile up to ridiculous amounts very soon. Select File/Empty Trash Folder, and they're gone.

Put It in a Folder

When you first install Gold, the Folder pane will consist of only the Inbox folder. In that folder will be a message from Netscape itself. When you first delete a message, the Trash folder is created, with the deleted message inside it. When you first send a message, Gold creates the Sent folder and stores that and subsequent sent messages inside it. All other folders are up to you to create, and you do so by choosing File/New Folder, then naming the folder whatever you like.

You create folders for the sake of storing messages you wish to keep. To move a message into a folder, click on the message in the Message Header pane and drag it to the folder in which you want to store it. Alternatively, you can choose the Message menu, then Move, and select the appropriate Folder name from the cascading list of folders that appears.

Note that you can also copy messages to a folder, using Messages/Copy. This is useful if you want copies in more than one folder.

Now that Gold can act as your Web browser and e-mail program together, it's as complete as most users need. Reading e-mail is always only a click away, and e-mail messages can look far better than they do in a typical mailer. In the next chapter we'll look at the mechanics of sending e-mail.

- *Guidelines for Writing E-Mail*
- *How to Compose an E-Mail Message*
- *The Message Composition Window*

CHAPTER

8

Composing and Sending E-Mail

IT'S ALL VERY WELL TO KNOW HOW TO READ YOUR E-MAIL (Chapter 7), but knowing how to send it matters every bit as much. Among other reasons, if you send e-mail you'll also start receiving replies; that's how the e-mail cycle goes. Send, receive a reply, reply to the reply, wait for the reply to the reply, and on and on and on. Many e-mail messages fly back and forth a dozen or more times, each time with new information added. And this can happen over the course of only a few days.

In this chapter, we look at all the features Netscape Navigator Gold has for composing and sending e-mail messages, both originals and replies. Gold offers a full-featured system, and it will suffice quite nicely for most e-mail users.

Guidelines for Writing E-Mail

If you already know everything you care to know about e-mail style and protocols—for example, the communicative aspects of e-mail—skip this minisection. If you're new to the e-mail game, or if you'd simply like a bit of a refresher, stick with us for a few paragraphs.

E-mail has no rules and no universally accepted standards. In this way, it's unlike letter writing, in which you're expected to provide a return address, date, salutation, closing, and a nicely formatted or carefully handwritten text body. It's also unlike speech, which has some very definite protocols, some established and nearly subconscious rules about turn-taking and interrupting, and all sorts of other socially agreed to "rules." E-mail offers freedoms and constraints of its own, and it's important to get to know them.

Message Length

Like everything else in e-mail, the length of your messages is entirely up to you. However, unless you're corresponding with a good friend or a colleague who's important to you, you should try to keep your messages to no more than five or six lines. In many cases, in fact, a single sentence will do.

Keep in mind at all times that many people on the Internet receive dozens—sometimes hundreds—of messages per day. If you spend two paragraphs explaining to them why you're sending your message, they won't likely stick around to read the whole thing. So get to the point (but see "Tone," below).

Tone

Tone is very difficult to master. The need for brevity of messages often leads to a tone of curtness or abrupt rudeness. Unless you know your audience, using a fairly light, somewhat colloquial style will set the right kind of tone. That's easy to say, but much harder to do.

Style

Your choice of style depends entirely on the audience. If the discussion uses professionally acceptable diction and style, reply in like manner. If you're writing to your best friend, write as you know they'd like you to write. And so on. The worst thing you can do is jump into an exchange on, say, a discussion list, changing a congenial style into something confrontational, or demonstrating impatience and disrespect. People express themselves quite openly on the Net, and it's very easy for someone to get upset at even a small, throwaway comment.

Humor

All of which brings up the subject of humor. Most people can't write humor. Period. Most comedians can't even write humor. On the Net, lots of people try, and almost all fail very badly. Generally speaking, strive for congeniality rather than humor, unless you know what you're doing. You can add comments like "ha ha" or symbols like "<g>" (for grin), but these things usually come across as extremely juvenile and can't be recommended. All of this advice goes out the window, of course, if you and the recipients already know one another's sense of humor and have established that this message thread will be humorous.

Smileys and Other Symbols

In e-mail messages, you'll often see a symbol called a *smiley*. (If you lean toward pretentiousness, you can use their other name, *emoticons*, but that usually produces guffaws from just about everyone.) The most common are :) or :-)—turn your head to the left, and the thing looks like a smiling face (with or without nose). There are many of these, and you can find a smiley dictionary on the Net itself. The advice is this: Don't use them indiscriminately. Many Internet users, including the author of this book, find them really annoying.

Replying with Original Text

All e-mail programs, including Gold, let you include the original text in the body of your reply. This allows you to respond to the original point by point and keep the individual discussions alive. It's all very wonderful, when it's done right.

Do not, under any circumstances, simply append the original text to the end of your message. That does nobody any good, and it chews up Internet resources needlessly. If you intend to include original text, include only as much as you need to make the comments you want, and delete the rest. Even more professionally, insert your comments directly where they belong in the original text, so that your message demonstrates how closely you've read the original.

If you're on a discussion list, get rid of the original text whenever possible. You can upset list members very easily by continuing to send the same stuff out to everyone, over and over again.

Using the Subject Line

Don't send e-mail messages without a subject line. Some users who get swamped by e-mail make messages without subject lines the first ones they delete without reading. Moreover, omitting the subject line is rude. It's a bit like phoning someone you don't know well and launching into a lengthy conversation without ever once stating why you're calling. It's also unprofessional. Send a memo to the president of your company tomorrow that doesn't have a subject line and see how far it gets.

One other recommendation about subject lines: Change them. When the topic of the message begins to shift after several replies, alter the subject line to reflect that change. Otherwise you keep getting messages that suggest one subject but actually contain another. This is especially important if you subscribe to discussion lists.

Pay Attention to the Address

There's very little more embarrassing in cyberlife than to mistakenly send a highly personal message out to 40 or 50 people on the Net, but it happens all the time. Someone will send a message out to multiple recipients. One of these recipients will reply to it and include highly personal content. But the reply will go not just to the original sender, but to all the original recipients as well. This is very often the case in discussion lists, but it happens in regular e-mail as well. The point is that it's worth the effort to make sure your messages are sent where you want them to go.

The other side of this issue involves messages that nobody except a particular user would want to read anyway. Why send a message to 30 people that says, "Nicely put, Mary!" Like, who cares? Instead, change the addresses so only Mary gets this fine commendation.

How to Compose and Send an E-Mail Message

To compose an e-mail message, you need to use (oddly enough) the Message Composition window, shown in Figure 8.1. You can get to this window in the following ways:

- From the Browser window, select File/New Mail Message (Ctrl+N).
- From the Browser window, select File/Mail Document (Ctrl+M).
- From the Mail window, click on the New Mail icon or select File/New Mail Message (Ctrl+N).
- While reading a message in the Mail window, click on the Reply icon or select Message/Reply (Ctrl+R).

- While reading a message in the Mail window, click on the Reply to All icon or select Message/Reply to All (Ctrl+Shift+R).
- While reading a message in the Mail window, click on the Forward icon or select Message/Forward (Ctrl+L).
- While reading a message in the Mail window, select Message/Forward Quoted.

Figure 8.1

Netscape Gold's Message Composition window lets you compose new messages or reply to old ones.

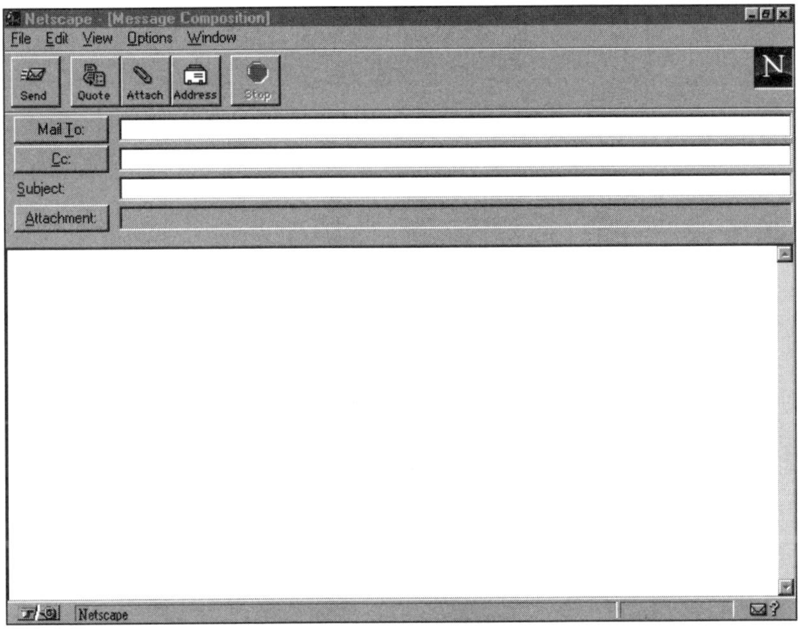

We'll now look at each of these options in greater detail. The Message Composition window and interface are covered toward the end of this chapter.

New Mail Message

You don't have to enter the Netscape Mail window if all you want to do is send a new message. Instead, you can call up the Message Composition window from the File menu of the browser by choosing the New Mail Message command. If you're inside the Netscape Mail window anyway, you can get to the Message Composition window by clicking on the New Mail folder or choosing File/New Mail Message.

In the Mail To field, enter the e-mail address of the intended recipient. This is mandatory. In the Cc field (if you wish), enter the e-mail address of the person to whom you wish to send a copy of the message. In both cases, you can click the respective button and select an address from the resulting Address Book.

In the Subject field, type a subject for the message. If you wish to attach a file to the message (such as a spreadsheet file or a graphic), type in the path and name of the file, or click the Attach button and browse your drives for the file you wish to send. This Attachments dialog box is shown in Figure 8.2.

Figure 8.2

The Attachments dialog box from the Message Composition screen

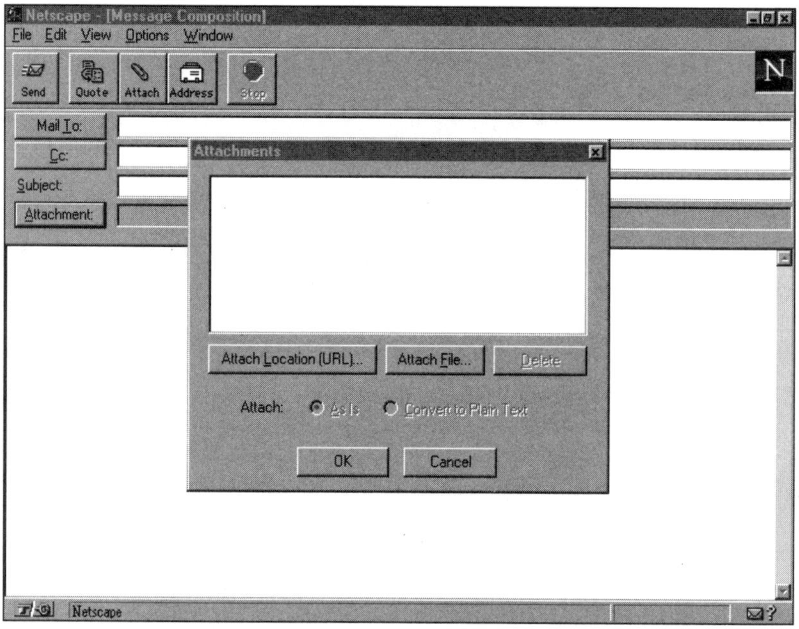

If you want to send your message to someone without the other recipients knowing it, choose Mail Bcc from the View menu. The Mail Bcc (blind carbon copy) field will appear, in which you can type the e-mail address of your "blind" recipient. If you want to send your message to a newsgroup as well as the recipient, choose Post To from the View menu and type the newsgroup name in the resulting field.

One other rather unusual possibility exists. By selecting Reply To from the View menu, you can change the e-mail address to which you want replies to this message sent.

You can select all these options by choosing Show All from the View menu. In such a case, the Message Composition window looks like Figure 8.3.

Finally, type your message. Then click on Send to send the message immediately, or click on Later to queue your message for later transmission.

Figure 8.3

The Message Composition window with all send and reply options enabled

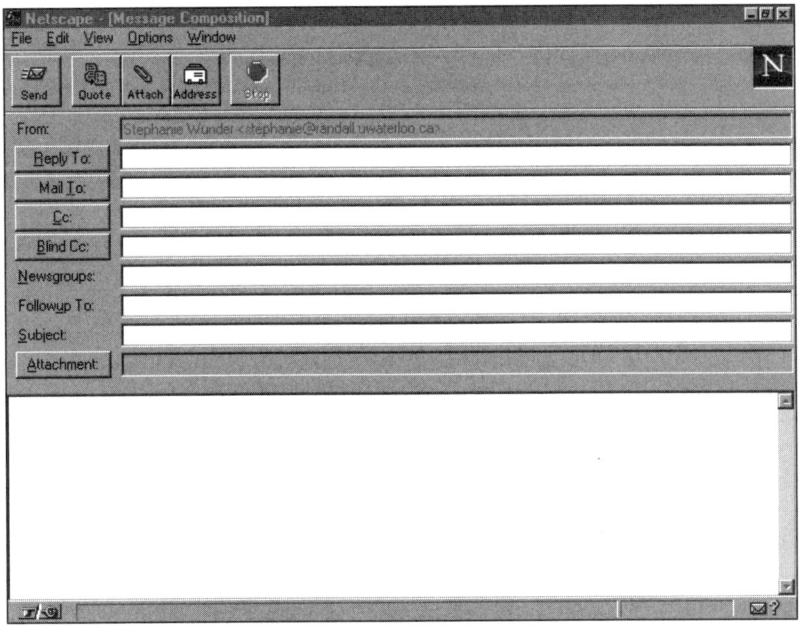

Attachments

By clicking on the Attach button you can locate a file to include with your message. The main reason for doing this is to send a *binary* file (that is, not a *text* or *ASCII* file). Text files can be included directly within the message area, but this area can't incorporate binary files. Binary files include such things as program files, graphics files, and sound files.

To attach a file to a message, click on Attach to bring up the Attachments dialog. You can attach a file from your hard drive, or you can attach a URL (or Web page) from an external Web. Clicking on the Attach File button will bring up the appropriate file selection dialog for your operating system, while clicking on the Attach Location (URL) button will yield a simple dialog in which you can type the desired URL (Figure 8.4).

The benefit of sending a URL is that Netscape's Mail window can display it as a Web page. In other words, you can send mail messages that bear full HTML pages, in order to get your point across even clearer. Sending an HTML page with the Attach File button also works this way; as long as it's HTML, Gold's Mail window will display it as a Web page, complete with graphics and working hypertext links.

Figure 8.4

Attatching a URL in Gold's Message Composition window

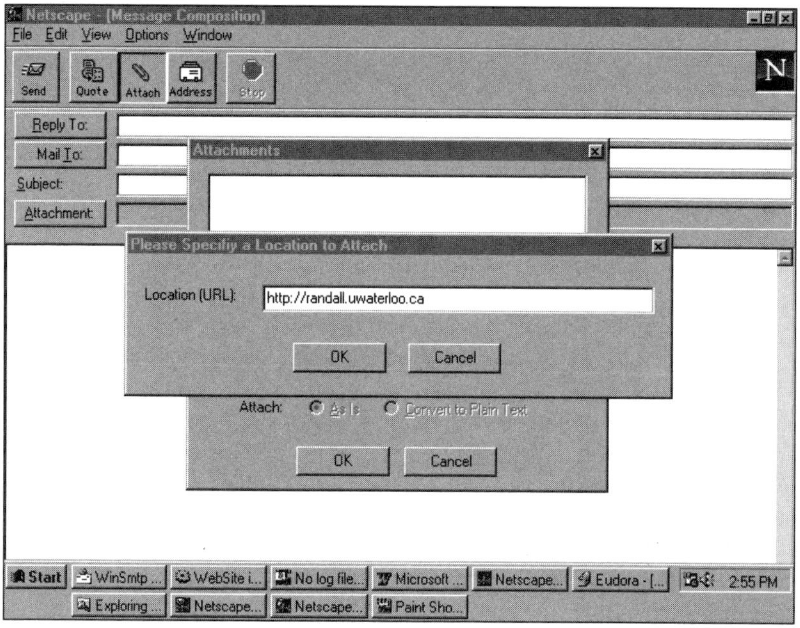

Reply

Most of the time, you're likely to reply to messages rather than create them from scratch. You read it, and then you want to write back and tell the sender what you think. In the Message Header pane, click on the message you'd like to reply to, making completely sure it's the right one. On the toolbar, hold the cursor over the Reply icon, or choose Message/Reply. You'll receive the Message Composition window, but this time with a difference (see Figure 8.5).

The name and e-mail address of the original sender automatically appear in the Mail To field, and the subject of the message you are replying to appears in the Subject field, prefixed with *Re:*. The subject can be changed if you like (in order to keep the message current), as can the name and e-mail address of the person you are sending a message to.

You can include all the same information and attachments in a reply that you can in a new mail message. The original message is not automatically included in the reply, but it can be. If you'd like to reply to the original message, go to the File menu and click on Include Original Text (not available on Macintosh). The original message will appear in the window, with each line prefaced by an angle bracket (>) and with the font appearance according to whatever you've established in Mail and News Preferences.

Figure 8.5

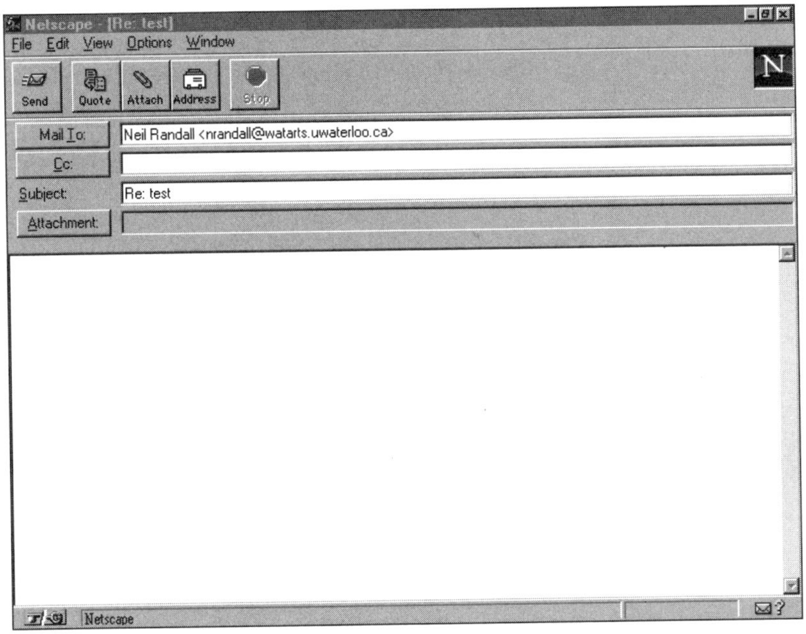

Replying to a message fills in the Mail To and Subject fields automatically.

As when sending a new message, when you're happy with your reply click Send. Keep in mind, though, that once you have done this, there's no turning back. The message is on the way to your recipient, and there is no Suck-Back-The-Message button. There will undoubtedly be times you wish there were.

Reply to All

You're reading your message, when suddenly lightning strikes and you have a great idea that everyone just has to know about. Whether you're doing a group project, organizing a meeting, or sharing a really good joke, you don't want to write it all out 50 times for each person to read. Instead, choose Reply to All to send your reply to all the original recipients at the same time.

To do this, click on the message in the Message Header pane to which you'd like to reply. Go to the toolbar and click on the Reply to All icon (envelope with two arrows). The other way to do this is to go to the menu, click on Message, and choose Reply to All. The resulting Message Composition window will show the original sender in the Mail To field and any other recipients in the Cc field.

The difference between Reply to All and the simpler Reply is that the latter sends the response only to the original sender. Unless you're absolutely sure you want everyone in the chain to receive the response, use Reply instead of Reply to All.

Forward

This time, you're reading your messages, and you realize someone *else* had a great idea. They wrote this big, long, wonderful message, and you know it would be helpful or useful to lots of people you know or work with, and you realize you can't just keep it to yourself. No problem: Just forward it to the people who should see it.

Click on the wonderful message. Read it again just to make yourself feel bad for not having thought of it yourself, then head for the toolbar and click on the Forward icon, or just choose Forward from the Message menu. The Message Composition window will appear, looking like Figure 8.6.

Figure 8.6

The Message Composition window showing a Forwarded message

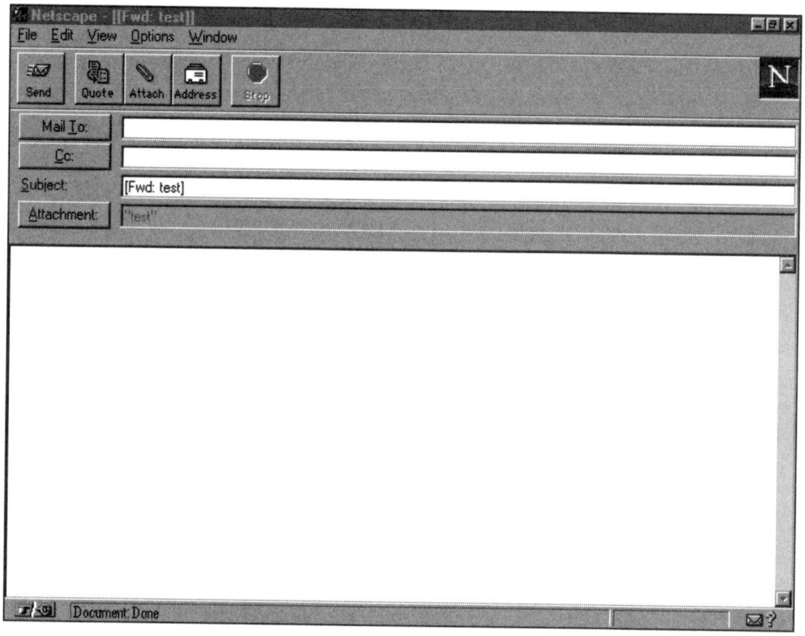

Note that the subject field states that the message is being forwarded, and the actual message is an attachment, not original text. You can write more if you like, and are not limited to only one attachment.

The attachment idea works great if you're sending to a recipient who also uses Gold's Mail system, but if not you should include the original message in the message area. To do so, click the Quote button or choose Include Original Text from the File menu. The forwarded text will appear as a quotation.

You can more easily forward a message with the original text appearing in the message area by highlighting the message and choosing Forward Quoted from the Message menu.

Mail Document

If you're in Gold visiting a Web page and you want to tell others about the site, choose Mail Document from the File menu. This will open the Message Composition window with the URL for the current document appearing in the message area, and the HTML document itself showing as an attachment. This is shown in Figure 8.7.

Figure 8.7

Gold's Message Composition window showing the URL of an HTML page, the result of a Mail Document command

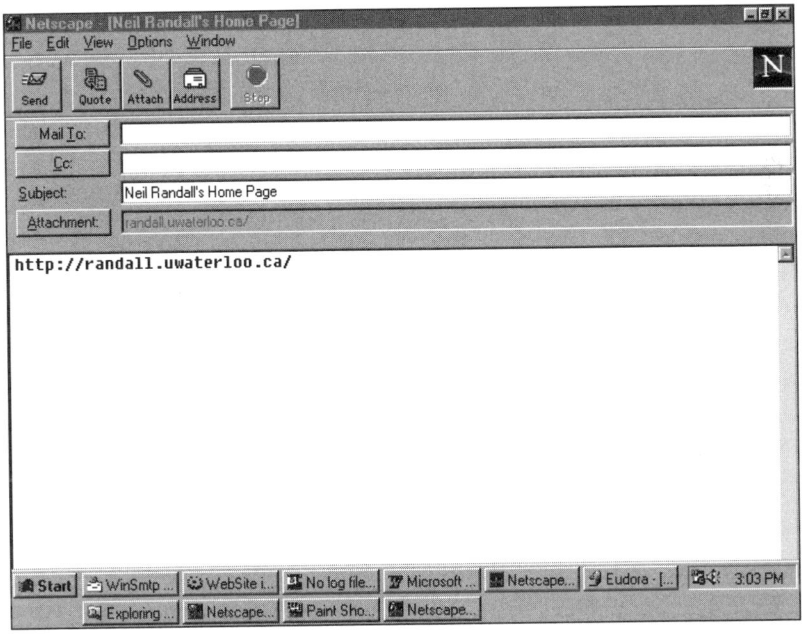

If your recipient is using Gold Mail system, the message will appear as a fully formatted HTML document. If not, it will be an attachment that the recipient can save and load into Gold manually (using File/Open File). Either way, it's a powerful tool.

■ The Message Composition Window

Figure 8.1 shows the Message Composition window. The window's menus include File, Edit, View, and Window; and four buttons on the toolbar—Send, Quote, Attach, Address, and Stop. By default, three message buttons are shown as well—Mail To, Cc, and Attachment—although this number can be increased. Five message fields are also shown—Mail To, Cc, Subject, Attachment, and the message area—but this number can also be increased.

The Menus

The menu items are as follows:

Menu	Command	Function
File	Send Message	Transmit the finished message to the mail server.
	Attach File	Attach a file to the message to be transmitted with the message.
	Include Original Text	In a Reply, include the text of the original message in the current document.
	Save As	Save the current message as a text file for later retrieval.
	Page Setup	Set up the page for printing the current message.
	Print Message	Print the current message.
	Close	Close the Message Composition window.
Edit	Undo	Undo the most recent command.
	Redo	Reverse the last undo.
	Cut	Cut the selected text from the message into the Clipboard.
	Copy	Copy the selected text into the Clipboard, leaving it in the message as well.
	Paste	Paste the contents of the Clipboard into the message at the cursor.
	Paste as Quotation	Paste the contents of the Clipboard into the message, using the quotation format.
	Select All	Select all the text of the current message.
	Scramble (ROT 13) Message	Scramble the current message according to the ROT 13 protocol, primarily for use when posting to newsgroups.
View	Show All	Show all the message buttons and fields in the Message Composition window (see Figure 8.3).
	Reply To	Show the Reply To button and field.

	Mail To	Show the Mail To button and field (included by default)
	Mail Cc	Show the Mail Cc button and field (included by default).
	Mail Bcc	Show the Mail Bcc (blind carbon copy) button and field.
	Post To	Show the Post To Newsgroups field.
	Followup To	Show the Followup field.
	Subject	Show the Subject field (included by default).
	Attachment	Show the Attachment field (included by default).
Window	Address Book	Open the Address Book.
	New Netscape Browser	Open a new browser window.
	Netscape Mail	Open the Netscape Mail window, or go to that window if already open.
	Netscape News	Open the Netscape News window, or go to that window if already open.
	Bookmarks	Open the Bookmarks window.
	History	Open the History window.

The Toolbar

The icons on the Message Composition window's toolbar function as follows:

Icon	**Function**
Send	Send the current message to the mail server for delivery to the recipient's mail server.
Quote	Put the current message into the quote format.
Attach	Attach a file for delivery with the current message.
Address	Open the Select Address window.
Stop	Stop the current Send attempt.

The Fields Region

The fields in the Message Composition window function as follows:

Default Field	**Function**
Mail To	The e-mail address of the intended recipient
Cc	The e-mail address of the carbon-copied recipient
Subject	The subject of the message
Attachment	Attach a file to be transmitted with the message
Optional Field	**Function**
From	The e-mail address of the message sender (set in Mail and News Preferences)
Reply To	The e-mail address to which replies are to be sent (set in Mail and News Preferences)
Blind Cc	The e-mail address of the recipient to be "blind" carbon-copied (no other recipient sees this address)
Newsgroups	The newsgroup(s) to which this message is to be posted
Followup To	The newsgroup and message to which the current message is a response

The Message Area

There really isn't much to be said about the message area, except that this is where you type. In the case of a reply or a forward, this area will contain text as soon as the Message Composition window appears.

Composing mail is something you'll spend a great deal of your Internet life doing. Gold's system is rich enough to suit most users, and extremely easy to access. Whether it's better than your current e-mail program is a matter of opinion, but since it's right there, why not give it a try?

- *Read This First*
- *Usenet Controversies*
- *Getting Started*
- *The Components of the News Window*
- *The News Window Menu*
- *The News Window Toolbar*
- *Posting Newsgroup Messages*

- *Some Basic Rules of Behavior*
- *Posting Messages*
- *Closing Words*

CHAPTER

9

Newsgroups

IF E-MAIL HASN'T PROVIDED ENOUGH OPPORTUNITIES FOR REACHING the horde of Internet users out there, Netscape Navigator Gold offers you another way of contacting the world. Newsgroups are discussion forums that, while technically originating through a separate network called Usenet, have become an integral part of the Internet itself. The idea behind newsgroups is that you subscribe to the ones you're interested in, read messages from a wide variety of subscribers who share your interest, and contribute to the discussions.

Each newsgroup is centered around a particular subject matter. Someone starts the newsgroup, and then Internet users with an interest in that subject join in the discussion. Then, as people on the newsgroup get to know each other's specific interests, subtopics, or *threads*, start appearing, and soon the group has numerous lines of discussions going on, engaging people from all over the world.

There are over 13,000 newsgroups in all, but it's up to the administrators of each news server to determine how many will be available to that server's users. Most servers offer only half or less of the total.

Next to e-mail and Web browsing, newsgroups are the most popular activity on the Net. The fact that Gold lets you do all three without leaving the program demonstrates why Gold is such a useful all-around tool for Net interaction. There really isn't any reason to close down Gold at all.

Read This First

Before you can start using Gold's newsgroup system, you must set your preferences properly. If you followed the Mail and News configuration section in Chapter 5, you'll already have this completed; if not, you might want to turn back there now. Establish your news server, your news identity, and other options by choosing Mail and News Preferences from the Options menu. Once you have these completed, you're ready to start reading and posting to newsgroups.

Usenet Controversies

Newsgroups offer a rich source of interaction. But as with any gathering of a few million people, things can get difficult, weird, and even completely out of hand. In fact, Usenet is in many ways the lawless frontier of the Net, and while the vast majority of users abide by the unstated rules of civility and cooperation, others aren't nearly as savory.

Most of the controversies surrounding the Internet are based on Usenet. When you hear about things like cyberporn, pedophilia, and hate-mongering, you're almost certainly hearing about activity in newsgroups. That's because Usenet is a place where all Internet users can say whatever's on their minds, and not everyone has nice things on their minds.

It's possible to remain relatively anonymous on Usenet. Gold's newsgroup preferences menu (see Chapter 5) lets you specify an identity that bears no relation to your real name and address, so if you really want to post controversial information you can do so without anyone knowing where it came from. It's not completely anonymous—nothing's *that* secure—but it's anonymous enough to hide from most users.

■ Getting Started

To access newsgroups from Gold, go to the Window menu and choose Netscape News. This yields a brand new window, similar to the one shown in Figure 9.1.

Figure 9.1

Gold's news window is nearly identical to the mail window.

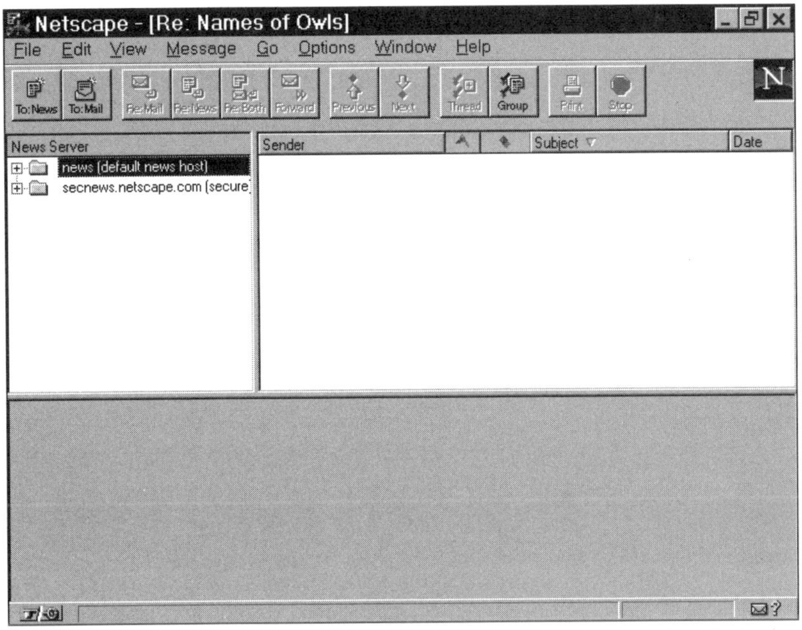

As with the mail window, covered in Chapter 7, the news window has three separate panes. All of the resizing, dragging, and interaction between boxes is the same as in e-mail. In fact, since the windows are so similar, this chapter will cover in detail only the different or additional features between the news and mail systems.

■ The Components of the News Window

The news window consists of three panes: the Newsgroup pane, the Message Header pane, and the Message pane. Most of the action, of course, occurs in the Message pane, where you read the actual messages.

Newsgroup Pane

In the top-left corner of the news window, you'll see the newsgroup pane. Figure 9.2 shows this pane expanded to show all newsgroups available on one particular news server. In fact, the figure shows only a small portion of the 6,000-plus groups available on this server; by scrolling, you can see the remainder.

Figure 9.2

The newsgroup pane displays the available newsgroups in hierarchical folders.

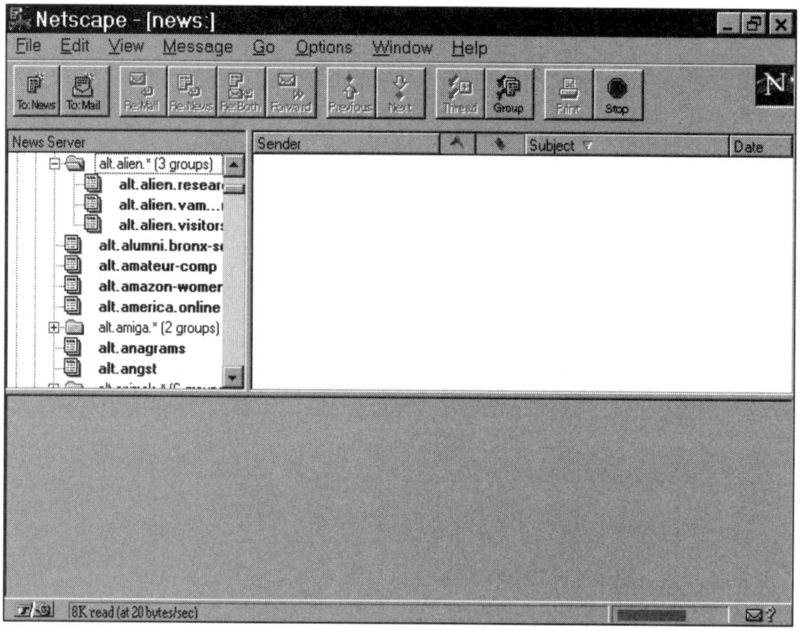

So how do you read what's in the newsgroup pane? First, you have to understand how groups on Usenet are named. Nomenclature is based on the concept of hierarchies, of which there are many. Some of the most popular are shown in Table 9.1.

There are many other hierarchies as well. Some, such as *de*, *fr*, and *uk*, offer newsgroups about and from those countries (Germany, France, United Kingdom). Most servers also offer local newsgroups, so that New York groups will begin with *ny*, Toronto with *tor*, and so forth.

Each newsgroup name begins with a hierarchy. Next comes a subject, and then, possibly, a set of refined subjects. For instance, *alt.stagecraft* is an alternative group about stagecraft (putting on plays), while *alt.supermodels.cindy-crawford* needs no explanation and *comp.os.linux* is a computer group with the subject area of operating systems and the subtopic linux

Table 9.1

Popular Usenet Hierarchies

HIERARCHY	DESCRIPTION
alt	Alternative—huge variety, almost any subject goes
bit	Bitnet—same as listserv mailing lists
biz	Business—often company oriented
comp	Computer—often technical
news	Newsgroups—info about newsgroups themselves
rec	Recreation—hobbies and recreation
sci	Science—amateur and professional groups
soc	Society—social issues

(a particular operating system). There are several comp.os groups, each dealing with a different operating system. To get a list of all the newsgroups your server offers, select Show All Newsgroups from the Options menu.

The newsgroup pane shows the newsgroups in hierarchical order, but it doesn't show all of them. In fact, Gold makes things fairly easy to find by showing only the top level of each hierarchy as a folder when you first open the news window. In other words, as Figure 9.1 shows, you see the folder named *alt.** in which you will find all other newsgroups in the *alt.** hierarchy, and inside that hierarchy will be other folders, each containing even more groups. Folders are represented by a plus sign (+) when they're open (thus revealing their contents), and by a minus sign (–) when they're closed. Clicking on the sign opens or closes them.

The Options menu gives you several other choices for what will appear in the newsgroup pane. You can show all subscribed, active, or new newsgroups. The ones you'll want most often are those to which you've subscribed, because those are the groups in which you have a particular interest. By default, Gold shows you those groups.

For now, in order to get started in your newsgroup adventures, display all your newsgroups, then click on the alt. group folder. Scan through them to find out what groups you may be interested in. Due to the number of groups, it may take a while for all of them to download; you can stop them halfway through by pressing the Stop button on the tool bar. Eventually, though, you'll want this list to be complete, so why not let it finish right now?

Along the top of the newsgroup pane are four resizable columns. News Server shows you the name of the current news server, as well as the names of the newsgroups themselves (depending on which "show" option you've chosen). The check box tells you which groups you've subscribed to, with a checked box indicating a subscribed group. The Total column tells you how many messages are currently on your server for each newsgroup. And the Unread column indicates how many of those messages you have not read.

Subscribing to a Newsgroup

You've seen it, and now you want a part of the action. You are looking forward to spending hours of your life reading countless posts, and occasionally sharing your precious insights with the world. And you want to keep tabs on everything that everyone's saying about the subject you're interested in.

The trick is to subscribe to the newsgroups that you wish to track. Actually, there isn't really a need to subscribe in Gold's system, since the program handles all groups identically and keeps track of which messages you've read. What subscribing does is to bring the newsgroup front and center: You see it when you launch the news window, without the need for showing all newsgroups and scrolling through and locating it.

Once you've determined which newsgroups you wish to subscribe to, find the name of the group in the newsgroup pane. Then click in the check box so that a checkmark appears. That's it—you've subscribed.

If you'd like to verify your subscription, or if you want to display only your subscribed groups, choose Show Subscribed Newsgroups from the Options menu.

Read and Unread Messages

The concept of "read" and "unread" messages is crucial to understanding newsgroups. When you open a message, it is considered to have been "read." Obviously, then, messages you haven't opened are considered unread. By default, Gold displays only the unread messages in each newsgroup. If you want to see messages that you've already read, select Show All Messages from the Options menu. This will display all messages from that newsgroup that still exist on the server. The messages will be displayed in the Message Header pane in a normal (not bold) typeface to show that they have, in fact, been read.

The Message Header Pane

Once you have chosen a group that tickles your fancy, double-click on it to see the messages in the Message Header pane. By clicking on the appropriate column, as with e-mail messages, you can rearrange the messages according to who sent them, whether they are marked as read, or by subject.

There is no real difference between the Message Header pane in the news window and the Message Header pane in the mail window (covered in Chapter 7). As a result, we won't spend time on it here. The only major point to make is that threading messages is much more important in newsgroups than in mail, and therefore the Subject column becomes a primary focus.

By default, Gold will display your news messages according to Subject line. Generally speaking, you won't want to change this, since typically you'll be interested only in certain subjects within the group. You can, of course, sort the messages according to Sender or Date by clicking on the appropriate column heading, but you will usually leave the Subject sorting active.

The Message Pane

If you'd like to read what someone has said about a certain topic, click on the posting in the Message Header pane, and it will appear in the Message pane. In other words, this works exactly the same as Gold's e-mail system. As with Gold, messages containing URLs will display them as hyperlinks, and you can click directly on the link to bring up the URL in the browser window.

Of particular use are hyperlinks to other newsgroups, usually shown in the Newsgroups section of the message's header (see Figure 9.3), which will take you directly to that group from the one you're currently reading. Since these are groups that the writer has selected for cross-posting, there's a reasonable chance you'll be interested in those groups as well. Keep in mind, though, that your service provider might not carry all the listed groups. In such a case, clicking on the group name does nothing at all.

To help you navigate the newsgroup, the toolbar provides Next and Previous buttons that smoothly take you through all the newsgroup postings. To read the message immediately following the current posting, click the Next button, and to read the message shown before the current one in the Message Header pane, click the Previous button. You can accomplish the same thing by selecting Next Message or Previous Message from the Go menu.

Gold keeps track of the read and unread messages in your newsgroups, but you have manual control over message status as well. To mark a message as read, simply click on it. To mark an entire newsgroup as read, highlight the group in the Newsgroup pane and click the Group icon in the toolbar (or select Message/Mark Newsgroup Read). To mark an individual thread as read, click on one message in that thread, then on the Thread icon in the toolbar (or Message/Mark Thread Read). Some threads get extremely large (usually the ones you're not interested in), so this command can come in very handy.

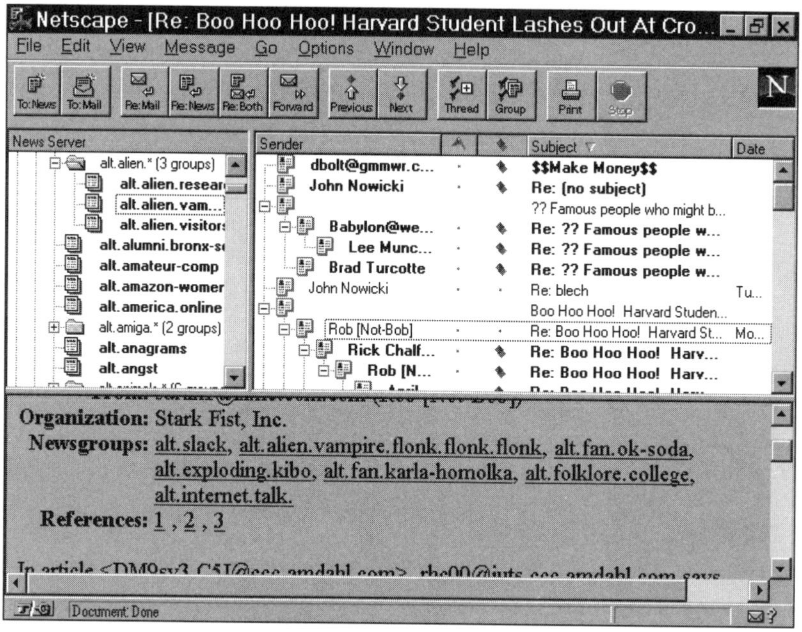

Figure 9.3

The hyperlinks beside the Newsgroup header are links to newsgroups to which the message is cross-posted.

■ The News Window Menu

You can control all of your newsgroup operations from the menus and the toolbar. Table 9.2 shows the menu items and their functions.

■ The News Window Toolbar

Most newsgroup operations—and certainly the most important ones—are available from the toolbar of the News window. Table 9.3 lists the toolbar icons and their individual functions.

■ Posting Newsgroup Messages

You've subscribed to newsgroups and you've read the messages. Some of them made you mad, some made you laugh—but for some strange reason, they all made you want to write back. You know you have something to add to the discussion, and it's time to stop lurking and get out there and speak your mind. Welcome to the addicting, infuriating, exhilarating world of real newsgroup activity.

Table 9.2

Menu Functions in Gold's News Window

MENU	MENU ITEM	FUNCTION
File	New Web Browser	Open a new browser window.
	New Mail Message	Open mail composition window.
	New News Message	Open news composition window with currently selected group in To: line.
	Save As	Open Save As dialog box for saving selected message to disk.
	Open News Host	Dialog box lets you specify news host to connect to.
	Remove News Host	Delete the current news host from the Newsgroup pane.
	Add Newsgroup	Add a specific newsgroup to Newsgroup pane—faster than scrolling through list of all newsgroups.
	Get More Messages	Retrieve new messages for the currently selected group.
	Page Setup	Set up the page for printing.
	Print Message(s)	Print the selected messages.
	Print Preview	Preview the printing of selected messages.
	Close	Close the newsgroup window (becomes Exit if newsgroup window is the only one open).
	Exit	Exit Netscape Gold.
Edit	Undo	Undo the last action.
	Redo	Reverse the last undo.
	Cut	Move the selected text into the Clipboard.
	Copy	Copy the selected text into the Clipboard.
	Paste	Paste the contents of the Clipboard at the cursor location.
	Select Thread	Highlight all messages in the current thread.
	Select Flagged Messages	Highlight all messages marked as flagged.
	Select All Messages	Highlight all messages in the current group.

Table 9.2 (Continued)

Menu Functions in Gold's News Window

MENU	MENU ITEM	FUNCTION
	Find	Find a text string in the current message.
	Find Again	Repeat Find.
	Cancel Message	Cancel the message you're currently typing.
View	Sort	Sort the messages in the current group according to date, subject, sender, or message number, or in ascending order. Also, toggle Message Threading.
	Unscramble (ROT-13)	Rarely used—for decoding messages scrambled by ROT-13 method.
	Load Images	Load images in current message (applies only to messages in HTML format).
	Refresh	Redraw the current message (applies only to messages in HTML format).
	Reload	Reload the current message (applies only to messages in HTML format).
	Document Source	Show the raw message text and source code for HTML-coded messages.
	Attachments Inline	Message attachments are presented as inline images in the Message window.
	Attachments as Link	Message attachments are shown only as hyperlinks in the Message window.
Message	Post Reply	Open Message Composition window with all relevant newsgroups addressed, and with subject line filled in.
	Post and Mail Reply	Same as Post Reply, except that original sender is addressed as an e-mail recipient.
	Mail Reply	Open Message Composition window with only the original sender addressed (not the newsgroups).
	Forward	Forward the message to another recipient.
	Forward Quoted	Forward the message to another recipient with original text shown as quoted text.
	Mark as Read	Mark the current message as having been read.
	Mark as Unread	Mark the current message as not having been read.

Table 9.2 (Continued)

Menu Functions in Gold's News Window

MENU	MENU ITEM	FUNCTION
	Mark Thread Read	Mark the currently selected thread as having been read.
	Mark Newsgroup Read	Mark the currently selected newsgroup as having been read.
	Flag Message	Flag the current message.
	Unflag Message	Unflag the current message.
	Add to Address Book	Add the sender's name to the address book.
Go	Next Message	Open the next message in the Message Header pane.
	Previous Message	Open the message immediately above the currently selected one in the Message Header pane.
	First Unread	Open the first message in the current newsgroup that is marked as unread.
	Next Unread	Open the next message in the current newsgroup that is marked as unread.
	Previous Unread	Open the previous message in the current newsgroup that is marked as unread.
	First Flagged	Open the first flagged message.
	Next Flagged	Open the next flagged message.
	Previous Flagged	Open the flagged message immediately above the current one in the Message Header list.
	Stop Loading	Stop retrieving messages from the server.
Options	General Preferences	See Chapter 3.
	Mail and News Preferences	See Chapter 3.
	Network Preferences	See Chapter 3.
	Security Preferences	See Chapter 3.
	Show Subscribed Newsgroups	In the newsgroup pane, show only the newsgroups to which you've subscribed.
	Show Active Newsgroups	In the newsgroup pane, show only the newsgroups which are active on the server.

Table 9.2 (Continued)

Menu Functions in Gold's News Window

MENU	MENU ITEM	FUNCTION
	Show All Newsgroups	In the newsgroup pane, show all available newsgroups.
	Show New Newsgroups	In the newsgroup pane, show newsgroups added to the server since the last Show New Newsgroups command.
	Show All Messages	In the Message Header pane, show all messages.
	Show Only Unread Messages	In the Message Header pane, show only the messages marked unread.
	Show All Headers	In the Message pane, show all headers.
	Add from Newest Messages	Selecting the Get More Messages command adds to the message list from the most recent messages on the server.
	Add from Oldest Messages	Selecting the Get More Messages command adds to the message list from the oldest messages on the server.
	Document Encoding	See Chapter 3.
	Save Options	Save the selected options.
Window		See Chapter 3.
Help		See Chapter 3.

You can post an entirely new message to a newsgroup on an entirely new subject, but that's a relative rarity. Usually, posting is the result of reading a message in an existing thread (or subject group). Some threads continue for months, even years, while others disappear after a few short replies. The thing to keep in mind is that posting a newsgroup message means that *everybody* who reads the newsgroup has access to it. So watch what you say, as many posters have discovered the hard way.

One of the interesting things about posting to newsgroups is that you don't actually have to subscribe to post a message. Go in, spew a little, and leave. That's useful, especially if you're not especially concerned with a reply, but it also means that anyone else on the Net can do the same thing. Any number of newsgroup battles—called *flames*—have been the result of some short-term visitor stirring up emotions. It's as if you're in a family gathering and some outsider makes a comment that sets everyone off. (Wait a minute—I've *been* at such a gathering!) Be careful not to get too worked up over a random comment.

Table 9.3

Toolbar Icon Functions in Gold's News Window

ICON	MENU EQUIVALENT	FUNCTION
To: News	File/New News Message	Open message composition window with current newsgroup addressed.
To: Mail	File/New Mail Message	Open blank message composition window.
Re: Mail	Message/Mail Reply	Open message composition window addressed to sender (only) of currently selected message.
Re: News	Message/Post Reply	Open message composition window addressed to currently selected newsgroup and cross-posted newsgroups.
Re: Both	Message/Post and Mail Reply	Combine Re: Mail and Re: News.
Forward	Message/Forward	Forward current message to another recipient.
Previous	Go/Previous Message	Select the previous message in the Message Header window.
Next	Go/Next Message	Select the following message in the Message Header window.
Thread	Message/Mark Thread Read	Mark all messages in the current thread as having been read.
Group	Message/Mark Newsgroup Read	Mark all messages in the current newsgroup as having been read.
Stop	Go/Stop Loading	Stop the transfer of new messages.

Some Basic Rules of Behavior

Usenet is a very public place. As such, it should be—and usually is—guided by basic rules of human behavior. Here are a few of the no-no's (and, for that matter, the yes-yes's).

Rarely cross-post: Try to avoid posting the same message simultaneously to more than one newsgroup (called *cross-posting*), especially if it doesn't apply to that specific topic. It just annoys people, particularly those who have subscribed to more than one of the groups. Cross-posting can be extremely useful if you carefully choose the destination groups, and where it's important that subscribers to all of the groups see what you have to say. Most cross-posts, though, are very poorly considered, and sometimes even malicious.

Don't "spam": The term "spam" means excessive multiple posting, or EMP. Basically, someone posts a single message not just to one newsgroup, or even to three or four relevant newsgroups, but to hundreds at the same time. (People have received death threats for doing this. Death, for some, is an even worse threat than cancellation of their account.) This kind of activity is infrequent, but when it happens most of Usenet seems to rise up in anger. There's a famous book available that tries to convince people to perform multiple cross-posts for the sake of making money, but even mentioning its name would cause our e-mail accounts to get flamed.

Test where the testing's good: Sometimes you want to test-post something. Perhaps a binary file, for example, maybe a picture of your cat just to see how it works. There are places to do your testing. Don't do it everywhere. Unfortunately, we learned this the hard way. Here's an approximation of a nasty little reply one of our posts received, back when we were learning all about newsgroup posting:

```
------
Please stop posting test messages to alt.coolstuff
[fictional group]. There are
specific newsgroups for test messages, e.g., news.test.
Posts to those groups are automatically acknowledged from
receiving sites.
     Our news spool is very restricted these days so every
test message that appears in alt.coolstuff pushes it closer
to the purge level. Once that level is reached articles I
haven't read yet are automatically removed from
alt.coolstuff. That is bad. Your posts also give new readers
the impression that alt.coolstuff is a trivial group for
trivial postings. That is also bad.
     Please take your testing elsewhere and `have a nice
day'.
------
```

We suspected that "have a nice day" bore a hint of sarcasm.

Don't offer MOTR: Coined specifically for this book, *MOTR* stands for *More Original Than Response.* What it refers to is a news reply that contains more of the original posting than new material. When you reply to a message, be sure to remove the irrelevant portion of the original, which is usually *most* of it. There's nothing more infuriating than scrolling through 40 lines of a quoted message, only to find the actual response, "I agree, Tim." What's the point?

Tell it to someone who cares: When you respond to a newsgroup posting with another posting, everyone on the newsgroup is subjected to it. If you simply want to say something to the poster him/herself, reply via e-mail instead. "I agree, Tim," is an example of such a reply. Nobody is even remotely interested in whether or not you simply agree, unless it's a survey of some kind (and even then...).

Posting Messages

Gold offers several ways to post messages to newsgroups. They're all included here. Methods for actually composing the replies are not, however, since the Message Composition window, the news composing tool, has already been covered in Chapter 8.

Post Reply

Activated by the Re: Post icon or through Message/Post Reply, this feature lets you post a response to a specific message to the entire newsgroup. As shown in Figure 9.3, the Message Composition window opens with the current newsgroup showing in the Newsgroups field, and with the current subject in the Subject line. If the original message was cross-posted, all relevant newsgroups will appear in the Newsgroups field. Be sure to edit this field if you don't want to cross-post to all these groups.

Post and Mail Reply

When you click the Re: Both button or choose Message/Post and Mail Reply, you are choosing to post a reply to the current message to the entire newsgroup *as well as* to e-mail a copy of the reply to the sender of the current message. Why do this? Often, people who post messages to newsgroups don't hang around to read the replies. Even if they do, there's a good chance that these people read e-mail more regularly than newsgroups. Finally, it shows the sender of the message that you felt strongly enough about the message to send them a directed response.

Mail Reply

Clicking on Re: Mail or selecting Message/Mail Reply sends a response to the current message to the original poster of the message via e-mail, and *not* to the newsgroup. This is a very useful option if you want to tactfully point out an error or a difficulty, or if you want to have a private chat with the person for any other reason.

Post New Message

If you want to post a message about a brand new topic to the current newsgroup, click the To: News button or select File/New News Message. This action begins a new subject in that newsgroup, with the hopes of opening a discussion about that topic.

Forward, Forward Quoted, Mark Message, and So On

These commands work the same with newsgroups as they do with e-mail. They're covered in Chapter 8, so please refer to them there.

Closing Words

Netscape Navigator Gold makes it extremely easy and convenient to participate in Usenet newsgroups. To many users of the Net, newsgroups are every bit as important as the Web itself, and there's no question that it's a way to meet a great many other Netters. The only thing to keep in mind is that newsgroup participation can be extremely time consuming, much more than Web surfing or answering e-mail. Still, newsgroups can be an excellent learning experience, social experience, and even professional experience, and having them available directly from your browser is a very good idea indeed.

- *Adobe Amber*
- *ASAP WebShow*
- *Astound Web Player*
- *Corel CMX*
- *Earth Time*
- *Envoy*
- *FIGleaf Inline*

- *Formula One/NET*
- *Lightning Strike*
- *NCompass*
- *Macromedia Shockwave*
- *RealAudio*
- *VDOLive*
- *Virtual Reality Players*

CHAPTER

10

Netscape Plug-Ins

AS YOU'VE ALREADY DISCOVERED, NETSCAPE NAVIGATOR GOLD is an extremely capable browser all on its own. But make no mistake, it has its limitations, primarily because of the inherent limitations of HTML itself. Those limitations are so extensive, in fact, that as of version 2.0, Navigator and Navigator Gold provided for the installation of *plug-ins*, programs that plug right in to Navigator's architecture to expand the browser's capabilities. The plug-ins are developed by companies and organizations around the world, and more are promised all the time.

What do plug-ins allow you to do? Any number of things, ultimately. If you have a means of viewing files of a particular kind that Gold doesn't have built in, you can develop a plug-in that will let readers view them in the browser itself. Of course, you can already add viewing capabilities to Gold by having your users download your viewer and configure it as a helper application (see Chapter 6 for details on using helper apps), but helpers are always a separate application, not part of the browser itself.

At the very least, in fact, plug-ins are helper apps that operate within Gold rather than launching externally. That would be a significant advantage all by itself, but plug-ins can do more. They not only can add to Gold's capabilities, but can make use of Gold's own strengths as well. In the case of Adobe's Acrobat plug-in (named *Amber*), you not only can view richly formatted Acrobat files, but also can interact with these files by clicking on them and moving to new Acrobat or HTML files. In other words, the Acrobat files become part of the Web itself.

So far, Gold plug-ins have been focused on multimedia presentations. That's hardly surprising, since HTML's great promise is multimedia, but it has a long way to go before fully realizing that promise. In addition to Adobe Acrobat files, plug-ins let you read Envoy files, Corel CMX files, and Macromedia Director Shockwave files (probably the single most impressive use of plug-ins to date). You can use plug-ins to view MPEG video or to listen to RealAudio real-time sound files. Several plug-ins take you into the futuristic world of virtual reality, through the Web-based Virtual Reality Modeling Language, better known as VRML.

As a Web designer, you'll want to consider developing pages for these browsers. It is beyond the scope of this book, however, to include information about how to do so. The URL for each plug-in is included here, though, and you'll find development material at each site. Once you find a plug-in that interests you as a designer, head for the home site and learn how to create pages that take advantage of it. It might very well give you a competitive edge, and on the overcrowded Web that can't be anything but good.

This chapter outlines many of the plug-ins available right now. For a comprehensive listing and the frequent updates, bookmark the Netscape plug-ins page at http://home.netscape.com/comprod/products/navigator/version_2.0/plugins/index.html.

Adobe Amber

Home Site: http://www.adobe.com/Amber/

Document Type: Fully formatted publications

Adobe Acrobat has been a favorite for cross-platform developers for a few years now, precisely because Acrobat's PDF documents can be viewed on Macs, PCs, and any other platform that supports them. The idea behind Acrobat was to be able to produce a graphically rich document and not have it restricted only to viewers who have the full Acrobat software package. The idea worked so well that Adobe developed Amber, an Acrobat plug-in viewer for Netscape.

Amber does more than just display PDF documents. Documents produced for Amber can be fully interactive Web pages, complete with hyperlinks. This is crucial, because otherwise an Amber document is nothing more than a very pretty graphic. With hyperlinks, it becomes a true Web page, and those links can be to additional Amber documents. In other words, you can create an entire Web site of nothing but Amber documents, but keep in mind that these documents take quite a while to download. As a Table of Contents and an impressive entry point, a PDF document can be stunning, but nobody should be forced to endure downloads of endless versions of these pages.

When you click on a link to a PDF file, Amber activates automatically. The PDF document is displayed in Gold's normal viewing window, and viewing controls appear at the top and bottom of the window. With these controls you can move through the document as you would in Adobe Acrobat itself.

After exploring these pages, then working your way through the remaining chapters in this book about creating Web documents with Gold, you might very well find yourself frustrated by Gold's lack of page-formatting tools. If so, consider developing PDF pages for users to view via Amber instead. However, you'll actually have to develop both, because you can't count on everyone having Amber plugged into their browser.

Figure 10.1 shows an Amber document at Adobe, complete with hyperlinks. Figure 10.2 shows another document, this time with a significantly different use, at the New York Times (http://www.nytimesfax.com/times.pdf). You can get a reduced version of the Times every day in this way, although there's nothing interactive here.

Figure 10.1

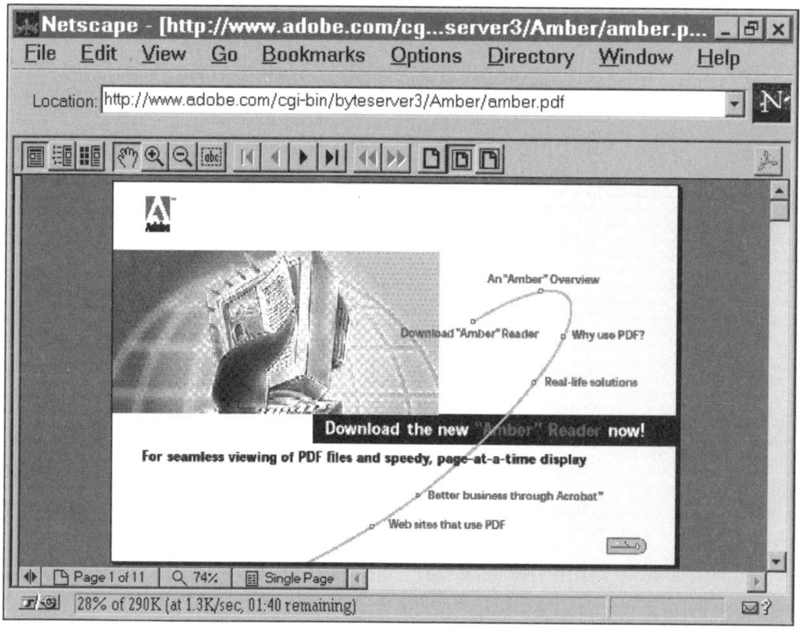

An Adobe Acrobat file, complete with hyperlinks, displayed using the Amber plug-in

Figure 10.2

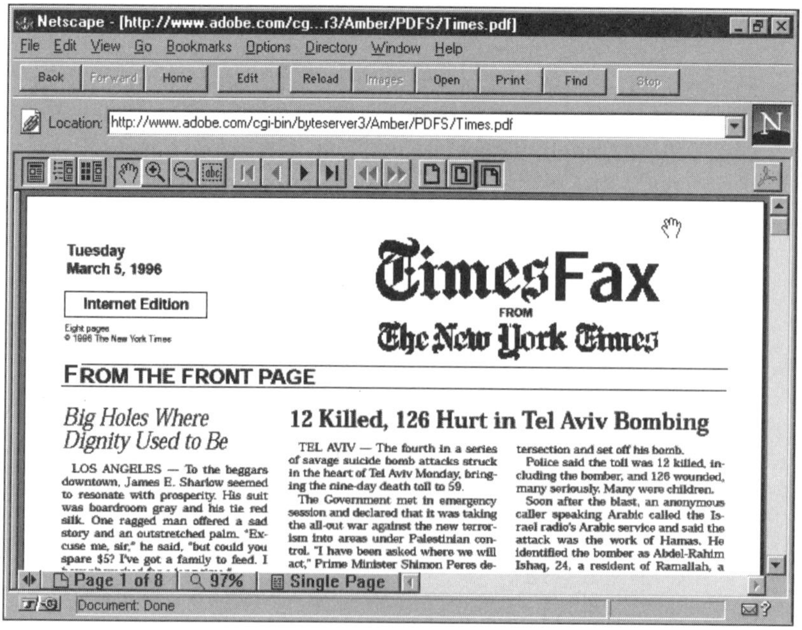

The New York Times Internet edition is available free every day in Adobe Amber format.

ASAP WebShow

Home Site: http://www.spco.com/asap/asapwebs.htm

Document Type: Slide presentations

The Web might be a hot business tool, but until now it's been pretty useless as a means of making business presentations. But it makes sense for the Web to be used this way, because presentations can be stored on your company's machines and then accessed by an entirely different machine, as long as it has Net access and the Navigator browser. In other words, there's no need to carry your entire presentation in PowerPoint or Presentations form on your notebook; moreover, if you don't have the notebook handy you can still access your show.

ASAP WebShow does exactly that—it makes your slide shows available over the Web. Slide shows are created in ASP file format, and these files are significantly smaller than those for other presentation packages. When you click on a link to an ASP file, WebShow loads the new page and, in a small window, the first page of the ASP demonstration. You can control the demonstration from slide to slide, or you can play the slide show continuously. You can also elect to expand the show to the full size of Gold's window.

Figure 10.3 shows a WebShow presentation with a larger HTML page (http://www.graphicsland.com/asapshow.htm). The following figure (Figure 10.4) shows the same presentation occupying the full Gold window.

Astound Web Player

Home Site: http://www.golddisk.com/awp.html

Document Type: Animated graphics

Gold Disk has been well known for its video and graphics tools over the years, and now they're among a growing number of companies attempting to expand the Web beyond its inherent static nature. Documents created with the Astound Web Player offer colorful animation, complete with sound effects, that can give your Web site a great deal of action. Even the most colorful HTML graphics, with all the best alignments, can't compete with stuff that actually moves and makes noise.

Astound files (ASN format) are produced by Gold Disk's Astound or M-Studio software. Once created, they can be embedded as links within HTML files, to be called up by your readers as they click on the site. Users don't actually have to do anything to access these animations; once they have the plug-in loaded, they need only wait until the Astound files appear and do

Figure 10.3

A WebShow presentation begins embedded inside an HTML document.

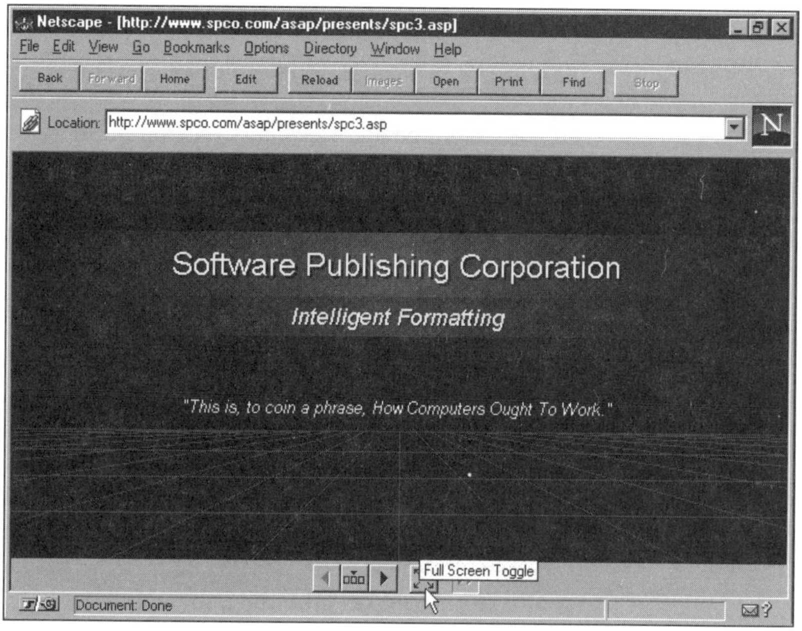

Figure 10.4

A typical WebShow presentation looks like a standard business slide show.

their thing. And the wait, surprisingly, isn't all that long. Even an ASN file with animation and sound together can be downloaded fairly quickly, and it can be programmed to continue offering its attractions.

If you enjoy producing action-oriented presentations, you should consider them for your pages. This is as good a way as any to start. Figure 10.5 (http://www.golddisk.com/awp/sample/alternate_home_page_demo/gd-home.asn) shows a high-impact Web Player offering from Gold Disk itself, and if you close your eyes you can imagine that all the characters are animated and fading in and out.

Figure 10.5

This Astound presentation includes animation and sound together.

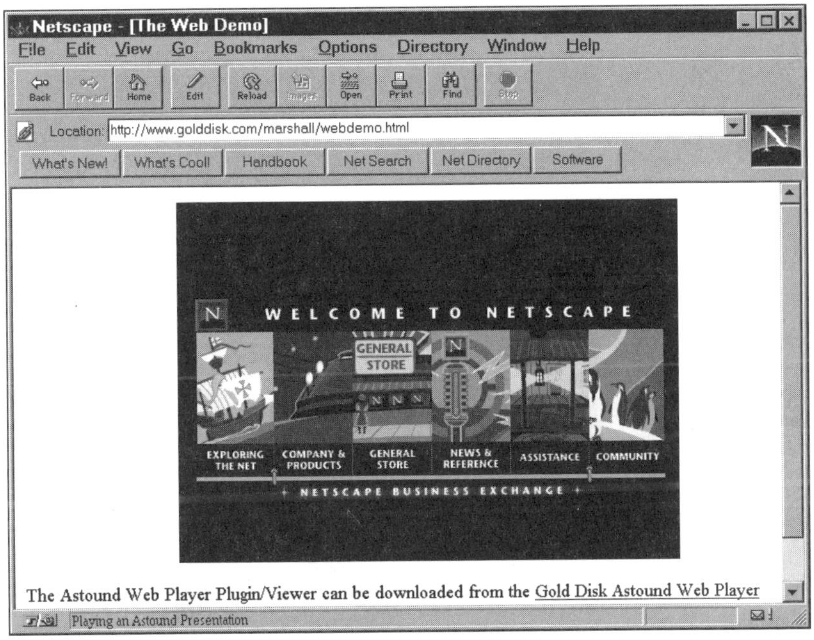

Corel CMX

Home Site: http://www.corel.com/corelcmx/

Document Type: Graphics

Corel specializes in graphics software for Windows users, but because Gold can show only JPEG and GIF files, many of the most impressive images created with Corel software can't be displayed directly on the Web. So, it's hardly surprising that they'd want a means of displaying Corel-created images directly on the Web.

Corel's CMX plug-in for Netscape does nothing more than allow CMX files to be viewed in the Navigator and the Gold browsers. As of this writing, not many sites had taken advantage of it, in fact, but its potential is obvious the minute you first see one of these images. They're highly attractive, and they add a kind of graphic luster to the Web you don't often see. They can't contain hyperlinks, but they can offer something most Web pages don't even approach—artistry.

Figure 10.6 shows an example of a full-screen CMX image (http://www.corel.com/corelcmx/cmx/unicorn.cmx). Figure 10.7 (http://www.corel.com/corelcmx/samples.htm) demonstrates the possibility of offering business presentations using Corel's imaging systems.

Figure 10.6

This unicorn is colorful, dramatic, and appealing, and would make a welcome addition to an appropriate page.

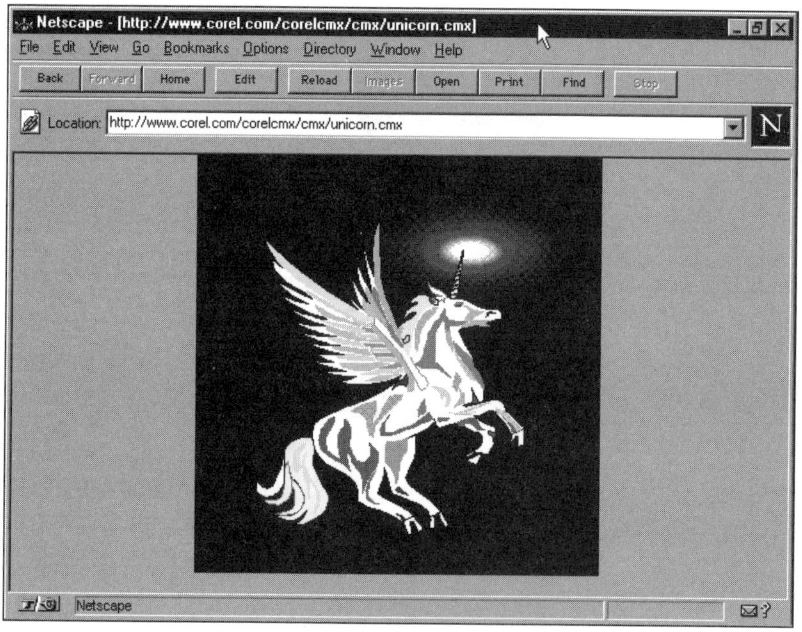

■ Earth Time

Home site: http://www.starfishsoftware.com/getearth.html

Document Type: Map

Here's something you probably didn't know you needed. Starfish Software's Earth Time plugs into Gold to give you the time of day in whatever cities you choose to display. You can show eight different cities around the perimeter of

Figure 10.7

Here we see a business presentation slide as a Corel CMX file.

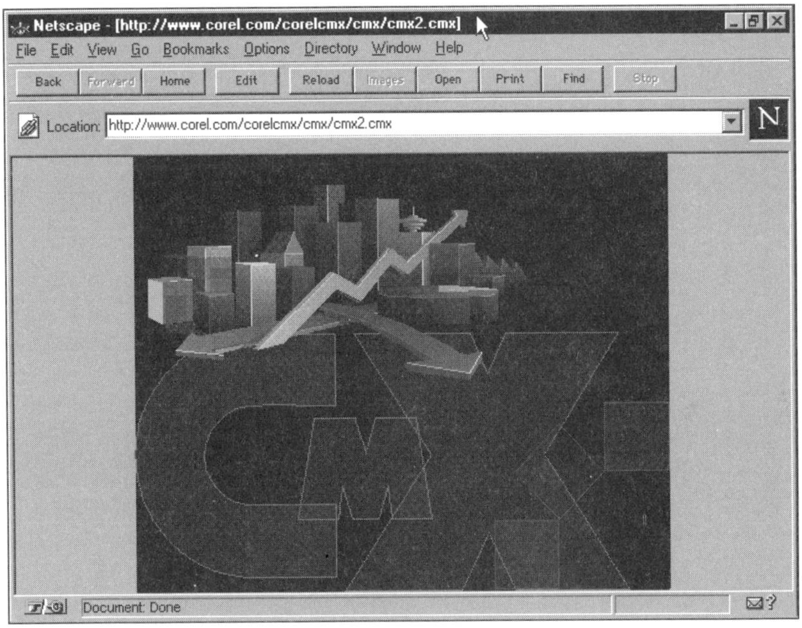

the map, and included in each is the most pertinent information—local time, currency, language, and current sunrise and sunset figures. You also get longitude and latitude, along with daylight savings information and the current phase of the moon. You can drag from one city to another to get time differences. Figure 10.8 shows the Earth Time map within Gold.

Why do you need this? First of all, it's interesting. Second, if you're planning business calls, especially conference calls, Earth Time can help you figure out the best times to call. The map even shows where it's currently day or night in the world, which could help as well. Finally, Earth Time ships as part of Starfish's well-known Sidekick personal information manager for Windows 95, and offers integration with that package's features.

Envoy

Home Site: http://www.twcorp.com/envoy.htm

Document Type: Fully formatted documents

Tumbleweed Software's Envoy plug-in operates much the same as Adobe's Amber—it gives you access to fully formatted, graphically rich documents developed from a variety of software sources. A stand-alone version of

Figure 10.8

The Earth Time map shows you where it's light and dark in the world.

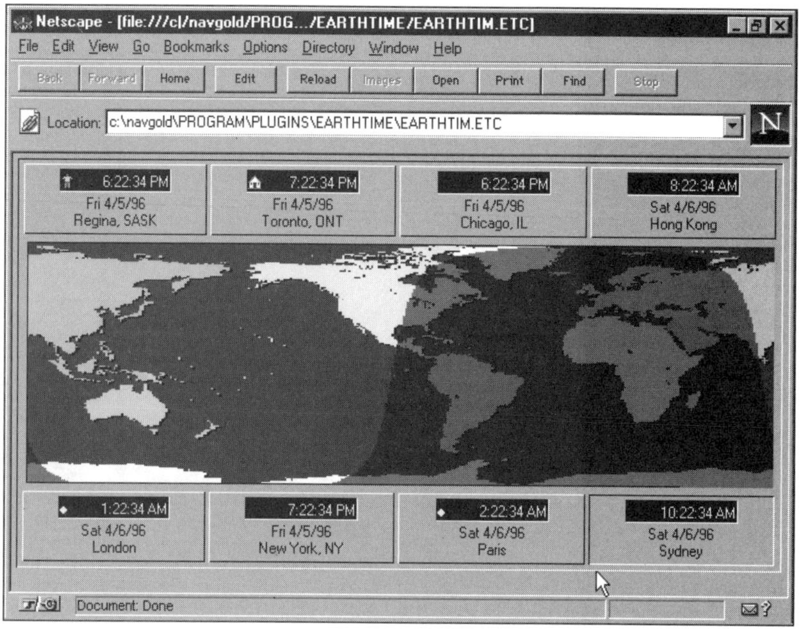

Envoy ships with WordPerfect Office (formerly owned by Novell but now part of Corel); like Acrobat, Envoy offers translation filters for a host of different types of programs. Install this plug-in, and you can access ENV documents around the Web.

Envoy documents are typically static, but they have the capability of containing links as well. Figure 10.9, the Envoy home page (http://www.twcorp.com/evy/home.evy), demonstrates this very clearly. The boxes surrounded by thick lines are all hyperlinks to other documents within the ENV document itself. Other possible document sources are accessible from Tumbleweed's sample documents page (http://www.twcorp.com/envoy.htm): Here you'll discover ENV files that began in Microsoft Word, Deneba Canvas, Corel WordPerfect, Quark XPress, AudoDesk AutoCad (Figure 10.10—http://www.twcorp.com/evy/autocad.evy), and Adobe Illustrator. There's even a document that displays scalable fonts that aren't part of HTML's limited font set.

For Web authors, Envoy's appeal is obvious. Create documents in most popular programs, convert them to ENV files, and they're ready for your Web site. Again, however, keep in mind that not all your readers will have access to Envoy, so standard HTML pages are still advisable.

Figure 10.9

The Envoy home page complete with hyperlinks

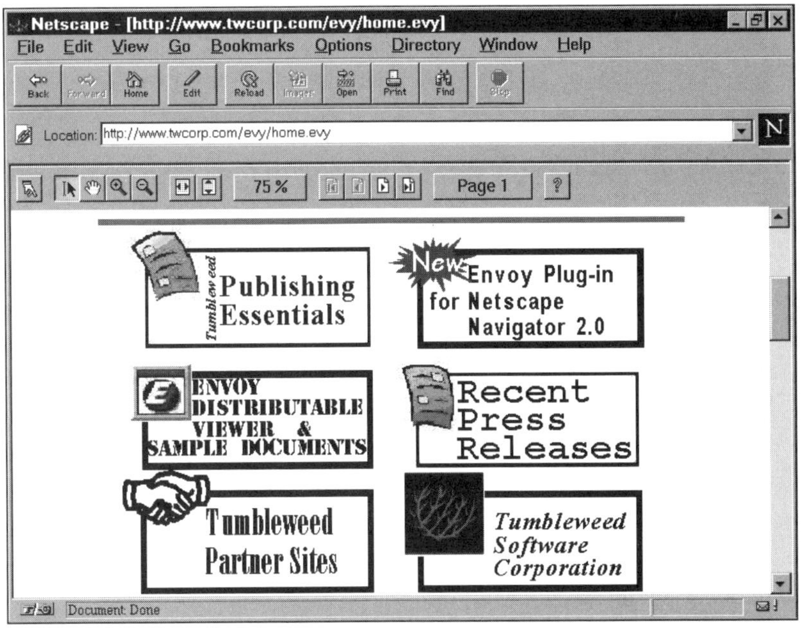

Figure 10.10

A sample Envoy page with an AutoCAD drawing

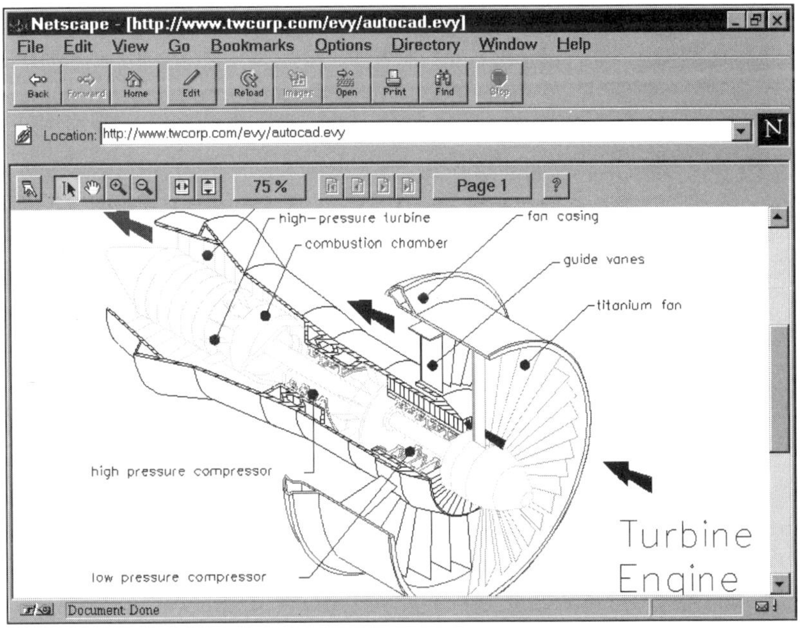

FIGleaf Inline

Home Site: http://www.ct.ebt.com/figinline/

Program Type: Graphics document viewer

As mentioned in the write-up of the Corel CMX plug-in, Gold as it ships can view only JPEG, GIF, and the little-used XBM graphics formats. Corel's plug-in adds CMX files to that list, but the world is filled with lots more graphic variety. Enter FIGleaf Inline, Carberry Technology's plug-in that not only lets you view more types of graphics, but also lets you zoom in to view them closer.

FIGleaf supports the following image types: CGM, TIFF, EPSI, EPSF, G4, TG4, BMP, WMP, PPM, PGM, PBM, SUN, GIF, and JPEG. Images can be displayed as inline images, embedded within an HTML document—the standard way of displaying inlines—complete with borders and either a dithered or a private color palette, or as full-browser images.

When you come across an image that FIGleaf supports, you can zoom in or out to show the image at larger or smaller scale, or you can fit the image to the window. FIGleaf adds menu items to Gold's right mouse button menu to accomplish these tasks.

Figure 10.11 shows a typical inline image as it appears on a Web page. Figure 10.12 shows a portion of the same image expanded by FIGleaf.

Formula One/NET

Home Site: http://www.visualcomp.com/f1net/download.htm

Document Type: Spreadsheets

Okay, we all know that the Web is great for demonstration, presentation, advertising, and downright silliness. But what about that great business application, the spreadsheet? If a technology can't do spreadsheets, does it have any hope whatsoever of winning the hearts of business?

Thankfully, we don't have to worry. Visual Components's Formula One/NET lets you display graphical spreadsheets over the Net that contain charts, hyperlinks, buttons and controls, and of course tables of numbers and calculations. With their companion program Formula One/NET Pro, you can create these goodies as well. Figure 10.13 (http://www.visualcomp.com/f1net/live.htm) shows a well-designed spreadsheet as seen through the Formula One plug-in.

This plug-in is important to the future of the Net as a business tool. But anyone designing Web sites with loads of data, charts, and other numerically

Figure 10.11

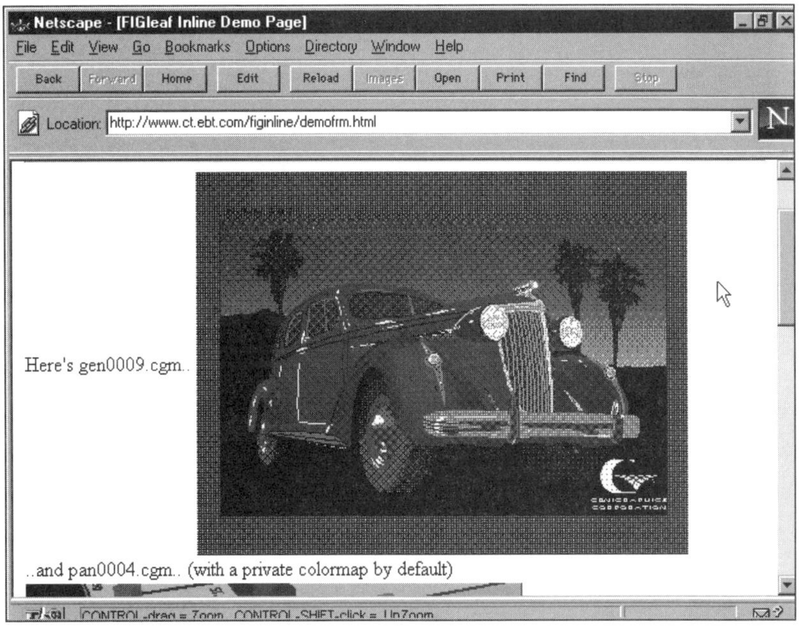

Inline image at normal size

Figure 10.12

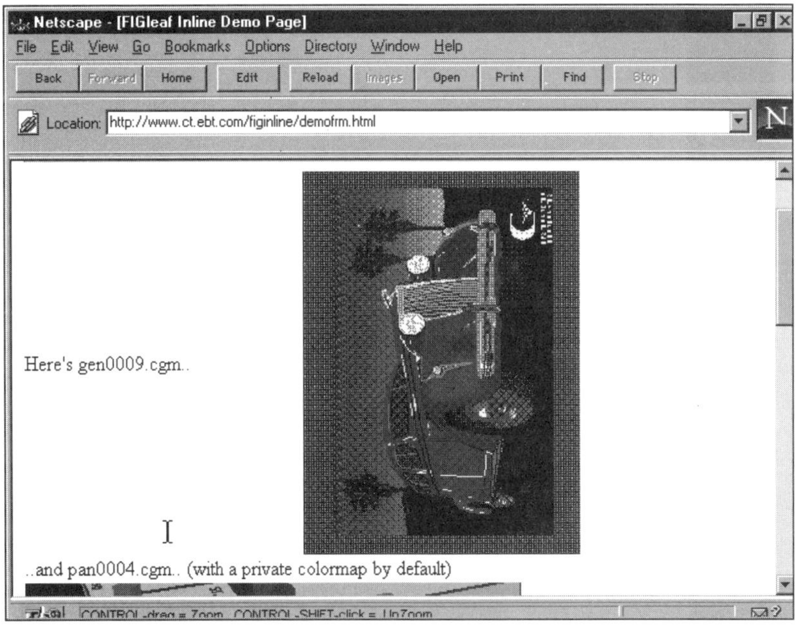

The same inline image as in Figure 10.1, turned on its side

based information will find it useful, whether or not it has anything to do with business. Any number of hobbies, tutorials, and online courses can make use of documents like these.

Figure 10.13

An interactive spreadsheet with buttons as hyperlinks

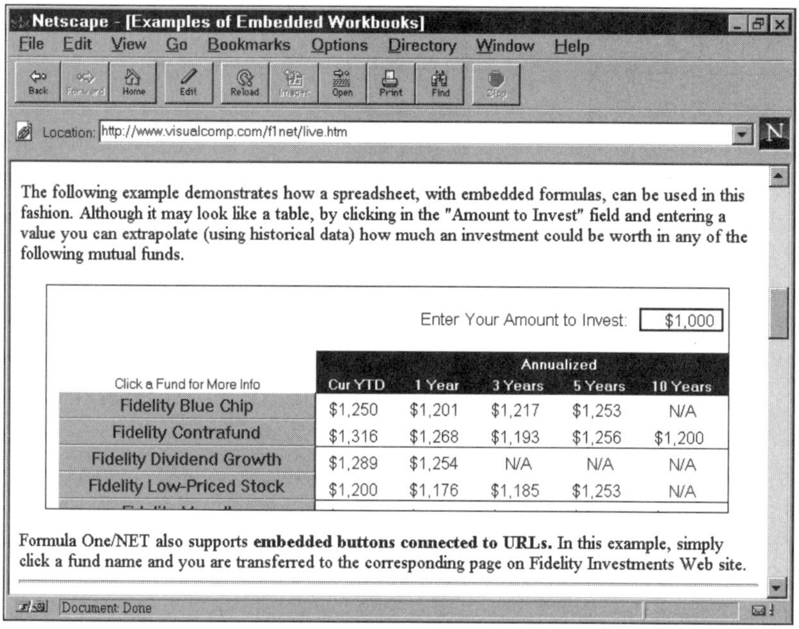

Lightning Strike

Home Site: http://www.infinop.com/html/extvwr_pick.html

Program Type: Graphics viewer

It takes a long time to download graphics files, right? Well, maybe not for much longer. Infinop's Lightning Strike offers file compression for graphics files that optimizes files for use with HTML documents. In order to offer Lightning Strike compressed graphics, you have to compress your graphics according to the Lightning Strike wavelet system, but once you've done so, and your readers have installed the Lightning Strike plug-in, the images on your Web site will load much faster than before.

NCompass

Home Site: http://www.excite.sfu.ca/NCompass/nchome.html

Program Type: OLE add-ins

If you're a Windows user, you've almost certainly heard the term *OLE*, short for *Object Linking and Embedding*. NCompass's OLE Control plug-in lets you view specially prepared OLE-based documents that can do whatever OLE itself can do. In other words, it's potentially unlimited.

In practice, NCompass offers pages that move, play music, and offer interactivity. It has much of the flexibility of the Java programming language, but it's easier to design for. You still have to be a programmer to create NCompass-capable pages, though, and since they're viewable only by Windows users you might turn your efforts to Java instead if that's a concern.

Still, as the NCompass home site shows, with its animation and background music, this OLE add-in offers some very strong possibilities. A few clicks around the demo page at http://www.excite.sfu.ca/NCompass/home.html will show you some of these possibilities, including the multiplayer game shown in Figure 10.14.

Figure 10.14

A multiplayer action game using the NCompass OLE plug-in

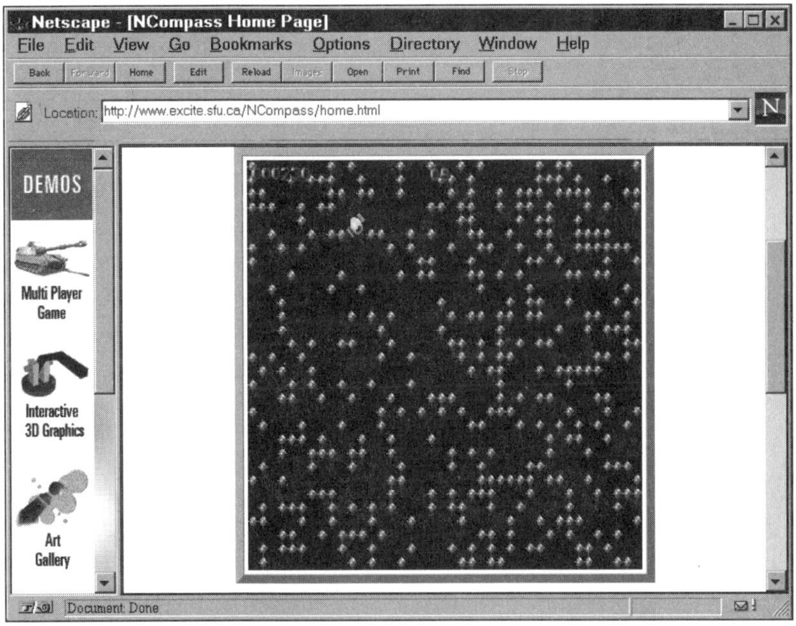

Macromedia Shockwave

Home Site: http://www.macromedia.com/Tools/Shockwave/index.html

Document Type: Macromedia Director presentations

Of all the early Netscape plug-ins, the one that's garnered the most attention is Shockwave. Shockwave lets you insert presentations created with Macromedia Director into your HTML files, and if you know Director you'll know how virtually unlimited its multimedia capabilities are. In effect, Shockwave gives the Web its first real multimedia authoring tool.

This doesn't mean that Shockwave pages don't have their problems. The major one is size: Shockwave pages take much longer to load than standard HTML pages. But they offer animation, special effects, and other possibilities that can set your site apart from others on the Web, and if that's a consideration then you should consider developing Director applications.

Even if you don't intend to design Shockwave pages, you can still get a charge out of seeing what other sites have done to "shock" their wares. Macromedia hosts a page pointing to a variety of existing Shockwave pages on the Net (http://www.macromedia.com/Tools/Shockwave/Gallery/index.html), and this page itself offers a spinning logo, one of Shockwave's many design possibilities. Figure 10.15 shows the MTV Shockwave site.

RealAudio

Home Site: http://www.realaudio.com

Program Type: Real-time sound player

RealAudio hit the Web in a big way in 1995, offering something new and useful—real-time sound. Until then, the only way to play sound files from Web pages was to download them and then launch an external player to hear what they sounded like. The problem was that sound files with anything to offer can be from 300K up to a whopping 2–3 megabytes, and downloading was hardly a practical idea.

What RealAudio offered was a means of listening to the files as they were downloading. Called streaming audio, this technology sacrificed sound quality for convenience, and it worked. The sound is only about as good as an AM radio with some static, but when it comes to speeches or live radio broadcasts such as baseball games, that's fine. Click on an RA file and the RealAudio player fires up, allowing you to listen as you continue navigating the Web.

Figure 10.15

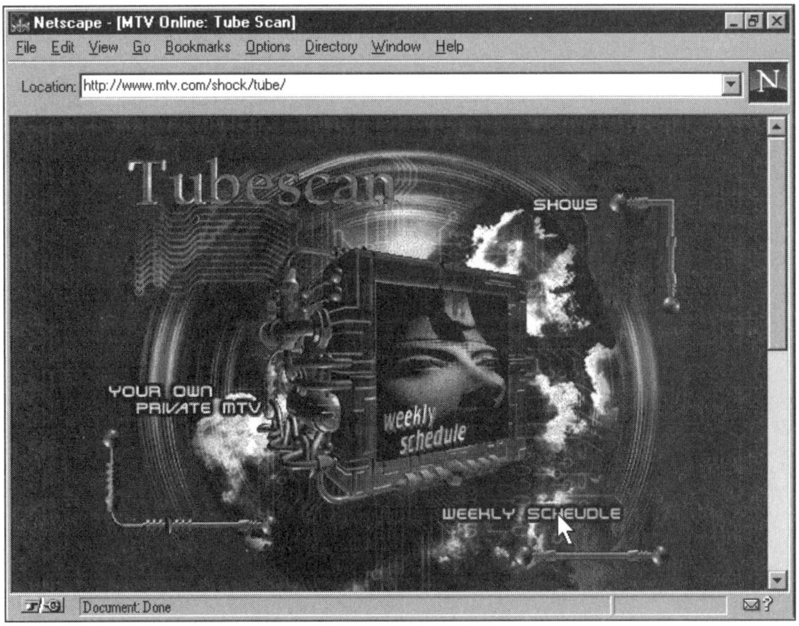

The MTV Shockwave site has all sorts of things bouncing around.

The RealAudio plug-in takes the idea one step further by building the player's controls—forward, rewind, pause, and volume control—right into Netscape, instead of launching an external player. It works well, and you should visit the RealAudio sites page (http://www.realaudio.com/products/ra2.0/sites/) to see who's serving up real-time sounds. In order to offer RealAudio on your Web pages you need the RealAudio server, of which there's a commercial and a personal version.

VDOLive

Main Site: http://www.vdolive.com/newplug.htm

Program Type: Real-time video player

What RealAudio did for sound on the Web, VDO does for video—delivers it in real time rather than forcing you to sit through lengthy downloads. Video streaming isn't as well advanced as audio streaming yet, however, and it will be a while before Web developers take advantage of this technology. Besides, with tools like Astound and Shockwave available, the whole idea of offering video over the Web might seem less attractive than it once did.

Still, VDOLive offers some very compelling solutions, particularly since, for many people, animation and special effects just don't cut it. Sometimes, video is simply necessary. A VDO-enhanced video downloads faster than most video, and you can control it as well. There's no point showing one in a screen capture, though, since the whole point—its speed—can't be represented by a picture.

Virtual Reality Players

The very first Netscape plug-in available was a virtual reality player, WebFX; more have appeared, and by the looks of things will continue to do so. The promise of virtual reality remains extremely strong, even though it hasn't exactly resulted in a large number of useful applications. We all keep waiting for the killer VR app that will immerse us in an alternate reality, and as you're trying out these viewers keep in mind that VR is only in its infancy.

Live3D

Main Site: http://home.netscape.com

Program Type: VRML player

Netscape believes in the future of VR on theWeb. It bought WebFX and has released that VR player as Live3D. VR players operate under the Virtual Reality Modeling Language (VRML), which lets developers program VR applications for the Web. The VRML plug-ins for Netscape allow the virtual worlds to be displayed in the main viewing window, along with controls for navigating through the worlds. Some of the early efforts are spectacular, but with anything less than a 28.8-Kbps modem they're extremely slow. Nevertheless, it's worth a look, and if you have a fast connection it's worth hanging around to play—uh, experiment. Figures 10.16 through 10.18 show a selection of VRML worlds, emphasizing some of the variety that's already begun to appear.

Live3D isn't the only VRML player available as a Netscape plug-in. Try them all and decide which you like. Bear in mind, however, that each occupies between 2 and 5 megabytes of hard-disk space. If you absolutely must choose only one, though, Live3D is probably your best start, since Netscape fully supports it.

Figure 10.16

This example shows a contoured 3-D terrain, just begging to be driven through.

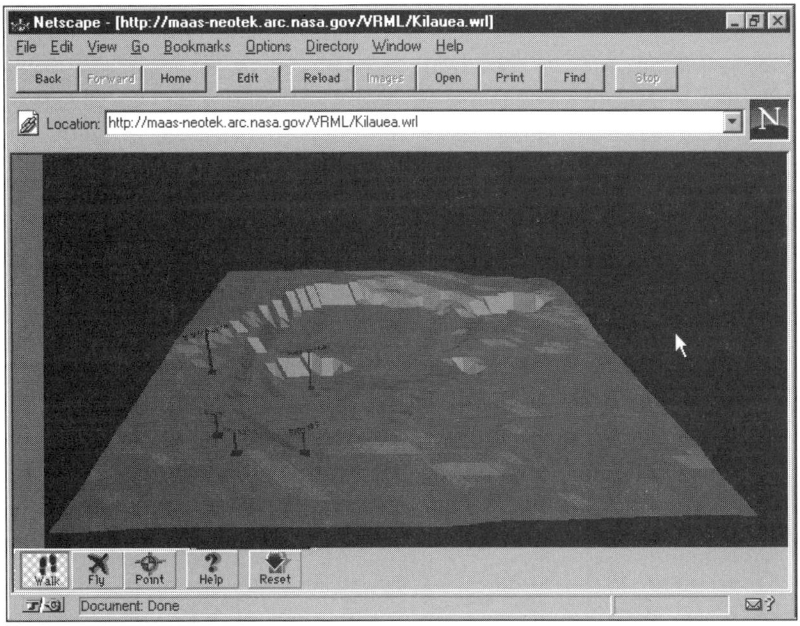

Figure 10.17

Virtual rollerskating hits the Web with this fine VRML world.

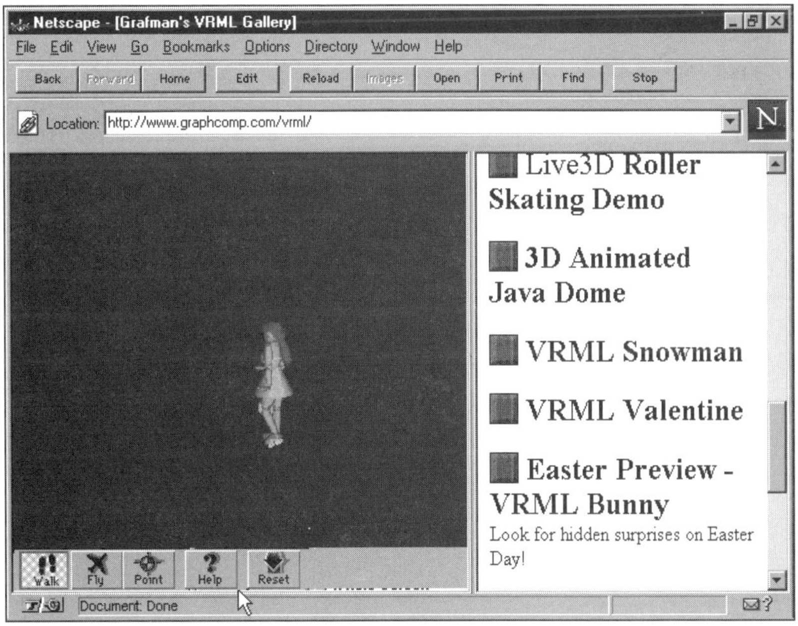

Figure 10.18

Just tell me you can resist walking through those archways.

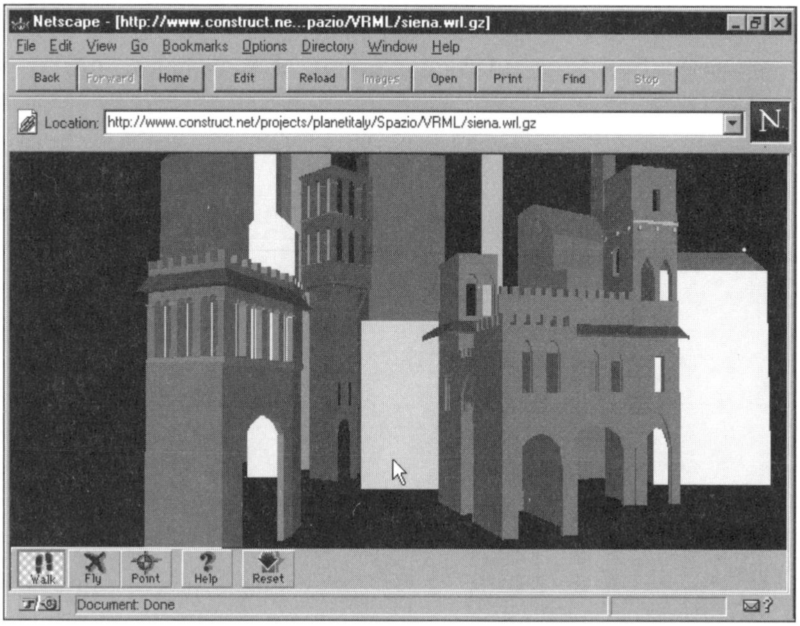

PART 2

Solid Gold: The Fastest Way to Create Web Pages

- *What the Editor Does*
- *Accessing the Editor*
- *The Editor Window*
- *The Workpane*
- *The Pop-up Menus*
- *The Dialog Boxes*

CHAPTER

11

Gold's Editor

UP UNTIL NOW, THIS BOOK HAS DEALT WITH NETSCAPE NAVIGATOR, not with Navigator Gold per se. Knowing as much as possible about Navigator is important because it's the browser you'll be designing your Web documents for, and you need to know its features, its quirks, and its specialties. But from this point on, you'll be spending most of your time in the Editor of Navigator Gold, from which you'll build your HTML files with all its bells and whistles.

Actually, you won't use all of them at first. Although Gold is supposed to handle all your HTML needs, its early releases won't be able to do so. Adding frames, tables, or forms to your pages isn't possible with the first Gold release, for example, nor does the program will ever handle such complex procedures as Java, which is actually a separate programming language. So if you're looking for an editor to take care of all possible HTML design work, Gold isn't it. Netscape promises that it will be within a few more releases, but right now, it's not quite everything.

However, Gold can handle most of your needs, and that's the major point. In fact, it handles all the needs that most users will ever have, increasingly so as it progresses from version to version. And if you need Gold to do something now that its WYSIWYG interface doesn't handle, it's easy enough to add it as raw HTML code. Right now you'll need raw HTML to handle frames; who knows if you'll ever be able to use Gold to add HTML extensions specific to Navigator's main competition, Microsoft Internet Explorer. But the bulk of HTML is already part of Gold, and it's extremely easy to use.

So fire up the Editor, take a look below to find out what you're looking at, and let's get authoring.

What the Editor Does

In the Editor window, you create and edit HTML files. This window is, in effect, an HTML editor, and if you've used other editors, such as HotDog or HoTMetaL, you'll recognize this one right away. Actually, though, the closest comparisons are to Microsoft's Internet Assistant and Quarterdeck's Web-Author, both of which are add-ons to Microsoft Word for Windows. All three editors treat Web pages as WYSIWYG documents that resemble word processing files complete with fancy formatting, and their main purpose is to hide the unsightly HTML codes from the user's eyes.

Everything in you do in the Editor creates HTML code. You can specify heading levels and hyperlinks, place images, create lists, and format text in any of the standard HTML or Netscape-specific formats. Note that you're not restricted to standard, sanctioned HTML. You have access to everything the Netscape browser can do, except for the features that it specifically can't handle with the initial releases. But Netscape-specific items such as font colors and DIV tags (Netscape's text alignment tags) are at your disposal, as are all of Netscape's useful image alignment options.

Accessing the Editor

There are several ways to open the Editor, depending on what you wish to accomplish. These methods are summarized here.

Option 1: Clicking the Edit Button, or Choosing File/Edit Document

If you click the Edit button on the toolbar, you'll open the Edit window and load, inside it, the document you're currently viewing in the browser window. As soon as the Edit window opens, the Edit Save As dialog box appears, as shown in Figure 11.1. This option is also available by selecting Edit Document from the File menu.

Figure 11.1

The special Save As dialog box offers several choices when the Edit window is accessed.

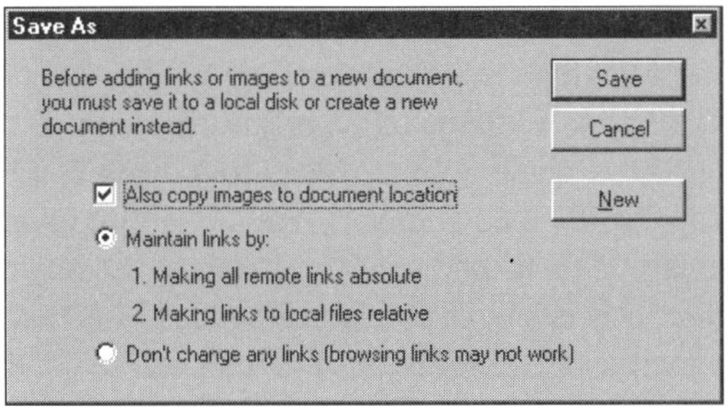

You can't begin to edit an existing document until you save it to your hard drive. The first button on the Save As dialog box, *Save*, lets you do exactly that. But it's not quite as simple as just clicking Save; instead, you have to make some choices.

Your first choice is whether or not to copy the document's images to your hard disk along with the HTML document itself. This is extremely useful if you want to make use of those graphics for your own document, or, in particular, if you're editing a document from your own Web site and you need the images for proper placement and formatting.

Next, you must make a decision about how to display the original document's hyperlinks. The choice you make will determine how the saved document stores link information.

The default choice is *Maintain links by:*, which does two things. First, it copies hyperlink information to the document in your Edit window and keeps links to remote documents absolute. This means that any hyperlinks in the original document that point to a document on another computer are changed, if necessary, to links that will maintain that specific pointing. That makes sense. The other function of this choice is to make links to local files relative, which means that hyperlinks in the original document that point to other documents within the same Web will now be replaced by remote links (in other words, to the same document as if it's on a remote machine, which it probably is). Unless you're editing documents on your own Web, and doing your editing on the machine on which that Web resides, it's almost always better to choose the *Maintain links* option.

You can elect to keep all links the same by choosing *Don't change any links*, but as the dialog box tells you, this might result in browsing links not functioning properly. What happens is this: If you change none of the links, Gold simply reproduces the HTML code of the original document exactly. In the case of relative URLs (see the discussion of relative versus absolute URLs in Chapter 14), *Don't change any links* maintains the reference to local files (file://) rather than to a remote machine (http://).

The only reason you'd ever *not* change the links would be if you're editing your own Web documents; when you're making use of a document from a remote Web, changing the links according to the *Maintain links* option makes more sense, and lets you use the links more easily in your own document.

Once you've made your choices, Gold displays a Hint box, telling you to beware of copyright issues. It reads: "You are about to download a remote document or image. You should get permission to use any copyrighted images or documents." This is an extremely good point—just because you can easily download documents and images doesn't mean you have the legal right to use them. Consider *everything* on the Web to be protected by copyright laws, and don't get caught using a document or image created by someone else. If you want to use it, e-mail them and ask permission, and be sure to save the response.

Option 2: Choosing File/New Document

Selecting New Document from the File menu in either the browser or the Editor window opens an empty document in the Edit window. This is the primary way of beginning a new HTML document. This option is also made available by selecting New from the Edit window's Save As dialog box, available after choosing option 1 above.

The New Document option gives you three choices—Blank, From Template, and From Wizard. Selecting Blank gives you a completely empty document in which you can start adding elements as you wish. Selecting From Template takes you to Netscape's templates page, where you can choose from a variety of styles to help you get started. From Wizard takes you to another page on the Netscape site, this one giving you a means of generating a portion of the page automatically. The options From Template and From Wizard war covered in Chapter 12.

Option 3: Choosing File/Open File in Editor

If you have an HTML document on your hard drive, you can load it into Gold's Editor to work on it. You'll be presented with your system's File Open dialog box to locate and select the file. You can achieve the same result by selecting File/Open in the Editor window itself.

The Editor Window

When the Editor opens, it resembles Figure 11.2. In this case, the browser has loaded Netscape's home page at http://home.netscape.com/; all graphics were saved locally and all links were maintained. Figure 11.3 shows the original browser window from which the Editor drew its document.

Figure 11.2

The Editor window, ready to work on Netscape Communication's main page

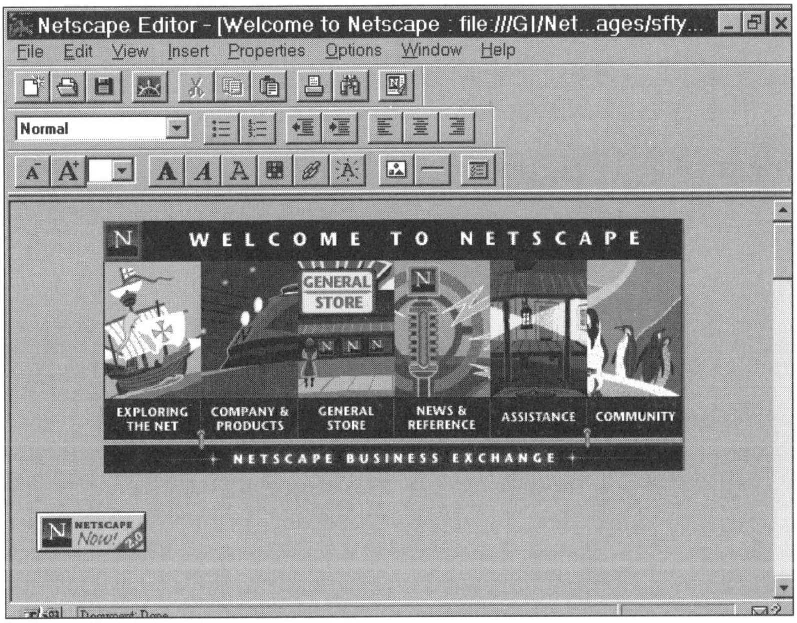

As you can see, the Editor window doesn't look much different from the browser window. In fact, it's not supposed to look any different at all, at least not the main viewing area. The Editor is supposed to handle anything that can appear in the browser, because the whole point of Gold is to allow you to edit documents specifically for Navigator. In the example shown in Figures 11.2 and 11.3, the Editor window looks slightly different (mainly in graphics alignment) because Figure 11.2 was shot using an early version of Gold's editor.

There are three fundamental differences between the Editor window and the normal browser window. First, when you switch to the Editor, you'll notice that the menus have changed. Second, the toolbars are entirely different. But the most significant difference isn't visible in Figure 11.2 at all. On the Editor screen is a blinking cursor, an insertion point of the kind found in word processors. In other words, you can *edit*, and that is precisely what makes the Editor worth using.

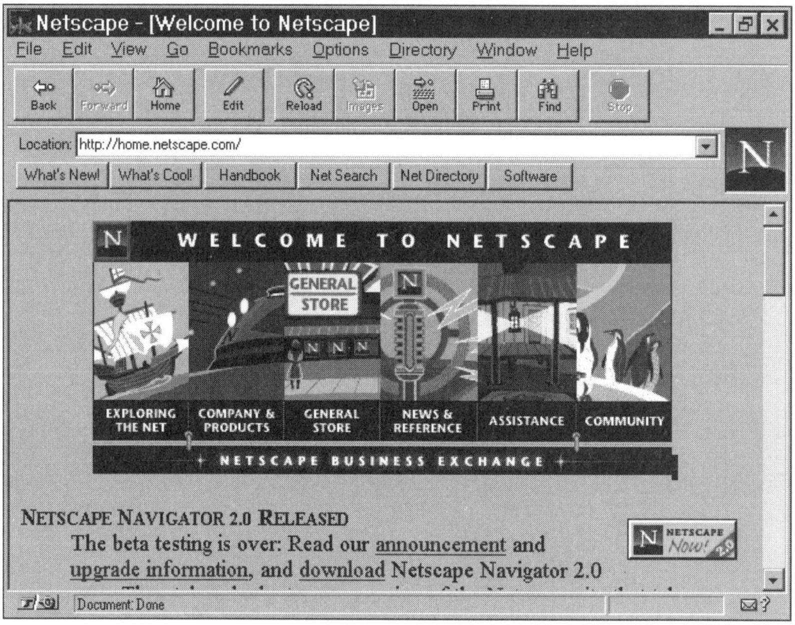

Figure 11.3

Netscape Navigator's window showing the same page

The Editor window consists of four major sections. The first three are always visible (unless you toggle them off): menus, toolbars, and a large area for viewing your work, which I'll call the *workpane*. From this point on in the book, whenever you see the word *workpane*, you'll know it's the area of the Editor in which you actually do something. The browser viewing area will simply be called the browser viewing area, or even just the browser. The fourth window section is the dialog boxes, which appear only under certain conditions. But understanding them is crucial to using the product to its fullest, so it's best to consider them a section of the window itself instead of simply an add-on.

Menus and Toolbars

Eight menus and three toolbars grace the top of the Editor window. The toolbars can be moved anywhere on the screen to maximize the workpane area. Table 11.1 summarizes the functions of each of the menu items, while Table 11.2 does the same for the toolbar items. Note, however, that only items specific to the Editor window are covered here. Menu items identical to those in the browser window are covered in previous chapters. Note also that the explanation for most toolbar items in Table 11.2 refers to the corresponding menu item in Table 11.1.

Table 11.1

The Menus in Gold's Editor Window

MENU	MENU ITEM	FUNCTION
File	New Document	Opens the Editor with an empty document
	Browse Document	Opens the browser window displaying the currently edited document
	Open Location	Opens a dialog box in which you can specify a URL, and specify whether or not you wish to load the URL into a browser window or into the Editor
	Open File	Opens a dialog box from which you can select a document from your hard drive to load into the Editor
Edit		All items identical to browser
View		All items identical to browser
Insert	Link	Opens a dialog box that allows you to create a hyperlink at the cursor location
	Image	Opens the image manipulation dialog box to insert a graphic at the cursor location
	Horizontal Line	Inserts a horizontal line at the cursor location
	New Line Break	Inserts a break tag at the cursor location
	Break Below Image(s)	Inserts a line break below the currently selected image
	Non-Breaking Space	Inserts a space, but not a line break, at the cursor location
Properties	Document	Opens a dialog box for manipulating the full document properties
	Paragraph/List	Opens a dialog box for adjusting the properties of the currently selected list
	Paragraph	Opens a cascading menu of choices for paragraph style (Figure 11.4)
	Character	Opens a cascading menu of choices for character appearance (Figure 11.5)
	Font Size	Opens a cascading menu for adjusting relative font size (Figure 11.6)
	Font Color	Opens a color palette allowing you to change the color of the currently selected font

Table 11.1 (Continued)

The Menus in Gold's Editor Window

MENU	MENU ITEM	FUNCTION
	Link	Opens a dialog box allowing you to adjust the properties of the currently selected hyperlink
	Image	Opens the Image Properties dialog box to adjust image appearance and details
	Horizontal Line	Opens a dialog box to adjust the characteristics of the currently selected horizontal line
Options	Editor Preferences	Opens a dialog box for adjusting default options for the Editor window
	Show File/Edit Toolbar	Hides or displays the File/Edit toolbar
	Show Character Format Toolbar	Hides or displays the Character Format toolbar
	Show Paragraph Format Toolbar	Hides or displays the Paragraph Format toolbar
Window		All items identical to browser
Help		All items identical to browser

Table 11.2

The Toolbars in Gold's Edit Window

TOOLBAR	BUTTON	FUNCTION	MENU ITEM
File/Edit	New Document	Opens Editor window with blank document	File/New Document
	Open File to Edit	Loads a file from your hard drive into the Editor window	File/Open File
	Save	Saves the currently edited file to your hard drive	File/Save
	Open Browser	Opens a browser window showing the currently edited document	File/Browse Document
	Cut	Cuts the current selection to the Clipboard	Edit/Cut
	Copy	Copies the current selection to the Clipboard	Edit/Copy

Table 11.2 (Continued)

The Toolbars in Gold's Edit Window

TOOLBAR	BUTTON	FUNCTION	MENU ITEM
	Paste	Pastes the Clipboard contents to the page at the cursor location	Edit/Paste
	Print	Prints the current document	File/Print
	Find	Locates a specified text string in the current document	Edit/Find
	NavGold Home Page	Opens a browser window with Netscape's home page for Gold	None
Paragraph Format	Style	Allows you to select a style for the current paragraph	Properties/Paragraph
	Bullet List	Creates an unordered list using the currently selected text	None
	Numbered List	Creates an ordered list using the currently selected text	None
	Decrease Indent	Decreases the indent for the currently selected paragraph by one tab space	Properties/Paragraph/ Remove one indent level
	Increase Indent	Indents or increases the indent for the currently selected paragraph by one tab space	Properties/Paragraph/ Indent one level
	Align Left	Justifies the currently selected text to the left margin	None
	Center	Centers the currently selected text	None
	Align Right	Justifies the currently selected text to the right margin	None
Character Format	Decrease Font Size	Decreases the size of the currently selected character(s) by one increment	None
	Increase Font Size	Increases the size of the currently selected character(s) by one increment	None
	Font Size	Allows you to choose the font size for the currently selected character(s)	Properties/Font Size
	Bold	Changes the currently selected text to bold	Properties/Character/ Bold

Table 11.2 (Continued)

The Toolbars in Gold's Edit Window

TOOLBAR	BUTTON	FUNCTION	MENU ITEM
	Italic	Changes the currently selected text to italic	Properties/Character/Italic
	Fixed Width	Changes the currently selected text to a fixed width font	Properties/Character/Fixed Width
	Font Color	Opens the Font Color dialog box	Properties/Font Color
	Make Link	Opens the dialog box for creating a hyperlink	Insert/Link
	Clear All Styles	Clears all character styles from the currently selected text	Properties/Character/Clear all character styles
	Insert Image	Opens the dialog box for specifying an image	Insert/Image
	Insert Hori-zontal Line	Inserts a horizontal line at the cursor position	Insert/Horizontal Line
	Object Properties	Opens the dialog box for the properties of the currently selected item	None

The Link Button

To the left of the Location box is a special icon called the Link Button. This is used to copy the URL of the current document into the clipboard, or to drag it to an Editor window to use as a hyperlink. To copy the URL to the clipboard, double-click and hold with the left mouse button, and drag it into the window.

■ The Workpane

There's not much to say about this section of the Editor window, other than to note the rather obvious fact that it's the largest single component. Scroll bars, title bar, and status bars appear according to what your operating system dictates, and while the workpane itself can't be resized, the entire Editor window can be whatever size you wish.

To get the maximum space for doing actual HTML work, consider dragging the toolbars to more convenient locations on the screen, or hiding them entirely through the Options menu. Figure 11.7 compares the workpane area of an Editor screen with all the toolbars displayed, and the same screen with

Figure 11.4

The cascading Properties/ Paragraph menu

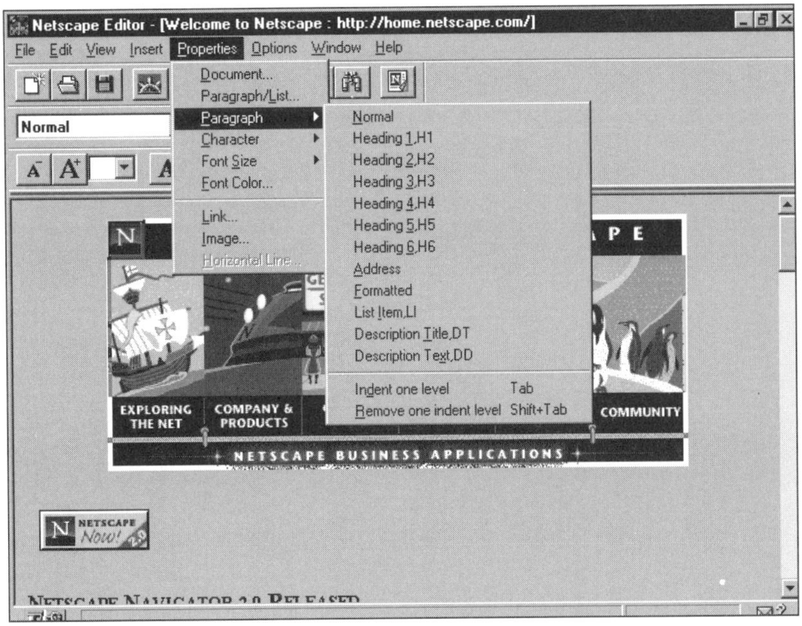

Figure 11.5

The cascading Properties/ Character menu

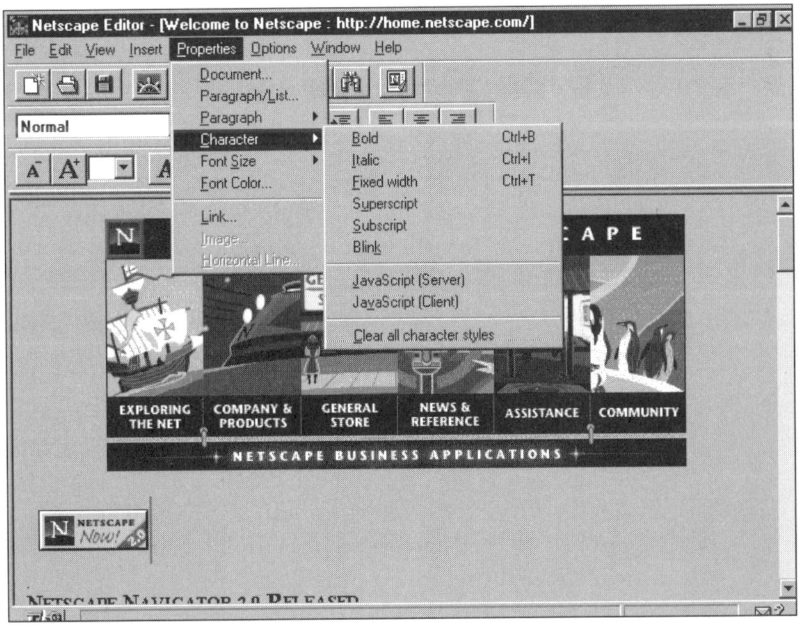

Figure 11.6

The cascading Properties/Font Size menu

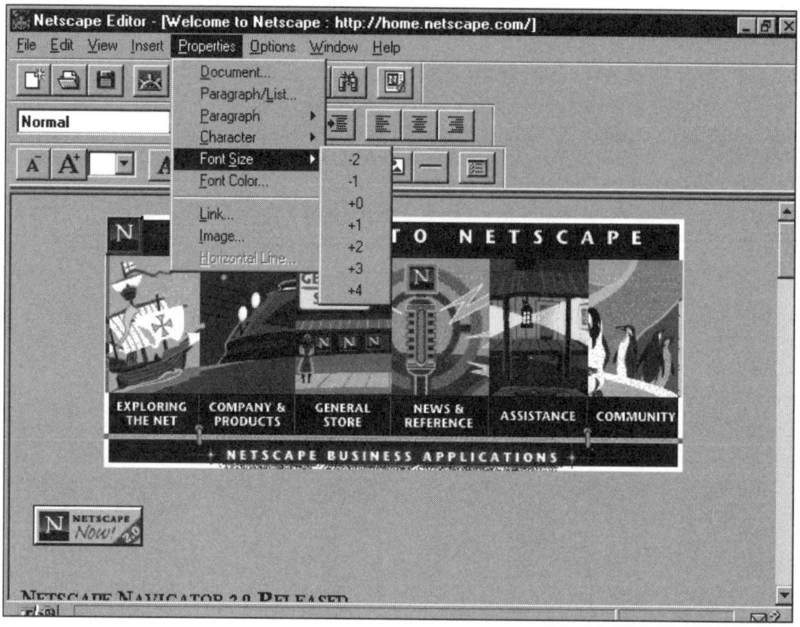

the toolbars hidden. Obviously, the screen with the hidden toolbars gives you a lot more working space. Hiding the toolbars makes much less difference, however, as you move to a larger screen and different resolutions.

The Pop-up Menus

One of the reasons you can comfortably hide the toolbars is Gold's use of pop-up menus. Accessed by the right-mouse button in Windows or UNIX systems and by the standard right-button emulation on the Macintosh, these menus contain all options relevant to the item on which you're currently working. Use them often, because they can be the fastest interface of all.

To access the appropriate pop-up menu, move the cursor to the item you wish to edit and right-click. The drop-down menu pertaining to that object type will appear on the screen. These are shown in Figures 11.8 through 11.10.

Figure 11.8 shows the standard document pop-up menu. This appears when you right-click anywhere outside an image, link, or other formatted element. From here you can create a new paragraph or list type, or you can create a new hyperlink or paste from the Clipboard, all at the current cursor position. You can also call up the Document Properties dialog box and change the features of the document as a whole.

Figure 11.7

A comparison of the workpane area with toolbars showing (a) or hidden (b)

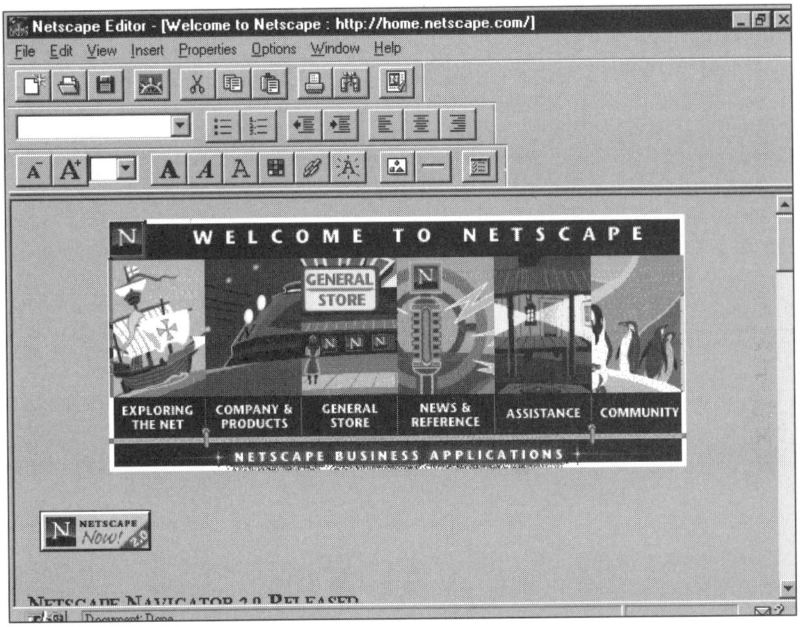

(a)

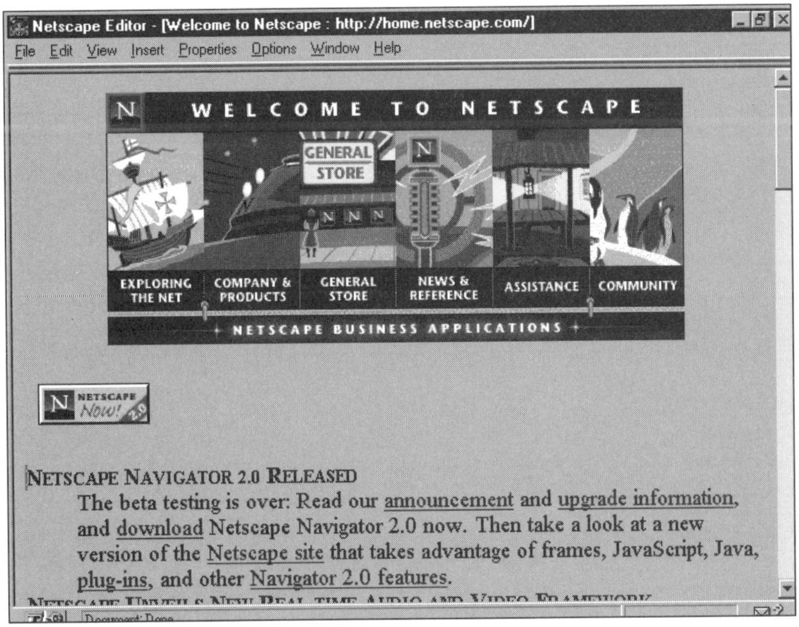

(b)

Figure 11.8

The standard document pop-up menu

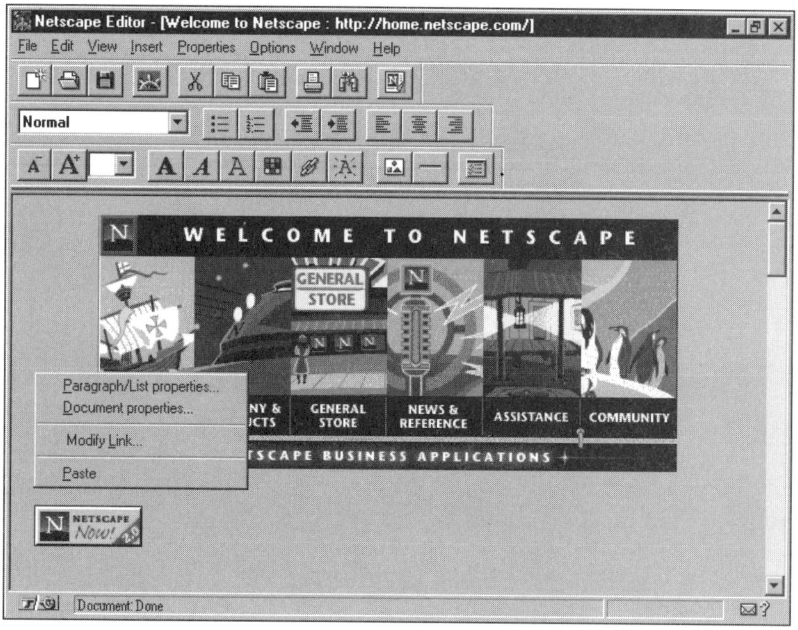

When you position the cursor over a standard text hyperlink and right-click, you receive the pop-up menu shown in Figure 11.9. From here you can modify the hyperlink (change its destination URL, for example), or you can copy the link to the Clipboard as you can in the browser. Furthermore, you can open a browser window with the destination URL loaded (browse to link), or you can bookmark the link in your Bookmarks file. Finally, and extremely usefully, you can open an Editor window with the destination URL loaded, all ready for your skillful editing touch.

In Figure 11.10, you see the pop-up menu that results from right-clicking on an image (you have to left-click to select the image first, however). You can call up the Image Properties dialog box to change the image's composition, you can save the image to your hard drive, or you can cut or copy it to the Clipboard. You can also make the image into a hyperlink by choosing Create Link Using Selected. If the image is already a hyperlink, you can also open the destination in a browser or an Editor window.

The Dialog Boxes

Several dialog boxes appear as the result of selecting options in the Editor window. These are covered in their respective chapters throughout the remainder of this book.

Figure 11.9

The hyperlink pop-up menu

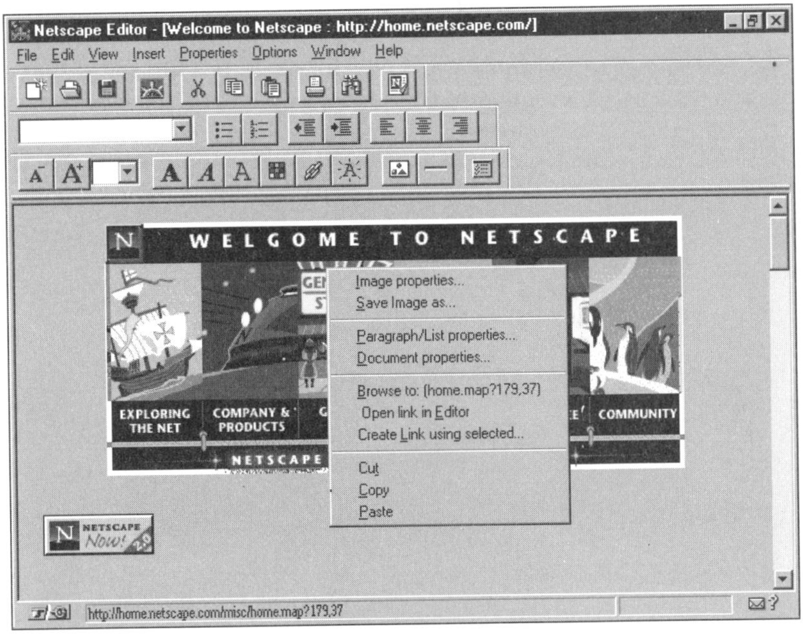

Figure 11.10

The image pop-up menu

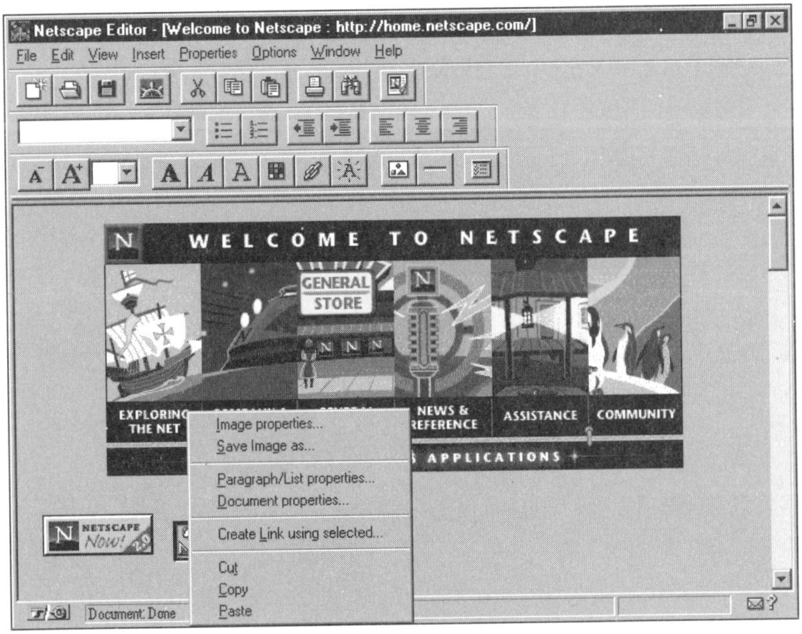

Gold's Editor is where your HTML action takes place. As you come to use it increasingly, you'll begin to see the many advantages it offers over other HTML editors. In particular, it offers the significant advantage of being Netscape Navigator itself. You can see instantly the effect your HTML additions and alterations will have on the way your users will see your pages, and you never have to leave your favorite browser. The Editor window makes Gold the extremely valuable product that it is.

- *Using the Wizard*
- *Using the Templates*
- *Using the Tool Chest*
- *Do You Need All These Things?*

CHAPTER

12

Starting a New Document: Wizards, Templates, and the Tool Chest

YOU HAVE THREE PRIMARY CHOICES WHEN CREATING A NEW WEB document with Gold. First, as you'll see in Chapter 13, you can start with an empty Editor window and add all the elements yourself. Next, as Chapter 15 explains, you can retrieve an existing document from the Web and edit it to hold your own information. But if you're just beginning your HTML career, why not get professional help instead? This chapter focuses on the wizards and templates Netscape has made available as part of the Gold package.

What's the difference between wizards and templates in Gold? The same difference as we see in just about all programs these days. Wizards are step-by-step walkthroughs, while templates are documents with pre-determined settings. The idea behind both is to help you get started efficiently and effectively, and even if you're an experienced Web author you might want to check them out.

Using the Wizard

Gold's wizard provides the easiest way to begin composing a new document. To use the wizard, click on the File menu, and from the resulting secondary menu select From Wizard. You'll be presented with the Netscape Page Wizard page shown in Figure 12.1.

Figure 12.1

From this framed page you can begin your document authoring.

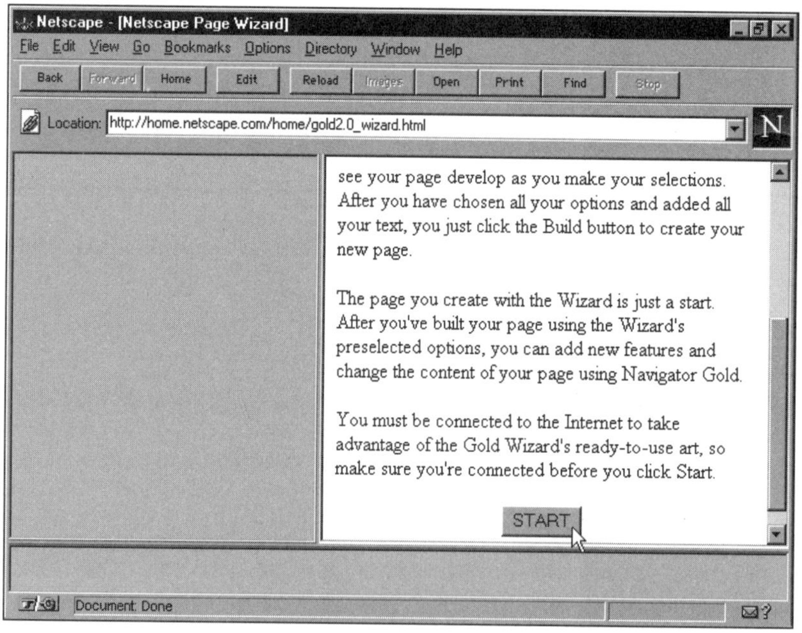

There's not much to do here but click Start, so click Start. This yields the instructions page shown in Figure 12.2. The frame on the left (the options frame) remains visible throughout your page creation, while the large frame on the right (the viewing frame) shows the results of what you've created. At the bottom is the fill-in frame, which you'll use to create your document's content and appearance.

Figure 12.2

Using a Wizard to create your page

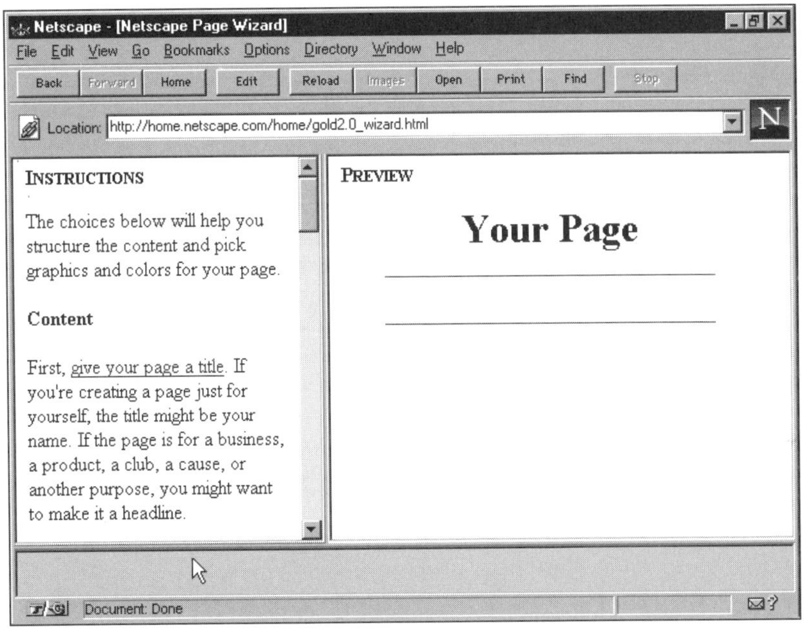

It's important to remember that you are not yet in Gold's Editor. At this point, you're still in the browser, and you'll create your page by clicking the Build button at the bottom of the options frame.

First you'll need a title a bit more spiffy than the default "Your Page." Click on the link entitled "give your page a title," and a one-field form will appear in the bottom frame. Call it whatever you want, then press the Apply button. The results frame will change immediately to reflect your choice.

Next, click on "type an introduction" in the left frame (options frame). Again, you'll be presented with a single-field fill-in form in the bottom frame (the fill-in frame). Type in the introduction to your page (if you want one), click Apply, and see the results in the viewing frame, the large frame on the right.

The next option is to add links to other Web pages. Although these might not be exactly where you want them in your document at this stage, remember that you'll have ample opportunity to alter your page once you click Build and thus launch the Editor. To create your links, click on "add some hot links" and fill in the name of the link (that is, how you want it to appear on your page) and the URL that will lead your readers to that site. Figure 12.3 shows the creation of a link to ZD Net, after having created one to Netscape's home page.

Your next choice in the options frame is typing a concluding statement for your page. Again, click on the link in the options frame, and type in your message in the fill-in frame.

Figure 12.3

The links you create appear in the viewing frame as a bulleted list.

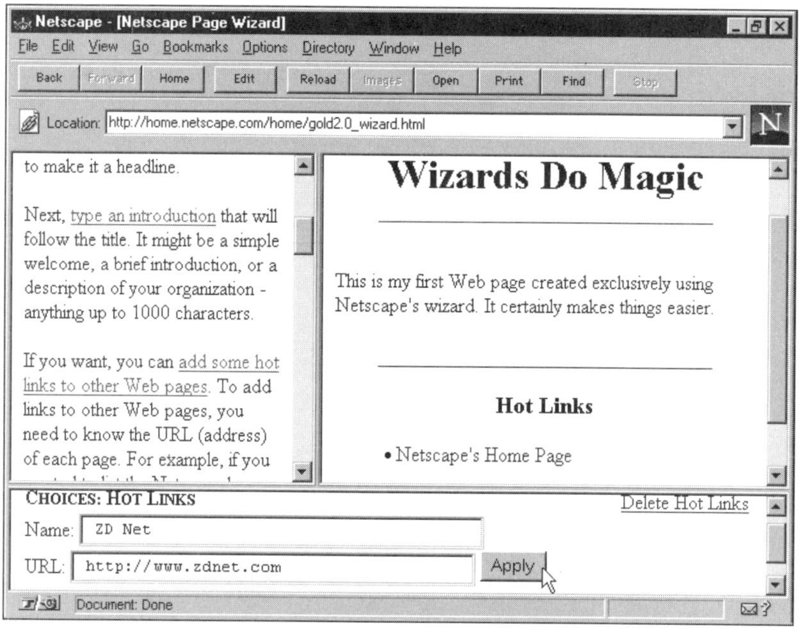

The last thing you can type in from this wizard is a link to your e-mail address. This will produce a link that will open Gold's message window, allowing your readers to send you a message. Type your e-mail address in the fill-in frame, and click Apply.

Now that you have all the text and links in your page, it's time to make some choices about the page's actual appearance. First up come the colors and patterns. Here you have a choice between selecting a preset color combination, or individually deciding on the background color or pattern, the text color, the link color, and the visited link color. (The visited link color is applied to links your user has already clicked on.)

Clicking on the "present color combination" link yields a bar of compatible colors in the fill-in frame. Click on one of them, and the viewing window will change to reflect your choice. Keep clicking until you find a combination you like.

If you prefer to make all choices yourself, including the option to have a background texture rather than a color, use the individual element links. Background color, text color, and the two link colors all offer a palette of colors from which to choose, while the background pattern link gives you a selection of textures instead (see Figure 12.4). Again, click on the one you want, and the viewing pane will change to show your choice.

Figure 12.4

The background texture you choose will be downloaded to your hard drive when you click Build.

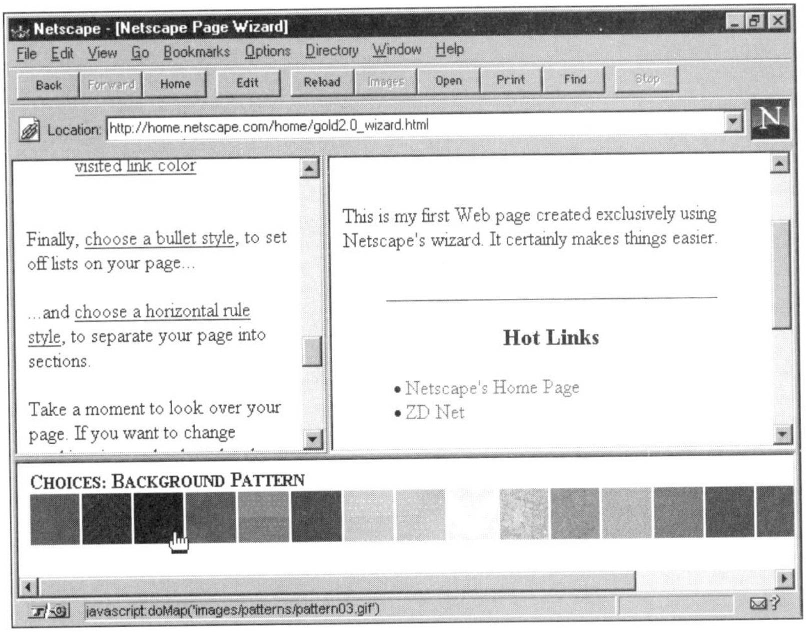

With your colors selected, the next step is to choose a bullet style and your horizontal rule style. Several are available, including some animated bullets; just click on your choice. A variety of horizontal rules is also available, and again it's simply a matter of choosing the one you want.

Go back over your selections and make whatever changes you desire, then scroll to the bottom of the options frame and click Build. Gold will construct the page, which will appear as a fully formatted page in a browser window. Click the Edit button (or choose File/Edit Document), and you'll be presented with the Save Document dialog to bring your page and graphics onto your hard disk. The Editor window will automatically open with your new document loaded, and you're ready to edit from there. See Chapters 13–17 for all your editing choices.

Using the Templates

Gold's templates are nothing more than preformatted HTML documents that you can load into an Editor window and change to suit your purposes. But that's precisely what makes them valuable. Because these documents are professionally designed, they spare you the task of working up an effective page from scratch. Most of us want to create our own pages, but very few of us are professional designers. We can often work better if we start from a template.

To begin a document with a template, click on the File menu and choose New Document/From Template. Gold will open a new browser window that takes you to the templates page on the Netscape site. As of this writing, Netscape offered 14 templates, with topics ranging from personal to business and hobby pages. In addition, there are a couple of pages to help you write JavaScripts (see Chapter 23). It's a very useful collection. A portion of these links is shown in Figure 12.5.

Figure 12.5

From Netscape's templates page, you can select the topic you're interested in.

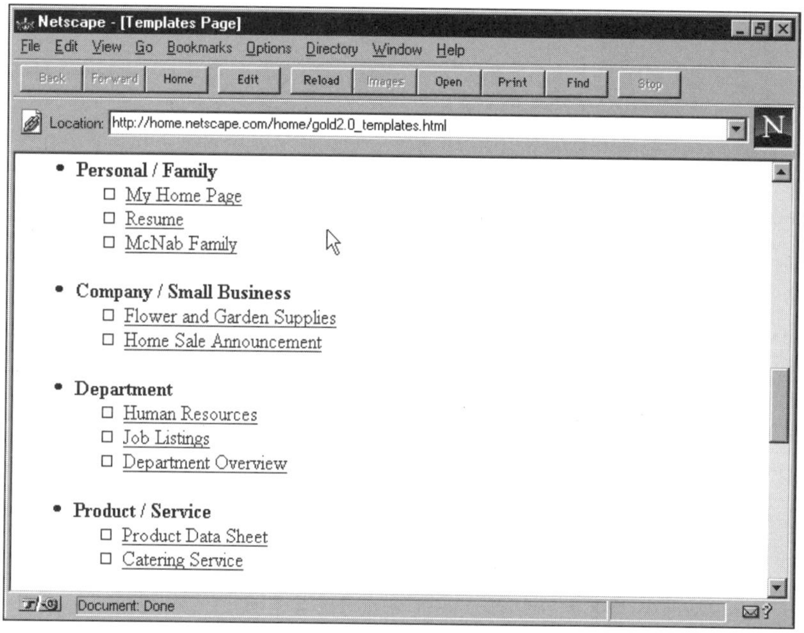

To choose a template, click on whatever link you wish. This will retrieve a page in the browser window displaying that template. When you have the template you want, click Edit (or choose File/Edit Document), and the Editor window will open with that document inside it. You'll be given the option of saving the graphics files and hyperlinks to your hard drive so that you can use them when editing the document to suit your needs. Figure 12.6 shows a small section of one of the template pages, complete with attractive graphic.

None of the hyperlinks on these pages is real; that is, they don't actually work. They exist purely for the sake of design, and you'll have to erase them or change them to make them usable. In fact, you won't want to retain any of the wording on the page, including the title. Instead, you'll want to make it your own, while retaining the elements of the design itself that you find suitable.

Figure 12.6

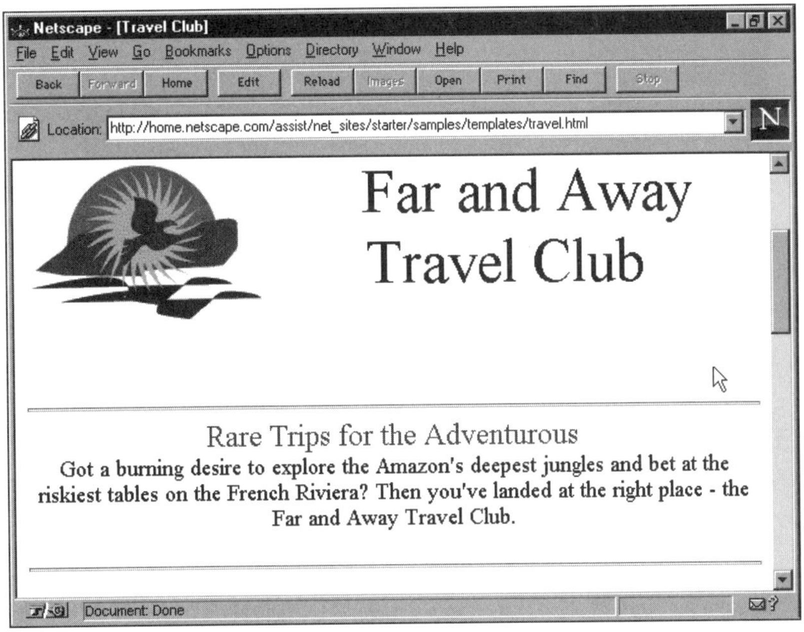

The template for creating a hobby club Web page

Using the Tool Chest

No matter what level of expertise you bring to your HTML authoring, you'll want to visit the Netscape Gold Rush Tool Chest immediately and frequently. From here you can get access to the wizard and templates pages described above, but more important you'll be presented with links to a wide range of valuable authoring resources. As Figure 12.7 shows, these include links to clip art, backgrounds, Java and JavaScript resources, and design tips. There's also an extremely useful section on copyright, to help you determine what you may and may not use as you find attractive designs on the Web.

Each link leads you to a page of samples. The Rules and Bullets page, for example, gives you a list of plain and fancy items, while the animated GIFs page presents you with a collection of graphics that actually move. All other links take you to similar pages, and you can download them according to the techniques demonstrated in Chapter 6.

Figure 12.8 shows one of these pages, a collection of illustrations featuring Netscape's mascot, Mozilla the dragon. As the page states, you are free to use these on your own site, but you must mention on that page that Mozilla is a Netscape trademark. Many sites featuring Web authoring tools require the same courtesy.

Figure 12.7

The Gold Rush Tool Chest page gives you the add-ons you need.

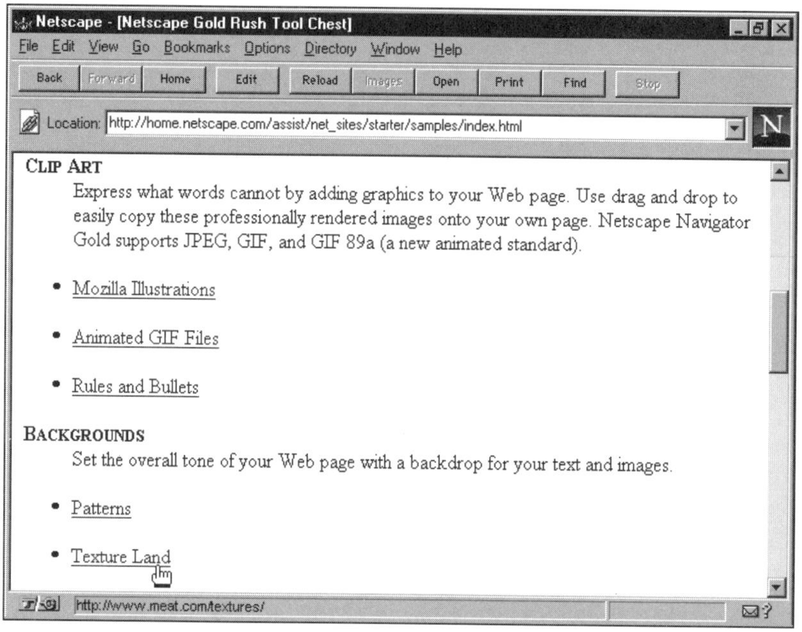

Figure 12.8

Mozilla in a variety of downloadable guises

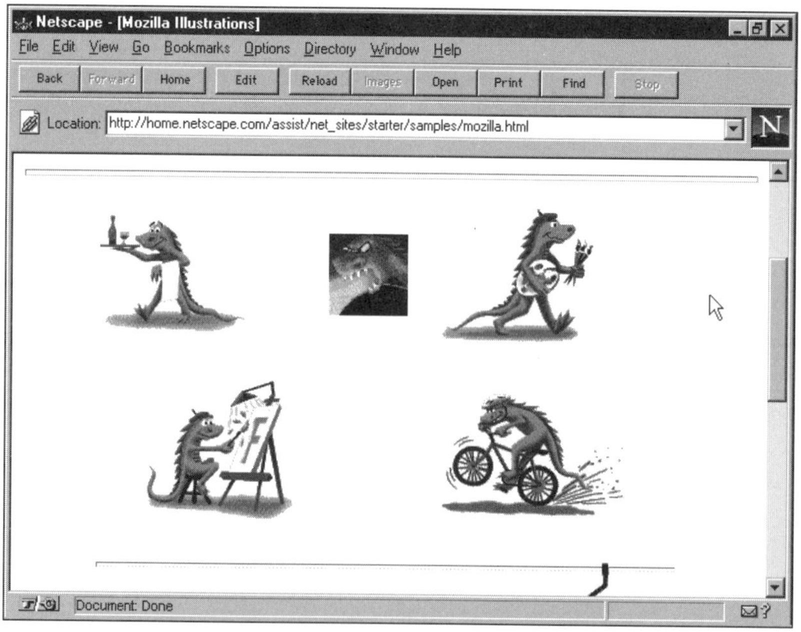

Do You Need All These Things?

No. You don't need any of them. But they can help you get started, and if you're pressed for time that's exactly what you need. In the future, Gold's designers should be encouraged to build wizards and templates into the program itself, so you're not forced to retrieve them over the Web, and they should be made more powerful as well. But they're useful as they stand, and you're encouraged to use them right off the bat.

- *The Basic HTML Elements*
- *Don't Forget Your Document Tags*
- *It's All Pretty Basic*
- *Basic Tags in Raw HTML*

CHAPTER

13

Starting It Off with HTML Basics

THIS IS IT! YOU'RE ABOUT TO CREATE YOUR FIRST WEB PAGES WITH Netscape Navigator Gold. This chapter will introduce you to all the basic elements of HTML design: everything from differently sized headings through document options to font colors, and even the various kinds of lists available to you. As with all remaining chapters of this book, you'll read about design decisions you have to make in using each element and how to put the elements into your pages using Gold; and then, to make you a true HTML expert, you'll learn the equivalent tags using standard, text-based HTML. By the time you've completed this chapter, you'll have a solid grasp of HTML basics. By the time you're done with the entire book, you'll be ready to tackle just about any HTML job asked of you.

The Basic HTML Elements

Several important and useful HTML elements have been around since the first few incarnations of Hypertext Markup Language, and Gold gives you access to all of them. In fact, it adds to the list elements established in subsequent versions of HTML, as well as a few Netscape-only tags. The basic elements will be introduced here, and each will be covered in detail as the chapter progresses.

Document Tags

While most of HTML is concerned with individual items on the page, some tags give you formatting options for the document as a whole. It's extremely easy to forget about some of these, since they don't all appear in your Editor window. Whenever you begin a new Gold document, therefore, you should be sure to set the document tags first.

Fortunately, Gold makes it easy to do all this, controlling the entire process through the Document Options dialog box. When you select Document Properties from the Properties menu (or from the default pop-up menu), you'll be presented with a dialog box with three tabs, General, Appearance, and Advanced. Together, these three tabs let you set all document-level options. These options are summarized in Table 13.1.

Basic HTML Tags

It's hard to determine which HTML tags should be considered basic and thus tossed into one chapter in a book like this. But the following tags have been around for most of HTML's existence, and have become not only standard, but often overused. In the case of lists, in fact, use is actually declining, because they're just not as attractive as tables or other formatting elements. Table 13.2 shows the elements covered in this chapter.

NOTE. *To see the HTML version of your work, select Document Source from the View menu.*

Don't Forget Your Document Tags

Document tags are those which force behavior on the entire document, rather than on one specific area. The document's background color or image, the link colors, the title, and other characteristics depend on these tags. Except for background colors and images, these tags do not, as a whole, have nearly as much impact on your work as the paragraph and character tags do, but they're important to complete nevertheless.

Table 13.1

The Document Tags in Netscape Gold

NAME	FUNCTION	HTML EQUIVALENT
Title	Sets the title of the document, appears in document information and in title bar depending on OS	<title></title> within <head></head>
Author	Sets the document author's name, which appears in document information	<meta name="Author"> within <head></head>
Netscape System Variables	Used to force HTTP server to convert META elements to HTTP headers	<http-equiv> within <head></head>
User Variables (META)	Used (somewhat rarely) to offer information for listing and cataloging not handled by regular HTML	<meta> - items added using name and value fields (within <head></head>
Normal Text	Sets color of normal document text	<body text=*color*>
Background Color	Sets color for solid backgrounds	<bgcolor=*color*>
Link Text	Sets color for hyperlinks	<link=*color*>
Active Link Text	Sets color for selected hyperlink	<alink=*color*>
Followed Link Text	Sets color for previously accessed links	<vlink=*color*>
Background Image	Sets image to display as background texture or graphic	<background=URL>
Keyword	Enter keywords to be found by Web search engines	None
Classification	Enter classifications to be found by Web search engines	None

Table 13.2

Basic HTML Tags in Gold

NAME	FUNCTION	HTML EQUIVALENT
Heading Level 1 through 6	Insert a heading level	<h1></h1> through <h6></h6>
Normal Text	Insert normal text	None
Address	Insert address-formatted text	<address></address>

Table 13.2 (Continued)

Basic HTML Tags in Gold

NAME	FUNCTION	HTML EQUIVALENT
Formatted	Insert formatted text	<pre></pre>
Ordered Lists	Insert a numbered list	<ol></ol>
Unordered Lists	Insert a bulleted list	<ul></ul>
Definition Lists	Insert a definition or glossary list	<dl></dl>
Menu Lists	Insert a menu list (rare)	<menu></menu>
Directory Lists	Insert a directory list (rare)	<dir></dir>
Block Quote	Insert an indented block quotation	<blockquote> </blockquote>
Indent One Level	Indent the selection one tab stop to the right	None
Decrease Indent One Level	Decrease the indent one tab stop to the left	None
Bold	Display the selection as bold font	<b></b>
Italic	Display the selection as italic font	<i></i>
Fixed Width	Display the selection as typewriter (nonproportional) font	<tt></tt>
Superscript	Display the selection as superscript (above the line)	
Subscript	Display the selection as subscript (below the line)	
Font Size	Change the font size by *x* number of increments from normal size	<font size=+*x*></font>
Font Color	Change the color of the selected text	<font COLOR=*color*> </font>
Paragraph	Start a new paragraph	<p></p>
Break	Insert a line break	 </br>
Break Below Image	Inserts a break below the current image	<br clear></br>
Horizontal Line	Insert a horizontal line	<hr></hr>

Fortunately, Gold makes it easy. One dialog box, consisting of two separate tabs, takes care of all your document-level needs. Figure 13.1 shows the Header Information section of the Document Properties box, while Figure 13.2 shows the Colors/Background section.

Figure 13.1

You can set document information from this dialog.

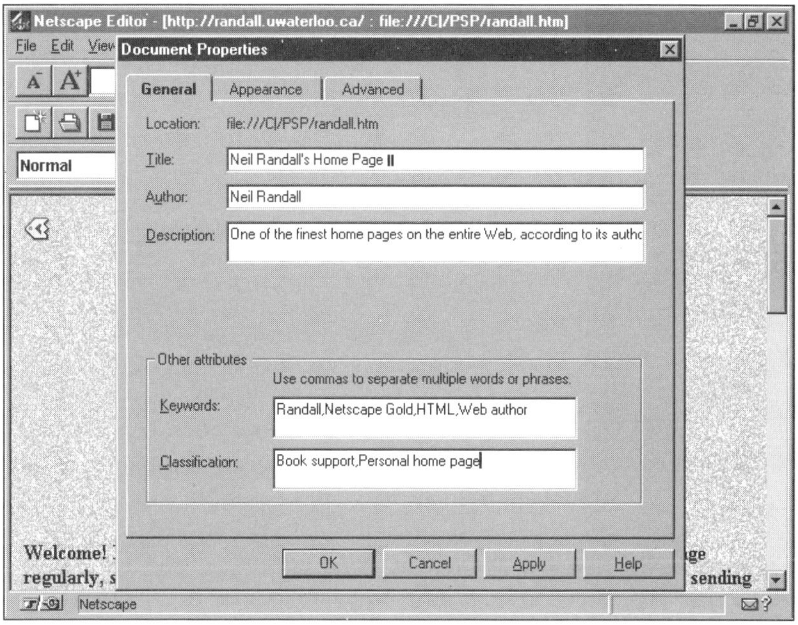

Setting Header Information

The Header Information areas of the Document Properties box, General and Advanced, offer several fields. All fields are entirely optional.

In the *Title* field, type the document's title. Note that this isn't the same thing as the major heading of the document itself. The title does *not* appear on the document itself. Instead, it is stored as part of the document's information, and it appears when you retrieve document information (View/Document Info) about the file you're viewing in a Web browser. Depending on your operating system, the title will also appear as part of the full browser window. In Microsoft Windows, for instance, the title appears on the title bar.

Make the title as descriptive as possible. Since it often displays before the actual document itself, a strong title can help users decide quickly whether or not they wish to view the entire document. The other major importance of the title is for Web search purposes. Search engines are programmed to search for words and phrases in titles as well as inside

Figure 13.2

Here are the options for setting colors and image backgrounds.

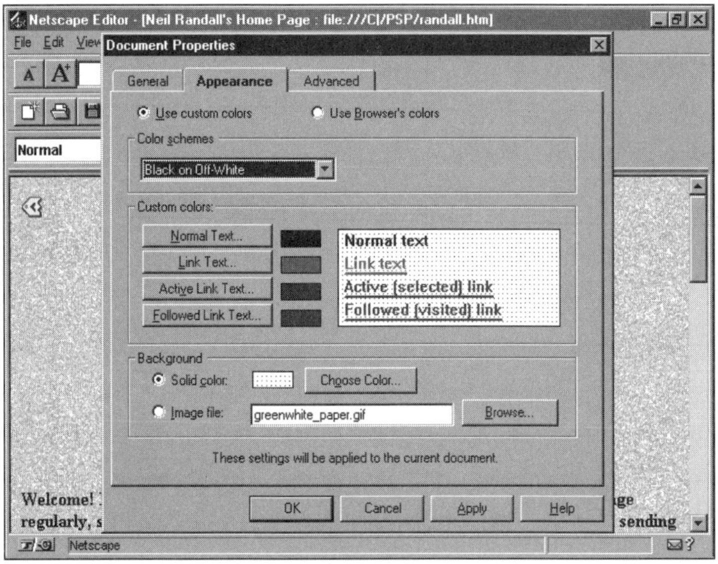

documents themselves, and in some engines you can specify titles as the search filter. Here, again, a descriptive title helps.

The *Author* field is designed to let you specify who wrote the Web page. It displays as part of the document information, not on the document itself. If you want users to be able to get in touch with the author easily, it's far more effective to put an e-mail link (see Chapter 14) somewhere on the document itself, usually at the end.

The Description field gives you a place to type information about your document; this information will appear when your readers choose Document Info from Gold's View menu.

The Other Attributes area includes two field, Keywords and Classification. In both, you can type words that you want search engines such as Yahoo to find in order to catalog your document.

The boxes labeled *Netscape System Variables* and *User Variables (META)* let you place tags that, in regular HTML, would bear the container <meta http-equiv ...></meta>. If you have no idea what these containers and attributes do, don't bother with them. They're covered briefly later in this chapter. You will notice, however, that Gold generates one META tag itself: GENERATOR=Netscape2.0Gold; this is a common META tag these days, and it shows users who choose to view document stats which HTML editor you used to create it.

To create an HTTP-EQUIV or a META tag, click in the relevant box. A new highlighted line will appear, but you won't be able to type directly in the box itself. Instead, you type the name of the tag in the *Name* field at the bottom of the Document Properties dialog, and you type the value of the tag that is, whatever you want it to say—in the *Value* field. Gold doesn't check for validity; you can type in anything you wish.

When you've finished typing Name and Value, click Set. This will place the information in the document header. If you want to add another tag, click New. if you want to delete a tag, highlight it and click Delete.

To complete the header information, click Close. Since you can't see what you've done (it's nowhere in the Workspace), select View/Document Source. There you'll see your titles and METAs, in all their resplendent coded glory.

Tutorial: Filling In Header Information

1. Choose Document Properties from the Properties menu.
2. Click the Header Information tab.
3. In the Title field, type **My First Gold Document**.
4. In the Author field, type your name.
5. Click in Netscape System Variables.
6. In the Name field, type **Expires**.
7. In the Value field, type **Wed, 05 Nov 1996 22:00 EDT**.
8. Click the Apply button. Your Document properties box should look like Figure 13.3.
9. Click OK. Select View/Document Source. The <head></head> container should look like the following:

```
<html>
<head>
<title>My First Gold Document</title>
<meta http-equiv="Expires" content="Wed, 05 Nov 1996 22:00 EDT">
</head>
```

Congratulations! You've just created your first Header information.

Setting Colors and Backgrounds—The Appearance Tab

You have two main choices when deciding on the text, link, and background colors for your document. First, by selecting the Use Browser's Colors radio button from the Appearance Tab, you can forget about setting these colors altogether; in this case, the colors and background will be determined by your

Figure 13.3

The completed Document Properties box

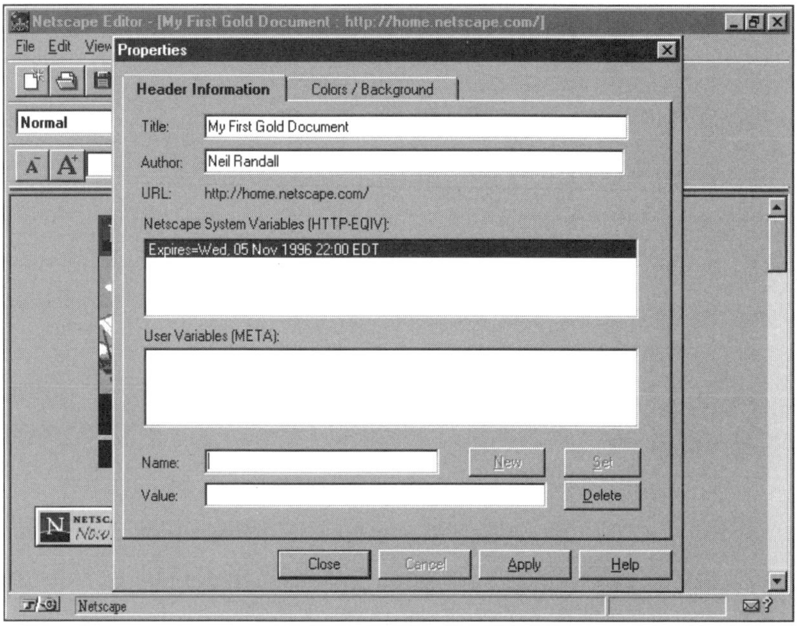

readers' Web browsers. Increasingly, however, Web designers are controlling these elements themselves, because they help with the full design of the document. Let's assume in this section that you want full control, in which case you would select the Use Custom Colors radio button instead.

Color Schemes

Gold includes two *color schemes*: Netscape Default Colors and Reverse Video. Choosing either of them, then clicking OK or Apply, sets all text and background colors to those specified in the scheme.

You can create your own color schemes by setting any or all colors and backgrounds, then clicking Save and naming your scheme in the resulting box. Create enough of them, and you can quickly set your colors and backgrounds by simply clicking on the appropriate background. This is especially useful if you're creating pages designed to have specific color themes and patterns (such as a site emphasizing a corporate image); when you add to the site, you can recall the color scheme easily.

To get rid of a color scheme, select the scheme and click Remove.

Choose Colors

Four selections are available in the *Choose Custom Color* section of the dialog box. Each works the same way. Click on the relevant button, then select the color from the resulting color palette, which is standard to your operating system. You can choose an existing color, or create a new color using the Custom Color palette.

Normal Text refers to all text in the document except links, and except text you've specifically colored using the Font Color button (or by selecting Properties/Font Color). All text except these elements changes to the color you select in Document Properties.

Link Text refers to the text in all the hyperlinks in the document, except the links that have already been accessed. Changing the Link Text color, of course, does nothing to graphics that have been set as hyperlinks.

The *Active Link Text* element refers to the text in hyperlinks on which you click. The active link is the currently clicked link, and it changes color only for a brief second after you click. It's a nice effect, but hardly a major design asset.

Followed Link Text refers to the text in hyperlinks that you've already visited. Your readers can set their browsers to maintain followed links for a specific length of time, and as long as those links are considered followed, when they appear on a page of your design they'll bear the color you've set in Document Properties.

With *Background Color* you can set the background of your document to a solid color or a background image. To set it as a solid color, click Choose Color in the Background section of the dialog. To set the background to an image file, see Chapter 14.

Tutorial: Choosing Document Colors and Backgrounds

1. Load a document, or get one from the Web.
2. Open the Document Properties dialog box.
3. Click the Appearance tab.
4. Note the changes as you run through each step.
5. In Color Schemes, choose Netscape Default Colors, then click Apply.
6. In Color Schemes, choose Reverse Video, then click Apply.
   Note the differences.
7. Switch back to Netscape Default Colors.
8. Click Normal Text. Choose a dark red or crimson. Click Apply.
9. Click Link Text. Choose a fluorescent green. Click Apply.
10. Click Active Link Text. Choose a deep blue. Click Apply.
11. Click Followed Link Text. Choose a brilliant red. Click Apply.

12. Click OK. Select File/Browse Document. Enjoy what you've done.
13. Go back to the Editor and open Document Properties again.
14. Under Background, click the Choose Color button.
15. Select a particularly ugly color, and click Apply.
16. Click OK, browse the document, and again note the changes.
17. In Color Schemes, click Netscape Default Colors, then Apply. You're back where you started from.

The danger, of course, is playing with colors for hours at a time.

It's All Pretty Basic

It's impossible to divide HTML code into basic and advanced, because no matter what you put in which category, someone's bound to disagree. For some users, imagemaps are the single most basic element of a Web page, and they wouldn't dream of publishing a Web document without one. For others, however, imagemaps are items of great complexity, and are well beyond what they need to know right this minute.

For the sake of this chapter, basic HTML elements are those that format the document's text. That's pretty much it. Headings, lists, font size and color, and the occasional formatting device such as the good old horizontal line—these are the basic elements of HTML. Graphics are undeniably a fundamental part of HTML documents, but they're sufficiently different that a separate chapter is devoted to them. And hyperlinks, the one true essential ingredient of the World Wide Web, are also given a separate chapter. This chapter, again, deals only with text formatting. And that's about as basic as you can get.

Headings

Headings were an early HTML invention that allowed content providers to offer different font sizes for various levels of headings. The heading for a major section of text could be one size, while those for the sections of text inside that major section could all be of the same smaller size. The heading for the entire page could be the largest of all.

NOTE. *Don't confuse* heading *with* title. *Even though the heading of a Web page is often what we'd normally call a title, in HTML lingo* title *refers to the <title></title> container, which is part of the HTML* header. *For that matter, don't confuse the <head></head> container with* heading *levels. The document's head doesn't display; the document's headings* do *display. You'd think someone would have thought this all out before naming them, huh?*

Headings come in six levels—H1 through H6. Although some browsers let users specify font sizes for all heading levels, the default has H1 as the largest font and H6 the smallest. When designing your page, the only thing you can really do is design it with your own browser set to its default heading displays; most users don't bother changing defaults, so they'll appear the same. If you're really worried about what the page will look like on your users' machines, use as few user-customizable elements as possible, in favor of graphics elements such as imagemaps (see Chapter 19) and graphics links (see Chapter 15). Headings, though, are well worth using, as they offer instant text formatting.

Gold offers two ways of using heading levels. First, you can select a heading level and then type your text. Second, you can type your text, then click anywhere within that text, and choose your heading level from the Style box on the toolbar or select the desired heading level from Properties/Paragraph. In other words, you can create heading-level text from scratch, or you can convert existing text into a specific heading level. Figure 13.4 shows the different heading levels in Gold.

Figure 13.4

The six heading levels

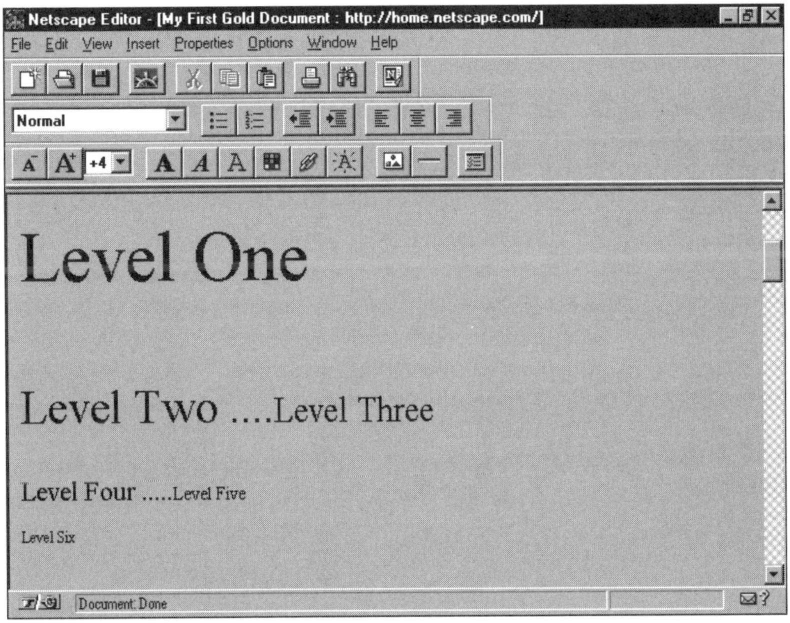

Tutorial: Creating Multiple Heading Levels

1. Open a new Editor document (File/New Document).
2. Type **My First Document** on the first line.

3. Drag the mouse over your typing to highlight it.
4. Click on the down arrow of the Style box and click Heading 1, H1; or choose Heading 1, H1 from Properties/Paragraph. Your text will immediately change size.
5. Click to the right of the typing to unhighlight it.
6. Press Enter to start a new line. The Style box still shows Heading 1, H1.
7. From the Style box or the Properties/Paragraph menu, select Heading 2, H2.
8. Type **Looking Pretty Good!** Notice that the font is now smaller.
9. On the next line, type something else, then highlight it and experiment with the heading sizes.

Text Styles and Alignments

Heading levels aren't the only means at your disposal for varying text styles. Other built-in font styles include Normal, Address, Formatted, and Blockquote. As with headings, users can usually determine how these styles will appear in their browsers, but since most users leave the defaults alone (especially Netscape Navigator users, since changing these elements is difficult), make use of them anyway. They can help give your document an even greater look of professionalism.

Normal, which is the default, is good ol' reliable Times Roman or Times New Roman. Normal simply means standard text, the stuff you get when you open a new document in Gold and just start typing. In fact, there's less and less normal text on the Web, since designers are opting for various individualized formats instead.

The *Address* style is used primarily for displaying an e-mail address in a small italicized font. By itself, it doesn't help your readers to send you an e-mail. But when used in conjunction with a *mail to* link (see Chapter 14), it can easily serve that function.

Formatted text in Gold is the same as HTML's preformatted option (<pre></pre>). Actually, it's not really formatted at all. It's simply rendered in nonproportional font (such as Courier), and therefore can be used to line up words, headings, and so forth. It originally was used to create tables, before HTML tables (see Chapter 17) came into being.

The *Blockquote* option renders the selected text indented in a block paragraph manner. A space above and below the quote is also inserted. Blockquote is used, as the name suggests, to display quoted passages of text from another source.

One thing you have complete control over is text alignment. Like a word processor, Gold lets you center a line of text, or justify it against the left or right margins. You can also indent the line inward from the left margin (but not the right).

Center Text is the most common alignment on the Web, and it's easy to execute. Simply place the cursor anywhere on the line with the text you want centered, and click the Center button.

To *Left-Align* a line of text, or align it with the left margin, click in that line of text and then on the Left button. To *Right-Align* it, or align it with the right margin, click on the Right button.

Aligning text is extremely easy, but there's one important point to remember. Gold aligns text by using the <div align= ></div> containers. It even centers text by using the <div align=center></div> container, not HTML's standard <center></center> container. Since as of this writing only Netscape Navigator actually interpreted <div> tags, this means that centering text using the Gold editor makes your documents readable only by Navigator.

To *Indent* the entire line by one tab space, place the cursor in front of a line of text and then click the Increase Indent button or select Properties/Paragraph/Indent one level. You can unindent by clicking the Decrease Indent button or selecting Properties/Paragraph/Decrease Indent one level. Note that Gold's Indent commands don't produce any special HTML code. Instead, Gold uses the Unordered list code <ul></ul> to accomplish this formatting.

Tutorial: Using Text Styles and Alignments

1. Open a new document in Gold's Editor window.
2. Type your e-mail address.
3. With the cursor anywhere inside the address, select the Address style from the Styles box or from Properties/Paragraph.
4. Press Enter to move to the next line.
5. Type the following: **Hamlet's famous soliloquy begins:**. Press Enter and then type **To be or not to be, that is the question.**
6. Click anywhere in the *To be or not to be* line, then select Properties/ Paragraph/List.
7. Select Blockquote and click OK.
8. Now type **Let's Align This**.
9. Click the Center button to center the line, then the Right button to right-align it.
10. Click to the left of your e-mail address and then click the Increase Indent button. Now click it again, and once more.

Easy, isn't it?

Emphasize, Emphasize!

In the print industry, one of the tried and true ways of capturing a reader's attention is through text emphasis. It's no different in Gold. As a designer, you have such elements as bold and italic text, and you can also adjust font sizes and font colors. You can also add superscripting or subscripting, and you can even make your text blink.

Bold and *italic* work much the same in Gold as in your favorite word processor. Highlight the text you wish to emphasize, then click the Bold or Italic button in the toolbar or select them from Properties/Character (or the reverse: Make the emphasis selection, then start typing). Be sure, however, to turn the selection off when your emphasis is finished.

Fixed Width works exactly the same, except that it changes the font style to a "typewriter" (nonproportional) font. It functions the same as the Formatted style, except that Formatted affects the entire paragraph, while Fixed Width changes only the selected characters.

Superscript and *Subscript* let you add, not surprisingly, superscripts and subscripts. Superscripts ride slightly above the line (such as the *squared* indicator in $E=mc^2$), while subscripts ride slightly below (such as the number symbol in H_2O). The super/subscripted character assumes the font style of the paragraph in which it resides, or the word of which it's a part.

Font Sizes can be adjusted by using Properties/Font Size, or by using the Font Size field on the toolbar. To change the size, highlight the word or characters you wish to resize, then select a font size different from the current one. This all sounds obvious, but it's a bit weird in practice. Normal font is the base size, and shows as +0. Other heading sizes automatically take a size larger or smaller than +0. Heading level 1, for example, is +3, while heading level 3 is +1. To alter a portion of a level 1 heading, highlight the characters and then select +4 for a larger font or +2, +1, +0, –1, or –2 for a smaller font. In other words, the font sizes are all relative, and the easiest way to determine the current size is to click on the characters and see what appears in the Font Size field on the toolbar. Note that not all browsers support Font Sizes.

Font Colors are adjusted by selecting the characters you wish to recolor, then clicking the Font Color button on the toolbar or selecting Properties/Font Color. In either case, you'll be presented with your system's standard color palette, and you can choose the new color from this palette. You can even change the color of a portion of an element whose color has already been set through the Document Properties dialog box. Note that not all browsers support Font Colors.

Blink lets you set certain characters as blinking (that is, they blink on and off). Highlight the desired text, then select Blink from the Properties/Character menu. Given the fact that any number of people absolutely despise blinking text, you probably won't want to do this very often.

Tutorial: Working with Text Emphasis Tools

1. Start a new document in Gold's Editor.
2. Type the following: **Peter Piper picked a peck of pickled peppers.**
3. Highlight *Peter Piper*. Click the Bold button, or select Properties/Character/Bold.
4. Highlight *picked*. Click the Italic button, or select Properties/Character/Italic.
5. Highlight *a peck of*. Click the Font Color button, or select Properties/Font Color. Change the color to a bright blue.
6. Highlight *pickled*. Click the Font Sizes field and change the font to +3. With the word still highlighted, change the color to a pickle green.
7. Highlight *peppers*. Change the Font Size to –1, and the Font Color to a burning red. Now select Properties/Character/Blink.
8. Select File/Browse Document and admire your work.

   A sample screen with a variety of character styles is shown in Figure 13.5.

Figure 13.5

All the text styles that fit

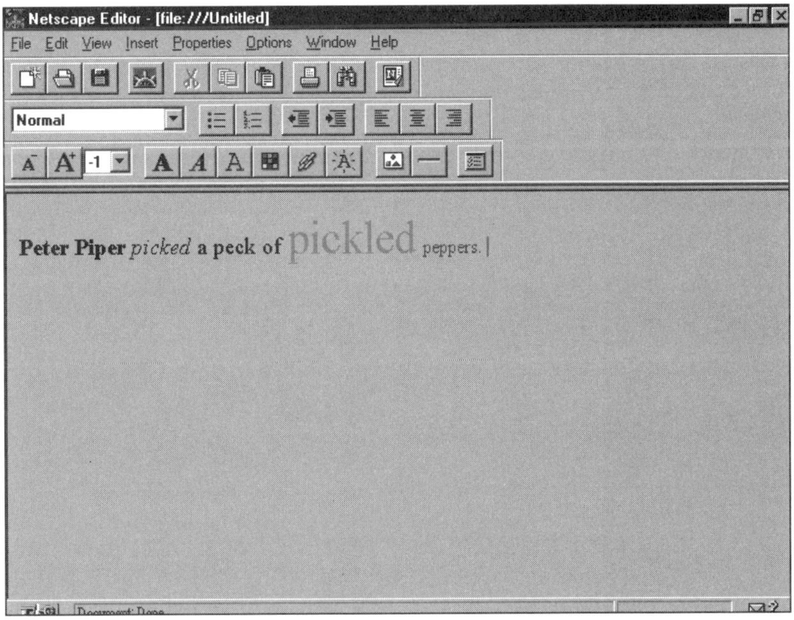

Horizontal Lines

Horizontal lines (officially called horizontal *rules*) are lines that extend horizontally across all or part of a Web document. They're used primarily to distinguish sections of the page. Early in HTML's history, there was only one kind of horizontal line, a thin one that stretched the entire width of the page. Now you can do much more with these lines, and Gold provides an easy-to-use line manipulator.

The first step is to create a horizontal line. To do so, position the cursor where you want the line to appear, then click on the Horizontal Line button on the toolbar, or select Insert/Horizontal Line. Presto! You have a line.

Once the line is in place, you can resize it and align it. Click on the line itself, then choose Horizontal Line from the Properties menu (or right-click on the line). You'll see the Horizontal Line Properties box shown in Figure 13.6.

Your first choice is alignment. You can center the line, or have it appear flush against the left or right margins. But in creating Web pages, often you won't make this decision until you've sized the line first. To size it, you choose width and height. *Width* refers to width of the screen; you can select either percentage (easier) or number of pixels. *Height* refers to thickness of the line, expressed in pixels. Finally, *3-D Shading* gives the line a three-dimensional appearance.

Figure 13.6 shows three horizontal lines. The first is the one that Gold automatically creates when you click the Horizontal Line button. The second is centered, occupying 75 percent of the screen, and with a thickness of 5 pixels. The third is right-aligned, 400 pixels in width, and 40 pixels in height, with 3-D shading turned off.

Figure 13.6

Gold's dialog box for editing horizontal lines, plus several lines

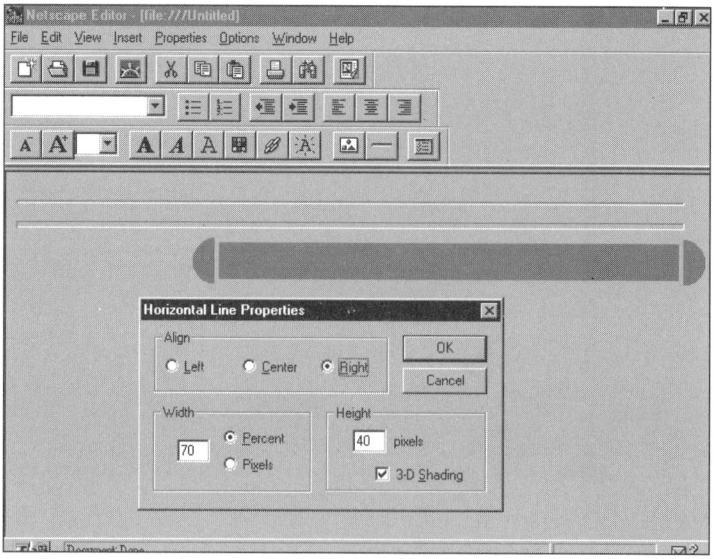

Tutorial: Creating and Formatting a Horizontal Line

1. Go to an Editor window (or open a new one).
2. Click the cursor on an empty line.
3. Click the Horizontal Line button on the toolbar (or select Insert/Horizontal Line).
4. Click on the newly created line.
5. Right-click and select Horizontal Line Properties.
6. In the Align section of the dialog box, select Center.
7. In the Dimensions section, replace Width 100 percent with Width 65 percent.
8. In the same section, replace Height 2 pixels with 10 pixels.
9. Ensure that 3-D Shading is on.
10. Click OK.
11. Select File/Browse Document and examine your work.

Lists

Lists used to be the Web's hottest design property. They made it easy to sort information into readable chunks, and in the Web's early days almost every page contained a list of either bullets or numbers. Today, with the advent of tables and other page-formatting tools, lists aren't nearly as prevalent as they were; used creatively, however, they can still be extremely effective. The most common are definition lists, bulleted lists, and numbered lists, but two other types are available for use as well.

Figure 13.7 shows the three main list types in Gold's Editor window.

Bulleted Lists (Unordered Lists) and Numbered Lists (Ordered Lists)

Lists of bullet points are the staple of the business presentation community, and you'll find them on the Web as well. Their function is to itemize points for clear and effective presentation, and as long as they're not overused they can be very useful. Their official HTML name is *unordered* lists, because bullets have no inherent ordering. Numbered lists, on the other hand (called *ordered* lists in HTML) imply an ordering with the most important item taking the number 1. They're mostly useful in such documents as a set of directions or a listing of placements.

To create a bulleted list using Gold's editor, type the list in the Editor window, pressing Enter after each point, then highlight the entire list and click the Bulleted List button on the toolbar. Alternatively, you can begin a bulleted list from scratch by moving to a new line in the Editor, then clicking on the Bulleted List button or choosing List Item (LI) from the Styles box on the toolbar.

Figure 13.7

From the top, a bulleted list, a numbered list, and a definition list

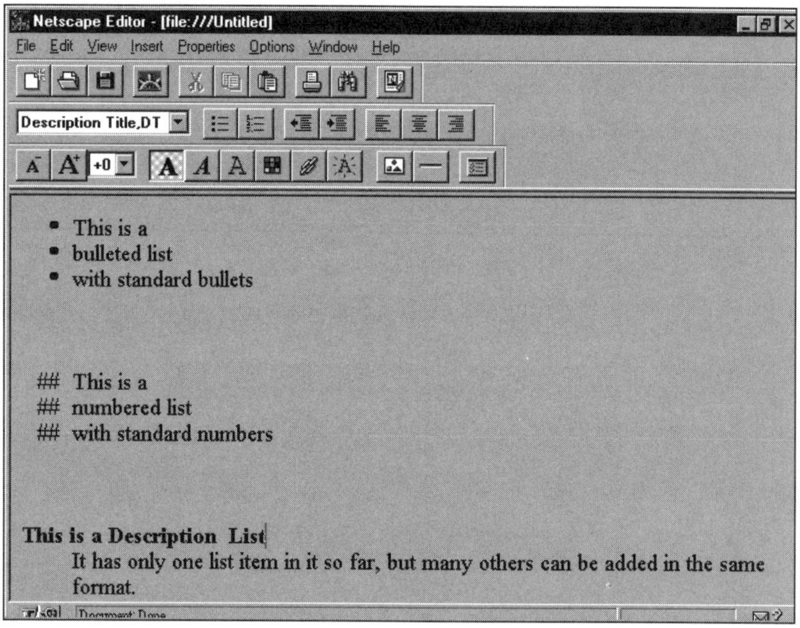

To adjust the characteristics of your bulleted list, click inside the list, then choose Paragraph/List from the Properties menu and click Unnumbered List from the Container or List Type pane, and then a bullet type from the Style pane.

While working in your list, pressing Enter begins another list item (in other words, creates another bullet). To end the list, select Normal from the Styles box.

Numbered lists are just what they say—lists of items separated by sequential numbers. Creating a numbered list in Gold is identical to creating a bulleted list, except that you click the Numbered List button instead. Once your list is created, use the Paragraph/List dialog box to set the types of numbers (Arabic, Roman, and so on) that will display.

Definition Lists

Without question, definition lists are the most useful type of list on the Web today. A definition list contains a title for each list item and then the "definition" of that title (for example, a text write-up of the title, immediately following and usually indented). A good example of such a list is from the Netscape home page, shown in Figure 13.8.

The items immediately below the Welcome to Netscape imagemap are constructed using the definition list capability of HTML. The description titles are all aligned with the left margin, while the corresponding description text, each a short paragraph, is indented below each title. If you download

Figure 13.8

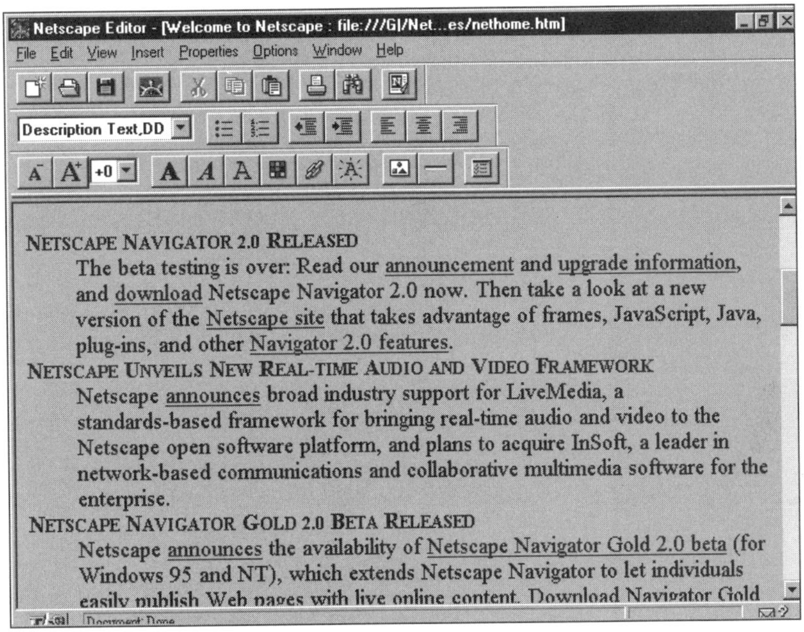

The constantly changing definition list from Netscape's home page

this page into your Gold editor, you'll see that the designers created the small-caps appearance by making use of differing font sizes.

Creating a definition list is best done from scratch—type each component one step at a time. To begin, move the cursor to a new line in the Editor window, then choose Description Title (DT) from the Styles box. Type the title, then press Enter to go to the next line. Select Description Text (DD) from the Styles box (this will indent the new line) and type the paragraph of text that corresponds to the title. When you're finished with the first entry, hit Enter to go to the next line and then select DT again. Repeat until you're finished.

Menu Lists and Directory Lists

Menu and Directory lists are used infrequently on the Web. A menu list is essentially a bulleted list with very short entries. A directory list contains items of no more than 20 characters, and can be arranged in columns. You can create both with Gold through the Paragraph/Lists Properties dialog, but since they're of little value in your Web designs we won't spend time with them here.

Formatting, Linking, and Embedding Lists

You can include character formatting and hyperlinks within lists. Each definition title can be a hyperlink, as can any number of list items or words within list items. Font sizes and colors, bold and italics, and all such features are available to you anywhere in the lists. Keep in mind, however, that paragraph-level formatting, such as headings, are not.

You can also embed lists, placing lists within lists. It's simply a matter of beginning a list of any type, then pressing the Tab key or clicking the Increase Indent button and beginning a new list type.

Tutorial: Designing a List in Gold's Editor

1. Open an Editor window.
2. Move the cursor to a blank line.
3. Type the following three items, pressing Enter after each: *Document Properties*, *Paragraph Properties*, *Character Properties.*
4. Highlight the three items, but only to the ending *s* in Character Properties (not the next line).
5. Click the Bulleted List button in the toolbar. You now have a bulleted list.
6. Move the cursor to the end of *Character Properties* (it should already be there).
7. Press Enter. A new bullet appears.
8. Type **Three Types of Lists** and press Enter.
9. Press the Tab key once, or click the Increase Indent button. Notice that the bullet shape has changed.
10. Create a three-part sublist by typing the following three items and pressing Enter between them: **Bulleted**, **Numbered**, **Definition** (do not press Enter after this last item).
11. Click beside the word *Bulleted.*
12. Select Paragraph/List from the Properties Menu.
13. Click on Numbered List, then on a,b,c.
14. Click OK.
15. Save your document and view it. You now have a bulleted list with an embedded numbered list.

■ Basic Tags in Raw HTML

You can, of course, perform all of Gold's document-level and body-level functions through raw HTML code. As always, Gold does nothing to change this code; it merely hides it and, in the process, makes page design a more intuitive, graphically based activity. Also as always, the reason to bother with raw HTML at all is, first, to see what Gold actually accomplishes, and, more importantly, to make troubleshooting your pages more precise; it also allows you to add new HTML tags and formats as they become available, before new versions of Gold can handle them.

Document-Level Codes

There are four major document-level codes in HTML—HTML, HEAD, BODY, and FRAME. Of these, the first three are standard HTML, while FRAME works only with Netscape or Netscape-compatible browsers.

The HTML Element

The <HTML></HTML> container is placed around the entire document. In fact, you don't even have to put it in until you've finished everything else, at which point you type the opening tag at the very beginning of the document and the closing tag at the very end. It's easy to forget, however, so the best thing is to type both tags when you first start, leaving the opening tag in place on the first line and continually moving the closing tag below the last line you've worked on. Gold places this container in the document automatically.

The HEAD Element

The <HEAD></HEAD> element contains a variety of information about the document. It surrounds the following tags, which are covered by Gold's Document Properties dialog. The only information actually required is the document title. Only the most common document elements are covered here.

Name	Description
<TITLE>	The title of the document. It does not appear in the document itself.
<ISINDEX>	Identifies the document as searchable by keywords. When accessed, it begins with a Search box bearing the caption, "This is a searchable index. Enter search keywords." If you're designing for Netscape, you have two attributes at your command. The first is PROMPT, which lets you change the caption. The second is ACTION, which lets you instruct the browser to call up a CGI script rather than execute the standard search.

Name	Description
<BASE>	The URL on which other references within the document are based. Used well, it allows you to offer truncated URLs throughout the remainder of the document. In practice, however, BASE isn't used very often, and the truncated URLs in the document depend on the directory structure of the server instead. There's one important exception to this when designing for Netscape, however. The BASE element can include the TARGET attribute, which gives every targeted URL in the document a default URL on which to act. This is covered in Chapter 20.
<META>	A container that offers a place to store information about the document that other elements don't cover. The purpose of META statements is to make information available that, given the right programs and scripts, can be catalogued and indexed. In practice, META information is useful primarily when constructing dynamic documents through such methods as server push, server pull, and JavaScript. The three main items within a META container are HTTP-EQUIV, which takes advantage of automated response headers; NAME, which gives the information a name; and CONTENT, which specifies the actual information that corresponds to the HTTP-EQUIV or the NAME attribute.

Here's an example of document-level code:

```
<HTML>
<HEAD>
<TITLE>Sample Code at Doc Level</TITLE>
<ISINDEX PROMPT="Type in a search string">
<META HTTP-EQUIV="Reply-to" CONTENT="nrandall@inforamp.net">
</HEAD>
[rest of document]
<HTML>
```

Body-level Codes

These are plentiful. In fact, most HTML codes, and certainly the ones everyone's most interested in, are at the body level. Included are anchors, formats, lists, horizontal rules, images, and so on. In this chapter we'll examine the basic codes for lists, rules, and character formats.

The body-level codes are always inside the <BODY></BODY> container. Typically, the opening tag of this container begins near the beginning of the document, following the closing </HEAD> tag, and ends at the very bottom of the document, immediately before the </HTML> tag that closes the entire file.

Paragraph Codes

These codes affect the entire paragraph of text that they surround. Some can be used in conjunction with each other in the same paragraph, but others, such as the varying heading levels, cannot.

Heading HTML offers six heading containers, <H1></H1> through <H6> </H6>. The text inside the container is displayed according to the font selections within the browser. This is completely controllable by the user, although generally the lower the heading number (<H1> is lowest), the larger the corresponding font.

The HTML 3.0 proposal gives an alignment attribute to headings. You can specify left, right, or center. A right-justified level 2 heading, for example, would take the code <H2 ALIGN=RIGHT>*text*</H2>

Address The address container—<ADDRESS></ADDRESS>—surrounds a text string you wish to specify as an address. Typically, it's an e-mail address, but you can use it for any text you wish. Generally it displays as small italicized fonts.

Preformatted Text inside the <PRE></PRE> container is formatted with a nonproportional typeface such as Courier. Its purpose is to present text characters that must be lined up for effective presentation.

Center One of the most popular HTML containers, <CENTER></CENTER> places the text in the center of the line, exactly as if it were the center button on a word processor. *Center* can be used inside heading tags, with the effect of centering the entire heading. Note that Gold's *center* command does not use this container; instead, it uses the Netscape-specific <DIV CENTER> container, which means that other browsers won't center the line at all.

Paragraph The paragraph container <P></P> instructs the browser to treat the enclosed text as a new paragraph. The browser adds a blank line below the container to separate the paragraph from the following text. Actually, only the opening <P> tag is actually needed, at least for this round of HTML updates, but it's habitual to use the entire container for when HTML demands it.

The HTML 3.0 proposal gives an alignment attribute to paragraphs. You can specify left, right, or center. A right-justified paragraph, for example, would take the code: <P ALIGN=RIGHT>*paragraph text*</H2>

Break
 is a tag, not a container (there's no ending tag), used to end the current line and begin another. Unlike <P>, it does not insert a blank line.

Gold supports the only <BR> attribute, CLEAR, which is used for floating images (see Chapter 14). When text is aligned beside an image and you wish to break that text, use the CLEAR attributes. CLEAR LEFT breaks the line and moves the rest of it down to the next line with a clear left margin. RIGHT does the same, only this time finding a new right margin. ALL moves the text down to where both margins are clear.

No Break You can insist that the browser *not* break text where it normally wraps by using the <NOBR> element (no ending tag). But keep no-breaks short or they'll extend beyond the right margin and force the user to scroll. You can counter the no-break with a *Word Break* <WBR>, which tells the browser to break a word if necessary (like a conditional hyphen in a word processor).

Basefont The basefont tag lets you set the default size of the document's font. All subsequent font size changes using <FONT SIZE> will then be based on this font. The syntax is <BASEFONT SIZE=*x*>, and *x* can range from 1 through 7 (3 is the default).

Div Netscape's exclusive <DIV></DIV> container acts as a means of aligning text strings. You can specify the alignment as left, right, and center by using the ALIGN attribute. For example, a centered string would be coded as

```
<DIV ALIGN="center">text string</DIV>
```

Note that Gold uses the <DIV ALIGN="center"> construction instead of the more common <CENTER></CENTER> container to do its centering. This means that your centered text created by Gold will render properly only in Netscape itself.

Horizontal Rule

One of the standard elements of HTML, the horizontal rule (or horizontal line) can be inserted simply by typing the code <HR> on a new line. That will give you a thin line across the page. To control the appearance of this line, use the SIZE, WIDTH, ALIGN, and NOSHADE elements.

ALIGN can be left, right, or center. NOSHADE tells the browser not to give the line a 3-D shading effect, instead rendering it as a solid line. A non-shaded centered line, for example, would be set as follows:

```
<HR NOSHADE ALIGN=CENTER>
```

SIZE controls the thickness of the line, and WIDTH specifies how far it extends across the page. Size always takes the form of a number, the default being 2. A size-5 line is substantially thicker, and a size-10 line is thicker still. WIDTH can be expressed in pixels or percentages.

A thick, right-aligned, shaded line extending across 250 pixels would be coded as follows:

```
<HR ALIGN=RIGHT SIZE=9 WIDTH=250>
```

Character Codes

Character codes are exactly that—codes that apply to individual characters. As with most software, you can adjust the appearance of the individual characters and words in an HTML document.

Code	Description
Bold	You can bold a string of text by enclosing it in the <B></B> container.
Italics	You can *italicize* a string of text by enclosing it in the <I></I> container.
Underline	You can underline a string of text by enclosing it in the <U></U> container.
Teletype	You can specify a typewriter-style nonproportional font for a string of text by enclosing it in the <TT></TT> container. Note that this is different from <PRE></PRE>, which sets the entire paragraph in a nonproportional font and can't be used for character sequences inside another paragraph-level container.
Strikethru	To render text as ~~struckthrough~~, enclose it inside a <STRIKE></STRIKE> container.
Subscript	To subscript a text string, enclose it in the container. The actual size of the subscript text depends on the font size and basefont size specifications.
Superscript	To superscript a text string, enclose it in the <SUPER> </SUPER> container. The actual size of the subscript text depends on the font size and basefont size specifications.
Font Size	You can control the size of individual characters or strings of characters through <FONT SIZE=*x*></FONT>. The choices for *x* range from 1 to 7 (the default is 3), or you can specify +*x* or –*x* instead. In this case, *x* means larger (+) or smaller (–) than the font size specified in the basefont tag.

Code	Description
Font Color	You can specify the color of individual characters or character strings by using <FONT COLOR=#*rrggbb*></FONT> or the much nicer <FONT COLOR=*color*></FONT>. For these choices, *#rrggbb* represents the hexadecimal number for an RGB (red-green-blue) color code (#ff0000 is red). Sixteen colors have been predefined so you can use the names instead of the codes—black, red, blue, navy, lime, white, purple, green, silver, yellow, maroon, olive, gray, teal, aqua, and fuchsia.
Blink	To drive your readers insane, have some text blink on and off by enclosing it inside the <BLINK></BLINK> container.
Citation	The <CITE></CITE> container renders the enclosed text as a citation, usually italicized, depending on how the browser is set by the user.
Emphasis	The <EM></EM> container gives emphasis to text, and usually appears italicized or bolded, depending on how the browser is set by the user.
Code	To display program or source code, use the <CODE></CODE> container. This will give the code a nonproportional font.
Strong	The <STRONG></STRONG> container gives bolded emphasis to the text.
Comments	If you want to put comments inside your HTML document that the browser won't display (usually to remind you of things later), start the comment with the <!> element (not a container).

Lists

Writing lists in raw HTML is tedious, but it's quite easy. Basically, you have to enclose the entire list in one of five list type containers, then use the list item tag to specify individual list items.

List Item

In all lists except definition lists, each item in the list is begun by the <LI> tag (no ending tag). For example, inside a bulleted list of favorite animals, the items might be coded as

```
<LI>cats
<LI>dogs
<LI>zebras
```

Unordered List

Unordered lists produce lists whose items are separated by bullets. Enclose all <LI> items inside a <UL></UL> container. Netscape lets you specify the bullet type by using the TYPE attribute inside the <LI> tag. The three types are disc (filled-in bullet), circle (open bullet), and square (open square).

Ordered List

Ordered lists produce lists whose items are separated by sequential numbers. Enclose all items inside a <OL></OL> container. You can specify the type of numbering you want, as well as what number begins the sequence, by placing the TYPE and START attributes inside the <OL> element.

The five TYPEs are:

A	uppercase letters (A, B, C)
a	lowercase letters (a, b, c)
I	uppercase Roman numerals (I, II, III)
i	lowercase Roman numerals (i, ii, iii)
1	standard Arabic numerals (1, 2, 3)—the default

To start at a specified number, use the START= attribute. For example, choosing START=4 will start the numbering, depending on the chosen TYPE, at D, d, IV, iv, or 4.

Menu List

Menu lists are unordered lists with only one line per item. It appears slightly more compressed on the page than a bulleted list. Enclose menu list items inside a <MENU></MENU> container.

Directory List

Directory lists offer a way to present columned lists, with each list item no more than 20 characters long. You can put multiple list items on each line of the code. Enclose all list items inside a <DIR></DIR> container.

Definition List

This is the most complex list, and it does not use the <LI> element. Instead, each list item is preceded with <DD>, and each <DD> can have a heading, or *term*, which is coded with the <DT> tag. The entire list is enclosed inside a <DL></DL> container. An example of a definition list is as follows:

```
<DL>
<DT>Shakespeare
```

```
<DD>The most famous playwright in the English language,
Shakespeare wrote numerous tragedies, comedies, and
histories.
<DT>Randall
<DD>Not nearly as famous as Shakespeare, Randall was
nevertheless more useful when it came to providing details
on how to do Web pages.
</DL>
```

In this example, the <DT> elements will be rendered as emphasized text, and the <DD> elements will be indented paragraphs.

At this point, you've learned enough about Gold to put together some functional, attractive Web pages. But there's lots more to this software, and indeed to designing Web sites. In the next chapter, you'll move on to the creation of hyperlinks, the Web's major distinguishing feature.

- *The Uses of Hyperlinks*
- *External Links versus Internal Links*
- *Golden Links*
- *Drag-and-Drop Hyperlinks*
- *Creating Links Using the Links Dialog Box*
- *Creating Links to Named Anchors*
- *Creating Image Hyperlinks*

- *Links in Raw HTML*
- *Linking to a Web Document*
- *Linking to an FTP Site*
- *Linking to a Gopher Site*
- *Linking to Telnet Sites*
- *Linking to an E-Mail Address*
- *Linking to a Newsgroup*
- *The NAME Anchor*

CHAPTER

14

Creating Hyperlinks

HEADINGS, LISTS, AND THE OTHER FORMATTING ELEMENTS discussed in Chapter 15 are all very well, and the graphics covered in Chapter 16 are essential to effective Web design, but the one single thing that has defined the Web from its inception is the hyperlink. Even Web browsers that can't display graphics or different font choices or heading levels (although they still exist) readily display hyperlinks, because from the beginning they have provided the Web's *raison d'être.* The whole point of the World Wide Web as it was initially conceived is to link documents, thereby creating a globally distributed database of information. The hyperlink makes it all possible.

The Uses of Hyperlinks

Hyperlinks offer a fast means for readers of Web pages to move from one piece or source of information to another. They can link items of information found in the same Web document, but more typically they're used to link information on other documents instead. These documents are sometimes found on the same Web as the current document (most Webs consist of multiple documents, but more often the documents are on another computer entirely). A hyperlink can link to any document being served by a World Wide Web server, or by a Gopher server, FTP server, or News server. In other words, a hyperlink can take you almost anywhere on the Internet.

In HTML terminology, when you construct hyperlinks you are constructing *anchors*. In raw HTML, anchors are enclosed in the <A></A> container. The anchors can contain references to several types of information sources on the Net. These include

- HTML or SGML documents
- A specific area in the same document or Web
- Gopher menus
- FTP archives
- Usenet newsgroups
- Telnet sessions
- E-mail sessions

This chapter covers all of these uses.

When you click on a hyperlink, you are instructing the browser to retrieve the referenced document, document portion, or Internet service, displaying the contents or results either in the current browser window or in a new window entirely. When retrieving an HTML document or a gopher menu, for instance, Gold will replace the contents of the browser window with the retrieved information. When clicking on an e-mail link (called *mailto* in raw HTML), Gold will open its message composition window with the recipient's e-mail address already filled in. When you click on a newsgroup link, Gold opens the News window and loads that newsgroup's content, and so on. By far the most common activity is the retrieval of other Web pages.

External Links versus Internal Links

One of the most difficult concepts to master in hyperlink design is the difference between external and internal links. Although there are several complexities to this issue, by far the most likely scenarios are as follows. An external link is a hyperlink that accesses an HTML document that is *not* part of your own Web. An internal link accesses an HTML document that *is* part of your own Web.

For example, let's say your Web page consists of ten different HTML documents. If you create a link that retrieves any one of those documents, you've created an *internal* link. But if you create a link that accesses a document outside your own ten documents, you've created an *external* link. All of this seems pretty obvious.

But there's more to it than that. First, you can create an internal link that doesn't actually retrieve a new document; instead, it jumps the reader to a specific place within the current document. These internal links are commonly called *anchors*, although technically *all* hyperlinks are anchors. We'll call them *internal anchors* in this book.

The other complexity is that, technically, it's entirely possible to create *external* links to documents that are part of your own Web. If your hyperlink is set to access a file, and thus uses the file:// prefix (explained in the Raw HTML section later in this chapter), then it's an *internal* link. But if you access the same file by using the http:// prefix (again, see below), then that's an *external* link, simply because of the http:// protocol decision.

There are other complexities as well. But for the sake of clarity, let's call a link *internal* if it retrieves a document from your own Web page, and all other links we'll call *external*. In the end, the only question is whether or not the reader gets to the right place.

Golden Links

Gold offers two means of constructing hyperlinks. The easier way is through drag-and-drop, while the harder (but more flexible) is through the hyperlinks dialog boxes. Both will achieve the same result: hyperlinks wherever you want them, helping your readers navigate to the information they need.

Drag-and-Drop Hyperlinks

Creating a hyperlink in a Gold document is as easy as clicking on an existing hyperlink (the source link) and dragging it into the Editor window (where it becomes the destination link). To do so, open the Editor, save your new (or existing) page, then click the cursor exactly where you wish to place the hyperlink. Place the Editor window side by side with the browser window from which you wish to drag the hyperlink, then click-and-hold the desired source link in the browser window and drag it into the Editor window. Release the mouse button and the destination link appears, complete with the correct title.

Figure 14.1 shows this process in action. Here, an Editor window overlaps a browser window. In the browser window you can see a list of source links. In the Editor window you can see some of the same links; these have already been dragged over and have become destination links.

Figure 14.1

Dragging a link from browser to Editor replicates the link in the edited document.

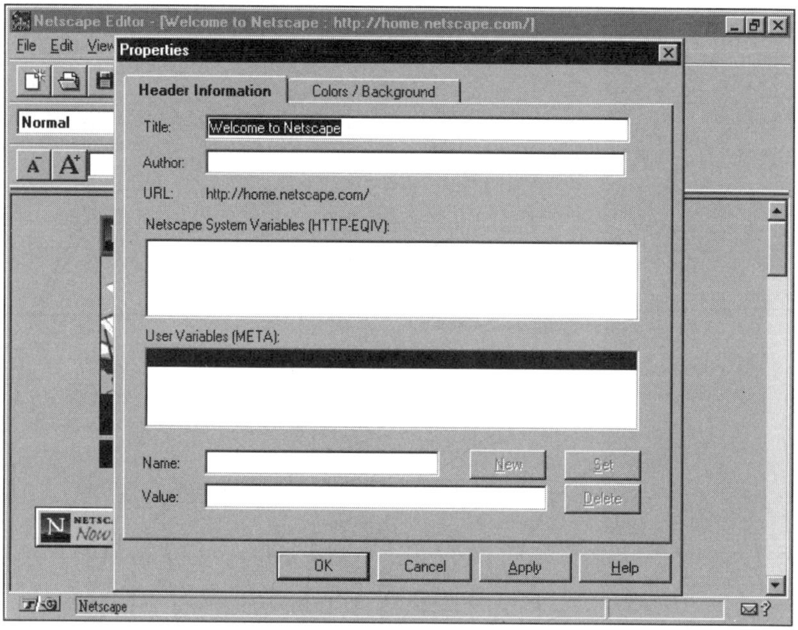

So far, the drag-and-drop process has let you copy links from inside Web documents into the Editor. But what if you want to create a link to the parent Web document, for instance to the document in which the copied hyperlinks reside (in other words, the open Web document). To do so, click on the link icon beside the Location box in the browser window, and drag it into the Editor. Or, if you prefer, double-click on the link icon, place your cursor where you wish inside the Editor window, then right-click and select Paste Link. Both methods achieve the same result.

You can create a hyperlink showing only the URL (not the link title) by right-clicking on the source link and choosing Copy Link to Clipboard.

Choose your location in the Editor window, then right-click Paste Link. This time, only the URL appears as the destination link.

Creating Links Using the Links Dialog Box

Drag-and-drop is a superb option when you have an existing hyperlink from which to draw, but often you need to create a link from scratch. The Links dialog box allows you to do so.

To create a link using the Links dialog box, place your cursor in the Editor window exactly where you want your hyperlink to appear, then select Link from the Insert menu. Alternatively, you can right-click and select Insert New Link, which does the same thing. Figure 14.2 shows the Links dialog box.

Figure 14.2

The Links dialog box allows you to specify internal or external links.

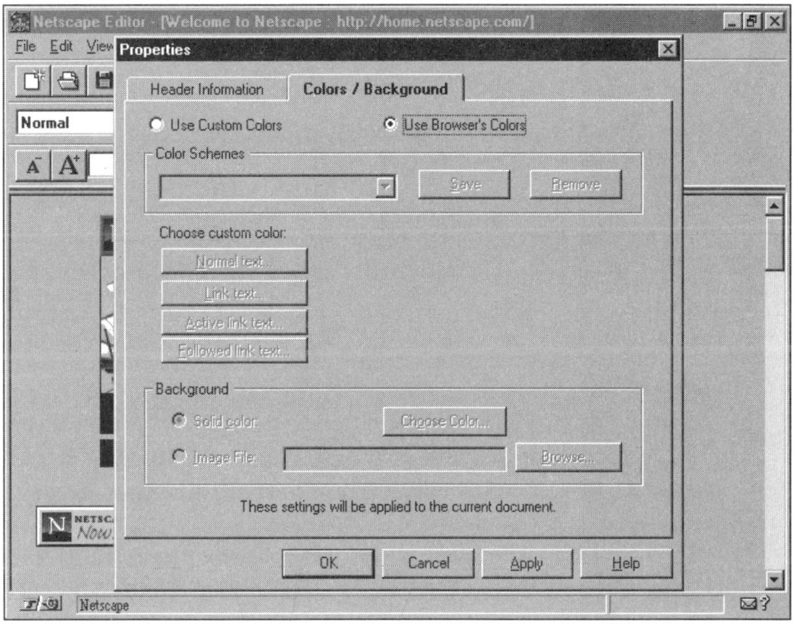

The first step is to name your link. The link name is the text that your readers will see in their browsers as a hyperlink. For example, to offer a link to the White House home page, your text might read "the president's nice home," which in your completed Web page might be part of a sentence reading, "Why not take a look at the president's nice home?"

If the text is already in place in your document, you don't need to retype it in the dialog box. To use existing text as the link text, highlight the word(s) in the Editor window, then choose Insert/Link. Or right-click and choose Create Link using selected text. The resulting Link dialog box will now show the highlighted text as the Linked text at the top of the box, and the Enter text field won't be there at all. Figure 14.3 shows a Link dialog box using existing text.

Figure 14.3

Although the Links dialog box with selected text is more convenient, you can't edit the Link text from here.

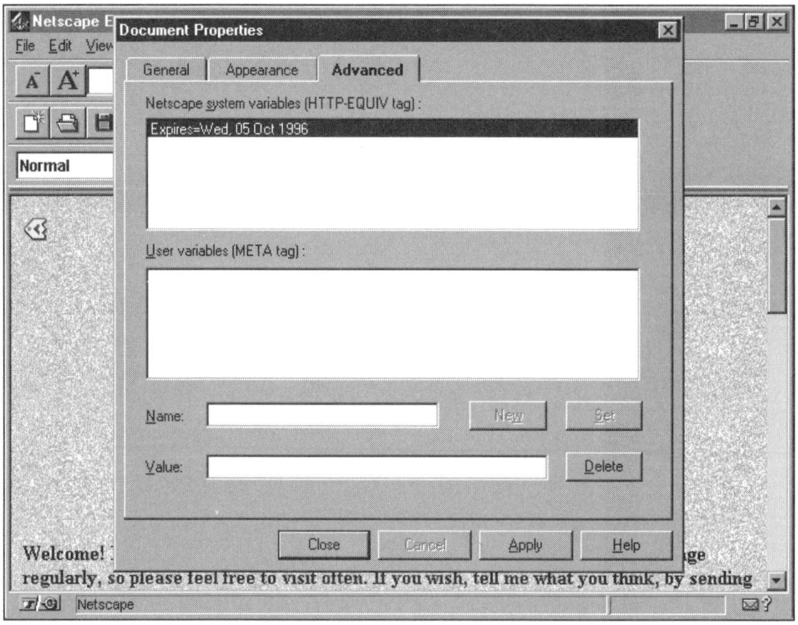

The next step, no matter which of the two text creation options you've chosen, is to fill in the Link to section of the dialog. The first field asks you to link to a page location or local file. In other words, you're asked to specify an external or an internal link.

To create an external link, type the URL of the destination document. For example, to create a link to the White House, type http://www.whitehouse.gov/ in this box. As soon as you finish the URL, your link is completed, and pressing the OK button places it in your Editor document.

In its initial release, Gold doesn't offer an archive of URLs, as some other HTML editors do. Such an archive would let you store URLs for future use, which you could then select from a list in the Links dialog. Hopefully, future editions will contain such a feature. What you *can* do, however, is make use of the standard copy-and-paste procedure of your operating system. Right-click on the URL in a browser window and select Copy Link to Clipboard, then right-click inside the Link dialog field and choose Paste.

To create an internal link, choose Browse File instead of typing in the URL. Locate the HTML file to which you want to create a link, then click Open or OK to enter it into the Link dialog box.

Creating Links to Named Anchors

To help your readers navigate your Web pages quickly and efficiently, you should supply them with links that lead not just to your documents, but to specific places within those documents. This is especially true if your documents are long and you want to reference particular sections of those documents.

To create these links, you first have to give names to the locations within the document to which the hyperlink will point. These names are called named anchors (or commonly just anchors). Then you return to the document you are editing and create a link to each named anchor.

(Actually, Gold calls these things *targets*, but since there's a specific HTML feature called targeted documents, let's stick with *named anchors* instead.)

For example, let's say you're writing an editorial about the implementing of amendments to the U.S. Constitution, and also that you have the entire set of amendments as one long HTML file on your hard drive. At one point, while talking about the Fifth Amendment, you want your reader to be able to jump immediately to the beginning of that amendment in the Constitution itself. First, you load the file containing the amendments, locate the Fifth Amendment, and create a named anchor at that point (calling it, say, "fifth"). Then, you return to your editorial and create a hyperlink pointing precisely to that anchor. When your readers click on that link, the amendments document will appear, and the Fifth Amendment will be on the screen immediately in front of them.

To create a named anchor in the document you're currently editing, place the cursor exactly where you want the link to take your reader (for example, the destination section). Highlight a word or two of the existing text if you wish. With the cursor in place, select Target (Named Anchor) from the Insert menu. This will yield the Target Properties dialog box, in which you can type the name of your anchor. If you'd highlighted text before opening this dialog, that text would appear in the field. Call your anchor whatever you wish, keeping in mind that it won't appear in the document itself.

To create a named anchor in a different document, load that document into Editor (File/Open File) and perform the same action.

Now that you have your anchor named (you can create as many as you wish in any HTML document), you can create links to them. To do so, open the document in which you wish the links to appear, then create a link as you normally would using the Links dialog box. This time, however, you treat the Links dialog somewhat differently.

If you have created named anchors in your current document, they will appear in the box labeled **Select a named target in current document** when you click the Current Document radio button. If your named anchors are in another file, you must first click Browse File and open that file, in which case the names of the anchors will appear in the **Select a named target** box when you click the Selected File radio button. To link to a specific named anchor, click on that anchor in the **Select a named target** box, and Gold will fill in the **Link to a page location** field appropriately. You may then click OK to complete the link.

Creating Image Hyperlinks

Images as well as text can be hyperlinks. When your readers click on an image, they'll be taken to the destination document as if it were a text link. Creating an image link is identical to creating a text link, except that if you right-click to create the link the appropriate menu item will read Image/Link Properties. Beyond that, all the linking options are available to you.

Note, however, that image links have nothing to do with imagemaps, which are covered in Chapter 19.

Links in Raw HTML

If you prefer to do your coding in raw HTML, you'll quickly discover that composing hyperlinks is among your least favorite activities. Anchor containers aren't too complex in themselves, but add the need to type the URL as well as the text that will appear as the hyperlink itself, and you end up with a fairly tedious activity. Once again, however, it can be easier to deal directly with the HTML text file, especially if you're working on your Web pages from a remote machine, so knowledge of raw HTML can be useful.

The HREF Anchor

HREF means *hypertext reference*. It is the most frequent attribute used in the <A></A> anchor container, and it tells the browser to treat all text between the opening tag and the closing tag as a hyperlink. HREF itself is always followed by a Uniform Resource Locator (URL) in quotation marks. The URL can access several different Internet protocols, the most common of which is the Web's own *http://*.

The construction of the HREF anchor is consistent throughout the protocols. It takes the following form:

```
<A HREF="URL">text of link</A>
```

What makes this syntax so easy to mistype is the URL itself, which can be long and drawn-out and consist of unusual characters.

Linking to a Web Document

Most hyperlinks take you to another Web document. These are constructed using the syntax

```
<A HREF="http://address/path">text of link</A>
```

For example, if you wished to construct a link to the Java home page, you would type the following on a new line in your HTML editor:

```
<A HREF="http://java.sun.com">Java's nifty home site</A>
```

This isn't too bad, obviously. But if you want to create a link to the famous What's New page at the National Center for Supercomputing Applications, the home of NCSA Mosaic, you'd have to type in this monstrosity:

```
<A HREF="http://www.ncsa.uiuc.edu/SDG/Software/Mosaic/Docs/whats-
new.html">NCSA's What's New page</A>
```

The difference, of course, lies in the length of the URL itself. In the case of Java, there was no path information to worry about; this is true of most corporate sites. For the What's New page, however, you need precise path information, keeping in mind that it's case-sensitive as well. If you create this type of anchor, it's always best to use your browser to find the page, then paste the full URL into your HTML editor.

Linking to an FTP Site

Your hyperlinks need not link exclusively to Web servers. In fact, you can link to several other types of server as well. Among the most common off-Web links are FTP sites, typically so that your users can download a file to their own computers. To the user, entering an FTP site through an FTP hyperlink is no different from logging into an FTP site via anonymous FTP, except that they don't need software other than the Web browser to do so. This is, obviously, a major convenience.

You need a user name and a password to get into an FTP site. To reach your own UNIX account via FTP, for example, you'd use your normal user name and password. To allow your readers to access your own account, therefore, would mean giving them your password, hardly a convenient solution. Instead, you can offer them anonymous FTP, in which they use the user name *anonymous* and their full e-mail address as their password. This is by far the most common use of FTP hyperlinks.

An FTP hyperlink takes the following syntax:

```
<A HREF="ftp://internet.address">Text of Link</A>
```

For example, to provide a link to Netscape Communications's main FTP site, you would construct an FTP link as follows:

```
<A HREF="ftp://ftp3.netscape.com">This will take you directly to Netscape's
FTP site</A>
```

As with links to Web sites, the complexity of the anchor depends entirely on the path for the FTP site. To provide a link to the multimedia downloads at The Oak Repository, for instance, requires the following anchor statement:

```
<A HREF="ftp://oak.oakland.edu/SimTel/win95/multimed/">You'll find good
multimedia files here</A>
```

In both these cases, when the hyperlink is clicked, Gold will automatically supply the user name *anonymous*, and will extract the password—your reader's full e-mail address—from the Mail and News Preferences dialog. If you offer a link to a site that does not allow anonymous FTP, your user will be greeted by the message "Could not log in to FTP server: user anonymous unknown."

You can provide links to standard FTP accounts (for example, those that don't offer anonymous FTP) with a somewhat different syntax. This time, the FTP address will include the user name as well as the site address:

```
<A HREF>="ftp://username@internet.address">Text of Link</A>
```

If the account bears the user name *jsmith*, for example, and is located at the address *dragon.upenn.edu*, you would link it as follows:

```
<A HREF="ftp://jsmith@dragon.upenn.edu">Why not get some files from Jill
Smith's account?</A>
```

When Gold logs into that account, it will provide a dialog asking for a password. This means that in order to provide a link to that account, you have to supply the password as well. In practice, then, nonanonymous FTP links are used only to access your own account, or an account shared by a restricted group within an organization.

Linking to a Gopher Site

Gopher was once king of the Net, and a great deal of information is still available out there in gopherspace; much of it which will never make it to the Web. Especially for educational, economic, industry, and government databases, you might easily find a reason for your readers to access gophers. Fortunately, HTML anchors handle these as well as Web documents and FTP sites.

The syntax for building a gopher link is as follows:

```
<A HREF="gopher://internet.address/path">Text of Link</A>
```

For example, a hyperlink to the Campus-Wide Information Server at the University of Southern California would look like this:

```
<A HREF="gopher://gopher.usc.edu/">Here you'll find world-wide Gopher
information</A>
```

With gopher more than any other link, the path can become enormous. It's usually imperative to copy and paste gopher addresses into your HTML editor for this reason. Here's an example of a real gopher address, from the gopher Jewels menu, pointing to computer-related resources:

```
<A HREF="gopher://cwis.usc.edu:70/11/Other_Gophers_and_Information_Resources/
Gopher-Jewels/internet/computers">Computer Resources through Gopher</A>
```

And this is hardly the worst example you could find.

Linking to Telnet Sites

So far, no Web browser has contained a built-in Telnet client program. But that doesn't mean you can't link to a Telnet location on the Net. You can, and it's easy, but if the link is important you should caution your readers that using the link will require setting up their browser to launch a Telnet program automatically. Gold users can do this through the Apps tab in the General Preferences dialog box.

The syntax for a Telnet link is as follows:

```
<A HREF="telnet://internet.address">Text of Link</A>
```

For example, to provide a link to the CARL document database, type the following on a new line in your HTML editor:

```
<A HREF="telnet://database.carl.org">The CARL database</A>
```

As long as the brower is configured properly, clicking on the link will launch the Telnet program and enter the site. In this case, no user name or password is required, but for most Telnet sessions they are.

Linking to an E-Mail Address

Gold and other browsers might not have a Telnet program built in, but they certainly have an e-mail program, at the very least one that lets you send messages. You can make use of this program to offer links to e-mail addresses, thereby letting your reader send e-mail messages to whomever you wish (presumably yourself).

A link to an e-mail address is called a *mailto*. Its syntax is

```
<A HREF="mailto:username@internet.address">Text of Link</A>
```

Note that, unlike all other HREF anchor statements, mailto (as well as *news*, covered next), does not contain the double-slash (//) after the protocol name. Just one of those delightful inconsistencies we've come to enjoy in our HTML coding.

To build a link to my e-mail address, for example, you would type the following on a new line in your HTML or text editor:

```
<A HREF="mailto:nrandall@inforamp.net">Send mail to the author</A>
```

Clicking on the link will open Gold's Message Composition window, with my e-mail address showing in the address field. Shortly after you've posted your page on the Web, I'll be besieged by endless e-mail messages. Oh well....

Linking to a Newsgroup

E-mail is not the only communications interactivity you can provide through your hyperlinks. If you want your readers to see discussions taking place about a certain topic on Usenet newsgroups, you can link to a specific newsgroup.

These links can be very useful, especially with Gold, which offers a full newsreader and posting system. But you should provide a warning to your user that their service providers might not carry that particular group. There are about 13,000 newsgroups these days, and providers carry anywhere from 5,000 to 11,000, so you can't possibly know which groups are on which server.

The syntax for a newsgroup link is

```
<A HREF="news:newsgroup.name">Text of Link</A>
```

Note that, as with mailto links, *news* links do not bear the double-slash (//) found with all other protocols.

For example, to provide a link to the well-known (and almost certainly available) new.answers group (which provides answers about newsgroups), type the following on a new line in your HTML or text editor:

```
<A HREF="news:news.answer">Here you'll find answers to your Usenet questions</A>
```

Keep in mind when creating news links that users can get lost in reading and answering them. If you want them to stay on your own pages, you might consider avoiding this type of link.

The NAME Anchor

The NAME attribute in anchors lets you target specific portions of Web pages, rather than the entire page, in your links. When your readers click on an anchor leading to a NAME, they will be taken precisely to that location on the page.

Typically, NAME anchors are used internally in a Web. That is, you want your readers to move easily from one topic within your Web to another, so you establish the topics as NAMEs and then provide links precisely to those NAMEs. The NAMEs can be on the same Web page as the hyperlink, or on another Web page entirely, within the same Web.

Creating a fully useful NAME anchor system is a two-step process. First you create the NAME, and then you create the hyperlink that takes readers to the NAME.

To create a NAME, use the following syntax:

```
<A NAME=name-of-NAME>Text of Name</A>
```

To create a hyperlink to a NAME requires the following syntax:

```
<A HREF=#name-of-NAME>Text of Link</A>
```

Note that here the anchor is an HREF type, not a NAME type. Note also that the name of the NAME is preceded by a number sign (#), and that there are no quotation marks.

Let's assume, for example, that you have a heading in your document you want to call *References to Other Works.* To make this heading into a NAME (which you can shorten to *refs*), you would place the cursor where you want the heading to occur, then type the following HTML code:

```
<A NAME=refs>References to Other Works</A>
```

The next step is to offer your reader a link to that name. In this case, you might do so in a Table of Contents at the top of the page, in a link called *Other References.* To do this, you would type the following HTML code:

```
<A HREF=#refs>Other References</A>
```

The HREF attribute points to the NAME *refs*, which is what you called the heading. When your readers click on this link, they will be taken to the section of the document called *References to Other Works.*

You can also link to a NAME from another document from within the Web. To do so, specify the file name of the document on which the NAME resides, in addition to the NAME reference itself. The syntax is

```
<A HREF=document.html#name-of-NAME>Text of Link</A>
```

To link to the above References example, which resides on, say, the maintext.html file, from a different page within the Web, you'd type the following:

```
<A HREF=maintext.html#refs>Here you'll find other references</A>
```

Netscape Navigator Gold supports one other attribute, TARGET, which allows you to specify a browser window rather than just a browser location. These are covered in Chapter 20.

- *But Isn't This Just Theft?*
- *Small but Mighty: The Edit Button*
- *Browse the Archives*
- *One Final Point*

CHAPTER

15

Working with Existing Documents

OVER THE YEARS, DOING THINGS ON THE INTERNET HAS BECOME continually easier. E-mail programs have been simplified to the point where sending a message is almost second nature, while even the early scourge of interactivity, newsgroup reading and posting, becomes much simpler with programs like Gold. Accessing information got easier with the development of gophers, and it has become simplicity itself with the advent of the World Wide Web and browsers such as Netscape Gold. Even FTP, once as arcane as anything in computing, is now an activity that takes very little time to learn.

Unfortunately, Web creation has not progressed as quickly toward full ease of use, even though Gold and other good editors are beginning to change that. The problem once lay in putting together the materials and then writing the code, and while Gold simplifies at least the latter of these two problems, it can't do much to solve the first. And there's an additional problem besides: Quite simply, most of us aren't designers, and we have almost no idea where to begin.

Creating video, sound files, animated graphics, and virtual reality sites is exciting but often unrealistic for a beginning Web artist. Instead, beginners resort to more bland creations, filling the Web with the standard HTML elements—heading, heading plus text plus links plus (maybe) simple graphics—and these pages often minimize not only the Web's multimedia capabilities but your own audience in the process.

But there's a tried and tested way that you can include even the most complex HTML elements in your home pages: Copy them. For most Web authors, the sites that wow and amaze are, for all practical purposes, beyond our capabilities and, indeed, our resources. They belong instead to professional designers that devote their careers to the exploitation of the capabilities of new technologies. The only way we can even begin to approach their excellence is to borrow the ideas we find most striking.

For example, consider the time and complex programming that was involved in the creation of the three sites shown in Figures 15.1 through 15.3.

These sites' interactive approach to Web design makes use of some of the best but most difficult HTML applications. Now compare the preceding pages with the impressive but generally more static counterparts shown in Figures 15.4 through 15.6.

If you have spent even a couple of hours exploring the Web, you're well aware of its enormous design potential, especially the visual excellence possible with this medium. Although hypertext links may always remain the foundation of the Internet and WWW communication, and although the simpler HTML strategies remain necessary elements in all Web pages, by this point they have become little more than the basic element upon which the more advanced and complex HTML applications can be built. Because of this, unfortunately, Web page creation can often be intimidating, and it's often very hard to figure out how to begin making your site even a fraction as strong.

But with Gold at your fingertips, mastering design has just become simpler. How? By not making you master it at all. Instead, by navigating the Web and then clicking the Edit button, you can bring the work of the best HTML designers right into your study.

Figure 15.1

Surf through the Internet Underground Music Archive to see some of the most complex sound and graphic features at their best. The IUMA archive is famous for its graphical appeal and audio options, all accessible through complex imagemaps.

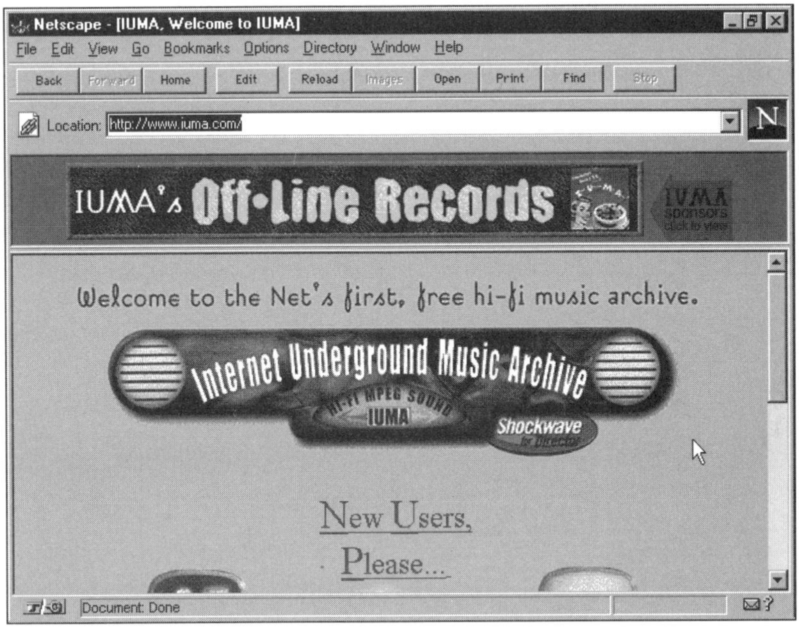

Figure 15.2

Check out the huge number of sound and video files maintained by the Disney Corporation in their television and motion picture archive.

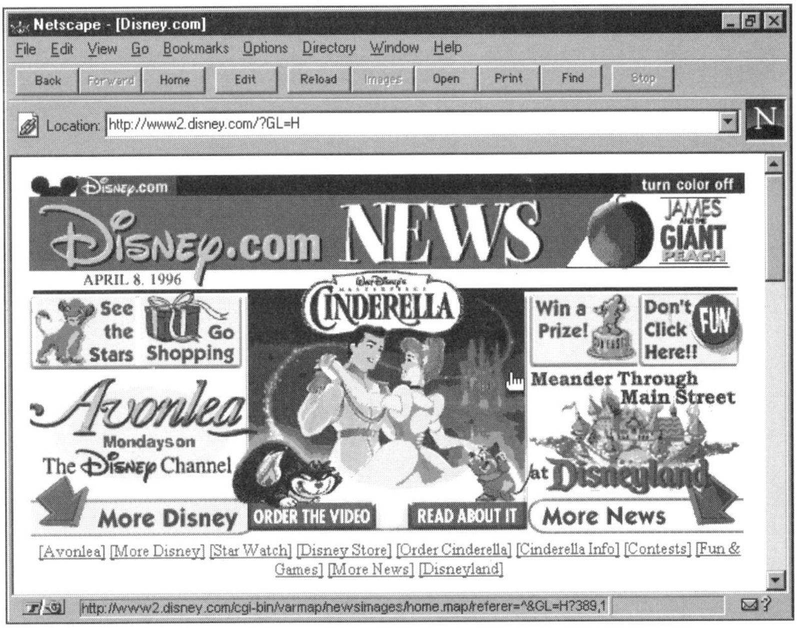

Figure 15.3

Who would've thought that Oscar Mayer would ever put the classic history of the Wienermobile online—using VRML and hot graphics?

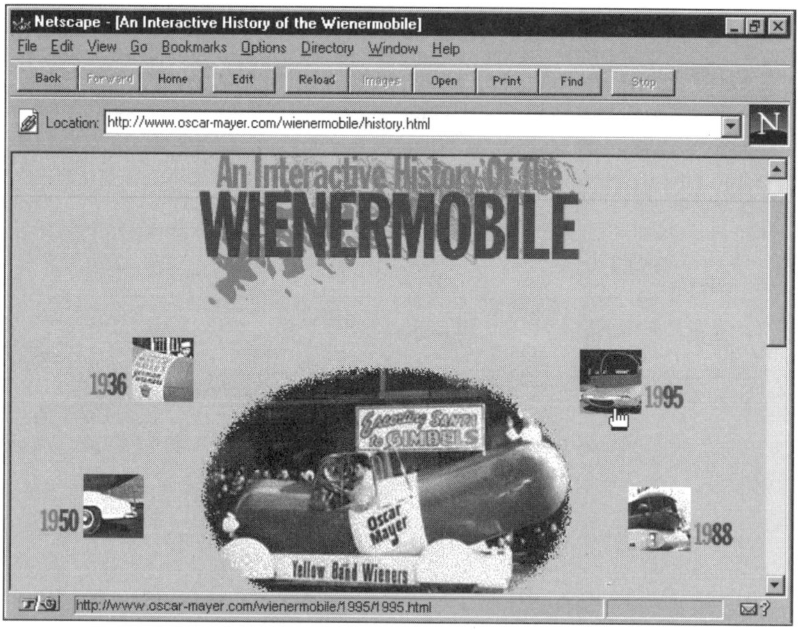

Figure 15.4

Mario's home page uses standard graphic and hypertext links to display the author's favorite sites and resource archives in a concise but unspectacular page.

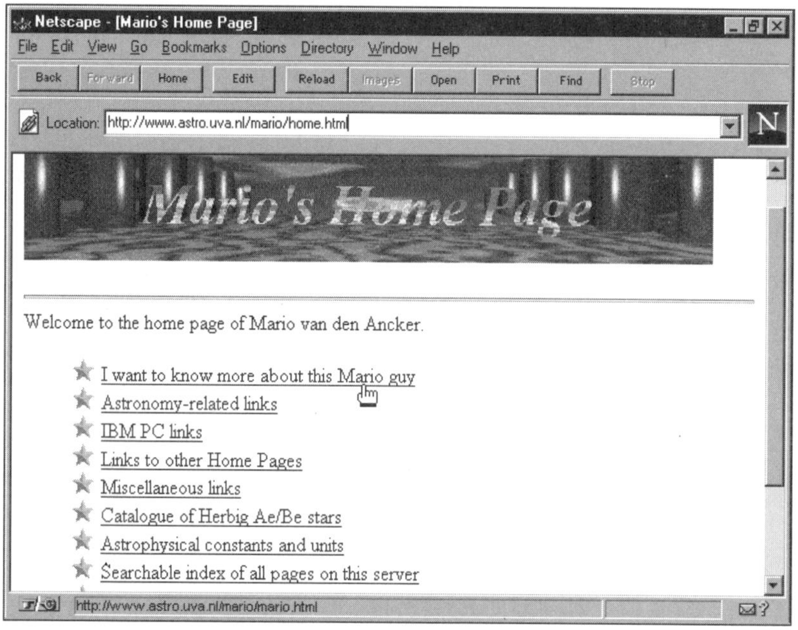

Figure 15.5

Directories and archive listings usually take a similar static approach to WWW display. Here, Yahoo focuses on ordering and grouping related pages, presenting them as simple text links.

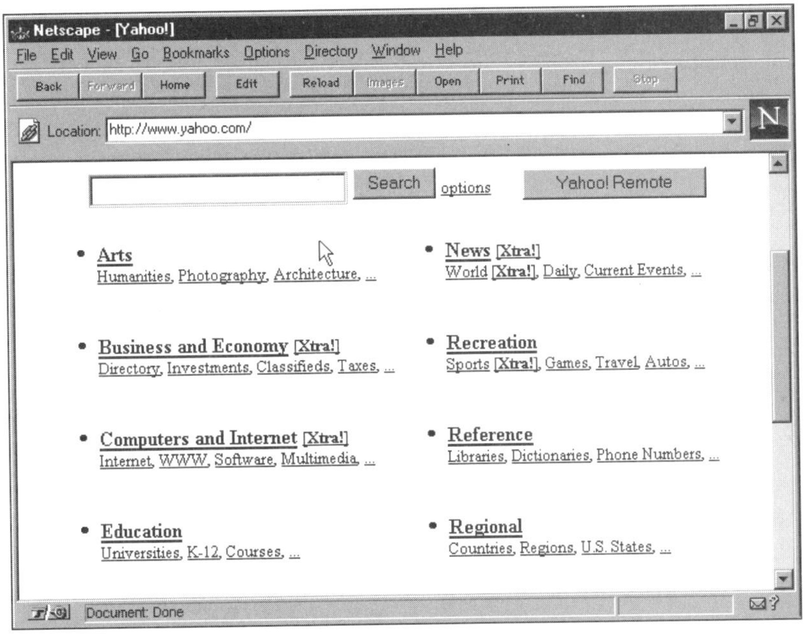

Figure 15.6

A large number of business and advertising links take a static approach to WWW design, listing favorite and relevant sites with textual links and avoiding graphic enhancement altogether.

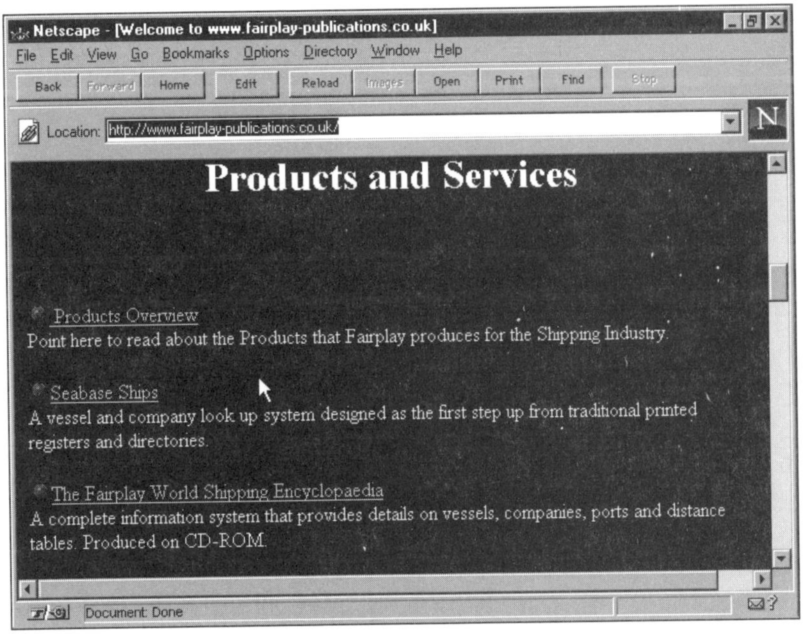

But Isn't This Just Theft?

Good question. The temptation is to say something flippant like, "Theft is in the eye of the new holder," but the question is far too serious for that. To some extent, taking a page off the Web to use for your own design is no different from designing a magazine from scratch using the tried and true formulas of the thousands of magazines that have used similar formats for decades. Or audio CDs, which almost always offer a photograph or piece of artwork on the front, and a listing of songs on the back. Or novels, which feature the title, the author's name, and a graphic on the front cover, and, in the hardcover versions, information about the book inside the front cover, and about the author inside the back cover. These are genre designs, and they get "stolen" all the time. How different, really, is the cover of the book you're holding from any number of other computer books in the store?

The idea of borrowing a design isn't theft. It happens all the time. What *is* theft is the borrowing or copying of text or graphics from other sites. In some cases, Web authors make it explicit on their sites whether or not you may use their graphics or scripts, and in that case simply abide by those instructions. If you're not sure, however, proceed according to the following rough guidelines:

1. If you're not sure, don't use it.
2. If you're not going to put it on the Web, don't worry about it.
3. If you're going to make money from your site, do everything in your power to avoid using other people's elements.
4. Things on the Web are protected by copyright laws. Period.
5. If you need to use it, e-mail the original Web author for permission. But make sure they have permission to use their stuff in the first place. Often, Web sites will contain pictures of Bart Simpson or Cindy Crawford, and you can rest assured they haven't asked permission in the first place.

Small but Mighty: The Edit Button

As you know by now, the biggest difference between Netscape Gold and all other Web browsers lies in the existence of one additional button—the Edit button. The Edit button is represented by a small pencil on your toolbar and serves the important function of switching modes in Netscape from the browser to the editing mechanism.

Essentially, what this allows you to do is locate a page on the Web that you like and that you wish to imitate or replicate in your own personal Web pages. Once you have loaded this page or screen into the Netscape Gold browser, simply click on the Edit button, and the page will automatically load into Gold's Web editor, ready for alterations and eventual implementation.

Although the simplicity of this copy and edit system raises some interesting copyright concerns for Internet users, the process allows beginning Web authors to create pages cold—without any background WWW experience or HTML programming expertise. To see just how simple and problem-free this process really is, let's create a graphically light home page that makes use of some standard HTML elements.

Editing a Simple Home Page

Before you can begin any copying or editing tasks with Netscape Gold, you should have a clear understanding of what you like and don't like to see on the World Wide Web. So take a few minutes (hours, days, weeks…) to familiarize yourself with the Web's capabilities and with the HTML elements that are most applicable to your particular site.

One of the most dangerous and unsuccessful ways of creating a Web site is to jump into the editing process immediately without properly planning and organizing your site's information and design strategies. The result is often a confusing, convoluted Web site that overlaps and overloads readers with irrelevant data.

Browse the Archives

The first step in creating a personal home page with Netscape Gold is to surf around and see what features work best for this type of electronic presence. Go into the archives at www.yahoo.com or any other collection of Web sites. Find a site that offers a good variety of elements, especially the ones you want, and bookmark it. Then start navigating again, bookmarking several sites that contain useful elements.

For demonstration purposes, I'll self-indulge and offer my own. Among other things, I can offer copyright permission to all readers of this book to use the site's elements in whatever ways you find useful. The site is located at http://randall.uwaterloo.ca, and while it's hardly a brilliant site, it's a good enough starting point (Figure 15.7). It offers

- Headline or title in large font and bold print.
- Image that breaks up text and catches the eye.
- Welcome text blurb.
- List of hyperlinks leading to favorite or relevant sites, e-mail link to offer commentary.
- Combination of graphics and links that explain the purpose of the site and tell the reader what to expect throughout their exploration. This

portion of most home pages acts as a what's new or what's cool spot that points new visitors to the site's best or most frequently accessed areas.

- The omnipresent "Under Construction" symbol typical of so many pages.
- Link to Yahoo's search mechanism, allowing visitors a useful exit point.

Figure 15.7

Whether good or bad, my home page contains most of the standard generic qualities featured in many WWW personal sites.

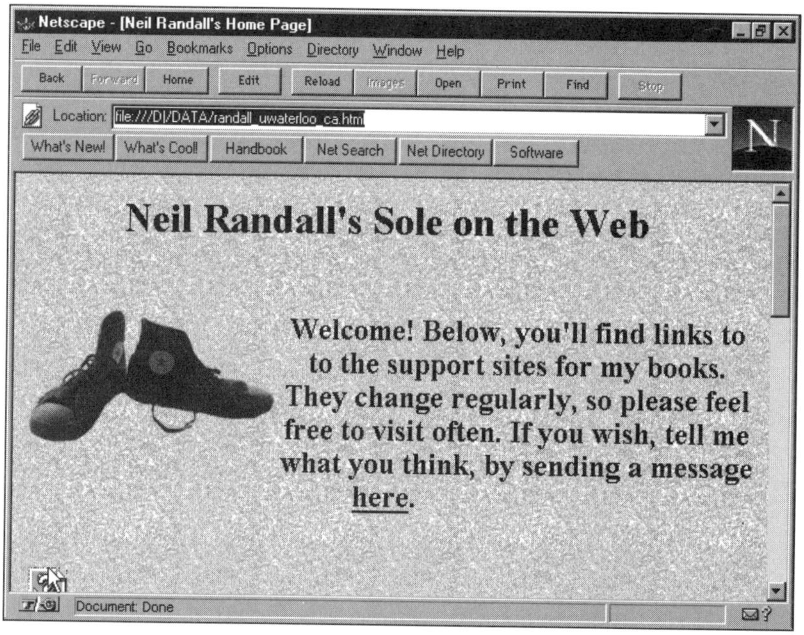

Now it's time to get started.

Using a browser window, retrieve my home page. Then, click on the Edit button that appears in the toolbar at the top of Gold's screen. Gold will now close the Web browser window and transfer an image of the current page to the Netscape Gold editing window. Your screen should look like Figure 15.8.

Netscape Gold gives you two important options with this save feature—the ability to preserve both links and graphics in the exact form that you viewed them on the Web. As you become more and more fluent in the Web creation process, you will undoubtedly acquire a collection of *favorite* or useful links and graphics of your own that you may wish to substitute for the original site's entries. But for now, check both these options and click the Save button.

You will then receive a copyright warning. In this case, we intend to copy the tags that structure the page, rather than the content itself, so click okay. And besides, I just gave you permission to copy (copyright means the "right to copy").

Figure 15.8

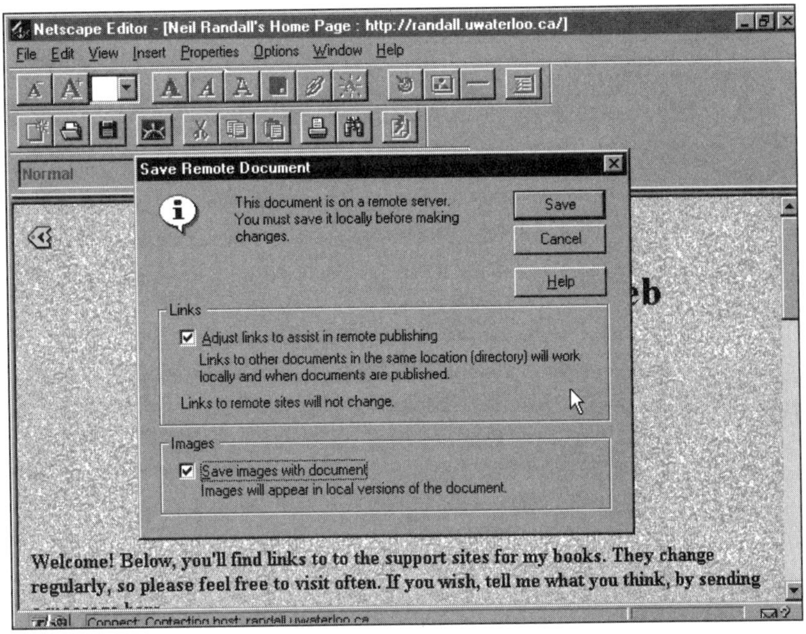

Because clicking on the Edit button simultaneously saves a copy of the original page to your computer, Netscape Gold presents this Save Remote Document message.

Gold will now show your system's standard Save As dialog box, which allows you to save pages in the appropriate directories and folders. This process saves all links and graphics contained within the site under their original names and formats on your local disk. If the graphics are large, and you're connected through a slow modem, the save process could take a few minutes.

All that's left to do now is delete and replace the text or graphics to mold the page to your personal tastes. There are a variety of ways to go about editing documents, the easiest of which is to simply delete text and graphics using the delete key on your keyboard, manually replacing data in the appropriate areas. But Netscape Gold also allows you to change the stylistic elements of imported pages, namely character or image properties and link locations. Scc Chapters 13–17 for details on altering all elements.

Since you are already familiar with the editing options that Netscape Gold makes available to your imported documents, you can proceed to create a personalized home page using the structure and style from parts of my home page. As you discover a need for different designs, import them as well from the Web. One of Gold's most powerful features is precisely this ability not only to view the best pages on the Web, but also to retrieve them for your own use, and doing so can dramatically reduce the time and effort needed to make the Web your own.

One Final Point

As I've stated before, publishing a Web page is a creative, artistic process and, as such, is best performed *from scratch*. While Netscape Gold's handy Edit button takes the time and effort out of Web editing, it also removes the expression of individuality that characterizes all "handmade" sites. The point of Web publishing and the World Wide Web itself is not to replicate what already exists—but to evolve and create in ways that are new to the medium. So while the Edit function may be beneficial for new Web authors or for publishing a series of documents that all conform to the same style, advanced Web users should be aware of the uniformity that reliance on this feature can spread, and strive to create rather than replicate.

But when you're just getting started, the Edit button is a great thing to have.

- *Varieties of Graphics*
- *The Image Properties Dialog Box*
- *Graphics In Raw HTML*
- *Design Decisions for Graphics*
- *Graphics Aren't Everything*

CHAPTER

16

Everything about Graphics You Could Even Begin to Ask

THE WEB IS A HOTBED OF GRAPHICS. YOU ALREADY KNOW THAT IF you've spent more than three minutes moving from site to site. In fact, Gold's default home page document, the Netscape Communications welcome page, offers rich graphics right off the bat. Start clicking anywhere, and you're certain to run into even more graphics. But that's hardly surprising; even more than hypertext, graphics are the reason the Web has become the most popular component of the Internet, and the amount of time and effort poured into creating new and exciting graphics reflects this popularity.

The World Wide Web was initially designed as a hypermedia forum (*hypermedia* = *hyper*text + multi*media*), but the first browsers weren't capable of displaying graphics. These browsers are still available—CERN line browser and Lynx for UNIX, Samba for the Macintosh—but their inability to display graphics pages makes them useful primarily to researchers accessing nongraphical documents. Even Lynx, which runs much faster than any browser you'll find on your desktop and offers a wide range of features, offers limited usefulness because of its graphics inability. The way pages are designed now, such an inability guarantees that a browser like this will see little widespread use.

Not until the release of Mosaic, the programming effort of Marc Andreessen (primarily) at the National Center for Supercomputing Applications (NCSA) at the University of Illinois, did the popularity of the World Wide Web skyrocket. Mosaic was released in 1993, and became an immediate hit on X Window and Macintosh systems. The Microsoft Windows version came later, and single-handedly spurred the explosion in Internet interest that continues today. The first Mosaic was nowhere near as capable as the browsers available today, but it displayed graphics and thus revolutionized what Internet information would look like. Andreessen, along with much of the rest of the Mosaic team, left to form Netscape Communications, and the result was the Netscape browser, which eventually became Netscape Navigator, and which eventually spawned Netscape Navigator Gold. And it remains a multimedia information system.

Varieties of Graphics

Web pages sport a variety of graphics types, each with its own purpose. Some of the basic types include bars, icons and buttons, inline images, backgrounds, and imagemaps. Bars come in different sizes, shapes, and colors, and usually act as an alternative to horizontal rules. Icons and buttons are generally quite small, and are commonly used as navigation aids or as alternatives to plain bullets in lists. Inline images are pictures, illustrations, logos, and other pictorial elements embedded into the document. Backgrounds are graphics files that display the rest of the Web page as a backdrop, and often have the appearance of three-dimensional textures.

Basically, there are three ways to get graphics. The first way is to browse the Web looking for graphics files you want to use in your own documents, and to save them to your hard disk directly from that page. Bear in mind, however, that these graphics might be copyrighted, and you should e-mail the page's Webmaster for permission to use them. In many cases, a statement on the Web page describes the use you may make of them, and some archives exist specifically to make graphics files available to you.

The second way is to make use of your artistic talent and create your own graphics. If you have access to a drawing program (Windows Paint will do) that will create pictures and images, you can create a graphic that is exactly what you need.

Third, you can scan graphics into your machine using a scanner, or you can get photographs developed on a CD-ROM. All of these are viable Web graphics.

The Image Properties Dialog Box

Netscape Navigator Gold handles its graphics primarily through the Image Properties dialog box. Two primary tabs—Image and Link—control your images' appearances and functions. The main portion of this dialog is shown in Figure 16.1.

Figure 16.1

The Image tab lets you control the major elements of your image.

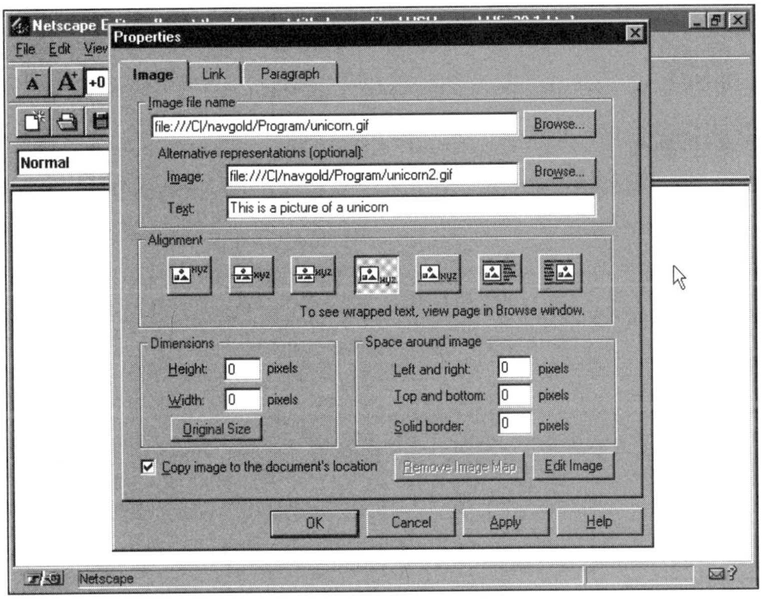

To activate the Image Properties dialog box, open Gold's Editor window and place the cursor in the document where you want the new image to appear. Then, select Image from the Insert menu. Alternatively, if an image already exists in your document, right-click on it and select Image Properties from the pop-up menu.

The Image tab of the Images dialog box presents the following choices.

Image File Name

Enter the path and name of the graphics file you want to place in your page, or click Browse to locate the file on your hard drive.

Alternative Representations

These two optional fields let you specify an alternative to the image. In the Image field, select a low-resolution version of the image file, which will appear in your readers' browser before the main image, giving them the option of stopping the retrieval process if they wish. In the Text field, you should type a short explanation of the image; this will appear in browsers that do not support graphics, or if your reader has a slow Internet connection and is operating the browser with the images toggled off. Neither of these fields is required, but they demonstrate that you care about your users' preferences.

Alignment

Alignment refers to the position of the image on the page, and to the position of the associated text in respect to that image. When you select an image, you have several aligning options to choose from. Each offers its own visual benefits.

In the interest of graphical clarity, Gold's designers have chosen to represent the seven alignment options as buttons picturing the resulting appearance of the text. In the interest of learning about HTML, however, this book offers the actual terminology as a means of referring to the options. From left to right across the Alignment section of the Image Properties dialog box, these options are as follows:

Align=TextTop: This choice (Figure 16.2) will align the top of your image with the top of the existing text. All text that does not fit on one line will continue *below* the graphic, not to the side of it. This is true for the first five options.

Align=Center: This option (Figure 16.3) aligns the middle of your chosen graphic with the middle of the existing text.

Align=Abscenter: This option (Figure 16.4) will align the middle of your graphic with the baseline of your text. *Baseline* refers to an imaginary line drawn across the bottom of the letters, and intersecting the extenders of letters that drop below that line (letters such as *y* and *p*).

Align=Baseline: This choice (Figure 16.5) lets you line up the bottom of the graphic with the bottom of the text. This is the default alignment

Align=Bottom: This option (Figure 16.6) is different from Align=Baseline in one way. Bottom of text includes the very bottom of all lowercase extenders, not just the baseline of the text. In other words, it's a wee bit lower.

Align=Left: Here (Figure 16.7), you can arrange the image on the left with the text wrapped on the right side of the entire image. This is as close to desktop publishing as HTML alignment gets.

Align=Right: Here (Figure 16.8), your image will appear on the right side of the text, with the text wrapped around the left side of the graphic.

Figure 16.2

TextTop alignment

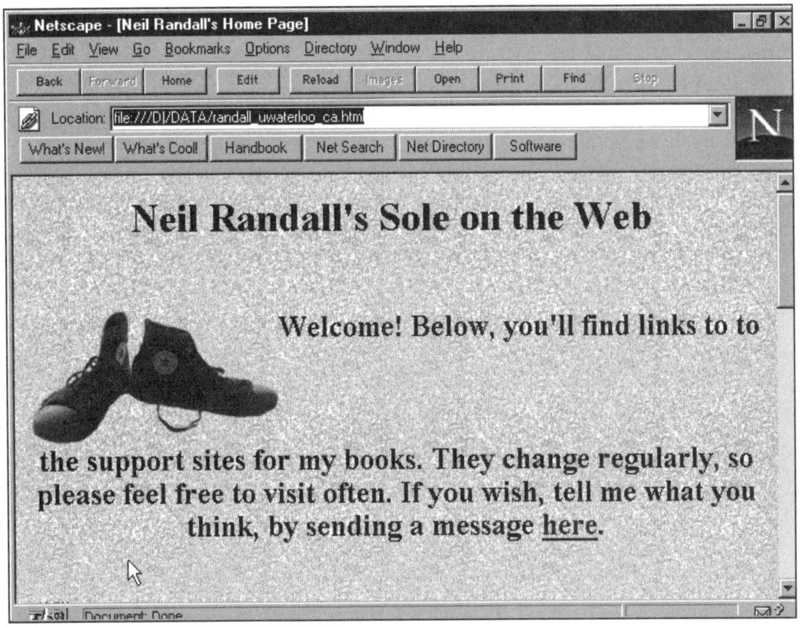

Figure 16.3

Center alignment

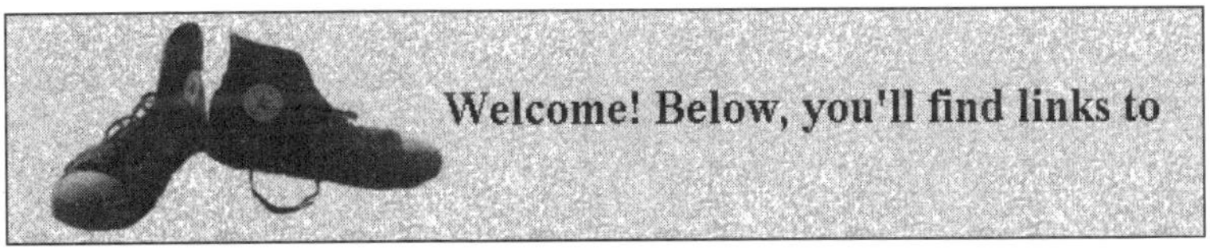

Figure 16.4

Absolute center alignment

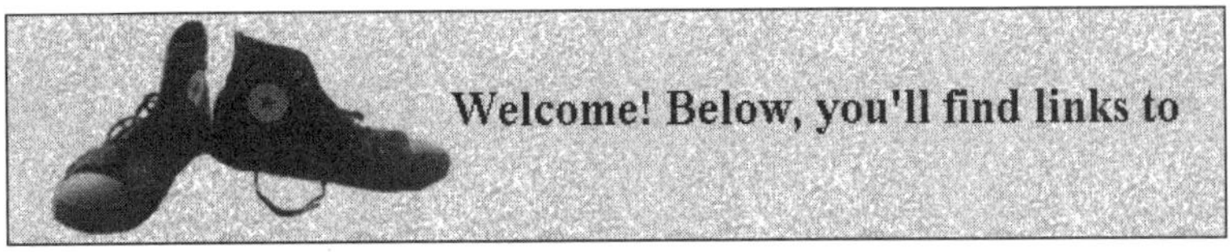

Welcome! Below, you'll find links to
to the support sites for my books. They change regularly,
so please feel free to visit often. If you wish, tell me what
you think, by sending a message here.

Figure 16.5

Baseline alignment

Welcome! Below, you'll find links to
to the support sites for my books. They change regularly,
so please feel free to visit often. If you wish, tell me what
you think, by sending a message here.

Figure 16.6

Bottom alignment

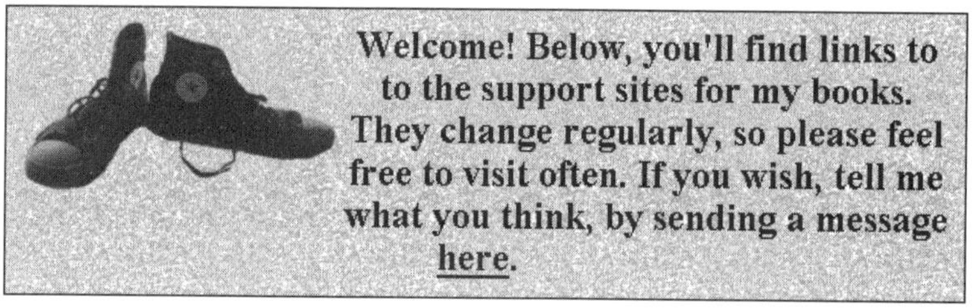
Welcome! Below, you'll find links to
to the support sites for my books.
They change regularly, so please feel
free to visit often. If you wish, tell me
what you think, by sending a message
here.

Figure 16.7

Left alignment

Welcome! Below, you'll find links to
to the support sites for my books.
They change regularly, so please feel
free to visit often. If you wish, tell me
what you think, by sending a message
here.

Figure 16.8

Right alignment

Dimensions

By adjusting the dimensions of your image, you change the size of the graphic on the finished page. You can experiment by typing in values (measured in number of pixels) for the height and width of the image, and if you end up dissatisfied you can click the Original Size button to return the image to its initial size. Figure 16.9 shows the image in Figure 16.8 increased in height from 104 pixels to 304 pixels, and the width unchanged.

Figure 16.9

The Resized image alters the appearance significantly.

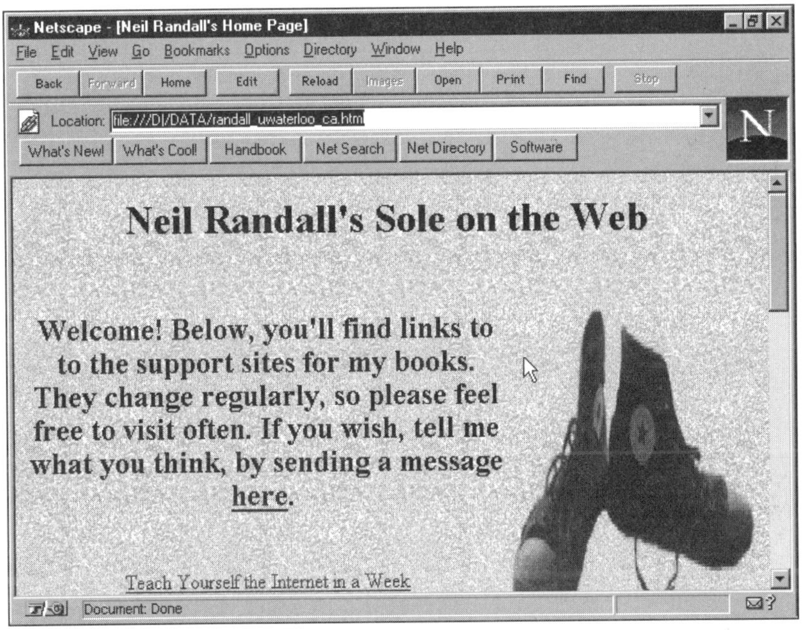

Space around Image

You can make a type of border around your images and graphics, to increase or decrease the spacing between image and text. The space is measured in pixels, and separate measurements can be specified for the spacing around the left and right sides of the graphic and around the top and bottom sides of the image. The Solid Border option places a black border around the graphic, which appears in the user's browser before the graphic begins to download. The border appears before the graphic, helping the user to decide if the image is too large to continue retrieving.

Copy Image to the Document's Location

Checking this box copies the image to the document's directory when you select Publish from the File menu. You can also choose to do this via the Publish dialog box during the uploading process.

Remove Image Map

If the image you're working with was originally an imagemap, you can remove the imagemap's link regions by clicking Remove Image Map. You use this feature if you've downloaded an imagemap that you want solely as an image, or if it's your own imagemap and you want to redraw the link regions. See Chapter 19 for the creation and use of imagemaps.

Edit Image

If you have an image editing program specified in the Editor Preferences dialog (see Chapter 5), clicking Edit Image will load that editor with the image inside it, ready for editing. After editing, save the image, and it will be ready for manipulation through the Image Properties dialog box once more.

Graphics In Raw HTML

Everything you can do in Gold's Image Properties box you can do with raw HTML code as well. Table 16.1 outlines the graphics functions. Note that the <IMG></IMG> container controls the graphics functions, and that the standard attribute is SRC (source). Thus, virtually all functions will begin with <IMG SRC=*x*>, with *x* representing the file name or the URL for the graphic file.

Design Decisions for Graphics

There are many things to take into consideration when you sit down and start to design your Web pages. Often, you will think you've made a good decision, until you actually see the results of that decision on the Web itself. The first suggestion, therefore, is to check and recheck the appearance of your new page before publishing it on the Web, and then check it again once it's placed on the server. Pink and orange pictures beside each other might seem like a good idea at first, but you won't likely find the combination appealing once you see it in your browser window. And the same holds true for a great many other graphics-oriented decisions. Remember that your graphics can make or break your entire Web page.

Table 16.1

HTML Graphics Functions

FUNCTION	HTML CODE
Inline Image	<img src = "name.gif">
Align Left	<img src = "name.gif" align=left>
Align Right	<img src = "name.gif" align=right>
Top:Top	<img src = "name.gif" align=texttop>
Middle:Middle	<img src = "name.gif" align=center>
Middle:Baseline	<img src = "name.gif" align=abscenter>
Bottom:Bottom	<img src = "name.gif" align=bottom>
Bottom:Baseline	<img src = "name.gif">
Left Right Spacing (10)	<img src = "name.gif" hspace=10>
Top Bottom Spacing (10)	<img src = "name.gif" vspace=10>
Borders (10)	<img src = "name.gif" border=10>
Link	<a href = "file or location URL"><img src = "name.gif"></a>

1. Using graphics well means using space effectively. You have a certain amount of space that should be used, and you should be careful not to overdesign. Try not to leave a large swath of empty space around your text, and try not to leave graphics isolated on the screen. If your readers enter your site and are greeted with little but blank space, they probably won't find your page very inviting. A large blank space at the bottom of the page is also a drawback, especially between the last essential element and the authoring comments at the bottom, because there is no sense of conclusion, or reason to continue to other links.

2. It's often a good idea to use graphics instead of text for your hyperlinks. If well designed, they can be much more attractive than text, but if poorly designed they can be much less informative. Your reader must be made aware that they *are* in fact links, because even though a linked graphic bears an outline that outline isn't always obvious. Usually, small icons that are simple and straightforward work well as hyperlinks. For example, when you see a picture of a little arrow at the bottom of the page, there's a good chance that it is a link to the next (or previous) page. Such links can also work well in the case of logos. But make sure such a logo isn't too big, or it might be mistaken for mere ornament, or for part of the background.

3. There is a danger in using too many or too few graphics on one page. Unless you are setting up a page of pictures and images (which take a while to download anyway), you'll want to be careful to keep your images to a decent level. For many users, graphics take a long time to download, and few people will wait to see them. What you may want to do in this case is downsize the pictures, or spread them out across many pages that link together.
4. Icons, bars, and other small graphics can greatly assist your reader in navigating your page. Used well, they can quite literally guide the user's eye down from one portion of the page to the other, or even from one page to the next. Unique and attractive icons make a good substitute for HTML's rather boring bullets, and colorful bars and lines can be used in place of plain horizontal rules to separate different regions of the page. A graphic down the right side of the entire page does not appreciably distract (provided it's not a overbearing picture), and it can encourage the reader to look down further, partially to see the rest of the graphic. You can also try to arrange to have one graphic in plain sight, while only a portion of another appears below the scroll line of the page. This can create curiosity, and everything across the page will get at least a little attention. The problem with this is that you have no idea how large the user's screen is, nor the resolution at which they are viewing your pages.
5. Color can be notoriously difficult to coordinate. If you have fairly light colored graphics, you will usually want a darker background to help then stand out a little more. But be careful that the text is not then too dark to be easily read. And be careful of the background itself; if it's too busy, make sure your page is correspondingly sparse.
6. Class counts. Simple icons and bullets are useful, and color schemes can be effective. Graphical themes running throughout a Web site show a touch of professionalism, as do tasteful and sparing images. If you're an artist, by all means create original art for your site. A great many Web sites, however, show far too many graphics, some of which are so distracting that they denigrate the content completely. Above all, consider the audience you're trying to attract, and put yourself in their place. And don't forget the value of actually studying the art of graphic design—pick up magazines and books on the topic.

Graphics Aren't Everything

There's no question that graphics have swept the Web. The sites that everyone talks about are graphically superb, to the extent that text-only sites, no matter how brilliant the prose or thought-provoking the content, have a hard time getting noticed. But when it comes right down to it, your graphics won't save you. If your site has nothing to offer beyond strong graphic design, people will visit it once but never again. Use your graphics to enhance your material, but make sure you have material worth enhancing. That's the ultimate secret of good Web design.

PART

3

Pure Gold: Advanced HTML

- *Why Doesn't Everybody Use Tables?*
- *What Do I Use Tables For?*
- *Design Decisions When Creating Tables*
- *Tables on the Web*

CHAPTER

17

Tables

HTML TABLES CAN BE EXTREMELY HELPFUL TOOLS. THEY CAN help you organize the information you're providing, and they can offer your readers a concise, readable means of accessing that information. Furthermore, they can be used as a means of getting around HTML's generic page design limitations. By no means are all tables out there on the Web well designed or constructed, but those that are enhance Web use considerably.

Future versions of Netscape Navigator Gold will allow you to create tables. For now, you must create tables by using raw HTML, or by installing a table-capable HTML editor. This chapter covers raw HTML only, although several good editors exist that allow reasonably easy table creation.

To place your created tables into your Gold documents, copy the entire HTML code into the Clipboard, then open the desired document in the Editor window. Place the cursor precisely where you want the table to appear, then choose HTML Tag from the Insert menu. Paste the HTML code into the HTML Tag box, then click OK.

Why Doesn't Everybody Use Tables?

There are two problems with tables on the Net. First, many Web designers seem to think that tables are just a rectangular assortment of boxes for displaying statistics or lists, like a word processing table. But tables on the World Wide Web offer many more possibilities; they can break free from this type of static compilation to allow for artistic design, colors, images, videos, links, and all the other interactive functions that make the Net what it is. Secondly, many basic Web editors do not yet support table formation, and one of these is Netscape Navigator Gold. As a result, tables are quite difficult to prepare. But Gold will soon let you build tables (apparently, WYSIWYG table features are notoriously difficult to program), and editors like Sausage Software's HotDog and Mediatec's Live Markup provide increasingly useful means of putting them together even now.

Of these two difficulties, the first is the more important by far. It's one thing to be able to create tables, quite another to figure out uses for them beyond the obvious technique of putting page elements inside a grid of little squares. The question, of course, is what you'll use tables for even when Gold can handle them directly.

What *Do* I Use Tables For?

Putting a table of information on the Web offers a number of interesting possibilities, but also a number of constraints. With a little effort, the overall effect can be quite impressive and very useful. HTML tables can display all sorts of information, and you can make this information as aesthetically interesting as you want by manipulating the table design. HTML tables are so flexible, in fact, that they can be used to format your pages to look as if they've been prepared with a desktop publishing program.

Tables that fail on the Web are usually extremely large and often contain lengthy portions of straight text. Since Internet users are confined to the viewing size of their monitors, they will only be able to view portions of large tables on a single screen. Of course, browsers do allow users to scroll both horizontally and vertically, but a table that extends beyond the physical limit of the screen can be difficult to actually use, because the headings will easily fall out of view.

Because of their elegance, flexibility, and visual appeal, tables are rapidly superseding imagemaps and the several types of HTML lists for the structured presentation of menus and data. The best tables on the Web combine text with graphics, links with sound, video, and animation to create a concise structure that explodes on your screen. Check out The Ultimate Collection of Winsock Software table (Figure 17.1) for an excellent use of the Internet's capabilities.

Figure 17.1

Software download sites such as this combine graphic, link, and downloading functions with the table format to organize information, making location of specific data easy.

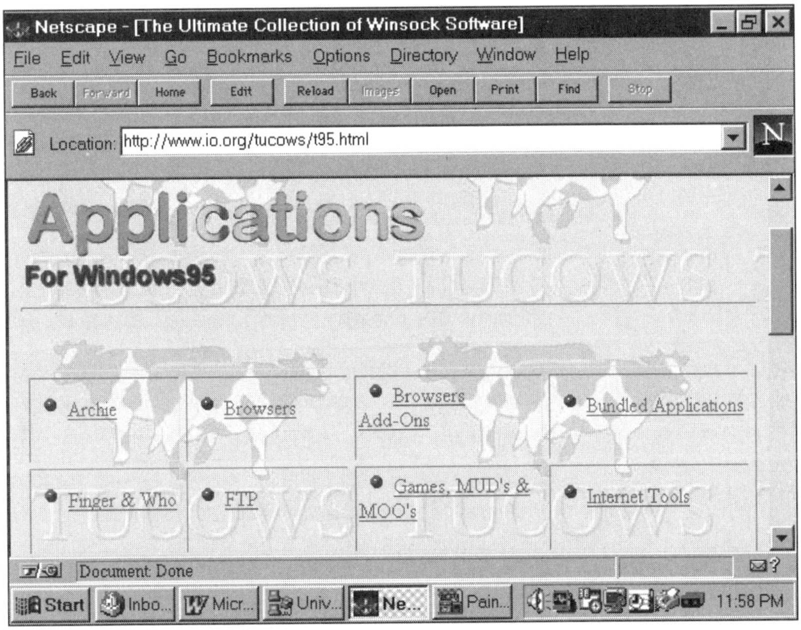

Undoubtedly, you have stumbled across tables of one sort or another in your Web surfing adventures—even if you didn't recognize them as tables the first time you saw them. Some advanced sites have incorporated tabular formats into their HTML documents with such ingenuity that you don't even realize that they lie behind the page layout (see Figure 17.2).

Here are some great uses for tables in your Web projects:

- Use tables to list travel tips and flight times, to organize class schedules, timetables, and daybooks, or to preserve your favorite recipes.

Figure 17.2

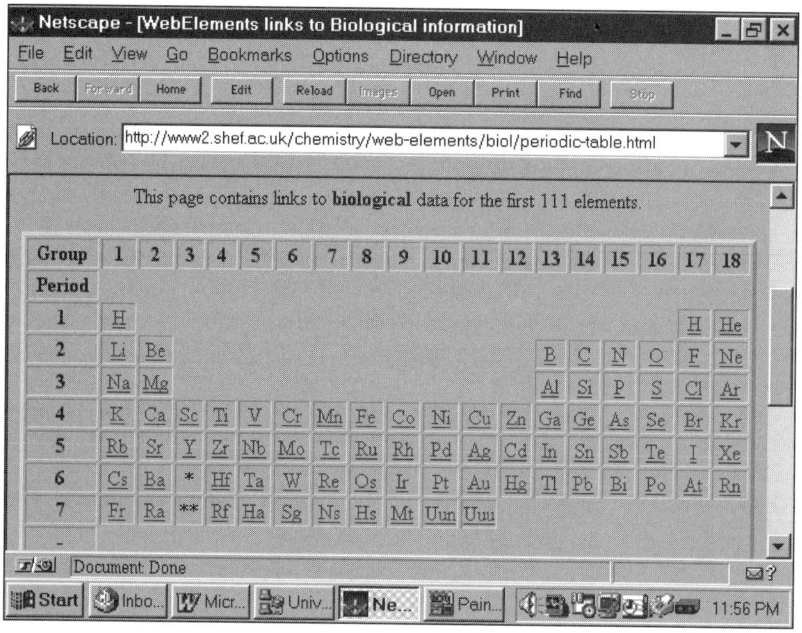

Some tables translate really well into HTML and onto the Web. The Periodic Table is a natural candidate, allowing users to link to information on the different elements.

- Tables act as aesthetic substitutes for items contained in bulleted lists or columns, for lengthy statistical data, or for complex imagemaps.
- Some of the best tables on the Net are incorporated as part of the page structure, often organizing the layout for e-zine articles, online magazines or directories, and surveys or questionnaires.

With Netscape Gold's new framed environments, tables take on even more functions, allowing users to display a full table of material in one frame while users surf among the table's links in the corresponding frames.

Design Decisions When Creating Tables

The tables you'll examine throughout this chapter are some of best examples I have ever come across, and the first time I saw them, I admit, I was tempted to copy the HTML code and immediately apply them to my personal online documents. However, what I soon realized was that it wasn't the table codes themselves that made the pages so great, was but rather the information those tables contained, the way the table was designed to support that information, and the activities that this information made available.

Without data that cries out for table formatting, constructing these visual listing devices on the Net is pointless.

So how do you know if your documents would be best displayed by tables? Here are a few simple guidelines that outline the types of users and pages most suited for table construction.

You should use a table if:

- You don't mind limiting your viewing audience to those who use Netscape Gold or another table-supported browser. Other viewers won't be restricted from all of the data contained in your tables, but will lose the basic formatting (which often makes data just as unreadable as if it hadn't been included at all).
- You have an unusually large amount of patience for tedious coding, testing, and experimentation in HTML, or, better, if you have access to a table-capable HTML editor (such as Gold in a later release). Creating tables by hand in HTML is no fun. The code for tables was designed to be easy to generate by programs like Gold, not to be written by hand, and as such it's rather confusing.
- The data you have included in your Web pages could be listed, grouped, or sorted in some coherent way to make it better understood. The second part of this tip is the most important—if your data works in a list or paragraph form, leave it as it is. Only use tables if they will help you get your point across.
- Each segment of the listed or grouped data offers users a number of additional options (links, graphics, downloads, sound, video applications, and so forth). Constructing a table that organizes information in a visual structure but doesn't actually go anywhere or do anything limits the advanced capabilities of the element itself.

Creating Tables Using Raw HTML

The HTML code for constructing tables is not impossible, but it's definitely not easy to learn; and, more than anything, it *looks* really hard. There are lots of little tags that must be implemented in a specific sequence, and the tediousness of the process may seem somewhat painful. In fact, creating tables from scratch may well be the worst HTML experience you'll come across. Still, the results often make it all worthwhile.

The Table Tags

The standard table containers used in the formation of all HTML tables are <TABLE></TABLE>, <TR></TR>, <TD></TD>, <TH></TH>, and <CAPTION></CAPTION>. These containers organize the basic structure of your tables, wrapping around the text you insert and building a standard table appearance. All of these tags must be used in even the simplest tables. Table 17.1 explains the function of each of these HTML elements.

Table 17.1

HTML Table Tag Functions

ELEMENT	FUNCTION
<TABLE></TABLE>	The main table tag is the wrapper for all other tags within the table structure and acts as a container for these tags, with <TABLE> occurring at the beginning of your table and </TABLE> at the end. All other tags will be ignored if these codes are not wrapped around them.
<TR></TR>	The number of table row commands listed in your table code specifies the number of rows that compose your table. TR can hold both the ALIGN and VALIGN attributes, which, if specified, become the default alignments for all cells in the row.
<TD></TD>	The TD command specifies a standard table data cell—the actual block portion of the table. Table data cells must only appear within table rows. Each row may vary the number of cells specified since shorter rows will automatically be padded with blank cells on the right.
<TH></TH>	Table header cells are identical to data cells in all respects except that header cells are printed in bold and are centered by default.
<CAPTION> </CAPTION>	The caption commands hug the phrase or comment that you would like to display above or below the table you are creating. CAPTION tags should appear inside the TABLE tags but not inside table rows or cells. Captions are always horizontally centered with respect to the table, and they may have their lines broken to fit within the width of the table.

A table in HTML is defined by the <TABLE> and </TABLE> tags. From there it is easiest to think of a table in terms of its individual cells. Your first task is to determine the maximum number of rows and columns your table will have, and start defining your cells one by one. As with spreadsheet or word processing tables, rows go across the screen, while columns go up and down. Every place where a row and column intersect, you get a cell. Hence, a table that has 5 rows and 4 columns will have 20 cells. Cells are defined from left to right in rows, and then from top to bottom.

The Big Picture

Before you begin inserting data in any of the cells you have chosen for your display, you'll want to consider the overall appearance of your table. HTML supports four attributes that give you added control over the appearance of your table.

Borders add a 3-D quality and shading, while *cellspacing* allows you to regulate the space between cells and *cellpadding* controls the area between the border of the cell and the contents of the cell. In addition, the HTML width command allows you to regulate the width of the table in absolute values, as a percentage, or in pixels. When the width attribute appears on either the TH or TD tag it is used to describe the desired width of the cell, either as an absolute width in pixels or as a percentage of table width.

To specify the border size to appear on your table, type *border=#* within the opening <TABLE> tag. If you do not insert the word border within the tag, no border appears, and if you do not insert a number after the border= entry, HTML specifies a single width by default.

Specifying the total width of the table simply requires placing the *width=#* command within the opening table tag. For example, if you want the width of your table to take up 80 percent of the space between your margins, you would insert the following line to begin your table coding:

```
<table border width=80%>
```

You may also specify the height of the table by inserting *height=#* in the same way that you determined the table width.

The cellspacing attribute is also inserted immediately after the <TABLE> command and specifies how much space lies between cells. The cellpadding default applies one unit of space between the cell content and the border, but for more control you may regulate the sizing using absolute values. Play around with some of these elements until you find the qualities that best display your individual table. Here is the first line of the HTML code that I used to create a table of contents page for an online book site:

```
<TABLE BORDER=10 WIDTH=400 HEIGHT=200 CELLPADDING=30 CELLSPACING=30>
```

Find the qualities you want your table to display, and then insert them into your opening table tag. Randomly altering the element values the first time you construct a table may be frustrating at first, but this experimentation will give you a better handle on what each command does and what best suits your page. Once you are satisfied with the results, you may use the same values over and over again in all of your tables. Finally you are ready to construct HTML tables.

NOTE. *Previewing your document before you have designed your table's data cells and concluded with the </TABLE> command is useless since neither the editor or the browser know what the opening table specifications are going to be applied to. Changing the values of the border, width, height, cellspacing, and cellpadding attributes will only produce results once your entire table is complete.*

The Heading Cell and the Data Cell

Since the heading cell (<TH></TH>) and the data cell (<TD></TD>) are so closely linked, we will examine their attributes together. Just as the <TA-BLE> command accepted internal specifications, heading and data cell tags also accept a number of additional attributes, the most important of which are the Align, Valign, Colspan, and Rowspan specifications.

The horizontal and vertical alignment of cell contents are determined by the ALIGN and VALIGN attributes, respectively. The ALIGN attribute can be used to explicitly specify the horizontal alignment of paragraphs within a table row:

- *align=left*—Paragraphs are displayed flush left. By default, data cells are aligned left.
- *align=center*—Paragraphs are centered. By default, header cells are centered.
- *align=right*—Paragraphs are displayed flush right.
- *align=justify*—Text lines are justified where practical, otherwise the justify value aligns text to the left.
- *align=decimal*—Text lines are indented such that the first occurrence of a decimal point on each line is aligned vertically. If a line doesn't contain a decimal point, the line is rendered flush left for data cells and centered for header cells.

A data cell that aligns its content to the right would look like this in HTML:

```
<TD align=right>insert cell content here</TD>
```

In the absence of the ALIGN attribute, text within cells is arranged according to the COLSPAC attribute on the TABLE element or by the presence of an ALIGN attribute on the parent TR element.

Conversely, the VALIGN attribute can be used to explicitly specify the vertical alignment of material within a table cell:

- *valign=top*—Cell contents are placed at the top of each cell. This is also the default vertical setting.
- *valign=middle*—Cell contents are centered vertically within each cell.
- *valign=bottom*—Cell contents appear at the bottom of each cell.
- *valign=baseline*—This is used when you want to ensure that all cells in the row with valign=baseline share the same baseline. This constraint only applies to the first text line for each cell.

In the absence of the VALIGN attribute, the align=top default can be overridden by a VALIGN attribute on the parent Table Row element. A heading cell that vertically aligns its content to the bottom would look like this in HTML coding:

```
<TH valign=bottom>insert cell heading here</TH>
```

The COLSPAN and ROWSPAN attributes are much less detailed than alignment specifications and function primarily to allow the merging of cells across columns and rows within your table. The COLSPAN value specifies the number of columns spanned by the cell that it defines, and allows you to merge cells across columns. The ROWSPAN attribute specifies the number of rows spanned by a specific cell, allowing you to merge cells across rows. Both COLSPAN and ROWSPAN default to 1.

The last command that you will need to become familiar with in order to create and understand HTML table codes is the DP specification. *DP* stands for *decimal point* and defines the keyboard character to be used for decimal points if you choose to include them in the ALIGN attribute. Most commonly, the DP code line looks like *dp*= ". " (the attribute's default setting) or like *dp*= ", ".

These other, less popular attributes are also specified by the TH and TD cells.

- The *ID* identifier is often used as the target for hypertext links or for naming particular elements in associated style sheets. Identifiers are NAME tokens and must be unique within the scope of the current document.
- *LANG* is one of the ISO standard language abbreviations (for example, "en.uk" for the variation of English spoken in the United Kingdom), and can be used by parsers to select language-specific choices for quotation marks, ligatures, and hyphenation rules.
- *CLASS* is a space-separated list of SGML NAME tokens and is used to subclass tag names. By convention, the class names are interpreted hierarchically, with the most general class on the left and the most specific on the right. The CLASS attribute is most commonly used to attach a different style to some element.
- The *NOWRAP* attribute is used when you don't want the browser to automatically wrap lines. After specifying NOWRAP, you may explicitly specify line breaks in paragraphs using the BR element.
- The *AXIS* attribute defines an abbreviated name for a header cell, which can be used when rendering to speech. It defaults to the cell's actual content.
- *AXES* is a comma-separated list of axis names which together identify the row and column headers that pertain to the cell. It is used when rendering to speech to identify the cell's position in the table.

Up to this point, you've received a lot of definitions and specifications that are the keys to table creation and must be examined, but that may seem slightly overwhelming and even confusing when viewed out of context. The best way to become familiar with these codes is to see how they work in a real table on the Web. Figure 17.3 is a good example.

Figure 17.3

Annette's Twice Baked Sweet Potatoes recipe looks great in simple table format and clarifies instructions in a concise visual display.

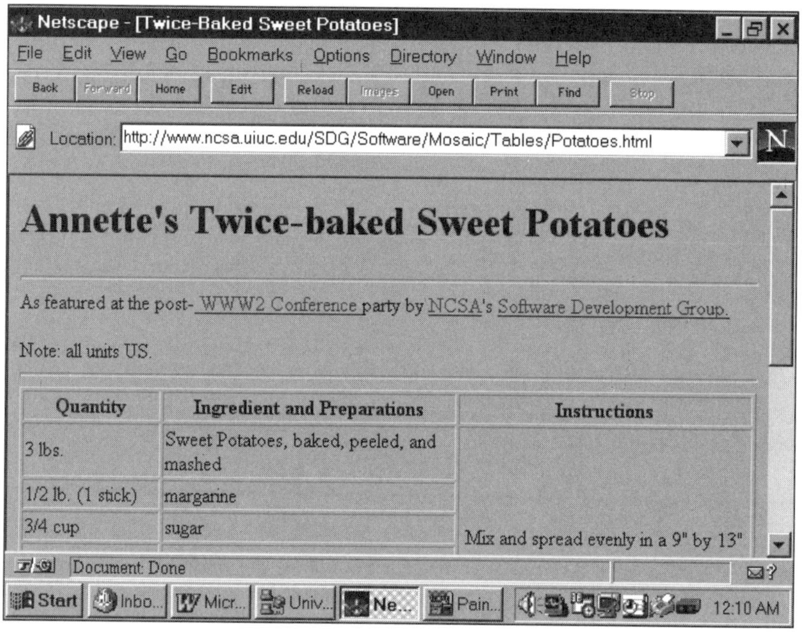

Here is the source code for Figure 17.3:

```
<TABLE BORDER>
<TR ALIGN=CENTER><TH>Quantity</TH><TH>Ingredient and Preparations</
TH><TH>Instructions</TH></TR>
<TR ALIGN=LEFT> <TD>3 lbs.</TD> <TD>Sweet Potatoes, baked, peeled, and mashed</
TD> <TD ALIGN=CENTER ROWSPAN=7> Mix and spread evenly in a 9" by 13" pan</TD>
</TR>
<TR ALIGN=LEFT> <TD>1/2 lb. (1 stick) </TD> <TD> margarine</TD> </TR>
<TR ALIGN=LEFT> <TD>3/4 cup</TD> <TD>sugar</TD> </TR>
<TR ALIGN=LEFT> <TD>1/2 tsp.</TD> <TD>Allspice</TD> </TR>
<TR ALIGN=LEFT> <TD>1 tsp.</TD> <TD>Vanilla extract</TD> </TR>
<TR ALIGN=LEFT> <TD>1/2 tsp.</TD> <TD>Cinnamon</TD> </TR>
<TR ALIGN=LEFT> <TD>3/4 cup</TD> <TD>Orange Juice</TD> </TR>
<TR ALIGN=LEFT> <TD> 1/4 lb. (1/2 stick) </TD> <TD> margarine</TD> <TD
ALIGN=CENTER ROWSPAN=3> Mix, then spread evenly on top of the first layer</TD>
</TR>
<TR> <TD> 1.5 cup</TD> <TD> brown sugar </TD> </TR>
```

```
<TR> <TD> 1.5 cup</TD> <TD> chopped nuts (typically Walnuts or Pecans)</TD> </
TR>
<TR ALIGN=CENTER> <TD COLSPAN=3> Bake at 350 degrees (F) for 25 to 30 minutes</
TD> </TR>
</TABLE>
```

Take a long look at this HTML gobbledygook line by line and you'll find, perpaps a bit to your surprise, that it eventually starts to make sense. The first line of the code tells the editor and browser that the following data will be presented as a table and that the table accepts the border default value of a single width measurement. The next line defines the first Table Row (TR), telling the browser to center the content of the following cells. Within this row, the HTML code defines three heading cells entitled *Quantity, Ingredient and Preparations*, and *Instructions.* All of these headings will appear as bold, centered text.

Follow through the rest of Annette's recipe to see how logical the structure actually is. Remember that tables don't have to include all of the specifications that we have examined above; in fact, it's a very good idea to limit the extras that you add to your tables in order to keep your pages clear and concise. The idea isn't to flaunt your knowledge of HTML specifications but to present data in an organized, creative way that is appealing and uncluttered.

Table Rows and Captions

The table row and table caption containers, <TR></TR> and <CAPTION></CAPTION> respectively, are extremely important in your table design. <TR> and </TR> control the appearance and function of each row in your table and act as containers for the table and heading cells and alignment attributes. The table row container tags tell the browser that the cells defined after <TR> and up to </TR> constitute a single row of data display. Since the TR tags envelop or surround the table and header cells, the closing cell tags—</TD> and </TH>—become rather useless. Browsers read the Table Data and Table Heading Cells as closed when the browser reaches the next <TD>, <TH>, or </TR> tag. The beginning of a new cell or the completion of a table row automatically assumes closure, so you really never need to include the </TD> and </TH> tags. The following lines would produce exactly the same results in HTML:

```
<TR ALIGN=LEFT> <TD>1/2 lb. (1 stick) </TD> <TD> margarine</TD> </TR>
<TR ALIGN=LEFT> <TD>1/2 lb. (1 stick) <TD> margarine </TR>
```

Captions are useful additions to most tables because they provide an accompanying dialog for the design and often provide users with instructions for the table's manipulation. Captions can range from witty remarks to titles and include any information that you want your readers to be aware of but that didn't fit within your table outline. Since tables are often introduced by a textual paragraph, captions often work well when aligned with the bottom of the figure, providing balance for the page. The default for caption alignment is align=top so to align to the bottom, type the following commands after the <TABLE> tag:

```
<CAPTION ALIGN=BOTTOM>This is the caption</CAPTION>
```

Tables on the Web

The Web is full of tables; in fact, they're everywhere you click. When they're well designed, they can make the difference between something boring and predictable and something that stands out as innovative and exciting. Here we'll look at a number of examples.

Although we've looked at some fairly plain samples throughout this HTML exercise, tables do not have to be static. In fact, the great thing about tables is that you can incorporate almost any Web function into cells, rows, and columns, creating a vibrant, active page that attracts and keeps readers' attention. HTML tables can include links, graphics, lists, forms, imagemaps, audio and visual files, and even other tables, But instead of reading about it, fire up your browser and follow along with Figures 17.4–17.8 on this WWW table tour.

TIP. *Remember—if you want to see just how the author of a page created a table, click on View Source. If you are using Netscape Gold 2.0, this will produce a new browser window that gives the complete HTML representation of the page.*

Figure 17.4

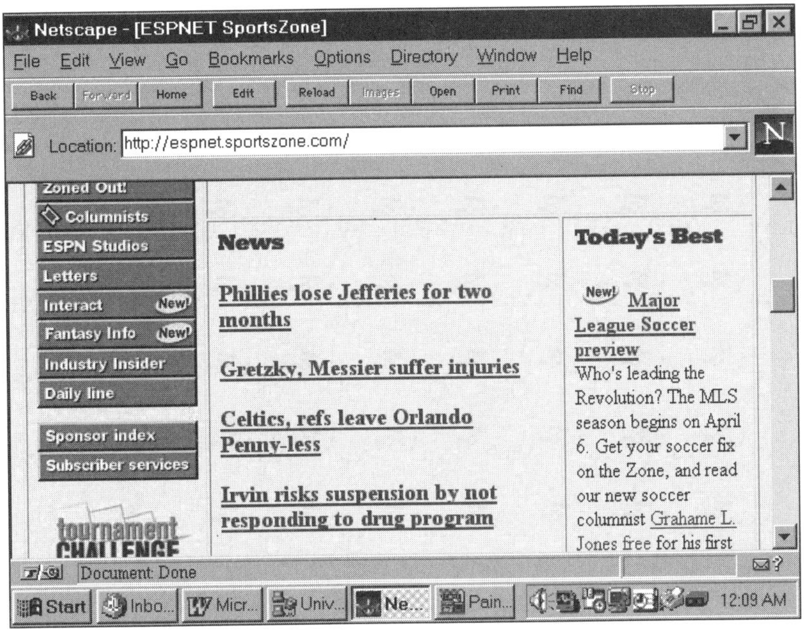

The ESPN Sports Page adopts the table format as the structural foundation for its main contents page, pushing the Web's current table applications to their limits in the process. This site makes evident the extreme differences between standard, static, word-processing type tables and their electronic counterparts. If you think this style might give your own pages that certain something that they're currently missing, examine the document's source code and modify the style to suit your personal communication needs. No, I did not just advise you to steal someone else's handiwork.

Figure 17.5

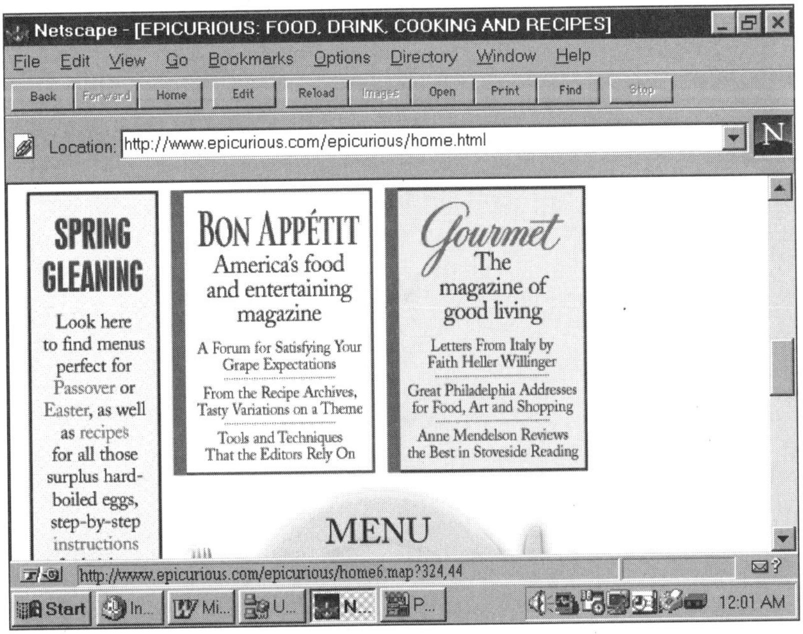

The Epicurious home page uses a table structure to provide users with a multimedia magazine-style document with thorough yet concise details of the archive's contents. The Epicurious page is updated daily but the basic format of the page usually remains the same. The issue featured here uses three separate table commands to produce the final document and shows the benefits of incorporating links, graphics, and imagemaps within table cells.

Figure 17.6

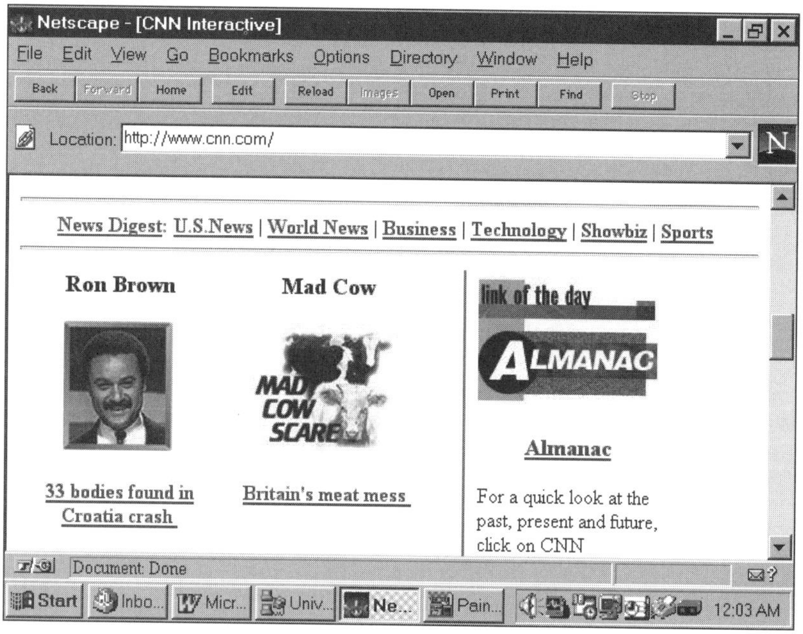

CNN Interactive uses a simple table to display the various sections of the archive, organizing their readers' options in a bold, graphic manner that attracts attention and makes them move. Tables like this one shift the reader's focus from the textual paragraphs on the page, encouraging us to browse the qualities, choose one that interests us, and click on it. Note the effect of the plain background and simplistic use of color—sometimes less is more effective. With smaller tables, cells are closer together and require a more moderate use of color, texture, and fonts in order to avoid clutter.

Figure 17.7

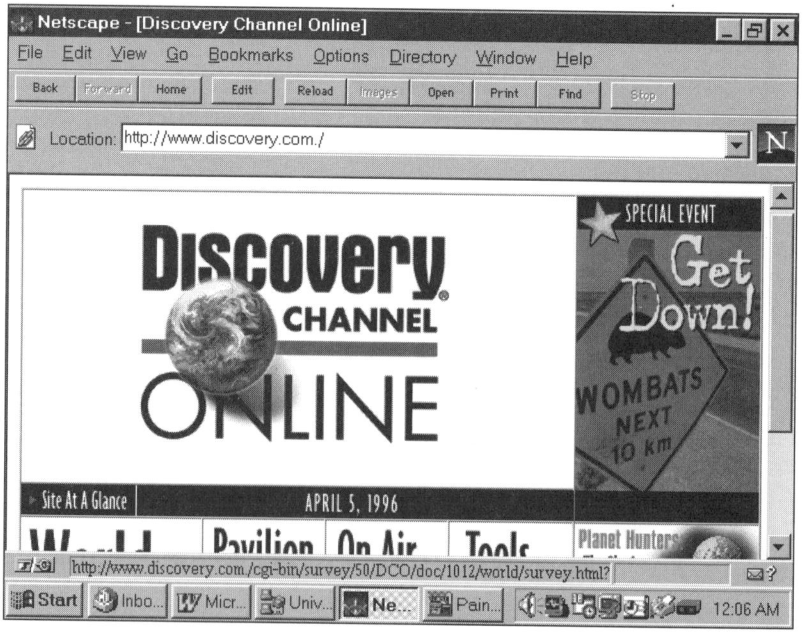

One interesting effect of table use is that it allows us to print large quantities of information on a single screen. In theory, with functions like linking, imagemaps, and graphics at our disposal, no HTML page should span more than a single screen. No one wants to wait while a lengthy page downloads, and it is even more frustrating when you have to scroll through numerous screens before you find a link that interests you. The Discovery Channel's home page table shows how effective single screen layouts can be when tables are used to display information.

Figure 17.8

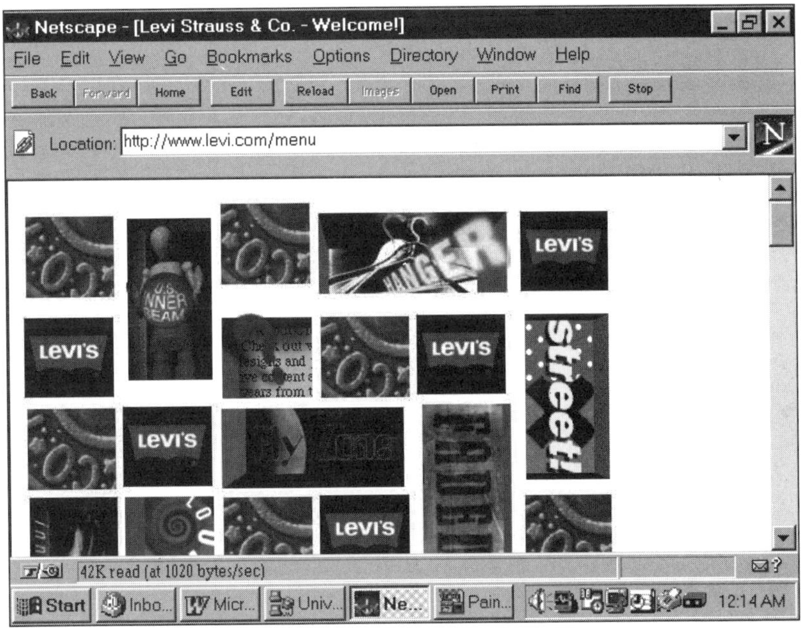

The Levi Strauss company home page provides a good example of multimedia table use. In this site, the graphic, video, and linking capabilities capture the reader's attention, enticing them to click on a jean image or a 501 graphic. But behind this mass of visual movement, a table structures the page's layout. Check out this document's source code to see how advanced multimedia capabilities can be incorporated into your own table cells.

- *Forms and Netscape Navigator Gold*
- *Forms and CGI*
- *What Are Online Forms and What Are They Used For?*
- *Design Decisions When Creating Forms*
- *Creating Forms with Raw HTML*
- *Putting It All Together*

- *Multiple Forms*
- *Forms on the Web*

CHAPTER

18

Forms

THOUGH YOU'VE ALREADY EXPLORED LINKS, GRAPHICS, AND TABLES and have practiced the use of these elements in both Netscape Gold and standard HTML format, you've only begun to scratch the surface of possibilities offered by Internet interaction. In fact, links, tables, and graphics do not allow full user-author interaction, focusing instead on the most appropriate means of moving between and through other Web sites. Only by creating forms do you begin to experience the true power of person-to-person electronic communication.

Forms and Netscape Navigator Gold

Future versions of Netscape Navigator Gold will support the creation of forms. For now, you must create forms by using raw HTML, or by installing a table-capable HTML editor. This chapter covers raw HTML only, although several good editors exist that allow reasonably easy forms creation.

To place your created forms into your Gold documents, copy the entire HTML code into the Clipboard, then open the desired document in the Editor window. Place the cursor precisely where you want the form to appear, then choose HTML Tag from the Insert menu. Paste the HTML code into the HTML Tag box, then click OK.

Forms and CGI

In some ways, a form on the Web is exactly like a form in the real world. It consists of fields to enter text, lists of options to check off, and choices to select from. The difference is that a Web form, unlike its paper counterpart, is instantly processed. When you click on the Submit or Send button after completing a form, the information you have entered is immediately sent to another processing program—and that's where CGI scripting takes over.

CGI stands for *Common Gateway Interface*; although grasping the programming techniques involved with this gateway interface can be difficult, the underlying principle of its use is fairly simple. CGI is a standard for interfacing external applications with information servers, such as HTTP or Web servers.

Essentially, you need CGI scripts that can be accessed by the Web daemon to process the information contained in your online form, receive the results of this processing, and display them once again to the client. So, while the actual form is the front-end to Web interactivity, where users enter text and make selections, CGI scripts are the "back-end," where the actual processing of data is performed. This means that while forms are fun to create and constitute an important part of Web interactivity, clicking on a well-designed form without supporting CGI applications will not actually do anything. CGI scripts typically act as the interface between your form and a database of information, and they allow your readers to access that preformed information.

Unfortunately, a book on Netscape Navigator Gold can't deal with the specifics of CGI scripting, any more than it can get into the nitty-gritty details of the Virtual Reality Modeling Language or, for that matter, the design of databases to which your Web forms can link. For information about creating CGI scripts and tying them to your data, see the Ziff-Davis Press book, *How the World Wide Web Works*, by Chris Shipley and Matt Fish.

What Are Online Forms and What Are They Used For?

Since forms not only give your site a professional appeal with interactivity built in but also allow businesses and services to have a real, interactive presence on the Web, they have become one of the hottest single features of Web design. The essence of form's power lies in the different ways that the documents can accept and organize the user's input. Including forms in your Web site moves Web creation from the static realm of one-way presentation to the dynamics of interactive relationships.

Forms have a number of functions on the Web, ranging from simple feedback or commentary pages to full-fledged purchase order forms. In fact, one of the primary uses of forms on the Web lies with electronic consumer shopping opportunities. Figure 18.1 shows an example of form implementation by Marketplace MCI.

Figure 18.1

marketplaceMCI is one of the Net's leading commerce sites, offering users membership privileges and innumerable shopping opportunities.

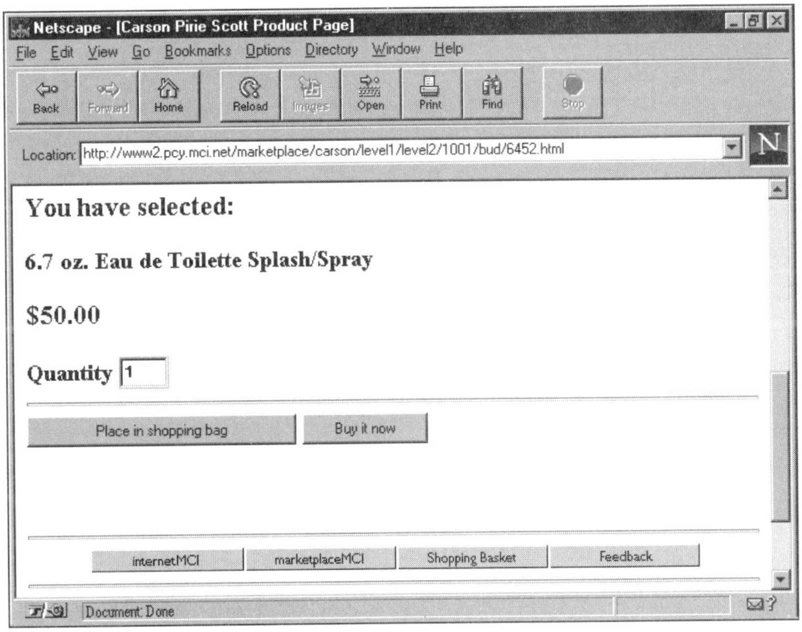

Despite its slow start, shopping on the Web continues to show great promise, and its growth is predicted to be strong once consumers begin to feel more secure about sending their credit card numbers over the Net (or once an alternative payment scheme becomes standard). As the Net's capabilities continue to expand, more and more companies are taking advantage of real-time commerce.

Most shopping malls work something like this. The store provides a small graphic and brief description of products and services that may be viewed by potential buyers all over the world, similar to mail order catalogs of the past. Buyers then indicate that they wish to purchase one or more of the particular item, and the mall places the product(s) in an imaginary shopping basket. Some more advanced Web store designs even provide a running cash total so that users are constantly aware of the total cost of their purchases. To see exactly how this shopping basket effect works go to the Netscape General Store at http://merchant.netscape.com/ and enter the bazaar for software sites.

Before you end your shopping experience, stores will require some assurance of payment, and this is where forms come in. Usually, shoppers submit a credit card number along with other personal information in an online form, which is immediately processed and maintained for future shopping excursions. For buyer protection and privacy, most commerce sites on the Web transmit information through a secure Web server such as Netscape's Commerce Server, meaning that the information is more or less safe from all but the best hackers.

However, shopping is only one of many possibilities for form use. Forms are also used

- To book hotels, send flowers, and make travel arrangements
- For feedback, opinion polls, surveys, and questionnaires
- In search mechanisms, order forms, and guest books

In reality, forms can be used on any Web page that requires the transmission of data from one recipient to the author or manager of the Web site. One example of the use of search forms appears on the All in One Search Page (see Figure 18.2), which offers a wide variety of simple interfaces to the Net's many search engines.

Design Decisions When Creating Forms

Forms range from single, one-item elements like search mechanisms to the complex pages required for service registration or questionnaire-style information. Learning to create even the most complex forms using Netscape Gold or any HTML editor is a simple matter of becoming familiar with basic tools and tags; what's more important than all of these technical factors is how you manipulate them. Your personal design decisions can make the difference between a welcoming, helpful page and a boring, static screen.

Figure 18.2

Search forms are one of the Web's most efficient and accurate uses of form principles. The All-in-One Search Page shows how clear and concise various means of requesting data can be.

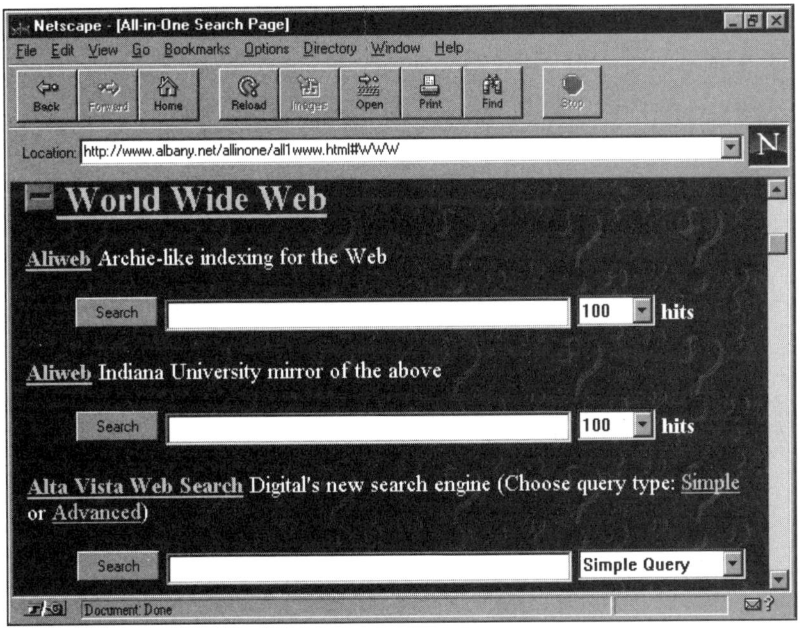

These are a few key issues that you should keep in mind when designing all forms, along with simple rules that help to make your forms inviting and useful.

1. Introduce yourself to your audience. Small explanatory phrases next to the form elements help readers immediately to determine exactly what you are asking and often result in more precise and accurate submissions.
2. Make use of white space. The space *between* fields offers room for introductory material, and can keep your forms readable.
3. Group information into classes. Sort all the information about a single subject in the same place and construct each field in proportion to the data you're requesting. Give readers enough room to supply the information that you are requesting without wasting space.
4. Use a logically progressive style. Ensure that the layout of your form requests appears in a naturally augmenting order, preferably starting with something familiar.

Perhaps the most important design issue of all concerns the size and length of your online forms. Since you are inviting Internet users to participate in your Web activity and consequently taking up some of their valuable online time, you must constantly be aware of the length of your forms and the time required to complete them. If faced with pages of registration information or screens requesting personal information or commentary, most users will opt to skip the process entirely. To avoid driving your readers away, request only that information which you specifically require in order to perform the function that your Web page was constructed to fulfill. Coupled with concise, accurate wording and the general principles of design discussed throughout this chapter, your forms will become active, inviting documents.

Creating Forms with Raw HTML

Creating a form using standard HTML codes and tags is a test of patience that requires the same type of tedious practice as tables. Most current Web editors that even consider offering forms as a functional element use advanced design systems with built-in tags and codes and automatic generation. However, since this type of form support is not yet available on some Web editors, and not until a later version of Gold, it's necessary to start from scratch and make your own interactive documents from scratch.

There are four standard form tags:

FORM	<FORM> </FORM>	The FORM container specifies where a form begins and ends as well as where the information inserted into the form will be sent.
INPUT	<INPUT> </INPUT>	INPUT containers accept up to six different input fields.
SELECT	<SELECT> </SELECT>	This container allows users increased selectivity by establishing a predefined list of options to choose from.
TEXTAREA	<TEXTAREA> </TEXTAREA>	The TEXTAREA container allows users to insert free-form text in an open-ended edit field.

A combination of these essential elements is all that you need to create fully functional forms for online use. However, just as the basic table elements hold different attributes, so do the form elements; this makes things more complex.

The FORM Container

The <FORM> and </FORM> tags contain all other form-related information, meaning that in order for additional form elements or attributes to contribute to the effect of your document, they must be contained between the opening <FORM> tag and the closing </FORM> tag. It's good practice to make these two tags the first thing you type in your Web editor, to avoid nonfunctional documents—remember that if one part of the FORM element is missing, nothing will work.

TIP. *In HTML, forms are not visually differentiated from the rest of a document; therefore, consider using the HR (horizontal rule) tag before and after a form to cleanly distinguish it from surrounding text and/or other forms.*

The FORM element can hold three main attributes—ACTION, METHOD, and ENCTYPE—which define where and how the form contents will be manipulated.

ACTION defines the URL of the query server to which the form contents will be submitted. If this attribute is absent, the current document URL will be substituted. The ACTION attribute is inserted in the following manner:

```
<FORM ACTION="URL"> insert form contents here </FORM>
```

The URL entry for the ACTION attribute specifies the location of a CGI script which will then take over the operation and functioning of the form data.

The METHOD attribute represents the HTTP/1.0 method used to submit the fill-out form to a query server. Inevitably, the method you choose depends on how your particular server works and how the CGI script you are sending the information to is written (a good CGI program will handle both).

Although your form will function correctly even without defining the METHOD element, it is a good idea to be as specific as possible throughout all of your Web creation projects and avoid relying on defaults that may become invalid in the future. The current METHOD attributes are

- GET—this is the default method and causes the fill-out form contents to be appended to the URL as if they were a normal query.
- POST—this method causes the fill-out form contents to be sent to the server in a data body rather than as part of the URL.

While GET is the simpler of the two METHOD attributes, it limits the amount of data that can be sent, usually to less than 1K. POST allows much more information to be transmitted, so if you anticipate that a larger amount of data will be generated by your form, you should use the POST method. Given the way many servers (for example, NCSA httpd) pass query strings from URLs to query server scripts, you run an excellent chance of having your form's contents truncated by hardcoded shell command argument lengths when using the GET method. With POST, you should be able to do a total end-run around such problems.

The METHOD option is used inside the FORM tag like this:

```
<FORM METHOD="POST"> insert form contents here </FORM>
```

Using both the ACTION and METHOD options within the opening FORM element looks something like

```
<FORM ACTION="URL" METHOD="POST"> insert form contents here </FORM>
```

or

```
<FORM ACTION="URL" METHOD="POST"> insert form contents here </FORM>
```

ENCTYPE specifies the encoding for the fill-out form contents. This attribute only applies if METHOD is set to POST, and even then, there is only one possible value (the default, application/x-www-form-urlencoded) so far.

When the submit button is pressed, the contents of the form will be assembled into a query URL, but remember that so far all you've done is direct the form contents to a specific CGI script in a specific manner. Now it's time to create the form itself.

The INPUT Tag

Form creators use the INPUT tag to specify a simple input element inside a FORM. INPUT is a standalone tag rather than a container, meaning that it does not surround anything and there is no terminating tag.

INPUT can be used to create six different input methods: TEXT, PASSWORD, CHECKBOX, RADIO, SUBMIT, and RESET. Each input method is specified by the TYPE attribute and all other options to INPUT are based on TYPE's value. The attributes to INPUT are given below.

TYPE must be one of the following:

- Text—text entry field; this is the default.
- Password—text entry field where entered characters are represented as asterisks.
- Checkbox—single-toggle button, on or off.
- Radio—single-toggle button, on or off; other toggles with the same NAME are grouped into "one of many" behavior.
- Submit—push-button that causes the current form to be packaged up into a query URL and sent to a remote server.
- Reset—push-button that causes the various input elements in the form to be reset to their default values

Other attributes within the INPUT tag include NAME, VALUE, CHECKED, SIZE, and MAXLENGTH.

- NAME is the symbolic name for the input field. This must be present for all types except for "submit" and "reset," and is used when putting together the query string that gets sent to the remote server after submission of the filled-out form.
- VALUE specifies the default contents for a text or password entry field. For a checkbox or a radio button, VALUE specifies the value of the button only when it is checked (unchecked checkboxes are disregarded when submitting queries), and the default value for a checkbox or radio button is "on." For types "submit" and "reset," VALUE can be used to specify the label for the push-button.
- CHECKED (no value needed) specifies that a checkbox or radio button has been checked by default.
- SIZE is the physical size of the input field in characters, and is only appropriate for text and password entry fields. The default value for SIZE is 20. Multiline text entry fields may be specified by the pattern SIZE=width,height—for example, SIZE=60,12. However, the SIZE attribute should never be used to specify multiline text entry fields now that the TEXTAREA tag is available.
- MAXLENGTH is the maximum number of characters that are accepted as input. The MAXLENGTH attribute is only appropriate for single-line text entry fields and password-entry fields. By default, the MAXLENGTH value will be unlimited. If MAXLENGTH is bigger than SIZE, the text field will scroll to allow the user to enter more data.

Single-Line Input Fields

If you specify the text option for the INPUT field, you will create a one-line text input field that resembles a single line of the TEXTAREA field that we will create later in this chapter. To construct a fully functional single-line input field you must identify the NAME, SIZE, MAXLENGTH, and VALUE.

```
Please enter your favorite color:
<INPUT TYPE="TEXT" NAME="color" SIZE="15" MAXLENGTH="13" VALUE="blue">
```

This simple one-line text field produces the screen shown in Figure 18.3.

Password Security with Hidden Transmission

When online forms request that users submit information that could be misused if placed in the wrong hands, such as passwords, increased security measures must be taken to protect the privacy of the individual user.

For this reason, characters typed into the Password field are hidden, visible only as asterisks on the screen. But this does not mean that your password is secure when transmitted across the Net. Once you press the Submit button

Figure 18.3

Requesting information such as first or last names or favorite colors can be represented easily by single-line textual fields such as this.

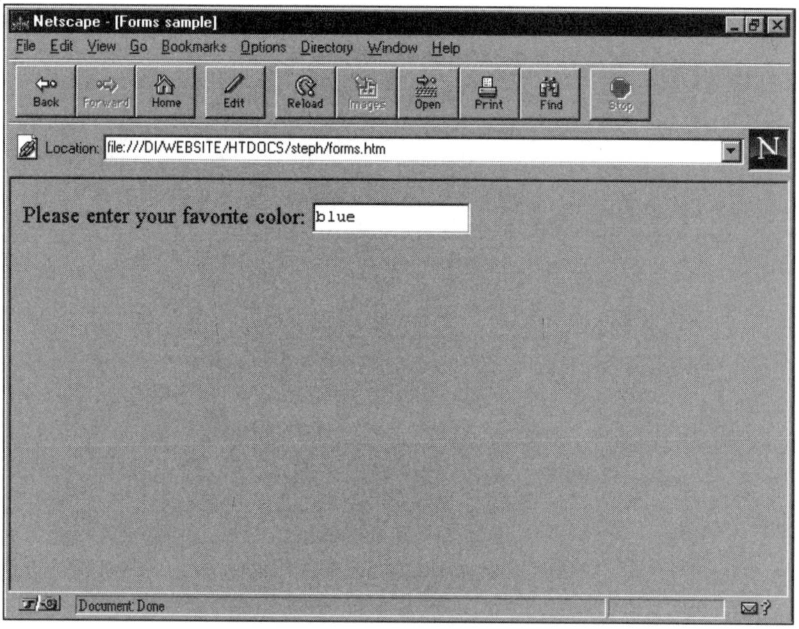

on any fill-out form, the data you have entered flow throughout the Internet's channels as plain uncoded text accessible to anyone with the knowledge and willpower to access your entry.

All other aspects of the Password field exactly resemble the single-line text field.

```
Insert your password:
<INPUT TYPE="PASSWORD" NAME="pass" SIZE="8" MAXLENGTH="8">
```

This simple HTML code produces the image shown in Figure 18.4.

Standard Checkboxes

Most yes/no type questions included in online fill-out forms are presented in standard checkbox format with an on/off or yes/no toggle switch. CHECKBOX takes three attributes—NAME, VALUE, and CHECKED—although VALUE is frequently omitted so that the default value dominates.

```
Select the items you take in your coffee:
<INPUT TYPE="CHECKBOX" NAME="cream" CHECKED> Cream
<INPUT TYPE="CHECKBOX" NAME="sugar" CHECKED> Sugar
<INPUT TYPE="CHECKBOX" NAME="white"> Whitener
```

This HTML code produces the screen shown in Figure 18.5.

Figure 18.4

Type your own password into the Password field to verify that all characters appear as asterisks on screen.

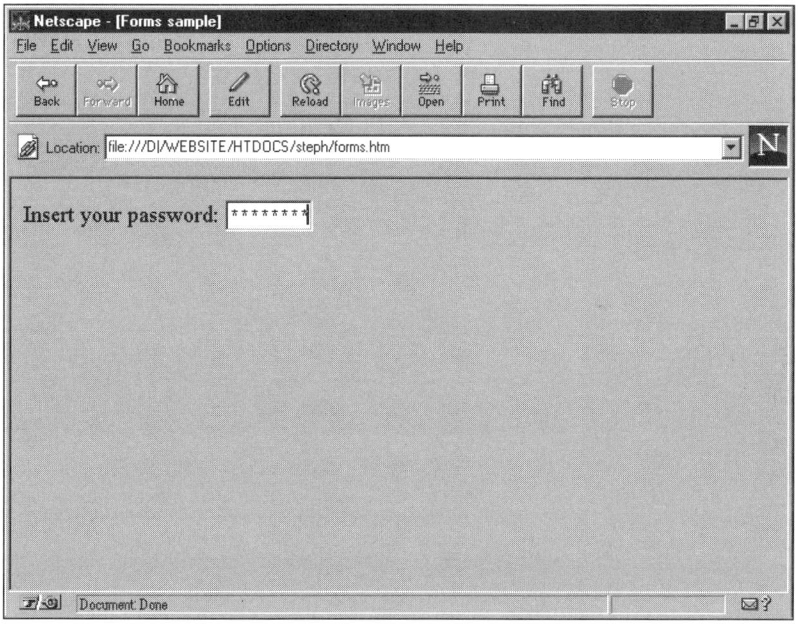

Figure 18.5

Checkboxes are great for yes/no questions and make filling out online forms easier and less demanding for audiences.

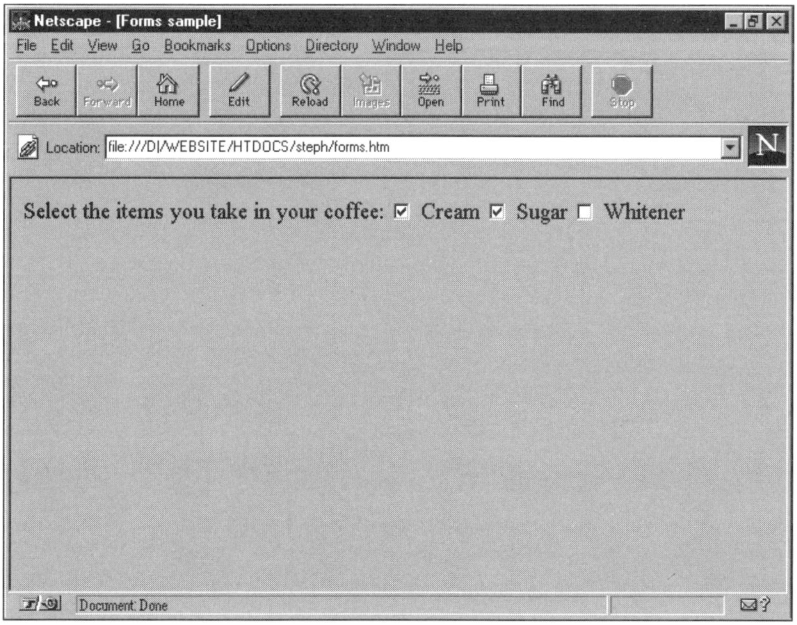

Narrowing Your Options

Checkboxes allow users to check or turn on as many items in a predefined list as they wish. However, some data require that only one option or toggle group be selected at a time, and this function is controlled by radio buttons. All RADIOs in a single form that share a NAME are considered members of a single group. If one button in the group is selected by a reader, any other button already chosen will be *deselected*, or turned off. This performs exactly the same function as the MULTIPLE SELECT option when it is *not* included in an HTML form.

```
Select your favorite flavor of ice-cream:
<INPUT TYPE="RADIO" NAME="ice-cream" VALUE="chocolate" CHECKED> Chocolate
<INPUT TYPE="RADIO" NAME="ice-cream" VALUE="vanilla"> Vanilla
<INPUT TYPE="RADIO" NAME="ice-cream" VALUE="strawberry"> Strawberry
<INPUT TYPE="RADIO" NAME="ice-cream" VALUE="heaven"> Heavenly Hash
```

This HTML code produces the screen of options shown in Figure 18.6.

Figure 18.6

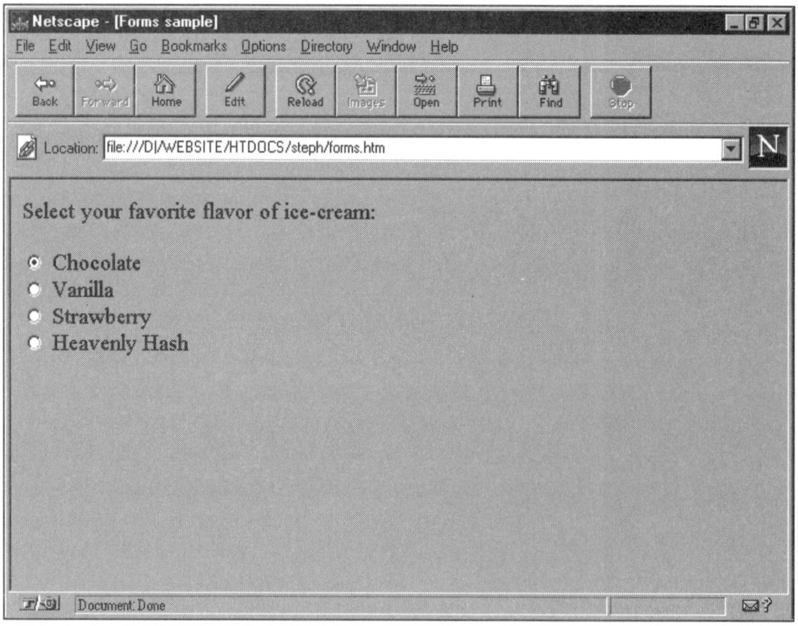

Although chocolate and strawberry are my two all-time favorite flavors of ice cream, radio buttons allow only one item to be checked at a time. Clicking on the strawberry button after chocolate was already checked would erase the chocolate selection, changing it to strawberry.

OOPS!!—The Reset Button

Inevitably, users will make mistakes or change their minds about information they have entered in their fill-out form; if the errors are large enough, it is often convenient to simply clear the entire form and begin again. RESET

TYPE produces a button that clears the screen of all typed entries and returns the form to its default positions, allowing users to retype their information.

Reset's only attribute is VALUE, an option which holds the text you want to insert with the Reset button.

```
<INPUT TYPE="RESET" VALUE="Press this button to reset the form to its
default positions.">
```

This HTML-coded sample produces the image shown in Figure 18.7.

Figure 18.7

A simple line of text augments this portion of the online fill-out form and informs readers of the button's function.

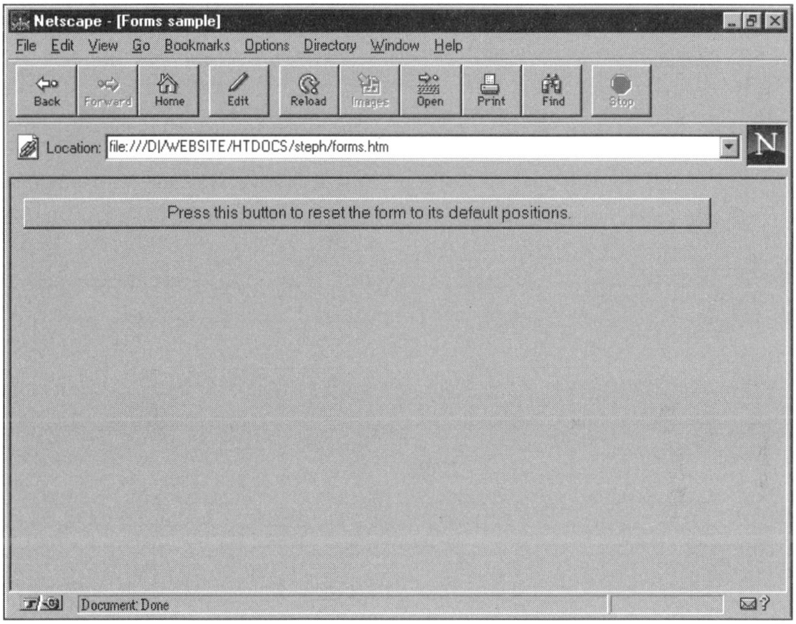

If VALUE is omitted from RESET TYPE, the default word "reset" will be substituted.

```
<INPUT TYPE="RESET">
```

The Submit Button

All of the buttons, fields, and boxes that you have been creating throughout this chapter are tools for identifying and retrieving information from your Internet audience. But what all of this data-gathering has been working up to is the Submit button. Once a form is filled in, users must press the Submit or Send button to transfer their entries to a CGI script where they will be processed. When the Submit button is pressed, the contents of the form will be assembled into a query URL and sent according to the METHOD attributes you included in the FORM element.

```
<INPUT TYPE="SUBMIT" VALUE="Press here to submit your input">
```

This coded sample produces the screen shown in Figure 18.8.

Figure 18.8

All forms must include a Submit or Send button which transfers data to the CGI script for processing.

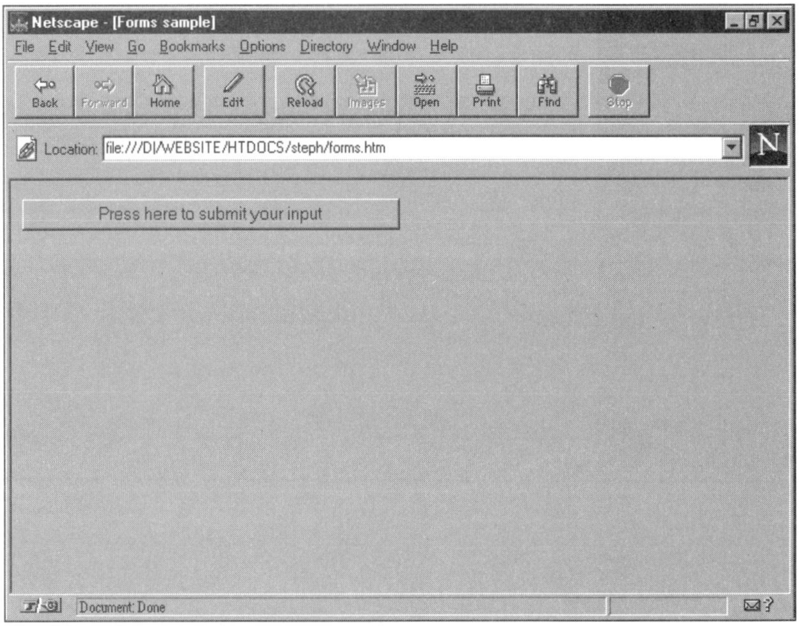

A SUBMIT element is not necessary in forms containing only a single INPUT element of type TEXT, in which case, pressing Return in the text entry area submits the form, or in forms containing at least one INPUT element of type IMAGE, in which case a click in the image submits the form.

The SELECT Tag

Though TEXTAREA allows Web authors to insert a multiline text entry field with optional default contents in a fill-out form, sometimes it is more practical to allow users to choose a specific number of options from a predetermined list. You may have seen this application in a number of Web sites which request users to rate a certain product or aspect of their work according to Poor, Good, or Very Good options.

The SELECT element acts as a container with both opening and closing tags. Within the <SELECT> and </SELECT> tags, users may add a sequence of OPTION tags, each followed by an arbitrary amount of plain text. A standard SELECT code follows this basic style:

```
<SELECT NAME="a-menu">
<OPTION> First option.
<OPTION> Second option.
</SELECT>
```

Here is a simple example of how you can use the SELECT element within your own form pages:

```
<FORM METHOD="GET">
Which type of animal do you prefer?:
<SELECT NAME="animals">
<OPTION>dogs
<OPTION>cats
<OPTION>birds
</SELECT>
</FORM>
```

Inside the <FORM> and </FORM> tags, any number of SELECT tags may be intermixed freely with other HTML elements including INPUT and TEXTAREA elements and text but excluding additional forms.

The attributes to SELECT include NAME, SIZE, and MULTIPLE.

- NAME is a mandatory attribute that holds the symbolic name for the SELECT element. The NAME value is used when assembling the query string for the submitted form.
- SIZE determines the height of the list of selections that will be displayed to users. If the SIZE value is set at 1 or if the SIZE attribute is excluded from the SELECT element entirely, SELECT will be represented as a Motif option menu or pop-up display. If the SIZE value is set at 2 or more, SELECT will be represented as a Motif scrolled list.
- MULTIPLE takes no value but, if included, indicates that the SELECT element allows multiple selections at one time. The presence of MULTIPLE forces the SELECT element to be represented as a Motif scrolled list, regardless of the SIZE value. If excluded from the SELECT attributes, users are required to make only one choice from the list of predefined options.

The OPTION tag defines each individual choice that the user will see and is only recognized inside a <SELECT></SELECT> pair. OPTION does not have to function as a container; that is, an OPTION's text does not need to be closed with </OPTION>, though it's always a good idea to maintain consistency and add the closing tag anyway.

OPTION takes only the SELECTED and VALUE attributes. SELECTED specifies that a certain option (usually the most common selection) is to be selected as default. If the SELECT element allows multiple selections (via the MULTIPLE attribute), multiple options may also be specified as SELECTED.

The VALUE attribute is what will be associated with the NAME if its option is chosen by the user. The CGI script uses the VALUE attribute to identify or label the option chosen. If omitted, the text that follows OPTION is inserted as a default value.

The Net is full of forms that include the SELECT tag as the primary means of gathering information from a variety of rather impatient readers. In the Computerama site, Web authors have used the SELECT form to list options that the user must choose from when filling out the mailing list application form.

This HTML code, taken from the Computerama site, produces Figure 18.9.

```
<SELECT NAME="mail" >
<OPTION>Yes
<OPTION>No</SELECT> I want to be on your mailing list.
```

Figure 18.9

Use the SELECT option to present yes/no options throughout your mailing list registration form.

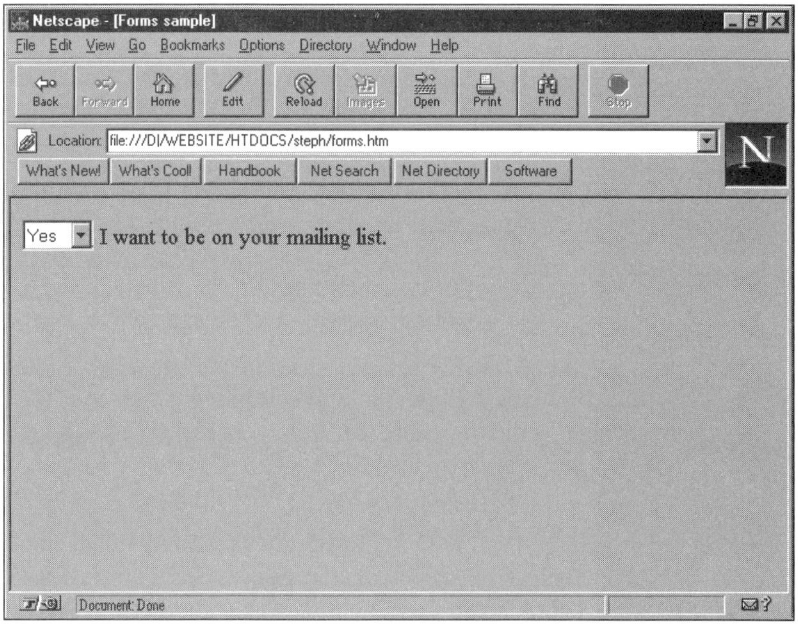

TEXTAREA

Like the FORM tag, the TEXTAREA element is used as a container for data and therefore requires both an opening and a closing tag, represented by <TEXTAREA> and </TEXTAREA>. The TEXTAREA tags can be used to place a multiline text entry field with optional default contents in a fill-out form.

A TEXTAREA with no default contents looks like this:

```
<TEXTAREA NAME="foo" ROWS=4 COLS=40></TEXTAREA>
```

A TEXTAREA with default contents looks like this:

```
<TEXTAREA NAME="foo" ROWS=4 COLS=40> Default contents go here </TEXTAREA>
```

As you can see above, the attributes to TEXTAREA include NAME, ROWS, and COLUMNS. The NAME of the TEXTAREA is the symbolic name of the text entry field and is paired with the contents of the area when the user submits the form. The NAME attribute is mandatory since this is how the CGI script identifies the control and retrieves its value.

The other two options, ROWS and COLS, define the size of the TEXTAREA in character heights and widths. ROWS represents the number of rows (vertical height in characters) of the text entry field, while COLS represents the number of columns (horizontal width in characters) of the same field. If excluded, the ROWS default value becomes 1 and COLS is set to 20.

The TEXTAREA option maintains a fixed-width font with all line breaks preserved to allow more control over the general appearance of the element. Here is a basic sample form that makes use of the TEXTAREA element without adding any attributes:

```
<FORM ACTION="/cgi-bin/form.sh" METHOD="POST">
Insert your comment here:<BR>
<TEXTAREA>I love your site!</TEXTAREA>
</FORM>
```

This HTML code produces the screen displayed in Figure 18.10.

The following HTML code makes use of all of the attributes discussed in this section:

```
<FORM ACTION="/cgi-bin/form.sh" METHOD="POST">
Let us know what you think:<BR>
<TEXTAREA NAME=COMMENT ROWS=50 COLS=70>
You have some great design strategies that I will use in my future Web
projects!
</TEXTAREA>
</FORM>
```

This HTML sample code produces Figure 18.11.

Figure 18.10

Default text should resemble the style and type of message that you expect from your readers.

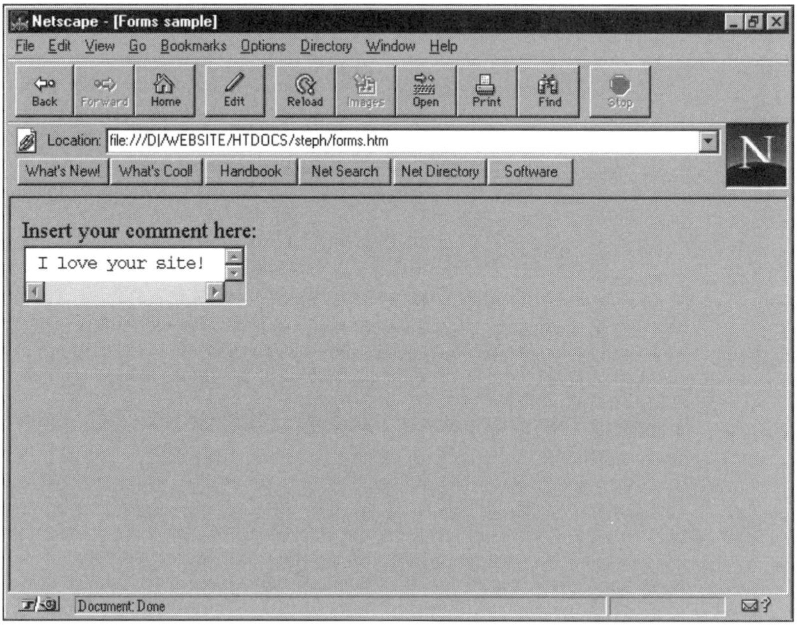

Figure 18.11

This TEXTAREA field allows users to type over the rather enthusiastic default columns in a TEXTAREA that is 50 rows long and 70 columns wide. The CGI script will identify this element by its NAME, which is *Comment.*

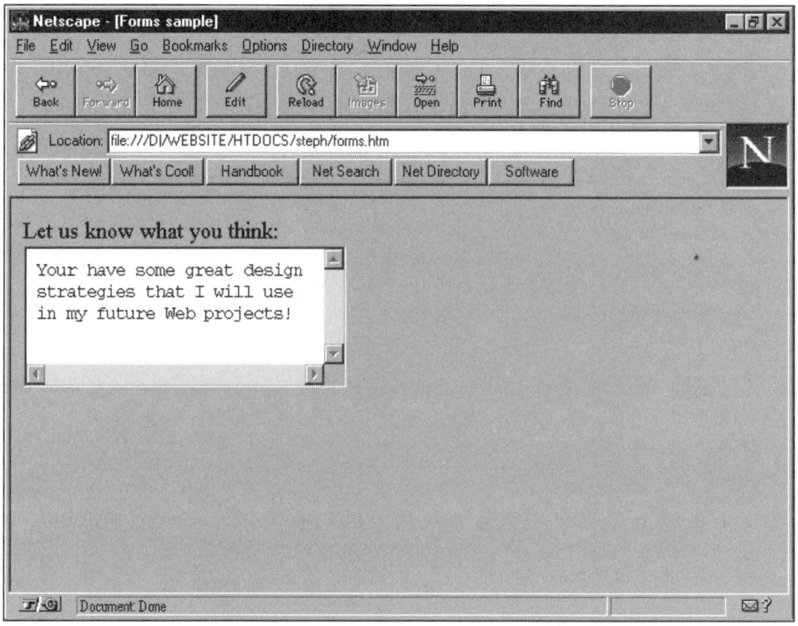

Since you can never anticipate the exact amount of room required for users to submit their comments or opinions, the ROWS and COLS attributes appended to the TEXTAREA element only regulate the size of the TEXTAREA field on your browser screen. If users type more text either vertically or horizontally within the field, scroll bars automatically appear to extend the number of rows and columns. In this way, the TEXTAREA element allows flexible, versatile, user-reader interaction.

Putting It All Together

With all these HTML codes firmly entrenched in your brain, creating your own forms using standard HTML code is now just a simple matter of putting everything you have learned together in an appealing and unique format. All forms differ according to the individual needs of their authors, and so no two documents are identical. Use the tools from this chapter to shape and reshape your forms until you find the format that best suits the information you are gathering and the audience you are attracting.

If you have spent any time at all surfing the Net, you have undoubtedly come across some type of registration or order forms, some of which are quite ingenious. To see how the authors of these form pages created such striking or attractive material, simply click on the View Source command contained in your browser menu and examine the HTML code. In fact, you may even copy the more complex codes or the entire source and tailor it to your own specific needs while maintaining some of the standard form entries.

Forms open up a new realm of design possibilities and the following section will teach you some of the more popular, easy-to-learn strategies employed by Web authors on the Internet.

The
 Tag

As with all HTML elements, the line breaks that you insert in your Web editor with the Return or Enter key are not preserved in the actual WWW presentation on your browser. To augment your design and provide aesthetics rather than standard HTML techniques, control your white space by inserting line breaks in the appropriate positions throughout your HTML codes.

Without line breaks, two input fields will take their default positions.

```
<FORM>
Height in inches: <INPUT TYPE="TEXT" NAME="height" SIZE="5">
Weight in pounds: <INPUT TYPE="TEXT" NAME="weight" SIZE="5">
</FORM>
```

This HTML code produces the screen displayed by Figure 18.12.

The same code with a line break tag (<BR>) inserted after the height input produces Figure 18.13.

Figure 18.12

Form default positions do not always provide the most appealing or appropriate visual displays and often make the form look cluttered and complex.

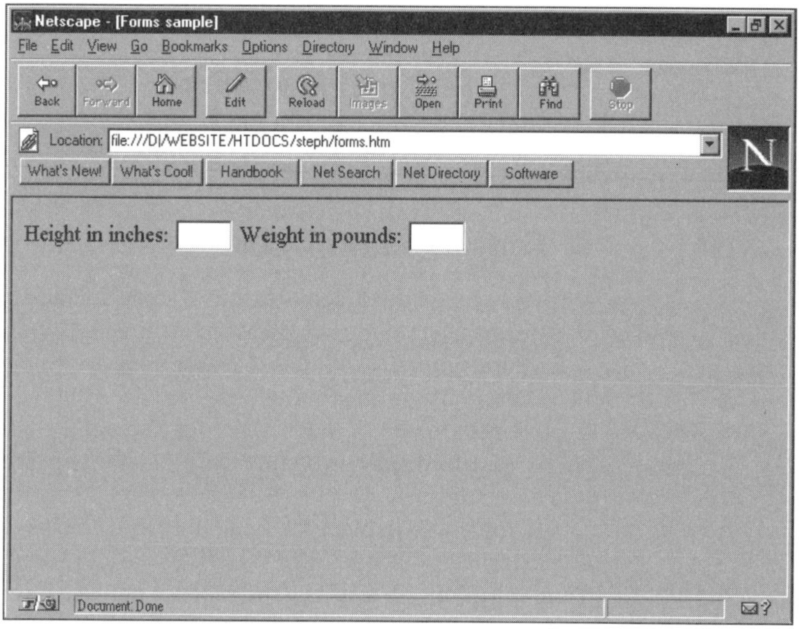

Figure 18.13

Line breaks can make a dramatic difference in the presentation of forms and make the document easier to fill out.

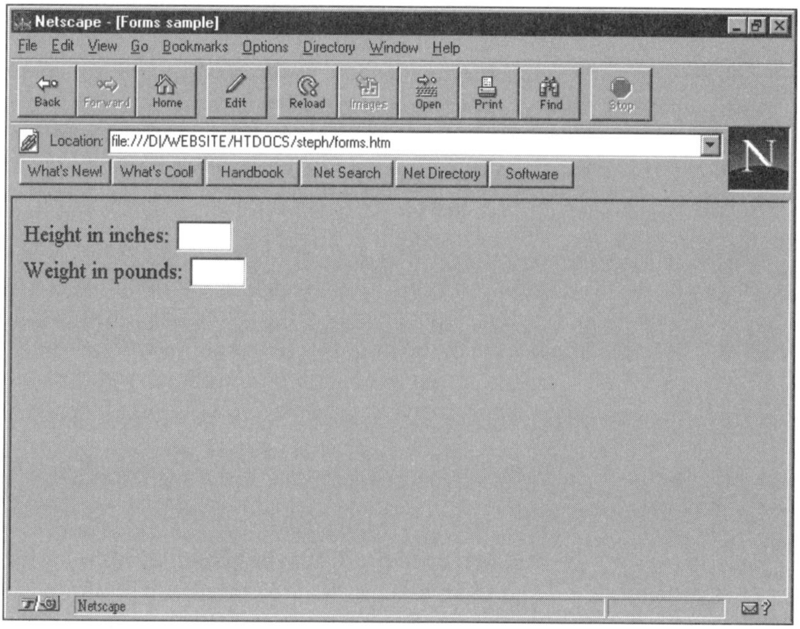

The <P></P> Tags

With the upcoming HTML/3 specification, the paragraph tag <P> will become a container, complimented by the closing </P> tag. Presently, most HTML editors accept either combination, but it's a good idea to become familiar with the new specification for added consistency.

With forms, the paragraph tags provide the same benefits as the line break tag, but instead of simply starting a new line, the paragraph tag inserts a line space before beginning a new line of text. You can see the difference between <BR> and <P></P> in Figures 18.13 and 18.14:

```
<FORM>
<P>Height in inches: <INPUT TYPE="TEXT" NAME="height" SIZE="5"></P>
Weight in pounds: <INPUT TYPE="TEXT" NAME="weight" SIZE="5">
</FORM>
```

This code produces the image displayed by Figure 18.14.

Figure 18.14

The Paragraph tags <P> and </P> mark the beginning and end of a paragraph of HTML codes. A blank space is inserted after the closing tag </P>.

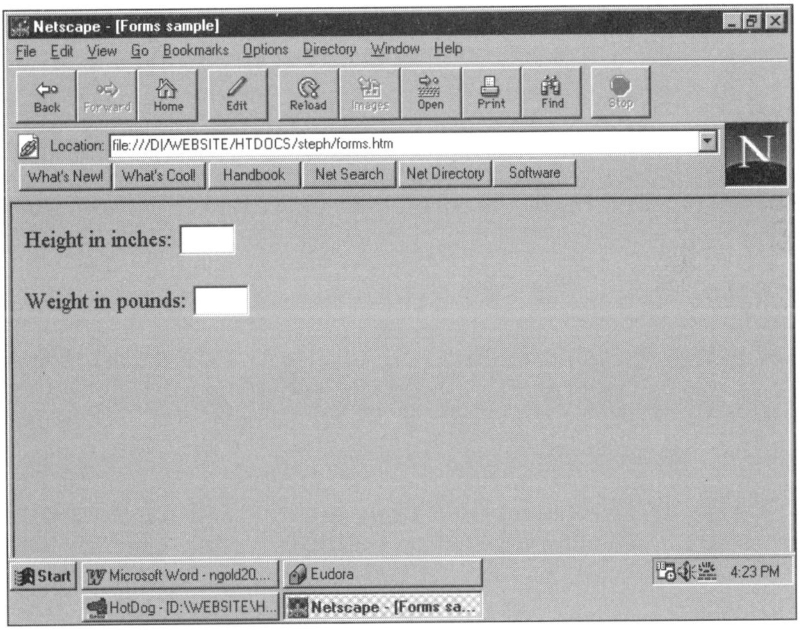

The best form pages on the Web use a combination of both line break and paragraph markers to control white space and separate cluttered text. The best judge of visual aesthetics is the artist's eye; therefore, you as the artist must judge the need for these elements throughout your documents.

The <PRE> Tags

One basic feature of all forms, whether electronic or paper-based, is strict alignment. Form elements almost always align vertically to create precise, linear documents that are easy to read and complete. Once you have inserted your line breaks and paragraph tags, you may notice that your alignment is still jumbled. Consider the following lines of HTML form code:

```
<FORM>
First Name:<INPUT TYPE="TEXT" NAME="first"><BR>
Last Name:<INPUT TYPE="TEXT" NAME="last"><BR>
Street Address:<INPUT TYPE="TEXT" NAME="addr"><BR>
Gender:<INPUT TYPE="RADIO" NAME="sex"> Male
<INPUT TYPE="RADIO" NAME="sex" CHECKED> Female
</FORM>
```

The alignment of HTML codes using the tab button and space bar produces the image shown in Figure 18.15.

Figure 18.15

Although the Web editor respects the tab and space bar inserts, browsers cannot recognize these keyboard attributes and the text lacks all vertical alignment.

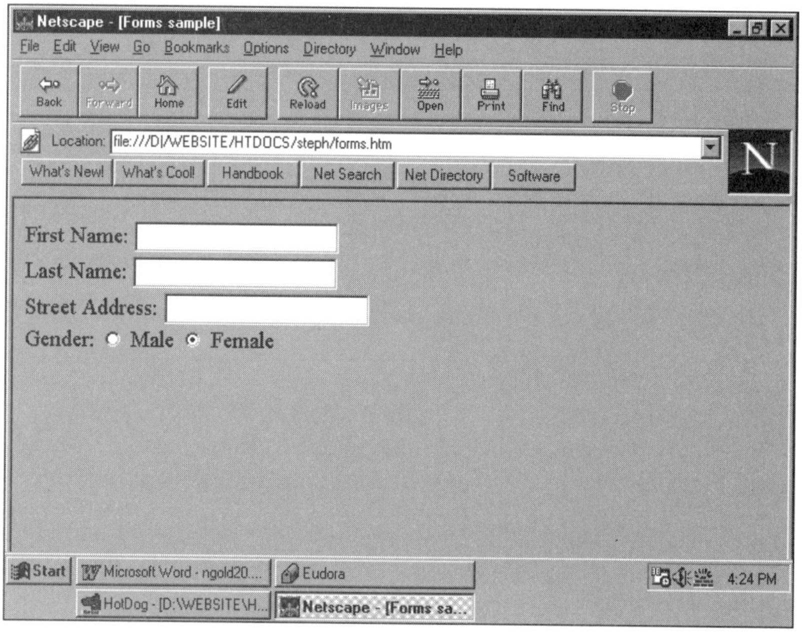

To remedy this situation, make use of the Pre-format or <PRE></PRE> container tags, which force the browser to use a fixed-width font while respecting the layout that you design within the Web editor itself. The above code would become

```
<FORM>
    <PRE>
    First Name:         <INPUT TYPE="TEXT" NAME="first"><BR>
    Last Name:          <INPUT TYPE="TEXT" NAME="last"><BR>
    Street Address:     <INPUT TYPE="TEXT" NAME="addr"><BR>
    Gender:             <INPUT TYPE="RADIO" NAME="gender"> Male
                        <INPUT TYPE="RADIO" NAME="gender" CHECKED> Female

    </PRE>
</FORM>
```

The <PRE> tag preserves all spacing, and because text entry fields also use fixed-width fonts, it would appear that you can create an even right margin by counting spaces, right? Wrong. Unless you limit yourself to precisely the same number of fields per line, and start counting out character and blank spaces, the border and internal padding of each text entry field still widens the line. You can control the vertical alignment of your HTML codes using preformatting techniques and produce Figure 18.16.

Figure 18.16

Appealing vertical alignment is one of the key features performed by the <PRE></PRE> tags throughout online form programming.

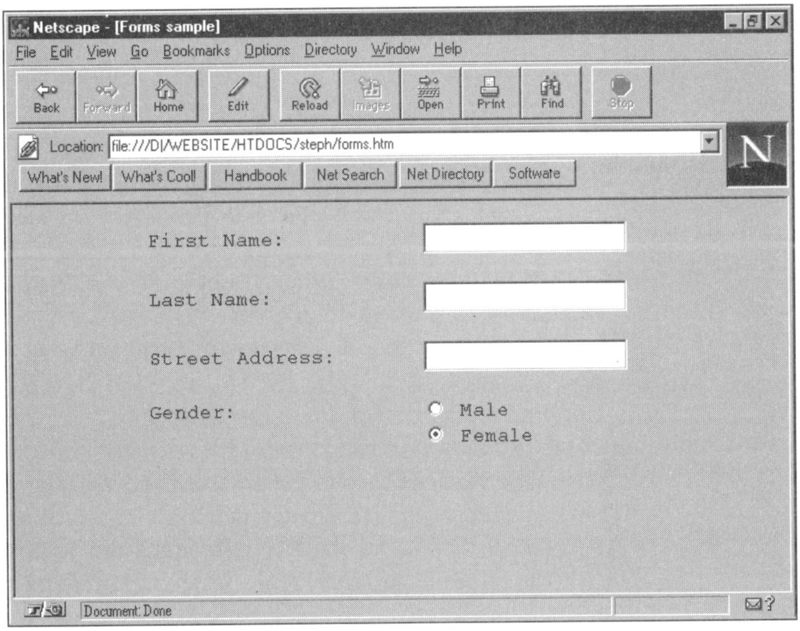

Multiple Forms

Once you have finally grasped all the tools of form creation, it's tempting to use the element repeatedly. However, in most cases, multiple forms on the same page are neither appropriate nor appealing. Web forms must be designed with a specific purpose in mind, and the information gathered by your form should reflect this goal. If your form does not accomplish the task you set out to achieve, the problem probably lies with the type of questions you pose to your audience and should be remedied with new word choice or ordering rather than an additional form.

Revamping your form is not always the answer, and in some isolated incidences, multiple forms are the best means of getting your point across. Multiple forms are appropriate when the forms you are using have only one or two fields and you want to give users a choice of search queries. (A good idea in this case is to insert a divider, such as a horizontal rule, between the forms.)

The biggest technical problem you'll encounter when you attempt to generate multiple forms from a single Web page is that sometimes the forms are presented as a single large form rather than two individual entities. If this happens, you have probably forgotten the </FORM> tag that should appear at the end of the first form to distinguish between the two bodies. Codes become more complex when mixed on the same page, so check and recheck your programming if problems occur.

Forms on the Web

The popularity of forms on the Internet cannot adequately be conveyed without taking a short tour of the Net's primary form users. Remember that at any time throughout this tour or your own Web surfing you may access a site's HTML code and design strategies by clicking on the View Source option in the View menu of most browsers.

The Internet Shopping Network's feedback page (Figure 18.17) provides a simple example of how effective and appealing feedback forms can be. The uncluttered, straightforward requests make it easy for users to give their opinions of the site without costing them a great deal of time or energy. The feedback page includes links back to the archive pages and shopping directories, making navigation throughout the pages automatic and inviting. Short introductory text informs users of the feedback requirements and purpose of the form fields.

The James Gang site (Figure 18.18) is a great location for those of you who are intent on improving the creativity and ingenuity of your forms. This entertainment archive uses the form elements we have discussed throughout this chapter in new and inventive ways to present material in a manner never before seen on the Net. The site presents both the graphic image and the list

Figure 18.17

The Internet Shopping Network's feedback page

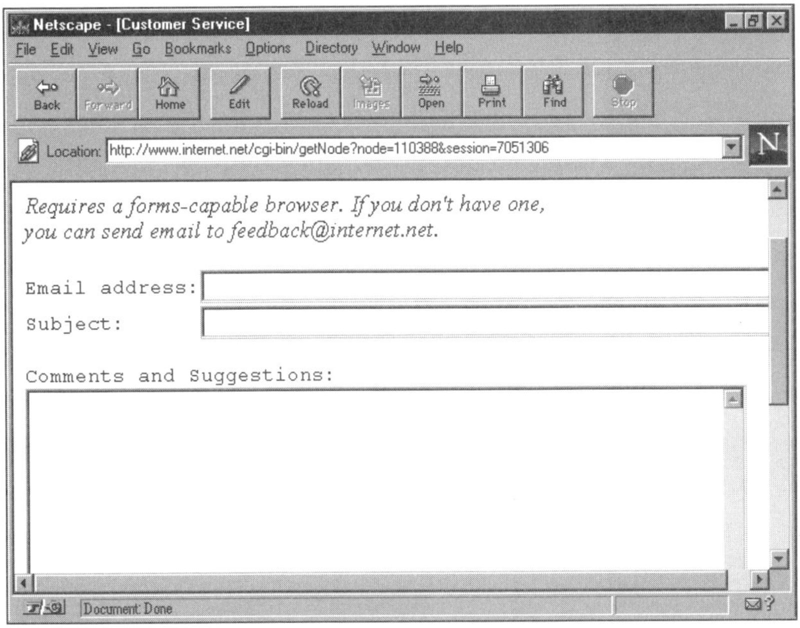

Figure 18.18

The James Gang site

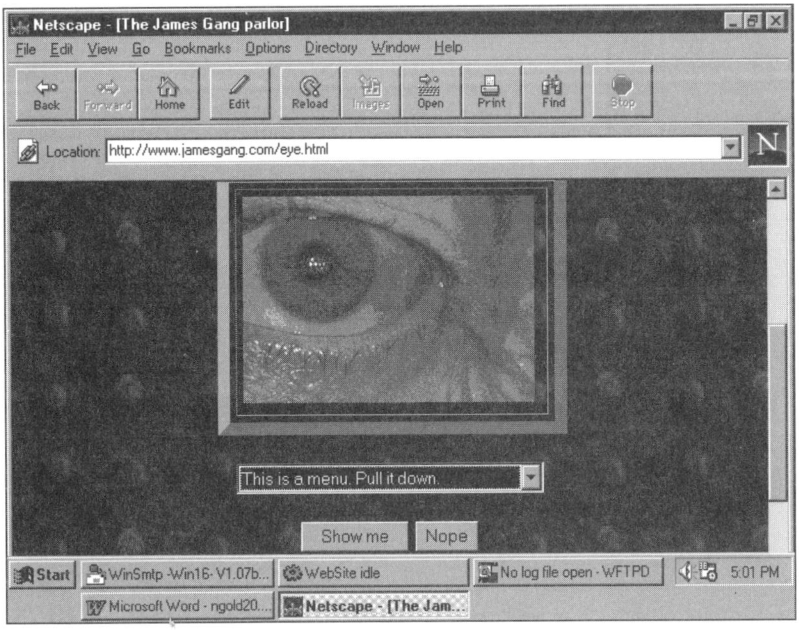

of options inside a form rather than implementing simple hyperlinks to perform the same task. The scrollable menu presents a set of options that are available to the user from this page in the archive. Visitors select the topic area that interests them and then send the information to a CGI script that transports them to the selected page. Notice the use of attention grabbing buttons that branch away from the boring Send and Clear commands commonly used in forms. Browse through the rest of the James Gang site and Nerdheaven to see even more creative uses of standard form elements.

Many sites on the World Wide Web require users to join or register before they are granted full access to all information contained in the archive. The membership form in the HotWired archive (Figure 18.19) presents the standard design and formatting of these registration requirements. This form uses all of the elements we have examined in this chapter in a straightforward, easy-to-use layout that makes it easy for readers to join the organization. Note the introductory and explanatory text as well as the page design. Information is sorted into categories or classes and presented in an organized style that makes efficient use of valuable white space.

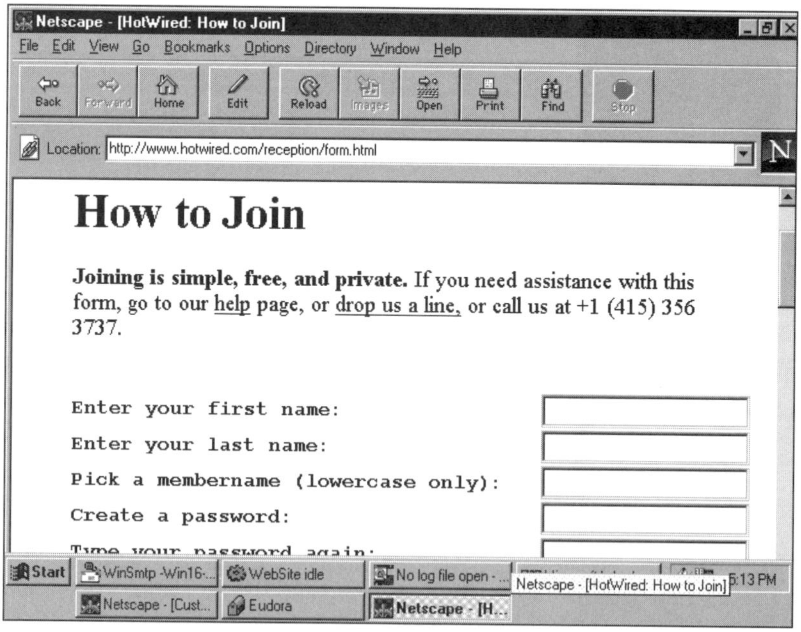

Figure 18.19 HotWired's membership form

Guest books are another popular use of electronic form elements on the Web and function much like feedback or commentary pages. The extent to which forms have bombarded the Net is evident by the fact that even the White House site has picked up on the feature in this guest book service. Simple graphic imagery can add aesthetic appeal to a basic form layout. The introductory text gives visitors directions pertaining to the use of this particular page while anticipating other locations that the user might want to visit.

- *imagemaps in Netscape Gold*
- *How Imagemaps Work*
- *Creating Server-Side Imagemaps*
- *Storing Your Imagemap*
- *Putting the Map in Your HTML Document*
- *Client-Side Imagemaps*
- *Design Tips*

- *Examples*
- *Software Tools to Help You*

CHAPTER 19

Imagemaps

IMAGEMAPS, IN THE SIMPLEST SENSE, ARE MULTIPURPOSE ICONS. What makes imagemaps different from most icons is that the result of clicking on an imagemap is dependent upon where on the imagemap you click. An imagemap is an HTML graphic that contains two or more clickable "regions." An imagemap is much like a hyperlinked image file, except that an imagemap is not limited to a single URL. The designer of the imagemap designates different URLs to different regions of the picture, so that when a Web surfer clicks on part of the image, an appropriate Web page is delivered to his or her screen.

Imagemaps have become such an integrated, common entity on the Web that it is difficult to navigate the Web without using them. The idea of clicking on an image as a method of navigation is part of the appeal of the World Wide Web. Almost all good Web sites make use of this tool, and the big graphic at the top of the Netscape home page (http://home.netscape.com/), which you've seen before in this book, is one example of their use. However, there are a number of intricate details which make creating imagemaps tricky even for the most experienced HTML authors.

Imagemaps in Netscape Gold

At this point, there is no special handling of imagemap editing built into Netscape Gold. It is expected that in one of the next releases there will be special editing tools for creating and modifying imagemaps from within Netscape Gold. Until that time, however, you'll have to resort to editing raw HTML tags in order to create and edit imagemaps.

How Imagemaps Work

Imagemaps work as a team effort between the user's browser and a program on the page's Web server that processes the pixel coordinates. Browsers are programmed to wait for mouse clicks. When they receive one, they send information to the Web server where the HTML page actually resides. In the case of an imagemap, the browser sends the pixel coordinates of the mouse click to the server. When it does so, the server software refers to the map file that is included in the Anchor tag to figure out what to do.

Map files are primarily a list of the links that correspond to each of the clickable regions in the imagemap. If the coordinates sent do not match any in the list, the software returns the page assigned as the default URL. If the pixel coordinates *do* match the list, then the appropriate URL is sent to the browser. Whatever URL is sent to the browser, it is then the browser's job to retrieve the specified page—the server doesn't automatically send the page. Figure 19.1 shows a good example of an imagemap, which really constitutes almost the entire home page for the delicious Epicurious site (http://www.epicurious.com/epicurious/home.html).

There are actually two types of imagemaps—client-side and server-side. What we've been discussing so far is server-side imagemaps, where the server does most of the work. These are more common, probably because they have been around longer. Client-side imagemaps, which place some of the onus on the client (that is, the browser), are a new twist on the old style, but work in much the same way. The difference in using and creating client-side imagemaps will be discussed at the end of the "Creating Imagemaps" section.

Figure 19.1

The Epicurious site changes the feature image (in this case "Silver Polish") each week, but the rest of the imagemap stays the same.

Creating Server-Side Imagemaps

Creating an imagemap involves selecting an image and dividing it up into clickable regions, creating a coordinate map file with URLs, storing the map image and coordinate files on the server, and linking these into your HTML document. The coding is complex, but after creating a few imagemaps, it becomes quite simple.

To create a working imagemap, you need access to a server. You also have to make sure that the server program handles imagemaps (but most do these days). Get in touch with your system administrator to learn how to construct your maps, because not all servers handle imagemap files in exactly the same way. The tips outlined in this chapter will work with all Netscape servers, and with most others (such as O'Reilly's popular WebSite, for instance).

The first thing to do is to find or create an image you want to use as your imagemap. Any graphics file will do, as long as you convert it into GIF format. imagemap GIFs can be in either GIF87a or GIF89a formats, and they may be interlaced. There are numerous freeware, shareware, and expensive graphics packages available that will allow you to convert just about any image into these formats, so this isn't much of a problem. Images can also be transparent (no visible background—a very nice effect) or regular. Again, many of the graphics packages available have mechanisms for converting images into transparent form. Shapes and objects that have well-defined edges work well for transparencies; pictures which have cluttered backgrounds do not.

Take care not to create imagemaps that are too wide for the typical browser window, or you may find that your readers can't access some of the linked pages. It is important to remember that many people on the Web may be viewing your pages at a lower resolution, which makes images much larger in proportion to the size of the viewing area. If users have to scroll horizontally in order to see an entire imagemap they may not bother with it at all because horizontal scrolling can be annoying.

As an HTML author, your job is to determine what regions on the imagemap you want your users to click on, and where each click will take them. Remember that each region is a hyperlink, and you can link internally or externally (see Chapter 14). Next, you must create a related MAP file (it has a .map extension in Windows) that tells the server what URLs to tell the browser to fetch for each region. The clickable regions can be round, rectangular, or, if you want irregular sides and shapes, polygonal.

The shape of a clickable region should follow intrinsically from what you want users to click on. If it's just a word within your image, make a rectangular region; if it's a globe, you can make the clickable region round. If your image is a map of the U.S. and you want to define a whole state as a clickable region, you'll probably need to use a polygon.

The entire image doesn't have to be defined in clickable regions. For instance, you could have an image that has a few objects on it. If the user clicks on or near those specific objects, the server tells the browser to fetch appropriate pages. But if the user clicks somewhere else on the image, then the server won't tell the browser to fetch any page, because there is no page to fetch. You can also set a default URL so that when the user clicks on an undefined region of the imagemap, the default URL is sent from the server to the browser and the browser then fetches that page. Try to avoid default pages that tell people they've either made a mistake or have not selected a clickable region. You're just wasting their time making their browser download another page that is irrelevant to what they wish to achieve. A good idea is to make the site's home page the default URL.

Once you've decided approximately what regions you wish to delineate on your imagemap, you then note the pixel coordinates of that image. You can do this manually, which is really tedious; you can use a graphics program such as Corel Draw or Paint Shop Pro and determine the coordinates using those programs; or (this is the best idea) you can download one of the many available imagemap utility programs, such as MapThis or MapEdit. They're available at most Net shareware sites.

The imagemap utility programs that are available are quite useful. You simply load the image into the utility and then draw shapes over it. The programs generally prompt you to enter a URL for each different area, plus a default URL, and then they produce the map coordinate file for you. Try them; they'll make you happy.

However, if you feel like creating the map file yourself, here is how you do it:

1. Create a text file using a simple text processor such as WordPad, and call your file *appropriatename.map*. It is important that this map coordinate file has an extension of .map, not .txt.

2. Comments may be incorporated into map files using leading **#** characters, to make obvious what it is you are trying to do. This is a good idea in case somebody else has to come along and modify the map file you've created.

3. At the top of your .map file list the default URL if you wish to specify one. Type

   ```
   default defaultURL
   ```

   Following this, you want to specify a clickable region on each line, until all regions have been specified. The components of a standard map file entry are:

   ```
   method URL x1,y1 x2,y2 . . . xn,yn . . .
   ```

   Here, *method* is the type or shape of the clickable region (circle, rectangle, polygon, or oval); *URL* is the URL to send back to the browser (another Web page, an FTP connection, gopher connection, and so on); *x1,y1* is the list of coordinates that describe the exact location of the clickable region in your imagemap.

4. Double check to make sure that you don't have any overlapping clickable regions. This could cause an error, depending on how your specific server program handles the situation.

5. For rectangular regions, you need to use pairs of pixel coordinates: upper-left and lower-right. Type

   ```
   rect URL_for_this_region upperleftX,upperleftY lowerrightX,lowerrightY
   ```

   For example, if the coordinates of the rectangle are 0,0 and 125,125 and the URL for the rectangle region is http://myserver/mypage.HTML, then the entry in the map file will look like:

   ```
   rect http://myserver/mypage.HTML 0,0 125,125
   ```

6. For circle regions, type **circle**, followed by the URL, followed by the coordinates of the center and then the coordinates of any edge point.

7. For ovals, type **oval**, followed by the URL, followed by the upper-right and lower-right coordinates of the rectangle that would just enclose that oval.
8. For a polygon, type **poly**, followed by the URL, followed by up to 100 pairs of coordinates that define the vertices of the shape.
9. For a point, type **point**, followed by the URL, followed by the point's x and y coordinates. The point method is useful as a "closest to" input (it's pretty hard to click on a specific pixel in an image). If two points are defined in your map file, the one that is selected is the one that the mouse click is closest to, as measured by a straight line. Be careful to not include a default URL in the map file for an imagemap that has a "point" clickable region—any clicks that are not in other clickable regions will be closest to the point, and the default URL will never be used.
10. Finally, make sure you save your file with the .map extension.

A note about absolute and relative URLs: You must be consistent in using relative or absolute URL links in your coordinate map file. If any of the URLs to which your imagemap refers are not at the same server as your imagemap, then you must make all URLs in the coordinate map file absolute. If all of the URLs to which your imagemap refers are on your server then you can use all relative URLs. Just make sure you don't mix the two conventions.

Storing Your Imagemap

Every imagemap actually consists of two files—the map file and the graphic file. Where these are stored matters. The map file must be located in a directory that is at the same directory level as the graphic file, but the two files must be in separate directories. For instance, put everything under a directory or folder called WEBDOCS. Under WEBDOCS create two directories or folders—HTML and MAP. In HTML, store all your HTML files and graphic files. Put all your imagemap files (the files that contain the imagemap coordinates and URLs) in the MAP directory or folder. Then use absolute links for the image (http://sitename/WEBDOCS/HTML/image.gif), and absolute links for the map file (http://sitename/WEBDOCS/MAP/ image.map). This rule generally works for most Web server programs. However, you may want to check with your system administrator to make sure that this is how your particular Web server works.

Putting the Map in Your HTML Document

Now that you've found a picture, converted it into the right format, decided on clickable areas, created a map coordinates file, and stored both this and the image file itself in the proper directory structure, all that remains is including links to these files in your Web page so that the imagemap will show up and work.

The ISMAP attribute in HTML works with the anchor element to signal to a Web browser that the current inline image is active, and that the browser should send the server the pixel coordinates of any mouse clicks on the inline image. The browser doesn't have to know if the user has clicked on a clickable region or not— that's the job of the Web server's imagemap program. The syntax for using ISMAP is:

```
<A HREF="MAP_file_URL.map"><IMG SRC=image_URL.gif ISMAP></A>
```

What you're basically doing here is anchoring your image to a URL, which is really just the map coordinate file. For example, if your image is called "picture.gif" and is located in the /web/pictures/ directory on your server, and the map file is called picture.map and is located in /map/mapfiles/, then your HTML tags will look like this:

```
<A HREF="http://www.company.com/web/mapfiles/picture.map"><IMG SRC=http://
www.company.com/web/pictures/picture.gif ISMAP></A>
```

There's nothing more to it, but be sure to test your map thoroughly to make sure all clickable regions do what they're supposed to do.

Client-Side Imagemaps

Client-side imagemaps do not use the server to process pixel coordinate clicks on an image. Instead, the database of coordinates and corresponding URLs is stored right in the HTML page containing the imagemap. This means less network traffic and a shorter wait for the user. Another benefit to client-side imagemaps is that as the user's cursor passes over the imagemap, the URL in the status bar at the bottom of Netscape Gold's window shows the actual destination URL instead of the map file URL.

There are obviously a number of differences in creating client-side imagemaps as opposed to server-side imagemaps. You still need to define clickable regions and get the coordinates, but unfortunately there are no utilities available that do this for you and embed the coordinates in your HTML file. You have to do the work yourself.

To embed a client-side imagemap in an HTML file, use the <fig></fig> tags. In the first fig tag, include the image name and URL as the "src="

value. Include the width and height of the image. Then, follow this tag by anchor tags containing the shape and coordinates for each clickable region in the image. You can only have one clickable region defined in each anchor tag. The anchor tag indicates the URL that should be retrieved if the user clicks within those coordinates with the "href=". You can include text between the anchor tag < A HREF="..."> and the end anchor tag </A>. This text will be displayed and will be clickable if the user's browser does not support graphics. (This is another benefit of client-side imagemaps, but not very important any longer because most browsers now in use do support graphics).

Let's look at an example of an imagemap and coordinates done with both server-side and client-side mapping. Assume you have the following clickable regions and URLs:

1. A rectangular region with upper-right coordinates 2,6 and lower-left coordinates 87,126. It should give the user http://mysite/rectanglepage.HTML.
2. A circular region with center coordinate 345,345 and edge coordinate 200,200. It should retrieve URL http://mysite/circlepage.HTML.
3. A polygonal region with coordinates 200,5; 220,20; 240,40; 285,50; 290,30; 285,20; 205,3. It should retrieve URL http://mysite/polygonalpage.HTML.
4. A default URL of http://mysite/defaultpage.HTML.

With a server-side imagemap, the map file would look like this:

```
default  http://mysite/defaultpage.HTML
rect  http://mysite/rectanglepage.HTML  2,6  87,126
circle  http://mysite/circlepage.HTML  345,345 200,200
poly  http://mysite/polygonalpage.HTML  200,5 220,20 240,40 285,50 290,30
285,20 205,3
```

If the map file is called myimage.map and is stored in the web/maps directory, and the image is called myimage.gif and stored in the web/images directory, then the HTML for the imagemap would look like this:

```
<A HREF="http://mysite/web/maps/myimage.map"><IMG SRC=http://mysite/web/images/
myimage.gif ISMAP></A>
```

For a client-side imagemap, there is no map file. The coordinates are stored in the HTML. Assuming the image file is again called myimage.gif and is stored in the web/images/ directory, the HTML will look like this:

```
<fig src="http://mysite/web/images/myimage.gif" width=500 height=300>
<a href="rectanglepage.HTML" shape="rect 2,6 87,126"></a>
<a href="circlepage.HTML" shape="circle 345,345 200,200"> </a>
<a href="polygonalpage.HTML" shape="polygon 200,5 220,20 240,40 285,50 290,30
285,20 205,3"></a>
```

```
<a href="defaultpage.HTML" shape="default">Default</a>
</fig>
```

This is all you need for the client-side imagemap. Just make sure that the image is actually located where you indicate that it is. Also, you can include alternate text in between the anchors if you wish, and make the list of anchors a bulleted list. None of this matters if the image does show up, but if it doesn't at least the user can read and click on some options.

Design Tips

Imagemaps let you create visual navigation guides, giving users the ability to click on different parts of a picture to do different things. This is one of the reasons that you so often see imagemaps taking the form of navigational toolbars at the top or bottom of all of a site's Web pages. When users want to go to the home page, they click on the part of the picture that has a house on it and when they want to e-mail the company, they click on the mailbox picture. This is useful, because the imagemap is seen over and over again, and the user becomes familiar with it very quickly.

If you are creating an imagemap for a commercial Web site, you may be provided with images to use by the company's advertising firm. If you *are* the company's advertising firm then you will already know what types of images work and don't work. For amateur Web designers, the idea is to pick an image which has immediate meaning to the viewer. The objects in the image should be recognizable so that the viewer can get a good idea of what might happen when he or she clicks on them. Also, the image should have clearly defined regions. If not, you may want to edit the image by adding words, so that users can tell that clicking in different areas will give them different results.

The image you pick for your imagemap is content-dependent. In other words, if you want to create a navigational toolbar that has links for a home page, for an e-mail link, and an FTP link, you'll probably want to include icons of a house, a mailbox, and a file folder. If you want to use your company's logo, you can do that too, and graphically edit it to contain words that can then be linked to different pages. If your site is divided up by information pertaining to different geographical regions, you may want to use a geographical map, so that people can click on the region that they are interested in.

On the Web, imagemaps must be created with a lot of care in order to ensure that readers don't get lost or overlook available hyperlinks because they didn't recognize something as "clickable." If your image has clearly defined regions then this probably won't be a problem. If not, ask a friend to point out all the different clickable regions on your imagemap to make sure that it's clear.

Imagemaps can be combined with other HTML entities. For example, an imagemap can appear in the cell of a table, or can appear in one frame of a page that is divided up into many. However, an imagemap cannot contain these items. The only HTML tag that can be included within the <img> tag is alt= for alternative text in case the browser doesn't display images. In the case of client-side imagemaps, any HTML can be included between the <fig> and </fig> tags, and this HTML will be rendered if the browser does not display images.

A final thing to be careful of is the size of your imagemaps. There are a number of issues here. First, an imagemap that is really large and complicated will take a long time to download. This will become less of a problem as access speeds increase, but for the next few years it is something you'll want to take into consideration. Second, if your imagemap is too big, some users may not be able to see the whole thing at once if they happen to be viewing at a lower resolution or if their browser screen is smaller. There isn't really any way to tell if an image might be too wide on different browsers other than by trying all of them out. Older machines with slower video cards often run at a lower resolution such as 800 × 600 or 640 × 480. These resolutions cause everything on the screen to be larger. If your picture works fine at 1,024 × 768, but is too large when you switch your resolution down to 800 × 600, you may want to rethink your sizing. Also, you're better off having a picture that is too long vertically than too wide horizontally, because people are used to vertical scrolling on the Web.

Examples

There are many good examples of imagemaps on the Web; we'll just look at a few.

The CompuServe home page shown in Figure 19.2 features an imagemap right at the top that is really easy for Internet customers to use. The image is pleasing to look at, but is explicit about how to get to different pages on the CompuServe site. This is a good example of using text as part of the imagemap.

Client-side imagemaps can look impressive as well. Figure 19.3 shows a client-side imagemap that you're probably quite familiar with. The Netscape site has been using a client-side imagemap for quite some time now, which is probably a good thing, considering the traffic the site gets.

Another good example of an imagemap is on the CNN Interactive site. This is shown in Figure 19.4. This page offers an imagemap as the main navigational tool, but also has a plain hypertext link to a text-only page for those browsers that can't handle images or imagemaps. The CNN imagemap actually looks like a table, but it is just an image created to look that way. The clickable regions are designed so that it seems like you are clicking on buttons.

Figure 19.2

A great example of an imagemap that is unambiguous and easy to use

Figure 19.3

The Netscape client-side imagemap shows users the URL, which will be retrieved when they click on a given area of the imagemap.

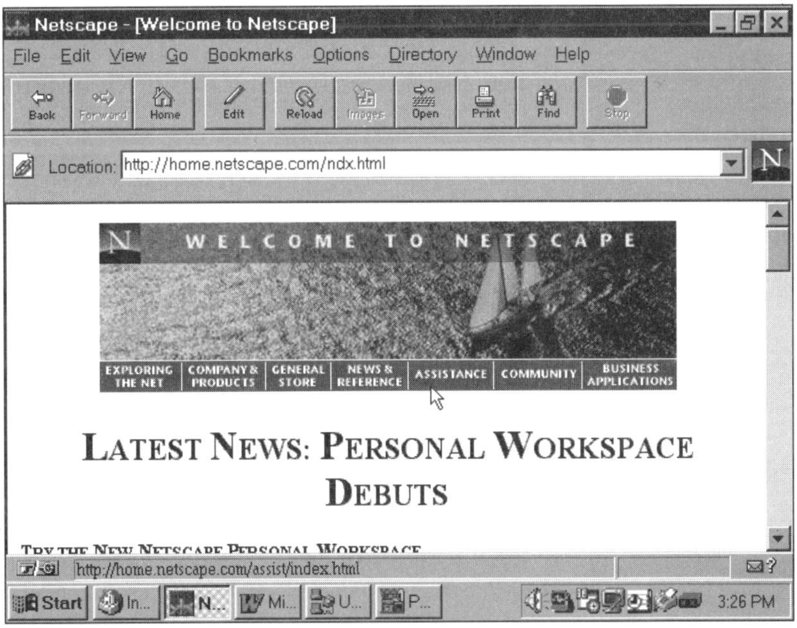

Figure 19.4

The CNN Interactive imagemap is also easy to use and attractive.

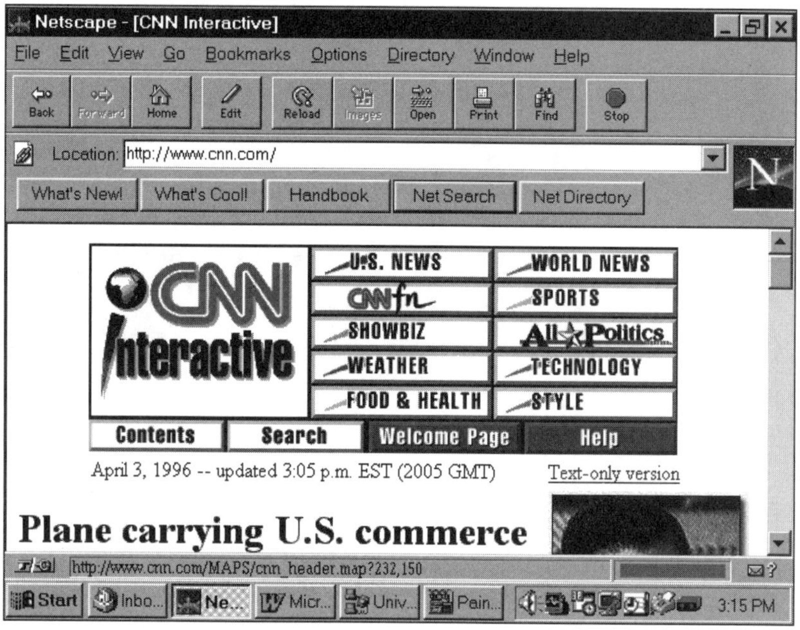

The U.S. Robotics home page has made good use of transparent images (see Figure 19.5). In fact, almost the whole page is one big imagemap that is made up of a number of smaller transparent images pasted together into one large image. The effect is quite dazzling. And again, the use of text is necessary here to help the user navigate with the imagemap.

Software Tools to Help You

The most complicated part of creating imagemaps is figuring out the pixel coordinates for each of your clickable regions. The following is a short list of tools which you can download off the Net to help you:

- UNIX—xv is an Xwindows viewer and editor that does everything you might want with your graphics—format conversions, interlacing, and transparency, as well as finding your pixel coordinates.
- Macintosh—WebMap lets you draw the clickable regions right on top of your image and then define the URL for each region. The program then saves all the information into your map file for you (http://www.city.net/cnx/software/webmap.HTML).

Figure 19.5

The U.S. Robotics home page consists of two separate imagemaps.

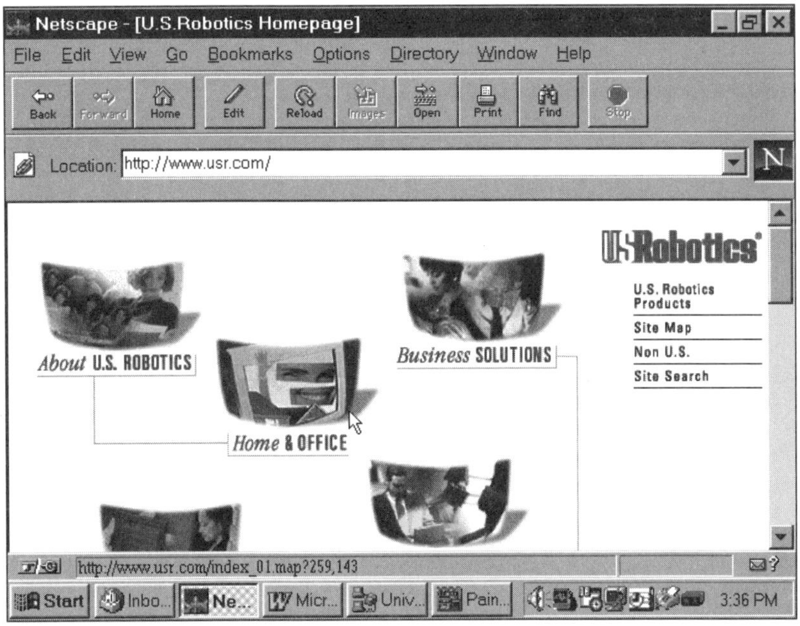

- Microsoft Windows—Mapedit, a 16-bit Windows 3.1 utility, and Map This!, a 32-bit tool for Windows 95 users.
- MapMaker—Available at URL http://www.tns.lcs.mit.edu/cgi-bin/mapmaker, this Web service helps you create an imagemap for any existing inline image on a Web page already up on the WWW. It asks for the URL of your page and then maps the clickable regions you fill in. This Web service is provided by Professor David Tennehouse and the Telemedia, Networks, and Systems Group at the MIT Laboratory for Computer Science.

- *Understanding Targets*
- *It's All in the Name*
- *Implications for Design*
- *Using Raw HTML To Create Targets*

CHAPTER

20

Targets

TARGETING WINDOWS IS A SIMPLE PROCESS THAT GIVES CORRESponding windows specific names to which you may direct your readers' clicks. Essentially, window targets allow the document writer to assign names to specific windows, so that clicking on these links opens the named document inside a new browser window.

Future versions of Netscape Navigator Gold will support the creation of targets. For now, you must create targets by using raw HTML, or by installing a target-capable HTML editor. This chapter covers raw HTML only, although several good editors exist that allow reasonably easy target creation.

To place your created targets into your Gold documents, copy the entire HTML code into the Clipboard, then open the desired document in the Editor window. Place the cursor precisely where you want the target to appear, then choose HTML Tag from the Insert menu. Paste the HTML code into the HTML Tag box, then click OK.

Understanding Targets

Sometimes it is actually easier to understand the function and purpose of elements when they are seen as raw codes. Here is the sample HTML code for a very simple target that opens up a new browser in which the specified document is displayed:

```
<HTML>
<HEAD>
<TITLE>Insert the document title here.</TITLE>
<BODY>
```

The syntax for the targeted windows is:

```
<A HREF="url.html" TARGET="window_name"> Click here and open a new window </A>
</BODY>
</HTML>
```

Copying this HTML sequence into your Web editor will produce the screen shown in Figure 20.1 when previewed.

Targeting grants Web pages a significantly improved level of sophistication, offering writers the ability to open new client windows at will, while maintaining the history of the client's browsing session in the original display window.

In the most advanced target applications, a Web page author may divide the viewing screen into frames of varying sizes (see Chapter 21 for a full discussion of frames) and instruct the browser to load a document accessed in region #1 for display in region #2 or #3. This is the principle that controls the Netscape home page, shown in Figure 20.2.

The element that stands behind both the implementation of simple targets and the creation of more complex styles, such as Netscape's target/frame interface, is the NAME attribute.

Figure 20.1

Clicking on the hyperlink produced by this HTML code will open a new browser screen—but until you replace "url.html" with the appropriate URL for one of your Web pages, the new browser window will remain void of content.

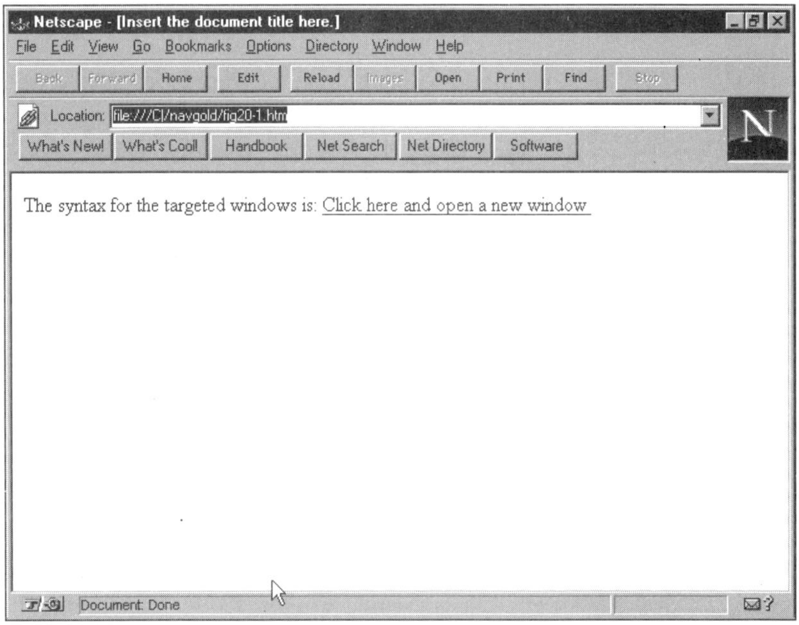

Figure 20.2

In Netscape's home page, all frame elements at the bottom of the screen are targeted to the main frame above.

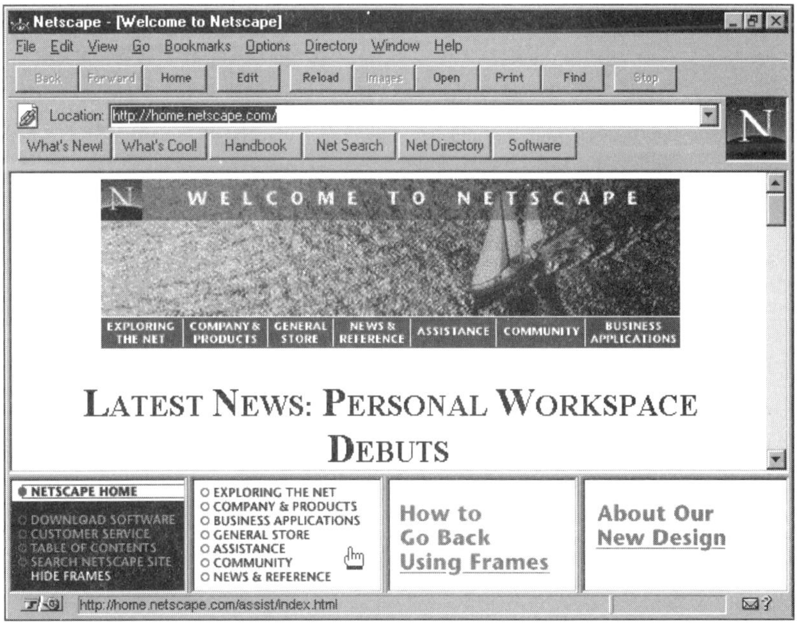

It's All in the Name

Naming simply involves giving a document the same name as that given to the corresponding display region or window. The naming process, key to all window and frame targets, can be accomplished in three ways.

Writers May Set a Document with the Optional HTTP Header Window-Target: Window_Name

When a document that has been named with the HTTP header format is accessed ("clicked on"), the browser loads the corresponding page in the window which has been named "window_name" by the author. The browser searches the archive for the appropriate location, and if this window does not exist, it creates one in which the page will be loaded. Since much of this naming process is automatically controlled by the browser, successful implementation of this feature is nearly foolproof, requiring very little technical knowledge.

A Document Can Be Accessed via a Targeted Link

Accessing a document from a targeted link requires an HTML sequence that assigns a target window_name to a corresponding link. The document loaded from the named link responds in the same manner as if it had the optional HTTP header Window-target: window_name, as discussed above.

A Window Created within a FRAMESET Can Be Named Using the NAME Attribute to the FRAME Tag

The NAME attribute is one of the FRAME tag's most functional elements (see Chapter 21 for a full discussion of frames). NAME="window_name" assigns a name to a frame so that it can be targeted by links in other documents or by other frames within the same document. The NAME attribute is optional; by default, all windows are unnamed. All names must begin with an alphanumeric character, except for the Magic Names discussed later in this chapter.

Whatever method of naming you or your editor choose to use to operate, your own targeted windows will perform essentially the same function. Names give your browsers corresponding windows into which they may load the appropriately labeled documents.

Implications for Design

As with the implementation of any new browsing or editing feature, the use of targets raises specific design issues that should be considered before happily peppering your documents with them. Although targets do provide additional control and visual appeal in some World Wide Web pages or archives, they may not be suitable for all occasions

Here are some guidelines.

First, multiple active windows can create confusion rather than clarification. If you label several links in a single Web page as targets, visitors to the site who access these links will end up with several open browser windows, forcing them to flip back and forth between them. Not only is this distracting, it can also be extremely annoying. Second, the writer's improved control causes a necessary loss of control among readers. The balance of control between authors and readers on the Web is directly affected by target implementation. As in all systems of balance, adding to one element takes from another; in this case, it is the reader who loses. Targets have a direct effect on the presentation of documents, manipulating a command that had previously been under the complete control of the viewer—the New Browser Command in the File menu. Readers now find new instances of their browser being opened without their knowledge or approval. Again, it can be off-putting.

Most pages suitable for targeting possess these three defining characteristics:

1. The document requires direction for comprehension. Some archives of material are best viewed in isolation, separate from the originating or parent document. Perhaps readers must continually refer to the parent page in order to fully comprehend the subsequent sites, or maybe readers will want to return to the parent page after viewing the linked archive without pressing the Back button and traveling through scores of previously visited material. Browse through your own World Wide Web pages to determine firsthand whether your readers will find it necessary to return to a specific document in your archive. If visitors must repeatedly back up to a central page, target the first document accessed from this home page location to be displayed in a new browser window.

2. The document is divided into frames. If you have chosen to implement the new FRAMES element among your World Wide Web projects, you will almost definitely require targets for truly efficient operating. Targeting frames allows a document that has been accessed in one region of the screen to be displayed in another region on the same page. In this way, browsers become more economic in their presentation of material and users may view both the parent- and child-linked documents on a single screen. To put it simply, if you have frames, you should have targets.

3. You want your readers to have continuing access to your main page. One of the problems with the nontarget hyperlink system is that once readers click, the original page is out of sight and possibly out of mind. Targets allow you some control over this problem by giving you a chance to use one page as a kind of ongoing interface to the rest of your

pages. Both pages remain active, and your readers can move back and forth between them. This is most effective, of course, for readers who have larger screens with higher resolutions, in which more than one window can always be visible.

Using Raw HTML To Create Targets

As you're already aware, Netscape Navigator Gold does not have the target creation features implemented. As a result, this section will deal exclusively with raw HTML codes for target generation. Fortunately, they aren't too difficult.

The TARGET Attribute

Target implementation is controlled by the TARGET attribute, which takes the form: *"TARGET=window_name"* and can be added to the <A>, <BASE>, <AREA>, and <FORM> tags.

Inserting the TARGET attribute in an <A> tag is the most straightforward of all targeting procedures. The anchor tag, <A>, is a marked text that is the start and/or destination of a hypertext link. The <A></A> containers can hold a variety of attributes, but either the HREF or NAME attributes are mandatory. If present, the NAME attribute allows the anchor to be the target of a link. In this sense, the value of the NAME attribute is an identifier for the anchor.

The optional TARGET attribute specifies a link to be loaded when the active item is clicked on. Adding the TARGET attribute to the anchor tag forces the load of that link into the targeted window. The following HTML sequence displays the format for inserting the TARGET element in the anchor tags.

```
<A HREF="url" TARGET="window_name">Targeted Anchor</A>
```

For more information on the anchor tags, see Chapter 13.

The TARGET attribute is added to the <BASE> tag when most or all of the links in a single document are to be targeted to the same window. In normal circumstances, the <BASE> element allows the URL of the document itself to be recorded in situations where the document may be read out of context. Where the <BASE> element is not specified, the HTML user agent specifies the URL it used to access the document to resolve any relative URLs. The BASE element holds the HREF attribute which identifies the URL.

Adding the TARGET attribute to the BASE element establishes a default window_name to which all links in the document will be targeted. This default is, of course, overridden by specific instances of the TARGET attribute in individual anchor tags. The HTML format for adding the TARGET attribute to the BASE element looks like this:

```
<BASE TARGET="window_name">
```

Establishing a target using the TARGET element in the AREA tag requires a more thorough understanding of HTML coding properties. As defined by the IETF Internet-Draft of Client-Side Image Maps, each <AREA> tag contained inside the map element specifies a single clickable area of the image.

Essentially, AREA describes a shaped area in a client-side imagemap and provides the link that should be followed when the user accesses this area. Adding the TARGET attribute to the <AREA> tag forces the load of that link into the targeted window. The HTML programming sequence that includes the TARGET attribute within the AREA tag looks something like this:

```
<AREA SHAPE="shape" COORDS="x,y,..." HREF="url" TARGET="window_name">
```

For more information on client side imagemaps, see Chapter 19.

The <TARGET> attribute may also be used within the HTML <FORM></FORM> container tags. When the TARGET attribute is missing from the FORM sequence, your browser displays the results of a form submission in the same window that the form was submitted from—the parent or originating window. Adding the TARGET attribute to the form tag causes the results of a form submission to be loaded into the targeted or specified window somewhere on your system. The HTML for adding the TARGET attribute to the FORM element follows this basic pattern:

```
<FORM ACTION="url" TARGET="window_name">
```

For more information on forms and form syntax, see Chapter 18.

Magic Target Names

We've already discussed the significance of the NAME attribute for targeting windows—specifying only that names must begin with an alphanumeric character. However, as with most rules, there are a number of exceptions which are classified as Magic Names.

Magic TARGET Names are names which may be successfully inserted into the TARGET="window_name" formula but that begin with the underscore character rather than an alphanumeric selection. The following four Magic TARGET Names may be used as window labels within your Web pages.

TARGET="_blank"	This Magic TARGET Name instructs the browsing mechanism to load the corresponding named link into a new "blank" browser window.

TARGET="_self"	The "_self" Magic TARGET Name instructs the browsing mechanism to load the corresponding link into the same window that the anchor was accessed from. This Magic TARGET Name is useful for overriding a globally assigned BASE target.
TARGET="_paren"	This Magic TARGET Name causes the browser to display the link it is attached to in the immediate FRAMESET parent of the same document. In the case that the document has no parent, this Magic Name operates in exactly the same manner as "_self".
TARGET="_top"	TARGET="_top" causes the link to load in the full body of the window. This defaults to acting like "_self" if the document is already at the top. TARGET="_top" is useful for breaking out of an arbitrarily deep FRAME nesting.

Any targeted window name beginning with underscore which is not one of these names will be ignored.

That's really all there is to the construction of targets. Targeting windows is probably the easiest task introduced with the Netscape 2.0 extensions, and it's truly amazing that such a simply formatted feature can provide such control and movement on the Web. But since the syntax and implementation of targets throughout your Web pages is so easy, it's up to you to use your creative inspiration to dress this feature up. One way to add invention to this feature is to use targets in conjunction with frames—and this takes us to Chapter 21.

- *Design Issues: When Should You Include Frames?*
- *Creating Frames with Raw HTML*
- *Nesting Frames*
- *Framed Sites on the Web*

CHAPTER

21

Frames

BEGINNING WITH THE RELEASE OF THE FIRST BETA VERSIONS OF Netscape Navigator, Web authors were given the capability of designing their pages around the idea of *frames*. This new feature meant that the Web no longer consisted exclusively of single pages in single browser windows. Instead, they now had a sophisticated page-presentation capability that allowed the display of multiple, independently scrollable frames within a single browser window, each with its own distinct URL. Since frames can function as both hyperlinks and targets, all within the same screen, Web authors were given the ability to incorporate more effective banners, ledges, tables of contents, and display panels into their designs. In effect, they now had a way of creating a fully functioning user interface right within the browser window.

Frames allow users to scroll through multiple sites without leaving the original page—something never before possible on the Web. Additionally, users may submit database queries in one frame while receiving results in another, or scroll through a page's related information while keeping the original interface, itself a frame, right in front of them.

Future versions of Netscape Navigator Gold will support the creation of frames. For now, you must create frames by using raw HTML, or by installing a frames-capable HTML editor. This chapter covers raw HTML only, although several good editors exist that allow reasonably easy frames creation.

What do frames look like? Netscape Communications maintains the basic framed page shown in Figure 21.1. As you can see, the page offers five different frames within the single browser window, a large frame occupying the top 75 percent or so, and four smaller ones running along the bottom.

Figure 21.1

Clicking on one of the special feature icons in the lower frame of this Netscape Navigator 2.0 and Gold page calls up information on that feature in the larger frame.

Although they're not yet a perfect solution, frames will undoubtedly change the face of the World Wide Web. No other supported feature has the power and ability to affect design decisions so radically, and no other feature has been adopted with such speed and efficiency. Frames offer Web authors (and their readers) three primary advantages:

1. Organization: Any Web page or screen can be divided into sections of various sizes. Each section or frame is given its own unique URL, so that a single page actually incorporates multiple sites. Because of this, readers can maneuver through more than one site from within a single page.

2. Navigation: Queries executed in one frame can generate results in another frame on the same page. This process simplifies navigation by obliterating the need to switch back and forth between screens to submit a query and preview results.

3. Ledges: Framed pages may also function as ledges that retain the most crucial information in the front of the screen while the user browses through alternate pages. A ledge is a frozen or constant area of the screen that may be horizontally or vertically altered to optimize viewing and can be designed to adjust or remain fixed in size. Orientation elements that the user should always see, such as control bars, copyright notices, and title graphics, may be placed in a static, individual frame. As the user navigates the site in "live" frames, the static frame's contents remain fixed, even though adjoining frames redraw. This feature is useful for design companies, advertising agencies, and all sites that offer users a consumer service, so that their logo or company name along with other critical advertising information will be constantly accessible to users. Figure 21.2 shows an example.

Table of contents pages become increasingly useful with frames. You can put major categories or units appearing in one frame and the subcategories appearing, as they are clicked, in the corresponding active regions of the page. This feature offers excellent possibilities for publishing sites, electronic magazines (e-zines), book sites, and any other site in which a guide or table of contents is a necessary feature. Figure 21.3 shows such a site.

The side-to-side design characteristic of all frames allows queries to be posed and answered on the same page, with one frame holding the query form and the other presenting the results. This design feature allows for more useful search engines, local search mechanisms, and form queries. An example of the design possibilities created by the side-to-side feature is displayed by Figure 21.4.

Figure 21.2

Silicon Graphics uses a static frame to make the company name and logo constantly available to potential customers.

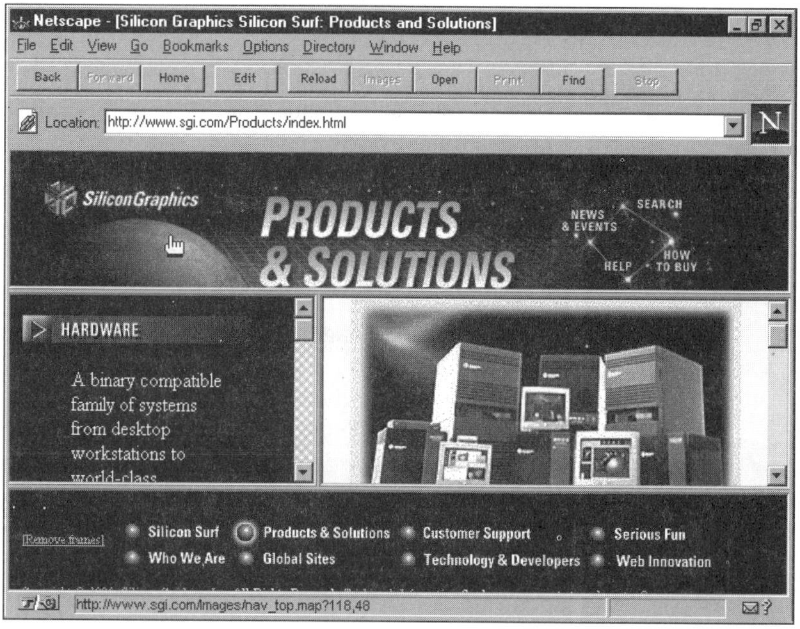

Figure 21.3

The Discovery Channel uses frame design strategies to display a guide to the channel's weekly programming while providing more specific information and articles in adjacent frames.

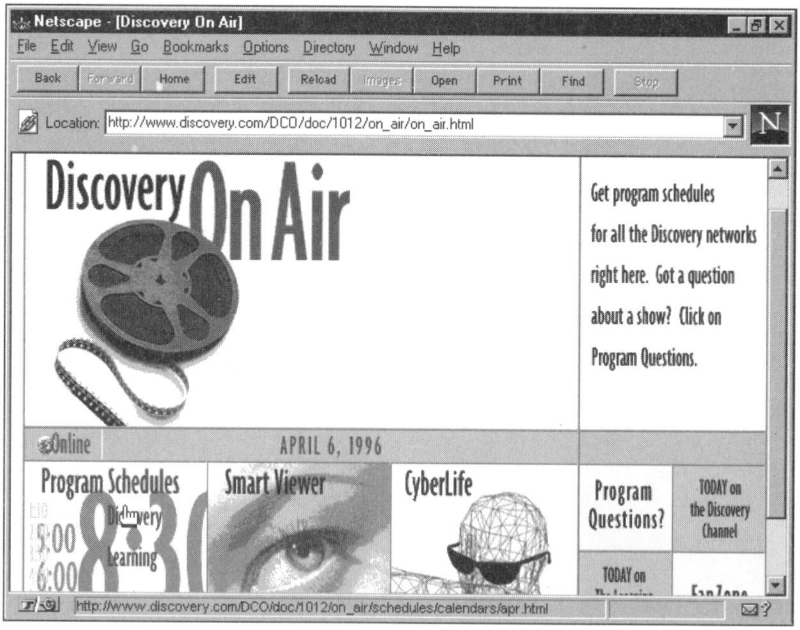

Figure 21.4

The Cool Site of the Day page utilizes the side-to-side design strategy provided by frames to organize and display their coolest sites. Clicking on the date icons in one frame reveals the coolest sites of that month in the adjacent frame.

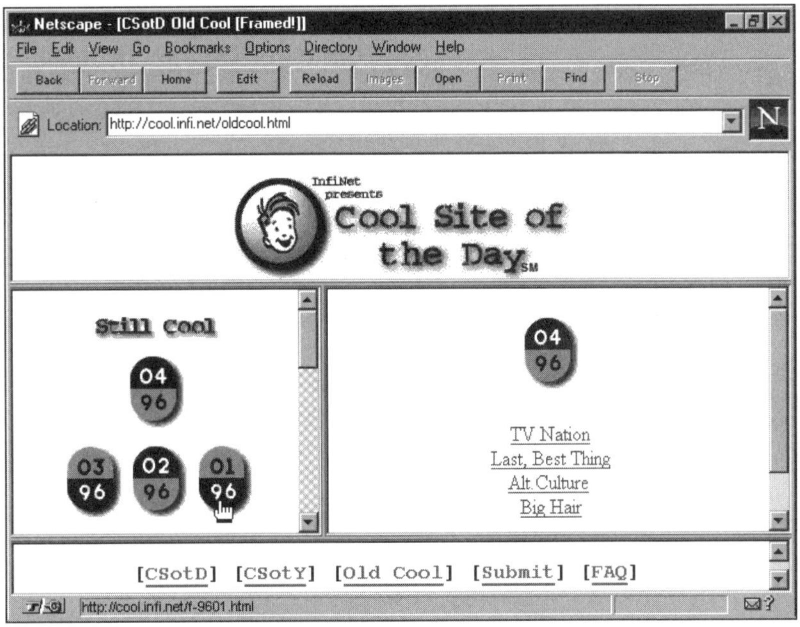

Design Issues: When Should You Include Frames?

Frames are suitable for just about any site on the World Wide Web, but before you implement them, ask yourself why you'd bother. Here are some possible considerations:

1. Does your site consist of more than one page of information? Frames are best suited to information archives where the reader or visitor to the site must browse through large quantities of information. Since one portion of the frame usually remains static or fixed while readers click through pages in another frame, sites with a large reserve of pages or data can be organized and simplified with frames.

2. Does navigation through your site require the repeated use of the browser's Back button? Are readers often required to return to a previous page or starting point to continue browsing? Sites that benefit most from frame implementation are those that require users to return to a previous document in order to continue browsing consecutive pages. With frames, you can eliminate the need for your audience to return to a previous page by making it visible to readers at all stages of their browsing.

But keep in mind that quite often you can accomplish the same result with well-designed navigation buttons and no frames at all.

3. Can the information in your Web documents be sorted and categorized easily? Since frame implementation requires that you chunk and sort your information, a good way to determine the feature's suitability for your site is to look for hierarchies or classes that would be fairly easy to restructure in a fully sorted manner. If you find a definite pattern or hierarchical structure within your pages, it is quite possible that the highest level of the hierarchy could best be presented in a fixed frame, with subsequent levels branching out from this static starting point.
4. Is it necessary for your pages to target the largest possible audience? Not everybody has access to frames. Not all browsers support them. Before long, all browsers will probably do so, but until then, implementing frames places intentional limits on your pages and reduces your target audience to only the most current users. If attracting a widespread audience is the most important goal of your design, then you may want to avoid framing. At the very least, you should consider offering a framed and a nonframed version of your site, and this requires extra time.

Creating Frames with Raw HTML

Frames are generated in HTML by three controlling elements: the Frame Document structure, the FRAMESET tags, and the FRAME tags.

The Frame Document

A Frame Document has a basic structure very much like your normal HTML document. Remember that a standard HTML page layout follows this tagged format:

```
<HTML>
<HEAD>
<TITLE>Insert document title here.</TITLE>
</HEAD>
<BODY>Insert document content here.</BODY>
</HTML>
```

With framed documents, the BODY container tags <BODY> and </BODY> are replaced by a FRAMESET container <FRAMESET> and </FRAMESET>, which describes the regions or partial HTML documents (frame) that will combine to make up the entire HTML page. The standard format for a framed page looks like this:

```
<HTML>
<HEAD>
<TITLE>Insert document title here.</TITLE>
</HEAD>
<FRAMESET>Insert FRAMESET attributes here.</FRAMESET>
</HTML>
```

The BODY element is not defined in any way for a framed HTML document; therefore, placing the typical BODY tags before the FRAMESET element will cancel everything contained between the opening and closing FRAMESET tags. Otherwise, frame syntax is similar in scope and complexity to table syntax and has been designed to be processed quickly and accurately by Internet client layout engines.

Frame Declaration—The <FRAMESET> Tag

The <FRAMESET> </FRAMESET> container holds all of the main information for a frame. Like tables, the FRAMESET element is defined by ROWS and COLS, attributes which specify the length and width of the proposed frame.

A Row list is a comma-separated list of values which tells the browser how to divide the document area into rows. The width of these rows is just the width of the document area, but the height and number of rows are determined by the actual values in the list. The number of rows is, simply enough, just the number of values in the list.

The ROWS height attribute is defined by a list of absolute pixel values, percentage values between 1 and 100, or relative scaling values that correspond consecutively to the number of rows in the frame.

- *Pixels. A simple numeric value is assumed to be a fixed size in pixels.*

  Since window sizes vary substantially from one viewer to the next, defining ROWS in terms of pixels can be dangerous. If you do decide to use fixed pixel values, you will almost certainly have to combine them with one or more of the relative size values described below. If pixel values are used exclusively, client engines will likely override specified values in order to ensure that the total proportions of the frame are 100 percent of the width and height of the user's window.

- *Percentages. A simple percentage value between 1 and 100.*

  If the total of all percentages in a ROW specification is greater than 100, the editor will scale all percentages down.

```
<FRAMESET ROWS="60%,60%,60%,60%">
```

If you define your ROWS attribute to total 240 percent as in the above example, your Web editor would scale each percentage down to 25 percent in order to create 4 rows of equal value.

If the total of all percentages in a ROW specification is less than 100, all percentages will be scaled-up to a total of 100 percent.

```
<FRAMESET ROWS="10%,10%,10%,10%,10%">
```

Defining your ROWS attribute to total only 50 percent, as seen in the previous sample, would cause your Web editor to double each value in order to scale up the total to 100. In all cases, however, if any relative-sized values accompany the percentage values, any extra space is divided between them.

- *Scalings. A single asterisk (*) indicates a "relative-sized" frame and is interpreted by the Web editor as a request to give the corresponding row all remaining space.*

  If the ROW attribute is defined with multiple relative-sized frames, all remaining space is divided evenly among them. Inserting a numerical value in front of the relative size character (*) causes that corresponding region to receive that much more relative space. For example, the value "2*,*,*" would give ½ of the space to the first frame, and ¼ to both the second and third.

As you have seen above, it is possible to specify a Row list such that the total height of all rows is not equal to the document area's height. This kind of Row list is called an *Improper Row list*, and though it is not necessarily bad, it can give unexpected results. The best way to avoid this problem is to use common sense and specify at least one row with an asterisk value. In fact, any Row list containing a pixel value but no asterisk value must be improper.

Since the total height of all the rows must equal the maximum height of the window, Row heights must sometimes be normalized. This means that whenever the sum of the specified row or column sizes does match the size of the area being divided, every frame is proportionately scaled until they all fit. Through normalization, a missing ROWS attribute will be interpreted by the editor as a single row and will receive the remaining value of the total window height.

ROW specification is really not as complex as it sounds since the Web editor automatically adjusts any errors you make, but it is important to realize how and why these adjustments are being made in order to have more control over the final appearance of your framed documents. A few examples will make the process clearer.

1. To construct a frame consisting of three rows, with the first and the last larger than the center row, the HTML code would look like this:

   ```
   <FRAMESET ROWS="40%,20%,40%">
   ```

2. The frame below consists of four rows.

   ```
   <FRAMESET ROWS="20%,48%,*,3*">
   ```

   The first row receives 20 percent of the total window height, while the second receives 48 percent. The third and fourth row divide the remaining 32 percent of the height with the third possessing a value of 8 percent and the fourth equaling 24 percent.

3. To construct a frame consisting of five rows, with the first, second, third, and the last maintaining a fixed height of 100, and all remaining space being assigned to the fourth row, your HTML code would look like this:

   ```
   <FRAMESET ROWS="100,100,100,*,100">
   ```

Now that you understand ROWS, COLS are easy. In fact, column specification follows exactly the same syntax as ROWS and functions in exactly the same manner. The only difference between ROWS and COLS is that while ROWS regulates the height of the rows in a frame, COLS specifies the width of frame columns. ROWS divide your HTML document into slices from top to bottom and COLS divide your page into slices from side to side.

Experiment with the attributes and values of the FRAMESET element until you have designed a screen that suits your WWW document. Here are the HTML FRAMESET values for the Boston Globe World Wide Web page.

```
<FRAMESET COLS="142,*">
```

This HTML coding separates the document into two frames, as shown in Figure 21.5.

Now check out the FRAMESET specifications for the NCompass site:

```
<FRAMESET ROWS="110,*">
```

This HTML code divides the screen in the manner illustrated in Figure 21.6.

The FRAMESET tag can be nested inside other FRAMESET tags. In this case the complete subframe is placed in the space that would be used for the corresponding frame if this had been a FRAME tag instead of a nested FRAMESET.

Figure 21.5

The Boston Globe presents all information in two frames that are defined by the FRAMESET COLS attributes.

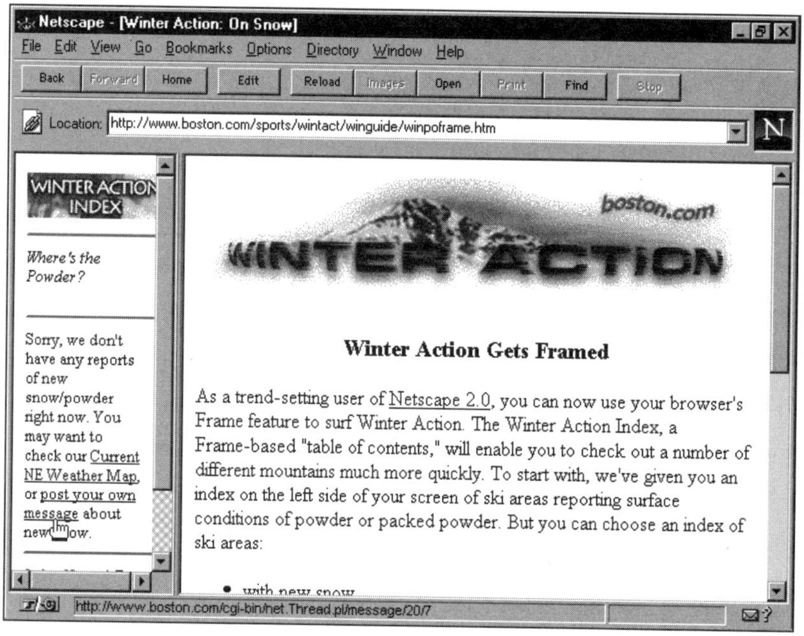

Figure 21.6

The NCompass site offers two rows, with the fixed frame showing an animated graphic

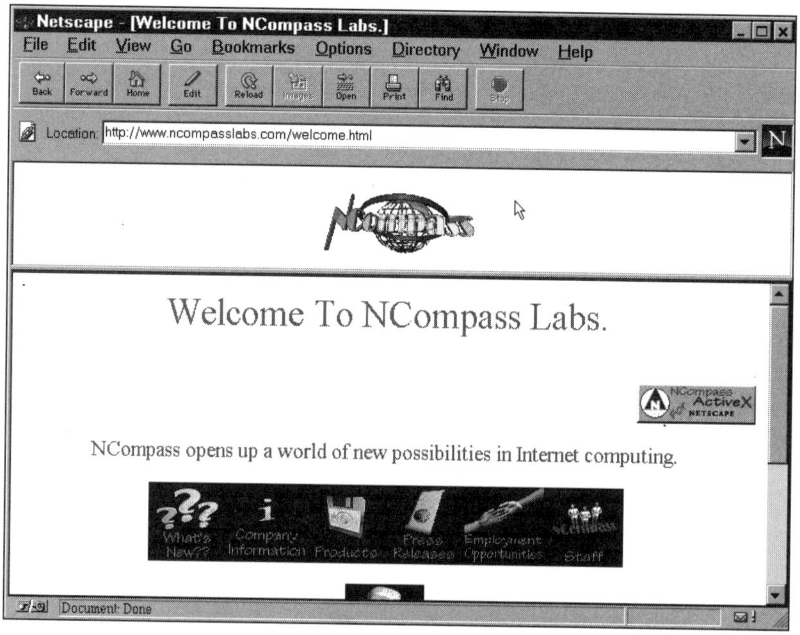

Frame Definition—The <FRAME> Tag

Now that you have used <FRAMESET> tags to divide the browser window into sections or regions, you must now tell the browser what information, text, and graphics to put in these frames. This is the function of the <FRAME> tags, which occur between the <FRAMESET> and </FRAMESET> container tags and define the contents of each frame declared in the row or column list of the preceding FRAMESET tag.

The <FRAME> tag defines a single frame in a FRAMESET and has six possible attributes: SRC, NAME, MARGINWIDTH, MARGINHEIGHT, SCROLLING, and NORESIZE. The FRAME tag is not a container so it has no matching end tag.

SRC="URL"

At the very least, each FRAME specification should contain a URL to another document. Frame URLs are specified within the <FRAME> tag by adding the tag property "SRC=URL". At view time, after the browser has laid out the document's frames, it will then use these URLs to load documents for display within the frames. If the specified URL points to another framed document, the frame will be further subdivided. Frames without SRC attributes are displayed as a blank space the size the frame would have been.

NAME="window_name"

You can assign names to frames by including the tag property NAME="window_name" in the <FRAME> tag. The NAME attribute assigns each frame a name that allows it to be targeted by links in any other WWW document or from other frames within the same document. If your particular application of frames allows all hyperlink targets to be specified through the relative, reserved names, then it is better to avoid frame name conflicts by not specifying frame names. By default all frames are left unnamed. Named frames can have their window contents targeted with the new TARGET attribute. For more on targets, see Chapter 20.

MARGINWIDTH="value"

The MARGINWIDTH attribute allows document authors more control over the margins for a particular frame. All MARGINWIDTH specifications must take a value greater than 1 in order to prevent frame objects from contacting frame edges and to allot space for the actual frame contents. When defined, the MARGINWIDTH value always appears in pixel format; if omitted from the <FRAME> specifications, the browser determines an appropriate margin width by default.

MARGINHEIGHT="value"

The MARGINHEIGHT attribute functions in exactly the same manner as the MARGINWIDTH attribute detailed above, but it controls the upper and lower portions of the frame margins instead of the left and right. To make things clearer, think of the MARGINHEIGHT value as the header and footer values in a standard word processing program.

SCROLLING="yes|no|auto"

The <FRAME> tag's SCROLLING attribute regulates the appearance of a side scroll bar. A "yes" value results in visible scroll bars on the frame whether scroll bars are necessary for viewing the frame or not; "auto" (the default value for the SCROLLING attribute) lets the browser determine if scroll bars are required for viewing and inserts them where necessary. The "no" value results in scroll bars never being added. Unfortunately, Netscape frame extensions do not provide independent control over horizontal and vertical scroll bars, nor do they allow the programmer to specify where on the frame the scroll bars should appear.

NORESIZE

The NORESIZE attribute takes no value, acting instead as a flag that indicates that the user may not resize the frame. Omission of the NORESIZE attribute is most common (the default) and allows users to manually resize frames by clicking on a frame edge and dragging it to a new location on the screen. However, if any frame adjacent to an edge is not resizable, as indicated by the NORESIZE attribute, the entire edge will be restricted from moving. This stipulation can also affect the resizability of other frames. This attribute often occurs in "menu bar" frames, whose sizes are usually given in pixels to accommodate inline graphics.

The NOFRAMES Tags

Since not all Web browsers support frames, the Netscape extensions provide the <NOFRAMES> and </NOFRAMES> container tags. This feature lets programmers place warnings such as

```
Warning! This document cannot be viewed without a frames-capable browser.
Please obtain a browser that supports Netscape's frame extensions before
attempting to view this page.
```

inside their framed documents so that frames-incapable viewers are aware of the cause of their visual impairment.

A frame-capable Internet client ignores all tags and data between the opening and closing NOFRAMES tags.

Presently, Netscape reads <NOFRAMES> tags only when they appear within the <FRAMESET> tags. This restriction makes it more difficult to for Web artists to construct pages that are viewable by both frames-capable and frames-incapable clients.

Nesting Frames

Now that you've become more familiar with the tags and attributes required for creating standard frame documents, there's really only one remaining concept that you must be aware of when creating more complex frames—nesting. A frame is nested if it divides another frame, called the parent frame, into multiple frames.

Rather than defining a <FRAME> tag with a URL to specify the frame's contents, you may replace the <FRAME> tag with an additional, nested <FRAMESET> declaration. Nested frames place the complete sub-frame in the space that would be used for the corresponding frame if this had been a FRAME tag instead of a nested FRAMESET.

Unfortunately, directly nested frames require nested <FRAMESET> tags. Since frame names are specified within the <FRAME> tag and not the <FRAMESET> container, it becomes difficult to assign names to collections of frames.

The HTML for a simple nested frame would follow this standard format:

```
<html>
<head>
<title> Insert document title here.</title>
<frameset rows=*,*>
<frame url=x.html>
<frameset cols=*,*>
<frame url=y.html>
<frame url=z.html>
</frameset>
</frameset>
</html>
```

In this scenario, x, y, and z represent source URLs that will appear nested within one single-framed document. However, this nested structure is flattened or meshed for display on your computer screen.

Framed Sites on the Web

As always, the best way to see what you can do with frames is to visit some effective sites on the Web. A very few of them are shown in Figures 21.7 through 21.11; surely enough to whet several appetites.

Figure 21.7

The Annex: Humanizing Technology site is one of the most interesting and innovative frame sites currently on the Web. Access the View Source option from your View menu to see the extent to which developers have embedded and nested frames in order to attain the visual effect they desired. Now click on the graphic images loaded in the alternating frame squares and notice the random loading of the appropriate text in adjacent frames. This site gives proof of the overwhelming possibilities for Web reconstruction that frames can offer.

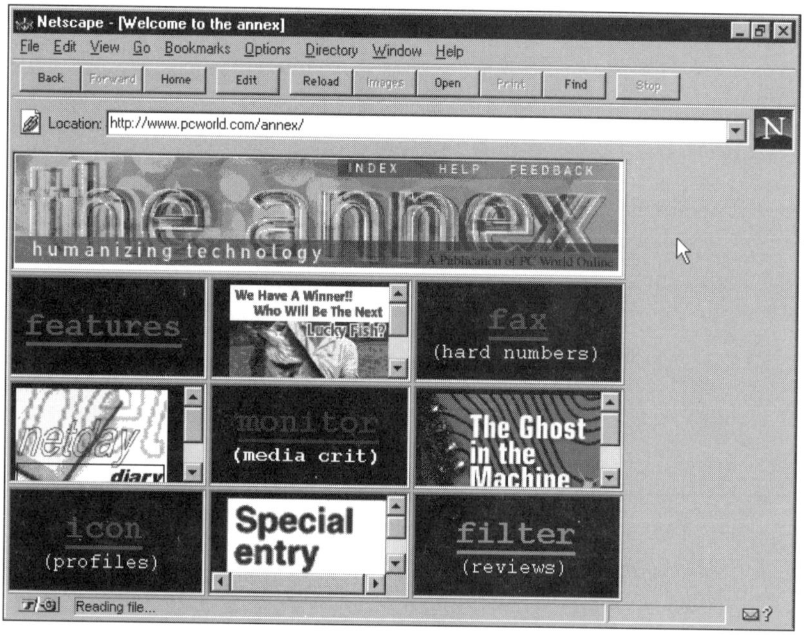

Figure 21.8

By its title alone, Designstein's Universe promises to be one of the more interesting Web influences. At first glimpse, Designstein's use of frames seems fairly simple, with three rows spanning the entire width of the page. However, browsing through the site will provide you with samples and variations for frame implementation in your own Web pages. Don't be afraid to copy the source code displayed with these sample pages for your own frame construction.

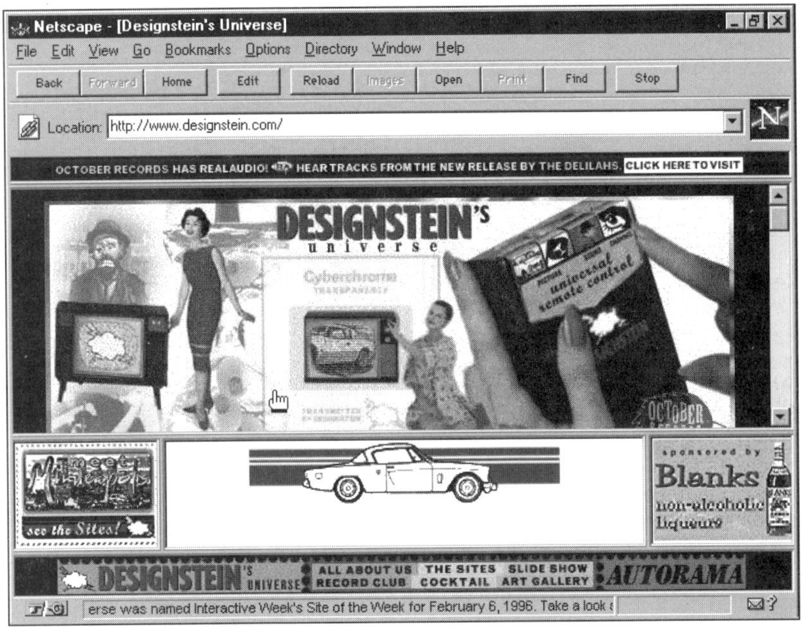

Figure 21.9

The HOTWIRED site is one of the Internet's most popular magazine archives, combining currency and accuracy with the most advanced design strategies and an innovative flair. The fact that HotWired has adopted a framed home page is, therefore, not surprising.

Figure 21.10

RockWeb has taken frame implementation to new heights by adding a simple form to the FRAME's content material. In this way, users need only access RockWeb's home page to find exactly what they need rather than spending valuable time searching the archive for the appropriate material. What this means for the "big picture" is that Web pages in general could become not only smaller, but more efficient with the correct implementation of frames.

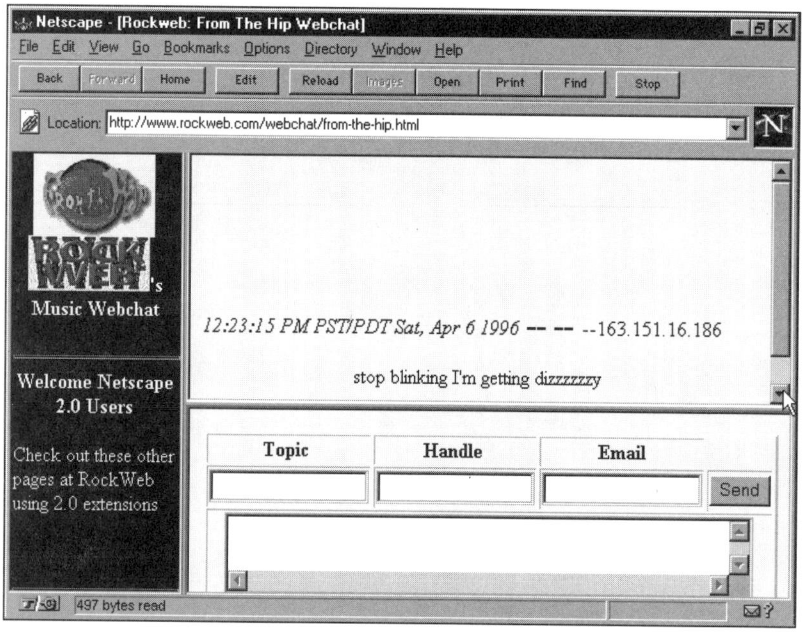

Figure 21.11

Dr. Bob's Virtual En-psych-lopedia shows one of the more educational uses of frames on the Web with pharmacological drugs and informative tips for just about any ailment you can imagine. What's truly amazing is the amount of information contained within the frames compared with the minimal HTML codes necessary to create the page itself. Frames will bring much-needed economy to the Web and maybe...just maybe...organization?

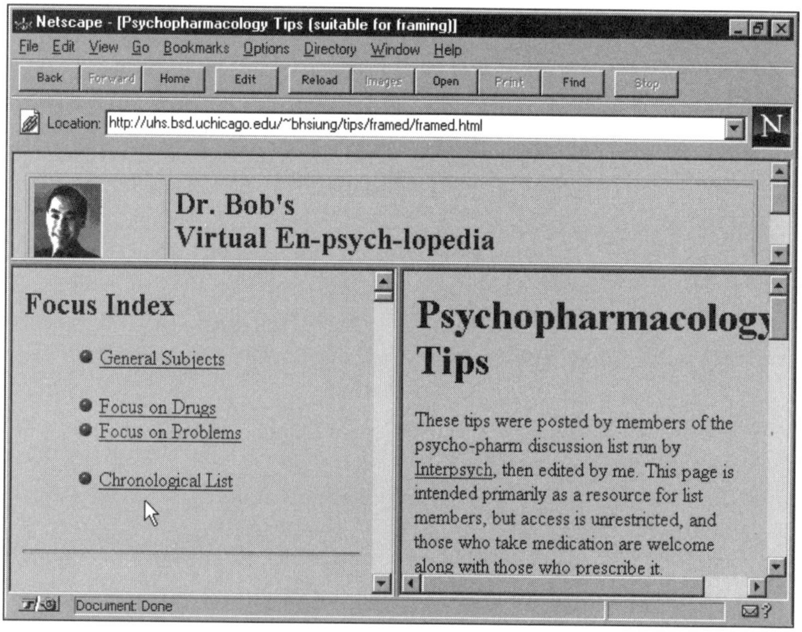

- *Java and Netscape Navigator Gold*
- *This Chapter Is Not Written for Programmers!*
- *What Are You Going to Do in This Chapter?*
- *Okay, Let's Talk about Applets!*
- *What Do You Need to Start?*
- *The Animator Applet*
- *Chapter Syntax*

- *The Java Language*
- *Operators*
- *Methods*
- *Control Structures*
- *Special Type: Arrays*
- *Object-Oriented Program— The Quick and Dirty Lowdown*
- *Attributes*
- *Interfaces*
- *Handling Errors—Throwing and Catching Exceptions*
- *Java Packages and Classes*
- *Creating the Hello World Applet*
- *Compiling Java Code*
- *Running Your Applet*

CHAPTER

22

Java

JAVA IS AN INTERNET BUZZWORD FOR A VERY GOOD REASON. THIS newly available language has the potential to completely revolutionize the way people interact over the Internet, not to mention the entire PC software industry. Okay, that may be a bit overzealous, but people who are using Java to enhance Web pages and develop interactive Web applications will probably support me here. Besides, *everybody*'s starting to implement Java in their Web pages.

So far, the Web has been seen by many Internet old-timers as a bandwidth hog that is attracting the masses with pretty pictures, but not really offering much in the way of content or interactivity. For a newcomer the Web in its present state does seem relatively interactive—you click on hypertext and pictures and another page or picture appears. The effect doesn't take too long to wear off, though, and soon the Web becomes...well, a bandwidth hog with pretty pictures.

Of course, the Web does offer some movie and sound clips, and even some other multimedia gimmicks such as animation. The problem is that all of these require special viewers or converters. The number of different file types that you can download from the Internet is growing every day, and your hard drive may already be getting crowded by multimedia viewers to support all of these formats.

What makes Java so revolutionary is that it allows you as a Web page developer to use any type of file format you want, without having to worry about whether or not the end user will be equipped to handle it. This is because Java allows the viewer to be downloaded at the same time as the file. Immediately visions of waiting ten minutes pop into your head, right? But this isn't the case. Java uses an intermediary format known as bytecode to transfer information to your PC. You'll hear more about bytecode later in the chapter, but for now, all you have to understand is that *bytecode* is efficient, and is interpreted by the end user's PC line by line, on the fly. Thus users don't have to wait for the whole thing to download, then compile, then run. Java applets can run as they download. There are many other great things about the Java language, and as this chapter progresses, you'll be sure to know them.

Java, in essence, lets your Web browser display and run entire programs. If you want your readers to be able to manipulate a spreadsheet, or play a game, or do a crossword puzzle, or do anything else a computer program can do, Java is the place to turn.

NOTE. *This chapter is written from a Windows 95 perspective. If you are using Windows NT, everything in this chapter applies, and the only difference is in the installation of the Java Developer's Kit, as I've specified. However, if you are using another platform such as a Sun workstation, keep in mind that things may be a little different, especially the information about installing and using the Java Developer's Kit.*

Java and Netscape Navigator Gold

Netscape Gold will run just about any Java program you create. But Gold has no tools for the creation of Java programs, and there's no guarantee it ever will. Java is *not* an HTML function; it's a separate programming language. For now at least, you need to create your Java programs independently, then bring them into your Gold documents through the HTML Tag command on the Insert menu.

This Chapter Is *Not* Written for Programmers!

Although Java is based on the C++ programming language, you don't need to know C++ to write Java programs. So, if you don't have any programming experience, don't worry about it. You're going to start by using an already available Java program that you can use to add animation to your Web page, and all you have to do is learn a few new HTML tags! Then you'll go on to learn the basics of the Java language, and you'll soon write an applet or two of your own.

Even though you need no real programming experience to continue this chapter, if you're a complete newcomer to programming and even scripting, you might wish to tackle Chapter 23 (JavaScript) and then return here. JavaScript is easier, although it's also more limited.

NOTE. *If you are a C or C++ programmer, you'll probably want to skip to the end of this chapter and read the second sidebar at the end of this chapter, "Differences between Java and C++ Types." From talking to a few C++ to Java converts, I have learned that experienced C programmers can generally figure out how to do something in Java by intuitively trying the way the thing is done in C, and it usually works! The sidebar outlines the main exceptions to this rule.*

What Are You Going to Do in This Chapter?

First you need to read the quick introduction to the Java applet. Then you're going to use an existing Java applet to add some cool animation to a Web page. The main part of the chapter follows with a brief outline of the Java language, and how it works. This will include an introduction to the concepts of object-oriented programming, and a description of some of the most important Java packages. Finally, youll finish up with a walk-through tutorial on how to create a Java applet.

If you're really not sure you're ready to start programming, just go through the first part of the chapter where you use an existing applet. This way you'll at least know how to embed somebody else's applet into your Web page, which can be useful. If you try this at home with other applets, make sure you have permission to use the applets first!

■ Okay, Let's Talk about Applets!

An applet is a small application. Using the Java language it is possible to write large applications, but the language has a number of added features that make it ideal for portable, small applications that can be downloaded over the Net. That's what youre going to concentrate on in this book.

People have written Java applets that do all sorts of neat and sometimes useful things. A good place to start is Netscape's Java page (http://home.netscape.com/comprod/products/navigator/version_2.0/java_applets/index.html); browse through some of the example applet pages that Netscape provides links to. I recommend checking out the Crossword Applet page, the "Work in Progress" animation, and the Graph Layout Applet page. Make sure you play with the Graph Layout applet, to see how it interacts with your mouse clicks and drags. Finally, check out a site that is using a Java applet in a very useful way: c|net (http://www.cnet.com).

Figure 22.1 shows a picture of the Crossword applet. The way it works is that users click on a square, and the clue appears at the top of the crossword. Then users type in their guess, and the letters show up in black if correct and red if incorrect.

Figure 22.1

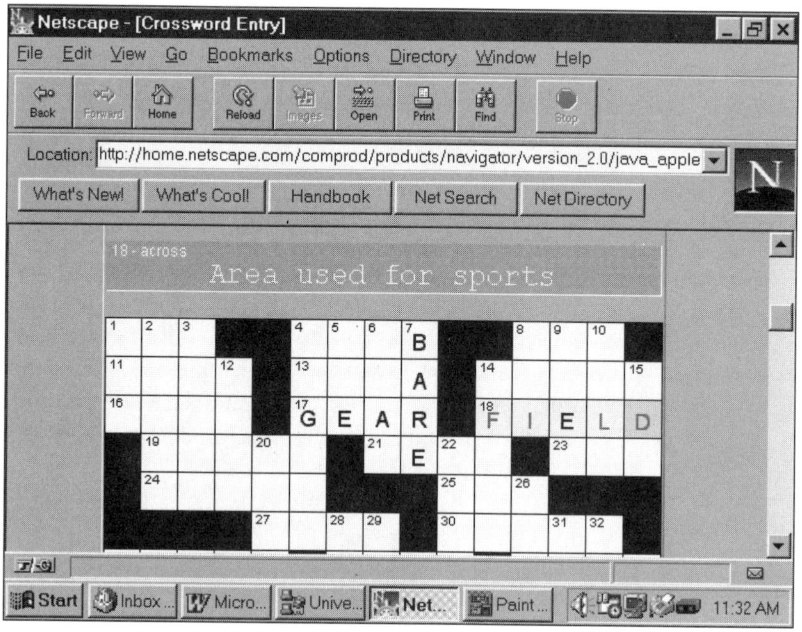

This applet runs an interactive crossword puzzle. The "Area used for sports" turned out to be an arena; that's why the "e" in "field" is black, while the rest of the letters are red to show that they are wrong.

When you use Netscape Gold to check out these pages, try out your View Source menu option, and look at how the applets are embedded into the HTML. Although Netscape Gold is designed so that you don't have to know what HTML even looks like, it's a good idea to familiarize yourself with it slightly because I'm going to be telling you all about the HTML applet tags a little later.

Figure 22.2 shows a picture of the HTML for the page with the crossword puzzle applet.

Figure 22.2

The tag for including an applet in a Web page is <APPLET></APPLET>. Imagine that!

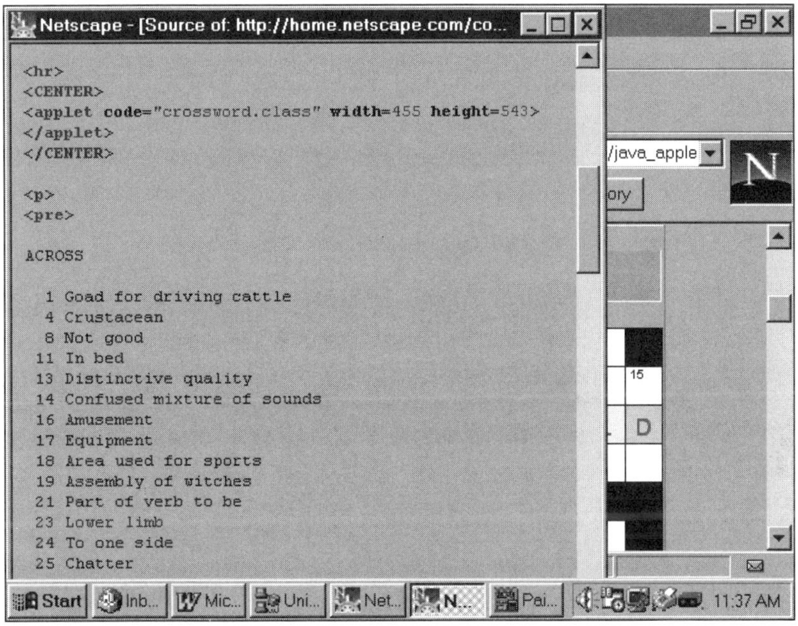

Netscape - [Source of: http://home.netscape.com/co...
<hr>
<CENTER>
<applet code="crossword.class" width=455 height=543>
</applet>
</CENTER>
<p>
<pre>
ACROSS
1 Goad for driving cattle
4 Crustacean
8 Not good
11 In bed
13 Distinctive quality
14 Confused mixture of sounds
16 Amusement
17 Equipment
18 Area used for sports
19 Assembly of witches
21 Part of verb to be
23 Lower limb
24 To one side
25 Chatter
/java_apple
ory
15
D
Start
Inb...
Mic...
Uni...
Net...
N...
Pai...
11:37 AM

Applets aren't just being used to show what the Java language can do. A fairly popular Web page on the Net that covers news about the computer industry is c|net. The c|net page has made great use of Java, to create an interesting applet. Figure 22.3 shows the c|net page.

By now you should have a vague idea of what applets are capable of. There are more and more Java applets appearing around the Net daily, so don't be afraid to go out and check them out. Navigator Gold should render all of the beta applets quite well.

NOTE. *A beta applet is an applet that was created using the beta 2 version of the Java Developer's Kit. There was an earlier version of the kit (the alpha 3 version), and applets created using this version will not show up in Netscape*

Figure 22.3

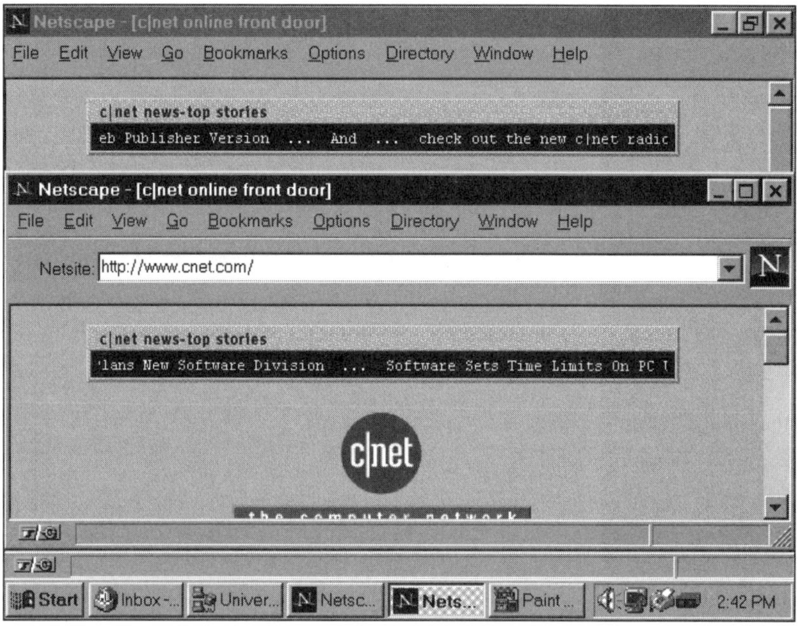

It's difficult to tell from the picture where the Java applet is. Look at the text that is in the black box near the top of the screen—it's a scrolling marquee which tells surfing visitors about what's new on the clnet site.

Gold. Not to worry, though; most of the alpha 3 applets are actually being converted to beta anyhow. And by the time this book comes out, Java 1.0 will be out, and Netscape will run Java 1.0 applets without a problem.

The big question you should be asking is how does a Java applet work within a Web page, and on the Internet. Let's take this one step at a time:

1. A Java applet runs from a piece of Java code that is saved in a file somewhere on the Internet. The file must have a .class extension.
2. When a Web page calls an applet, it must specify where to get the applet code, unless the code for the applet is in the same directory that the HTML page is in.
3. The applet doesn't necessarily have to be located on the same machine (or for that matter the same country) as the HTML page, although you'll see later why it may be necessary in some cases.
4. The applet is like an executable file embedded in the Web page. The applet keeps on running for as long as the browser has the Web page loaded. When the user clicks on a link to a new page, or closes the browser, the applet frees up any resources it has been using and then stops running, and only then does the Web page disappear.

5. The applet doesn't necessarily download to your hard drive the way other executable files do. In other words, it doesn't get automatically saved to your hard drive. Just like a picture on a Web page, it resides in your computer's temporary memory, and then it disappears when it is no longer needed.

The only way for part of an applet to actually reside on your hard disk is if the browser caches some of the information (such as the graphics) from the Web page. Thus, if you've just visited the crossword puzzle applet page, and you go back to it, it may load more quickly because some of the information about the page has been temporarily cached. However, if you go back after a few days of surfing, it probably won't load as quickly anymore because your cache has been filled up with information about more recently visited pages.

Readers with a lot of computer experience should by now be wondering about the security issues of downloading executable files that actually run on your machine temporarily. These are valid concerns, which are addressed in the first sidebar at the end of this chapter. For now, suffice it to say that the people at Sun Microsystems Inc. (the company from which Java originates) have some pretty neat tricks up their sleeves when it comes to avoiding security problems.

A Java applet becomes part of a Web page in the same way that a picture becomes part of a Web page. You simply add HTML tags that define the applet. The following syntax display gives you the basic, cut and dry information about including an applet in an HTML tag. You'll see this syntax display a lot in this chapter, and I'll explain why I use it and how it works right after this section.

Syntax Display: HTML Applet Tag

Form: `<APPLET [codebase=URL] CODE="Name.class" WIDTH=#pixels HEIGHT=#pixels></applet>`

Example: `<applet CODEBASE="http://java.sun.com/JDK-prebeta1/applets/NervousText" CODE="NervousText.class" WIDTH=400 HEIGHT=75 ALIGN=center> <PARAM NAME="text" VALUE="This is the blinking text applet"> </APPLET>`

This HTML coding is pretty standard. You always start with the keyword <APPLET>, and end with the keyword </APPLET>. The CODEBASE URL is only necessary if your Java code is located on a different machine or in a different directory than the HTML page itself. You must include the class name, as well as the width and height, but the alignment attribute is optional. The middle sentence which begins with PARAM is only necessary if the applet you are using takes input from the HTML page. There are many applets which don't have any input parameters, while there are some which will have a few different parameters—you can have as many as you wish. Parameters will be discussed when you use the Animator applet.

This is enough information for us to get started. Just so you know, however, the blinking text applet does exist—it's shown in Figure 22.4. The source code, showing the input PARAM tag in use, is shown in Figure 22.5. If you want to look at this applet running, point Netscape Gold to http://www.javasoft.com/JDK-prebeta1/applets/Blink/example1.HTML.

Figure 22.4

This is a screenshot showing four instances of Netscape, all aimed at the page with the blinking text applet, so that you can see it really does blink.

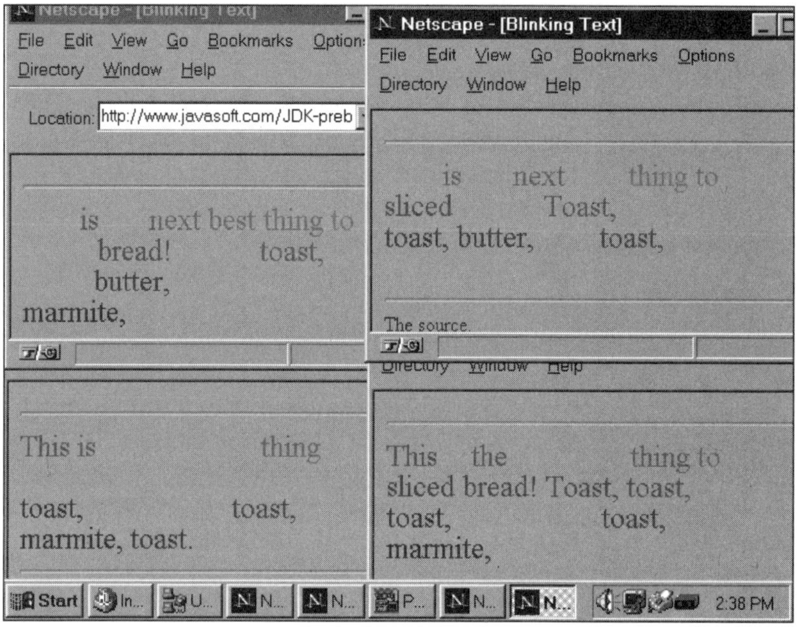

■ What Do You Need to Start?

You need to have a PC or a workstation to work on, and at least an Internet account. It definitely helps to have access to Web space on somebody's server so that you can upload Web pages with applets and test them out over the Web. Many Internet access providers are including Web space in their connection packages, so if you don't have Web space or access to a server, contact your Internet service provider.

There are two ways to run Java applets. You have to create the applet, then embed it in an HTML file. After that, you have to either upload the HTML file to a Web server and load the page with Netscape Gold, or use the appletviewer which comes with the Java Developer's Kit (discussed below). It is not actually possible to open an HTML file that has a Java applet embedded in it by using the Open Local File command of Netscape Gold. So, if you can't

Figure 22.5

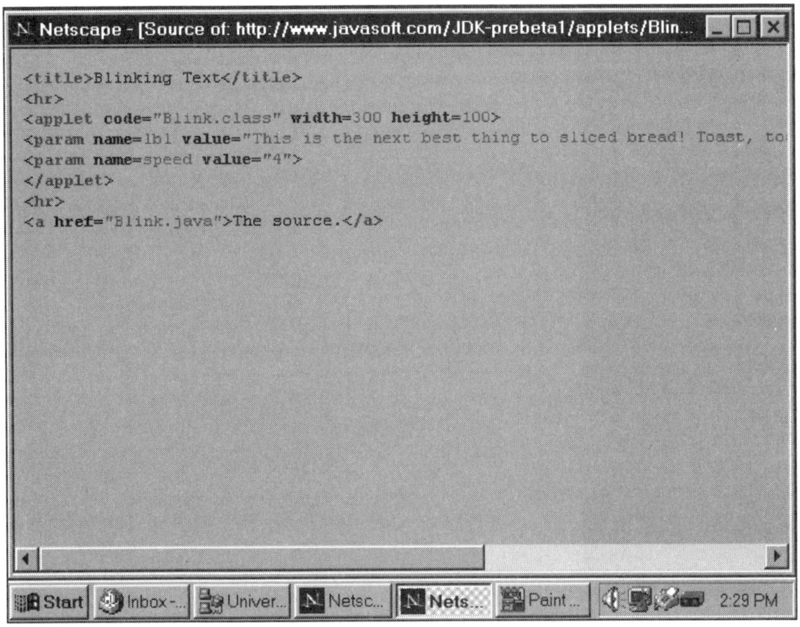

Here is the source code for the blinking text applet. Note that the text which blinks is actually a parameter label, and the speed at which the text blinks is also something which can be controlled by whoever writes the applet into the HTML page.

get access to a Web server, you'll be stuck viewing Java applets using the appletviewer, which isn't as interesting as viewing them as part of a Web page.

Now, assuming that you have all that, what you really need is the Java Developer's Kit, known as the JDK for short. You can download this kit from http://java.sun.com/JDK-beta/. The kit includes:

- Java Applet Upgrade Utility, for help in converting alpha 3 applets to the new beta 2 API. Unless you have been using the old alpha version of the Java programming language, you probably won't need to use this.
- Java Applet Viewer, for testing and running applets. This allows you to test your applets locally, without the necessity of putting them onto a remote Internet server.
- Java Debugger API and Prototype Debugger.
- Java Compiler.
- Java Interpreter.

You'll need to install the JDK, but as of January 1996, the help file for downloading the JDK is confusing and less than helpful for Windows users. I finally got things running after I followed the instructions posted at http://www.io.org/~mentor/setup_win95.txt. A summarized version of these instructions follows.

- Download the file for the JDK (by this time it will probably be called something like JDK-win32-x86.exe for the Windows NT and 95 version). Execute the file in the root directory. It will create a c:\java directory and subdirectories under java.
- Go to a DOS box and get to the java directory. At the prompt, type **c:\java> md .hotjava**. This will allow you to run the appletviewer without getting a nagging license screen every time you open it! (Note that you'll still get the license screen the first time you run it.)
- Run sysedit (in the file menu of NT or the Start menu of Win 95), and edit your autoexec.bat file. If you are a Windows NT user, you'll need to make the exact same changes to your autoexec.nt file. You need to add the following two lines (assuming you unloaded the JDK file in your root c: directory):

  ```
  set CLASSPATH=c:\java\classes;c:\html\classes
  path c:\java\bin;%path%
  ```

  You need to save the changes and reboot your machine.
- Make a directory off the root directory called HTML, and within that, make a directory called classes. This is where you will put your HTML and Java class files after you have created them, so that you can run them using the appletviewer.

I highly recommend that you download the Java API specification in HTML format. API stands for Application Programmer's Interface, and it describes the language and class libraries of a language. In other words, the API describes what has already been built into the language, so that you don't have to code everything from scratch. This is like having a language reference manual, but it's on screen instead of on paper. The easiest way to work on Java programs is to use a text editor to write them, and to keep a browser open at the same time, with your local version of the Java API documentation loaded in. You can download this from ftp://java.sun.com/docs/. I don't know what the exact file name is that you will have to download, as the only one there now is for the beta 2 version of Java. The file will probably be called something like JDK-apidocs.exe. Just download this file and then execute it to expand it. It will create a number of local HTML files in whichever directory you executed it. Finally just use the Open File command in the Netscape File menu to open up the file called packages.html or API_users_guide.html, and click away! The best part is that because Netscape will be using local documents, you don't have to be online.

You may be wondering about whether or not you need that thing called HotJava. HotJava is a Web browser developed by the people at Sun. The interesting thing about HotJava is that it was written entirely using the Java language.

At the time of this writing, the HotJava browser is only able to run alpha 3 Java applets. However, as soon as Java 1.0 comes out, HotJava will be updated, and should be able to run all current Java applets. If you have trouble getting an applet to run in Netscape Gold, you may want to try loading your HTML page into HotJava to see if it works there. You can get the HotJava Web browser from the Sun Web site: http://java.sun.com/.

The Animator Applet

The Animator applet was written by Herb Jellinek, and is copyrighted by SunMicrosystems. The Animator applet has been made available for public use, although it is still owned by Sun.

Before you start trying to create an animation, you should have a look at the Animator applet in use. Go to http://randall.uwaterloo.ca/celine/celine.htm. At the top of this page you'll see a small animation which uses the Animator applet. I created the pictures for this animation in Paint Shop Pro, a shareware graphics program. This is a pretty simple use of the applet; there are many more complicated and interesting animations around the Web. But this is the type of animation that anyone with access to the Animator applet can create—it just takes a bit of time to create the pictures!

Now, let's get started. Open a graphics program and draw a stick figure. If you don't have a fancy graphics program, don't worry about it. Paintbrush in Windows works fine, and most other systems have small graphics utilities that are easy to use. Your figure doesn't have to be beautiful or complicated; in fact, the simpler it is, the better! Now make a copy of your figure, and change it a little bit. For example, my little animation cartoon has just three pictures, one with the little guy's arms waving and his mouth open, and the other with his arms not visible and his mouth closed, and the final with his mouth in a frown.

Save one of the pictures as T1.gif, and the other as T2.gif. If you have a third and a fourth, they need to be called T3.gif and T4.gif. Go back to the Web page with my animation on it, and use the View menu to look at Document Source. You should see all of the HTML for my Web page, and about eight lines down you'll see the beginning of the applet tagging. It should look something like this:

```
<CENTER><APPLET CODEBASE="classes" CODE="Animator.class" WIDTH=150 HEIGHT=150>
<PARAM NAME=imagesource VALUE="pics">
<PARAM NAME=endimage VALUE=3>
<PARAM NAME=pause VALUE=200>
</applet></center>
```

Don't worry about the <Center></Center> tags. They're just being used as normal HTML to center whatever is in between them. The CODEBASE has a value of "classes" which doesn't look much like a URL. That's because it is a relative URL, reflecting that the code is on the same machine as the HTML page, but it is in a lower level directory called classes. The code is Animator.class, and there is a file in the directory classes which has the name Animator.class. The width and height are pretty self-explanatory; the idea is to choose a width and height which reflect the size of your pictures because the applet is clipped to this size.

The following three lines of HTML reflect the fact that the Animator code can take input values from the HTML page. In this case you are passing three parameters to the Animator class, including a directory for finding the location of the pictures, a number which indicates the number of the last picture to be shown, and a pause value, which tells the code how long to wait before moving on to the next picture. The way these parameters work is that somewhere in the Animator code you'll see something like:

```
String param = getParameter("imagesource")
```

So the value of imagesource (in my HTML it is "pics") gets assigned to the string variable called param, and the variable param can be referenced in other parts of the applet, whenever there is a need to know where the imagesource directory or URL is. If you don't really understand this, don't worry about it; you will when you start learning about the Java language.

Now you need to get a copy of the file Animator.class. The file is available for downloading from ftp://randall.uwaterloo.ca/java/Animator.class. Once you have Animator.class, you'll want to ftp your Animator.class file, as well as your saved images (T1.gif, T2.gif, and so on) onto a Web site that you have access to. The easiest thing to do is to create a directory structure for yourself. For example if your name is Jane Doe, and you've been given some Web space at http://www.machine.com/users/jdoe/, then create a structure as follows:

```
/users/jdoe/java/classes/
```

and

```
/users/jdoe/java/pics/
```

Now copy the file Animator.class into the java/classes/ directory, and make sure that the full file name is preserved. Java was developed on UNIX systems which permit really long file names, and so Java uses long file names and extensions. You'll have to be careful of this if you're working on a platform that doesn't support long file names well. (If your file does get concatenated to Animator.cla, you'll have to rename it after you've copied it. Using a 32-bit FTP program can really help avoid this type of situation.) Finally, copy your pictures to the java/pics/ directory. You are now ready to write an HTML file that will include your animation applet.

Your HTML file doesn't have to be anything special. Try this:

```
<HTML>
<BODY>
<H1><CENTER>My First Animation Applet</CENTER></H1>
<P>
<CENTER><APPLET codebase="classes" CODE="Animator.class" WIDTH=150 HEIGHT=150>
<PARAM NAME=imagesource VALUE="pics">
<PARAM NAME=endimage VALUE=2>
<PARAM NAME=pause VALUE=200>
</APPLET></CENTER>
<BR>
<P>
<STRONG><BIG>Isn't this cool?!!!</BIG></STRONG>
</HTML>
```

If you have more than two pictures, then you'll want to change the value for endimage from 2 to however many pictures you have. You may have to change the width and height, depending on how large your pictures are. (If your pictures aren't all the same size, set these attributes to reflect the size of the largest of your pictures.) If you've used the directory structure that is specified above, then the rest of the HTML should be fine.

Now save this HTML file, and copy it to the java directory you created in your Web space. For example, if you save your file as Jane.htm, and copied it correctly, you should have the following structure in your Web space (where an asterisk indicates a directory name, and a dash indicates a file name):

```
*users
   *jdoe
      *java
         -Jane.htm
         *classes
            -Animator.class
         *pics
            -T1.gif
            -T2.gif
```

If everything is in the right directory, you should now be able to use your Web browser to access the page, and hopefully, you'll see your animation. Just type your machine name, your directory name, and your HTML file name into the URL field at the top of the Netscape Gold screen, and press Enter. In our example this would be http://www.machine.com/users/jdoe/java/Jane.htm.

If it doesn't work, here are a few things to try:

- Make sure that your classes and pics directories are subdirectories of java, and not at the same level as java.
- If you are getting an "Error 404, file not found" message, then you haven't typed in your URL correctly, or your HTML file is not in the right place.
- Depending on the type of Web server, your HTML file will have a .html extension or a .htm extension; make sure you have the right one, and that you are typing in the write extension.

Once you do get it working correctly, you'll probably want to bookmark your page, so that you can show off to your friends and find your page easily if you go back and modify it often.

Congratulations...you've just used your first applet! You can spend some more time playing around with the Animator applet. There is much more you can do with it—make images move across the screen, give a background for your image, add sounds to the animation, and so on. All you have to do is check out the Java Animator information page at http://java.sun.com/applets/applets/Animator/index.html. This page will tell you all about the many features of the Animator applet, as well as what the plans are for future modifications and additions to the applet.

The next challenge is to create your own applet. But first you'll have to learn about the Java language. You'll learn some basics, and then you'll write our own simple applet. Before you read about the Java language however, make sure you read the next section on the chapter syntax. This will explain the format I use in showing different parts of the language.

Chapter Syntax

In this chapter, I will be using a syntax display to introduce different aspects of the Java programming language. An example of this is below, followed by a short explanation of how to use this syntax display.

Syntax Display: Comments

```
Form:    //comments
Example: //The purpose of the next three lines of coding is to test the input
         //data for any errors or invalid responses.
```

Comments are used to aid the programmer in remembering the purpose of different parts of code, and to help other people (who may have to maintain or update the code later) to understand the code. Comments must always be preceded by double backslashes. Comments should be used generously in programming code, to help make the code more readable and easier to maintain.

The above syntax display should give you all the information you need about the language syntax being discussed. In more difficult examples of coding syntax, I will use the custom of underlining keywords, enclosing necessary parts of code in arrow brackets: < >, and enclosing optional code attributes in square brackets: [ ]. For example, an assignment statement will be presented as follows:

***Syntax Display:* Variable Assignment Statement**

```
Form: [attributes] <type> <name> [= some value];
Example: public int coffee = 3;
```

The above example declares an integer variable with the name coffee, gives it a public access attribute, and assigns the value of 3 to coffee.

From this you can assume that the very least you need for a variable assignment statement is the variable type followed by the variable name, and that the statement may begin with one or more attributes (a characteristic of a variable), and may end with the assignment of some value to that variable.

Note that I will always underline keywords. You should get to know the keywords, so that you don't make the mistake of using them as variable or object names. However, you do not actually underline the keywords when you write your Java code. I am simply underlining them in this text so that they stand out.

The Java Language

Java is case-sensitive. This means that if you have a variable called foo, and you later refer to Foo, you won't get the results you expect.

There are no constants per se in the Java language. There are variables and there are objects. To create something that works as a constant, you create an object that is static and final. Objects will be explained after some Java basics are explained.

A statement in a Java program always ends with a semicolon, and compound code statements are surrounded by curly brackets: {, }.

Every variable and some methods (collection of code which does something) have types. For instance, a variable called Count which takes on values such as 3 and –497, but not values such as 2.37, is of type *int*. When a method has a type, such as an integer, it means that once that method is called, and has performed the tasks it was supposed to do, depending on how the performance of the tasks succeeded, the method returns a value. For instance, if you have a method that is supposed to draw a line on the screen, and you call it, and it draws the line, it might return to you a *Boolean* value of true, to tell you that the line drawing went well. So the method's return type would be *Boolean*.

The Java language is multithreaded. Many programming languages are sequential, with a beginning and an ending, and a predefined order of what will happen. When you look at a Java applet, you are watching a multi-threaded program. A thread is like a single sequential program—it has a beginning, an ending, and a certain predefined order as to what it will do. The difference between Java and many other programming languages is that Java allows multiple threads to run concurrently. Thus, one thread in Java may be downloading pictures, while another is downloading audio files, while yet another thread is displaying something on the screen. Using threads in Java is slightly complicated, but worth the effort. You will find a more detailed explanation of threads later on in the chapter when interfaces are discussed.

Common Types

The class is the single, unifying type in Java. If you are not familiar with classes or object-oriented programming, you can temporarily think of a class as a record data type with a number of fields which can contain variables or methods. A full discussion of object-oriented programming and Java's classes and packages will follow.

When you write an applet, the applet itself is one class, which may contain instances of other classes. Unlike traditional programming languages such as Pascal and C, in which the program often has a sequential layout with an identifiable start and finish, Java applets have threads and classes which appear throughout the program, and which interact in nonlinear ways. The Java language itself is not necessarily nonlinear, but the applets are.

Many of the traditional atomic types that you would see in Pascal or C are still used in Java. The difference is that these variables are found within the classes, as fields. In Java there are no global variables.

- *Boolean*—This is a variable that takes on a true or false value. No other values may be assigned to a Boolean-type variable. You can also have methods which have a Boolean return type.
- *Int*—This is an integer variable that can take on any value between –2,147,483,648 and 2,147,483,647.
- *Float*—This is a real number, which takes up four bytes of space. The Java floats are almost a complete implementation of the IEEE floating points.
- *Char*—A type of variable for storing a single keyboard character. In Java, a char is not limited to ASCII; it can be any unicode character. Thus European characters with accents and so on can be used. However, it is probably a good idea to stick to the standard ASCII set because

many platforms and operating systems won't know how to handle the extended characters available in unicode.

- *String*—There is a special class in Java for the manipulation of strings. For information on strings, check the API documentation under the java.lang package.
- *Array*—An array is a very powerful data type used when you wish to group a bunch of objects together. Arrays in Java are dynamic, and are referred to by pointers. For this reason, an array is a special data type, and it will be discussed at detail in a later section.
- *Object*—An object takes the form of an instance of a class in Java. If you are familiar with object-oriented programming, you will only need to breeze over that section to understand how the access specifiers work in Java. If you are unfamiliar with objects, don't worry; there is a whole section on object-oriented programming coming up.

Other variable types found in Java include byte, short, long, and double. These are numeric types.

Operators

Operators in Java are fairly standard, and for those who are familiar with C or C++, you'll find little that is different. I've only included the most common operators here, so if you're looking for something a little more complex, such as an XOR operator or the ? operator from C, you'll want to look through the specifications document on the Sun site. In general, all operators are the same as in C, except for the new operator, which will be discussed later when arrays are described.

Syntax Display: Assignment Operator

Form: `=`
Example: `character='s'`

The assignment operator assigns the value of s to the variable *character*, which must be either a char type or a string object. The assignment operator is an equal sign. This should not be confused with the equality test operator, which is a double equal sign. This is the cause of many programming errors in languages such as C and C++. However, Java will not let you make the following type of error:

```
if (character='s')  {
     //some code in here
     } else {
```

```
    //some other code
    }
```

In C or C++, this would always evaluate to true, and the first set of code would be performed, because every time the if statement is executed, the assignment operator will assign the value s to character, rather than testing to see if character has a value of s. However, if you tried to compile this code in Java, you would receive an error, and the code would not compile. The equal sign can only be used as an assignment operator, and cannot be used with the selection control operation if, which only evaluates Boolean expressions.

Syntax Display: Equality Test Operator

Form: `==` (a double equals sign)
Example: `number == 5`

This will test to see if the variable number (which must be of some numeric type) currently holds a value of 5. Note that the example shown in the syntax display for the assignment operator would work properly if the double equal sign was used:

```
if (character=='s')  {
     //some code in here
     } else {
     //some other code
     }
```

Syntax Display: Other Logical Operators

Form: `!, &&, ||,`
Example: `booleanvariable = ((number == 5) || (number == 7)) && (!otherbooleanvariable)`

The exclamation mark is a *not* operator, the double ampersand is an *and* operator, and the double line is an *or* operator. *booleanvariable* is a Boolean variable which will take on the value of true or false depending on the value of the expression on the left. The first thing that will be checked is whether or not the variable number has a value of either 5 or 7. If this is true, then the first half of the expression is true, and you go on to evaluate the part of the expression after the && sign. The double-ampersand sign means that both parts of the expression must be true for the whole expression to have a value of true. If the first part of the expression did not evaluate to true (if number == 8), then the second part of the expression wouldn't even be evaluated, because you already know that one part of the expression is false, and so booleanvariable will take on a value of false. This is known as short-circuit evaluation. The exclamation sign in front of otherbooleanvariable signifies a not operator; in other words, if otherbooleanvariable has a value of true, for the purpose of the expression, it has a value of false, and so again booleanvariable would take on a value of false. Only if the variable *number* has a value of either 5 or 7, and the variable otherbooleanvariable has a value of false, will the whole expression (and therefore booleanvariable) evaluate to true.

Other operators are self-explanatory: +, -, *, /. The BEDMAS precedence rules (brackets, exponents, division, multiplication, addition then subtraction) apply.

Methods

A method is a set of code statements which can be called and executed repeatedly. Using methods is a very important way to cut down on the length of your code. If you need to find the area of different rectangles and squares frequently throughout your code, then you would want to create a method that takes two integer values as parameters and returns an integer value that is the product of the two integer values. Then, every time you need to find the area of some square or rectangle you could just call your area method, and pass in the width and length of the rectangle you are currently working with.

The area example may seem a little silly, since the only calculation is a simple multiplication, but there are many instances where what you need to perform would take 12 or 100 lines of code. If you can type in the 12 lines once as a method, and then just type in one line of code every time you need to use those 12 lines, you'll save yourself a lot of trouble.

In Java, methods turn out to be inside of classes. For instance, the Java language has a package known as java.lang, and that package contains a class called Math. In Math there are many mathematical calculations for which there are predefined methods. So, as long as you have imported the java.lang.Math class into your code, then you can call on any of these predefined mathematical methods, instead of creating code yourself to perform these functions. You'll hear all about packages and classes later on; for now all you need to know is that every method is a field within a class, and cannot stand alone.

However, at some point you'll probably need to create your own method to do something, because there isn't already one in the Java package to do it. The following syntax display will show you how to declare your own method. One important convention to take note of is that method names are never capitalized.

Syntax Display: Methods

Form:
```
[attributes] <returntype> <methodname> (parameters) {
    //code containing instructions for method
    }
```

Example:

```
public static int max(int a, int b) {
  //some code which compares a and b and
  //returns the larger of the two
  }
```

This is an actual method found in the java.lang.Math class. There are two attributes for this method: public and static. These attributes will be discussed later on. int is the return type, thus the method max will return an integer value. If the method doesn't actually return a value (maybe it just does something, but doesn't give any input back to the code), then the return type would be void. There are two parameters for this method, both of which are integers. Every method must be followed by brackets containing the method's parameters, and if there are no parameters, the method must be followed by empty brackets. Note that in Java, parameters are passed in by reference. This means that if the value of the parameter changes within the method, that change is preserved beyond the scope of the method.

Control Structures

In many traditional, non-object-oriented programming languages, the if-else selection structure, and the repeating loop structure made up the skeleton of much of the program. However, because Java is object-oriented and multi-threaded, there is less usage of these structures for control of the program. In Java, control structures such as else-if and for loops are found only within classes and methods.

Syntax Display: If-Else (Selection Statement)

Form:

```
if <(some expression to be evaluated)> {
    //some code to be executed if the expression evaluated to true
    } else {
    //some code to be executed if the expression evaluated to false
    }
```

Example:

```
if (number==3) || (found) {
        done = true;
        if (othernumber == 9) {
             search = false;
             }
        } else {
        done = false;
}
```

Here you have a nested if statement. Note that an expression following an if is always surrounded by brackets. What happens in this example is that you test number to see if it has a value of 3; if it does, you don't need to bother testing to see if found (which must be a Boolean variable) has a value of true. The idea is that at least one of these two expressions must evaluate to true, in order for the statements done = true and the other if statement to be evaluated. So if one of these two expressions is true, the variable done gets assigned a false value, and you go into the next if statement. Now you test to see if the variable othernumber has a value of 9. If it does, search gets assigned a value of false. If it doesn't, nothing happens, because there is no else after the bracket following false. After this, the first if statement is finished—because you found one of the expressions to be true, you evaluated the first part of the if statement, and you ignore the second part (the part after the else). If number did not have a value of three and found was not true, then the whole expression is not true, and you would skip down to execute the code after the else keyword. So you would set done equal to false, and our if statement would terminate. In case this has been more confusing than helpful, the following table will show you what happens to the Boolean variables done and search, depending on the values of number, found, and othernumber:

number	**found**	**othernumber**	**done**	**search**
3	true	9	true	false
3	true	(some other number)	true	?
3	false	9	true	false
3	false	(some other number)	true	?
(some other number)	true	9	true	false
(some other number)	true	(some other number)	true	?
(some other number)	false	9	false	?
(some other number)	false	(some other number)	false	?

So, if number ==3, found == true and othernumber ==9, then done will get assigned true, and search will get assigned false. In some cases, you don't know what value search will hold, because the statement in which search occurs doesn't get executed. In these cases the variable search will contain whatever value it contained before the if statement was executed.

Note that there is no such thing as elseif in Java, as there are in some other programming languages. Instead, the syntax is simply *else if*. Thus, you are really creating a new *if* statement. This can be rather confusing, and takes some getting used to for those of us accustomed to compound if statements.

Another selection structure which is very useful but not as common as the if-else structure is the switch structure. The switch structure is much the same as the case statement in some other languages. The switch structure is used when you have a variable which can take on only a small, finite number of values. For instance, suppose you had a variable called FamilyMember, which can only take on the string values of "Mother," "Father," "Daughter," and "Son." Depending on which value the variable takes, you want different code to be executed. In this case you would use a switch statement, with the variable FamilyMember, and four cases: Mother, Father, Daughter, and Son. The following syntax display will use this example to show you how the switch statement works.

Syntax Display: The Switch Statement

Form:

```
switch (<variablename>)  {
case "1" :
     //some code if variable has value 1
case "2" :
     //some code to be executed if variable == 2
default  :
     //some code to be executed if variable doesn't fit any
     //of the other cases.
}
```

Example:

```
switch (FamilyMember) {
case "Mother" :
     //some code here
case "Father"  :
     //some other code here
case "Daughter"  :
     //some other code here
case "Son"  :
     //some other code here
}
```

Switch statements are found within class methods. Unless this switch statement is part of a repeating loop structure, it will only be executed once each time the method is called. Suppose the method is called, and Family-Member has a value of "Father". In this case the switch statement will execute, and the code on the line after case "Father" : will be executed. After that code is executed, the next code to be executed will be whatever code comes after the last parenthesis. Note that in my example, I didn't use a default case. I could have used "Son" as my default case, but if for some reason the value of FamilyMember took on some other value such as "lsjfakljZ", then the code for Son would be executed, and I probably wouldn't want it to be. A good thing to do is to include an error message statement as the default case, if you're sure you only want your variable to take on the specified values. Thus I should have added the following:

```
.......
        default :
              system.out.println("Invalid value for variable FamilyMember");
  }
```

This would give a system error if something had gone wrong.

The loop structure is a common programming structure, and is used whenever there is a need to repeat a set of instructions a number of times. There are two main types of loop controls that can be used within Java. The first is a simple incrementation and count, and this is known as a *for* loop in Java. If you want the loop to repeat 10 times, set the incrementer to 1, initialize a counter to 0, and when the counter gets incremented to 10, the loop will terminate. The second type of loop is a *while* loop and for this structure it is not necessary to know how many times you need to repeat the instructions, as long as you have some kind of known event after which you want the loop to terminate. For this type of case, you have a Boolean variable, and you create the *while* loop so that it will keep on repeating until your Boolean variable becomes true. You just need to make sure that you have something in your code that will check for your event and change the Boolean to true when the event occurs.

Syntax Display: for Loop Structure

```
Form:    for (<variable initialization>; <test expression>; <incrementation
expression>) {
          //some code here
         }
Example: for (int  i = 0; i < maxnumber; i++) {
                int x = i;
                imageUpdate(image imf, int flag, int x, int y);
         }
```

The *for* loop is a very powerful operation in Java, allowing the programmer to repeat steps a specified number of times. The structure in the above example basically means initialize i to 0, execute the two inner statements, then increment i by 1, and execute the two statements again. Keep on incrementing i and executing the statements as long as i is less than the variable maxnumber. So if maxnumber happens to have a value of 8, then the two inner statements will be executed eight times. So the first expression in the *for* brackets declares a variable i, and initializes its value to 0. The second statement tells the computer when to stop repeating the inner statements, based on an expression involving i. The final part of the *for* statement is an incrementer; the two plus signs signify that every time the *for* loop is executed, add 1 to the value of i. If the last part were i--, then it would mean that every time the loop was executed the value of i should be decreased by 1.

Syntax Display: While Loop Structure

Form:
```
while (<BooleanVariable>) {
//code to be executed while Boolean variable is true
//should be some code in here which will eventually
//cause the BooleanVariable to be false, to prevent
//an infinitely repeating loop
}
```
Example:
```
while (test) {
      //some instructions to be performed
      if (NumberOfGuests > 25) {
            test = false;
      }
}
```

A very important thing to remember in creating a *while* loop is to make sure that the Boolean variable being tested is initialized to true before the loop code. This will ensure that the loop will execute at least once. Each time the loop executes, the computer will check to see if the variable NumberOf-Guests is larger than 25. If it is, then test will get assigned the value of false, and the while loop will terminated. This may seem like a repeat of what you did with the *for* loop, but there is a slight difference. In this piece of code, you cannot tell how many times the loop will execute, because you don't know what the value of NumberOfGuests is before the loop executes. If NumberOfGuests has a value of 34 before the loop executes, then the loop will only execute once. If it has a value of three, then the loop should execute 22 times. All you know is that you want the set of instructions to be repeated until NumberOfGuests is equal to or greater than 25. This is known as an event-controlled loop.

Another very important control structure which is often overlooked are the begin and end parentheses. These items can make the difference between code that works correctly and code that doesn't.

Syntax Display: Begin and End Parentheses

Form:
```
{
      //some code here, can be just one line, or it can be twenty {
            //some more code here in the nested parentheses
            }
      //some more code here
      }
```
Example:
```
static void isWon (int pos) {
            for (int i = 0; i < DONE ; i++) {
                  if (i == pos) {
                        won[i] = true;
```

```
            }
        }
    }
```

In this example, you are looking at the code for the method isWon, which has an integer parameter, pos. The entire code for the method is enclosed between the first open parenthesis and the last close parenthesis. The method consists of a single *for* statement. i is initialized to 0, and the *for* loop will repeat, with the value of i incrementing by 1 each time, until the value of i is equal to or greater than the value of the integer variable DONE (which would have been declared previously in the code). Every time the loop is executed, the *if* selection statement will be checked. If, for the current value of i, i has the same value as the parameter pos which was passed in, then the statement in the innermost set of parentheses (won[i] = true;) will be executed. Notice that the *if* statement itself is surrounded by parentheses, and that the number of open parentheses is equal to the number of closed parentheses.

Special Type: Arrays

Now that you've gone through control structures and assignment statements, you have a basis on which to explain the implementation of arrays. As mentioned earlier in the section on types, arrays are special. Because they are implemented dynamically (which means that the amount of memory they use can change as the array changes size), they must be both declared and assigned, as follows.

Syntax Display: Array Declaration

```
Form: <type> <arrayname>[ ] ;
Example: int i[ ];
```

This is a declaration of an array of integers, called i. This is a one-dimensional array; a two-dimensional array would have two sets of square brackets ([ ] [ ]) after the array name. Arrays in Java are always length-checked, so you do not need to specify how many elements will be held in the array. Declaring an array does not actually create it, however, and it is because of this that arrays are special cases. Because an array can vary in length, you must actually allocate space for an array by calling the new operator. The new operator is explained in the next syntax display.

Syntax Display: New Operator for Arrays

```
Form: <array declaration as above> = new <type>[<number of elements>]
Example: int i[] = new int[10]
```

In this example the array is declared, and assigned space in memory for ten integers. Each element in the array can be accessed individually. For example, if you wanted to test to see if the third element has a value of five, your expression would be:

```
if i[3] == 5 { ….
```

You can also explicitly assign values to the array in this way. For example, if you wanted the array to have values from 31 to 40, you could use the following:

```
final static int firstvalue = 31;
for ( a = 0, a > 9, a++) {
    i[a +1] = a + firstvalue;
}
```

What you are doing here is declaring a constant using the final and static attributes. This constant holds the number which you want to have as the first value in the array. Then you create a *for* loop. Note that in this for loop, you use *a* as your integer instead of the usual i. This is because you've already used I as the name of your array, and you don't want to confuse the situation. So the *for* loop will execute 10 times, and each time it executes it will put a number into the next spot in the array. For instance, on the first execution of the loop, *a* has a value of 0. You assign the value of 0 + firstvalue (31) to the array i, at the index a + 1, which is 1. Thus, you can picture the array so far as looking like this:

```
i[31, , , , , , , , , ]
```

Only the first element in the array has been assigned something. The array has been declared in such a way that there is room for nine more integers. So, on the next execution of the loop, a is incremented by one, and now has the value 1. You assign a + firstvalue, which now is equal to 32, to the a + 1 element in i, which is now the second element. This process will continue until the array looks like this:

```
i[31, 32, 33, 34, 35, 36, 37, 38, 39, 40]
```

Note that you'll probably never actually see the array printed out with all of its elements like this. But this is what you should be picturing in your head when you think of an array of 10 integers. It is also important to realize that the array doesn't have to hold sequential data. In fact, the array could just as easily hold integers that look like this:

```
i[478, 32, -790, 33, 8, -2, 435, 1000, 289, 43]
```

The biggest difference is in the assignment. In this case, you couldn't just use a *for* loop to assign these numbers to the different elements of the array as you did in the previous example. You would need to have individual assignment statements for each element, as follows:

```
i[1] = 478;
i[2] = 32;
i[3] = -790;
       .
       .
i[10] = 43;
```

Finally, remember that arrays don't have to hold integers. They can hold characters, strings, and, most often, objects. And now were finally going to learn about objects, classes, packages, and methods, in the following discussion on object-oriented programming.

Object-Oriented Program—The Quick and Dirty Lowdown

Although you may expect that the code for an applet such as the "Work in Progress" Animation would be really long, it's not. That's because the code depends on already developed Java code that has been developed at Sun Microsystems. This code takes the form of classes which are contained in packages, and these packages are embedded into Netscape Gold. For example, if you look at the code for the animator class you'll see lines at the top that say such things as import java.io.InputStream, import java.awt.image.ImageProducer, and so on. These lines tell the Java compiler that certain methods held within the classes above will be needed. Thus when the compiler gets to some code that says read(), then the compiler looks through its information about the imported classes and says, "Aha, the read method is defined by java.io. Input-Stream...now I know what to do!" (Okay, so the Java compiler doesn't actually talk, but you see what I'm getting at.) Being able to import previously defined classes means that you don't have to figure out how to make the computer do everything; a lot of stuff is already figured out for you. (For those who care, this means that Java is a "high level language" as compared to a "low level language" in which strange people write things in series of 1s and 0s).

The idea of importing classes is Java's version of object-oriented programming. Let me explain. Java has a main class, which is called Object. From Object there are subclasses, and from those subclasses there are more subclasses. You should be picturing a hierarchical structure. Let's make up an example so that you have an idea of what all this means. Suppose that under the class Object, there was a class called Shape. Shape is Object's "child" and

Object is Shape's "parent." Now suppose Shape has two more subclasses (children) called Square and Circle. So far you have the following:

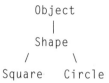

```
        Object
          |
        Shape
       /      \
   Square   Circle
```

Every class can contain two different types of information: methods and variables. So let's say that the class Shape has a variable that defines what color it is: Color. And let's say that it has a method called Area, that calculates how big the shape is. Because Shape has this variable Color and this method Area, Square and Circle also each have a variable Color and a method Area. If the variable Color is assigned a value of "purple" within the Shape class, then Circle and Square inherit the Color "purple". *Inherit* is the key word here.

Every subclass inherits all of the variables and methods of its parent class. Inheritance is a very important concept. If our original class, Object, has an initialization method, then the Shape class inherits that method, and therefore Square and Circle also inherit the initialization method. However, inheritance only goes one way. Suppose you declared a new subclass of Circle, and called it LittleCircle, and you added a variable to LittleCircle that limited the size of its radius. This would have absolutely no effect on the Circle class. In other words, classes do not inherit from their children or subclasses.

An important thing to note is that each class can inherit from only one parent. This is known as single inheritance, and is one of the main differences between Java and C++. In C++ it is possible to have multiple inheritance, which can get very complicated. Java's single inheritance is a blessing for those of us new to programming; it keeps things nice and simple.

Every time you create an applet, you define a new class, and the name of your Java code takes on that class name. For example, suppose you created an applet that caused words to flash on the screen. You would probably start your Java code by creating a class called Flash. Then your Java code would have to be saved as Flash.java. Then, when you compile your code, it would compile into a file called Flash.class. In other words, your applet code basically creates a new Java class, and the HTML page runs that class.

When you define your class, you may wish to make it a subclass of some already existing class in the API library. If you don't define it as such, the compiler assumes a default inheritance from the main Java class, Object. To define a new class you need to use the keyword *class*, and to define your class as a subclass of some other class, you must use the keyword *extends*. Let's take a look at the class definition syntax display.

Syntax Display: Defining a New Class

```
Form: [attributes] class <name> extends <superclassname> {
        //some code here
    }
Example:     public class Myapplet extends applet {
               int MaxSize = 5;
          }
```

In this example, you are declaring a new class, and calling it MyApplet. MyApplet is now a subclass of Applet, and therefore it inherits all of Applet's characteristics and methods. If Applet has a method init(),then MyApplet also has that, but you don't need to type that into our code; it is implicit because MyApplet *extends* applet. MyApplet is different from Applet in that it has the added characteristic of MaxSize. The word public in this example is an access attribute, and it means that any other classes in other packages can "see" the class MyApplet. Some common attributes which you will discuss include access attributes such as private and public, as well as the final, static, and abstract attributes.

You can only inherit or extend a superclass which is your own, is in the same package as the class you are creating, or is public. If the class you create inherits another class which is your own, that other class must be in the same package, and thus the .class file for the superclass must be in the same directory that you are currently working in. All of the classes in the Java API are public classes and can be extended. However, it is not necessarily true that all of the methods and variables within those classes are public.

It is important to realize that when you write Java code, you don't usually operate on classes except when you use the static attribute, which will be discussed in the next section. Instead you operate on instances of classes. As an example, let's look at our class structure above. If you wanted to have a square as part of our applet, you would create an instance of the class square. You might call it *sq*. Then you could perform operations on sq, or do things with sq. Calling a new instance of an object is the same as declaring a new variable. The only difference is that instead of using a predefined type such as int or float, the variable type is the class name. Let's look at the syntax for calling an instance of an object.

Syntax Display: Calling a New Instance of an Object

```
Form: <classname> <instancename>;
Example: Square sq;
```

This example creates a "variable" called sq. sq is an instance of the class Square, and thus the variable sq has all of the characteristics that are part of the class Square (perhaps the color purple), and all of the methods that are part of the class Square can be performed on sq. For instance, if Square has a method for initialization that looks like init(); then you can now call sq.init(). This would initialize sq, the instance of the class Square. It is important to understand that you can't actually call the object Square. Whenever you have an instance of a class you can call methods and variables of that class using the format <instancename>.<methodorvariablename>.

Attributes

Access Attributes: Packages and Classes

One of the reasons that the Java language has become so popular for networking applications is because of its security features. Every class, and every method or variable within a class, can have an access attribute. Access attributes include private, protected, and public. What these attributes mean is somewhat complicated, and the differences can be quite subtle and difficult to comprehend. You'll look at definitions of these attributes first, and then you'll go through a number of examples. Before the definitions, however, it will be necessary to go through an explanation of how packages and classes work together.

A Java package is basically a grouping of Java classes that are related to one another in some way. When you look at the Java API documentation, you'll see that everything is divided up into packages such as java.net and java.applet. In java.net, you'll find all of the Java classes that are specifically related to using Java over the Internet, such as the class URLConnection and the class ServerSocket.

If you create a few Java classes that you think are related and that you'll want to use again, then you should put them together as a package. The way to do this is to change your directory structure. Remember when you put together a directory structure in order to run the Animator applet? It looked like this:

```
*users
      *jdoe
          *java
                 -Jane.htm
                 *classes
                       -Animator.class
                 *pics
                       -T1.gif
                       -T2.gif
```

Now, let's suppose that you have written three new Java classes, called FlashingText.class, ColorText.class, and SizeText.class. You could just put them into the classes directory with Animator.class, but these three new classes are related, so you should make them a separate package. Note that right now, Animator.class is not specified as part of a package, and so by default it is part of the "unnamed package."

In order to make the three text-related classes a separate package, you need to add a directory to the classes directory, and include the three classes within that directory. The new structure should then look like this:

```
*users
     *jdoe
        *java
            -Jane.htm
            *classes
                -Animator.class
            *text
                -FlashingText.class
                -ColorText.class
                -SizeText.class
            *pics
                -T1.gif
                -T2.gif
```

Now, all three text-related classes should be considered part of the text package. For the purpose of examples later on in this section, I'm going to add another package to this classes directory, called display, with two classes in it called BackgroundPattern.class and Border.class. Now the directory structure looks like this:

```
*users
     *jdoe
        *java
            -Jane.htm
            *classes
                -Animator.class
            *text
                -FlashingText.class
                -ColorText.class
                -SizeText.class
            *display
                -BackgroundPattern.class
                -Border.class
            *pics
```

```
-T1.gif
-T2.gif
```

Adding package structure to your classes directory changes the way the applet HTML tag works, but only slightly. The difference is that now when you specify "code = Something.class," you have to add the package name and a slash before you type the classname. So, if I had an applet based on the FlashingText code, the HTML tag would look like this:

```
<Applet codebase=classes code=text/FlashingText.class width = 200 height =
75></Applet>
```

Now that you have a package directory structure to work with, let's look at the access attribute definitions.

Public

A class that has a public access attribute can be imported. So, if you create a class, and you want to be able to import that class into some other Java code you write, you had better make sure that your original class is public. There are many public classes in the Java API, but many of these public classes depend on other private classes which you don't see unless you look at the source code. Variables and methods can also be public, although you can only have public variables and methods in a class that is public. (This makes sense, because if you make a class that is not public, it won't be able to be imported into other code. If it can't be imported into other code, then there isn't any point in making one of its methods or variables public, because nothing outside the class will be able to use it anyhow.) If you have a variable or a method that is public, then that method or variable can be called from some other code, as long as the class the variable or method belongs to has been imported into that other code.

Private

A private class is one that cannot be imported. This will not often be very useful, but there is one exception. This is when you wish to create a helper class within another class file. If you create a class file that has a number of different classes created in it, the compiler will break up the file into separate .class files. Thus, there could be a private class called FlashingMechanism within FlashingText.java. Because FlashingMechanism.class is created within FlashingText.java, it is basically a field of FlashingText.class.

Although private classes are not used very often, private methods and variables are quite common. The idea behind making a class public, but making some of its methods or variables private, is to protect code. Suppose you have a variable in your FlashingText.class called maxStringLength. The purpose of this variable might be to prevent people from using FlashingText.class with really long strings (maybe the class only works with strings that are less than 200 characters long). You want this variable to be part of FlashingText.class, so that when a user enters a string as a parameter you can check the string against maxStringLength to ensure it is not too long. However, you don't want users to be able to import FlashingText.class, and change maxStringLength from 200 to 1,000, because you know that FlashingText.class won't work with strings that long. The answer to this problem is to make maxStringLength a private variable. Then write a method called StringLengthCheck which is public, but which uses the variable maxStringLength. StringLengthCheck can call on maxStringLength because they are both in the same class. However, any code which imports FlashingText.class can only call on the StringLengthCheck method, and can't explicitly call maxStringLength.

A common convention you should be aware of is to make data fields private, and to make methods which can access those data fields public. In this way, other users can import your classes, and use your data, but they can only access that data indirectly, and therefore they cannot change or corrupt your data, because you are controlling the methods by which they access it.

An interesting question is what happens to subclasses when the parent class has private methods or variables. Suppose you create a new class called SlowlyFlashingText.class, which extends FlashingText.class. SlowlyFlashingText.class inherits everything that FlashingText.class has, and that includes private fields. However, because maxStringLength is a private variable, SlowlyFlashingText cannot access it directly. It too can only access StringLengthCheck. Thus, private methods or variables are inherited, but cannot be overwritten in subclasses.

No Access Attribute

A class must be either private or public. However, a field within a class (a variable or a method) can have no access attribute, the private access attribute, the public access attribute, or the protected access attribute. You'll talk about the protected access attribute later on. For now let's look at what it means for a field to have no access attribute specified.

A field which has no access attribute specified can be seen and used by any class that is within the same package. For instance, in our structure above, FlashingText.class and ColorText.class are both in the text package. Thus, the code for ColorText.class can actually use methods and variables within FlashingText.class that have no access attributes specified. Of course, fields within FlashingText.class which are public are also available to ColorText.class, but fields that are private are not. You may be wondering what the purpose would be of giving a field no access attribute, when other classes are going to be able to access it; why not just give it the public attribute? The answer is that you may have a variable or method which you want to make available for all the classes within the text package, but which you don't want made available to other classes in other packages which extend FlashingText.class.

Protected

The protected access attribute is pretty much the exact opposite of having no access attribute. You cannot have a protected class, only protected methods and variables. When a variable or method has the protected attribute, only descendants (subclasses) of that class can have access to the variable. Thus classes which are in the same package as FlashingText.class do not have access to protected fields within FlashingText.class, unless they actually extend FlashingText.class.

An interesting twist can be found here. The protected access attribute can be paired with the public access attribute. If a subclass of FlashingText.class is in a completely different package then that subclass can access a public protected method within FlashingText.class, but not a protected method within FlashingText.class.

After reading the four definitions above, you should be thoroughly confused. Let's draw some diagrams using the example package and class structure from above. This way you'll go through a number of examples, and show what each access attribute actually allows.

Figure 22.6 is a visual representation of our two packages, and the classes that make up those packages. Note that almost all of the classes are public. The only exception is FlashingMechanism.class, which is private. This private class is actually a field of FlashingText.class. It is only accessible in the FlashingText.class code. Thus, you could not refer to the object FlashingMechanism.class in the code for the ColorText applet, even though the ColorText.class and FlashingText.class are in the same package. The only way that the class FlashingMechanism.class is accessed is indirectly through the use of FlashingText.class. So, if some other class (say, Border.class in the display package) extends FlashingText.class, then it can call on methods in FlashingText.class which may use FlashingMechanism.class, but it cannot directly call on any methods or variables within FlashingMechanism.class.

Figure 22.7 is a visual representation of some of the code which you might find in FlashingText.class. You'll look at this code in terms of what it means to the other package and classes.

In this figure you see that FlashingText.class has, among other code, two fields with access attributes. The first field is an integer variable called maxStringLength, with a private access attribute. The second field is a public method called StringLengthCheck, which has a Boolean return type. Now, ColorText.class can call on the method StringLengthCheck because the method is public, and because the class in which the method is found is public and in the same package as ColorText.class. If BackgroundPattern.class or

Figure 22.6

Visual representation of a set of packages and classes

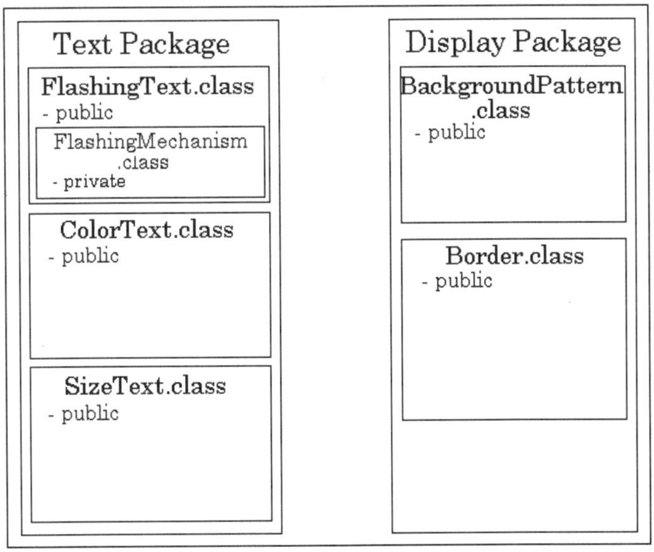
Text Package
FlashingText.class
- public
FlashingMechanism
.class
- private
ColorText.class
- public
SizeText.class
- public
Display Package
BackgroundPattern
.class
- public
Border.class
- public

Figure 22.7

An example of the type of code that might be found in FlashingText.class

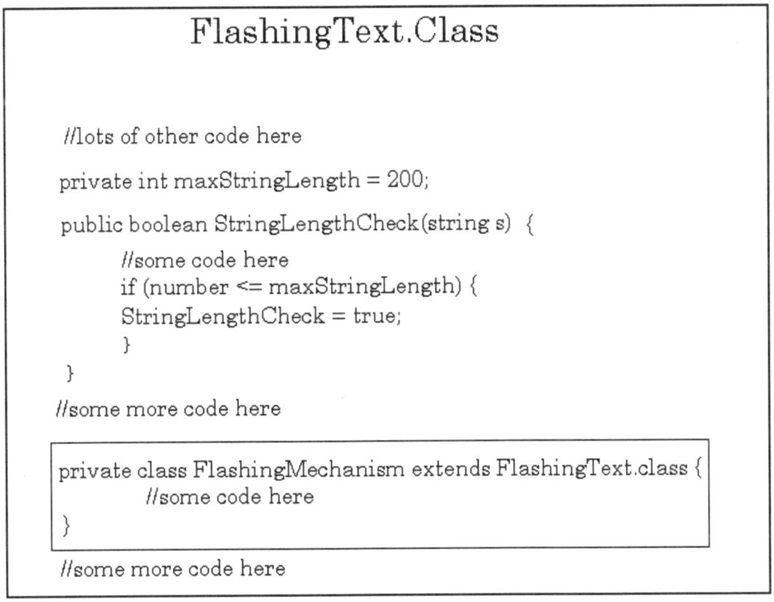
FlashingText.Class
//lots of other code here
private int maxStringLength = 200;
public boolean StringLengthCheck(string s) {
//some code here
if (number <= maxStringLength) {
StringLengthCheck = true;
}
}
//some more code here
private class FlashingMechanism extends FlashingText.class {
//some code here
}
//some more code here

Border.class either were to import the Text package, or were to extend FlashingText.class specifically, then they too would have access to the StringLengthCheck method. Note that maxStringLength can not be accessed by anything except instances of FlashingText.class. If another class extends FlashingText.class, it still cannot directly access maxStringLength.

Concept: Polymorphism

When you create a subclass, it is often necessary to adjust the methods which the subclass has inherited from its parent. For example, you may have a class called Square, which has a method called Area. That method basically consists of multiplying the length of a side by itself. This is fine until you create a subclass of Square called Rectangle. For a rectangle, the area is defined as width times length, not the square of one side. Thus, you would want to override the area method that was inherited from Square. You can still keep the name area; all you have to do is re-declare the method. The idea of using the same name for a method which varies throughout a hierarchy to suit each particular class is called polymorphism. This is a very important and useful concept to understand.

Concept: Virtual Methods

The concept of virtual methods is slightly more difficult to explain than the concept of polymorphism, although the two are very much related. Figure 22.8 sets the scene.

In the figure, you have two classes, A and B. Note that B extends class A, and thus B inherits all of A's methods and variables. You can see in B that Method D has been inherited, but the code for Method D is different in Class B than it is in Class A. Thus Method D has been overridden in Class B. The tricky part comes when an instance of Class B calls on Method F. In other words if 'littleb' is an instance of Class B, then you could call littleb.F, because the method F is inherited. However, you'll notice in the Figure 22.8 describing all this that the method F itself calls on Method D. The question is, which version of Method D will be used in this case? The version in Class A or the version in Class B? Well, the method F, which is calling the method D, was originally called from Class B, and therefore, the version of Method D which is in Class B will be used. This is known as a virtual method. Java keeps track of where in the class hierarchy methods and variables are called from, and uses the method which is closest in the hierarchy to the original call.

Figure 22.8

Visual representation of a virtual method

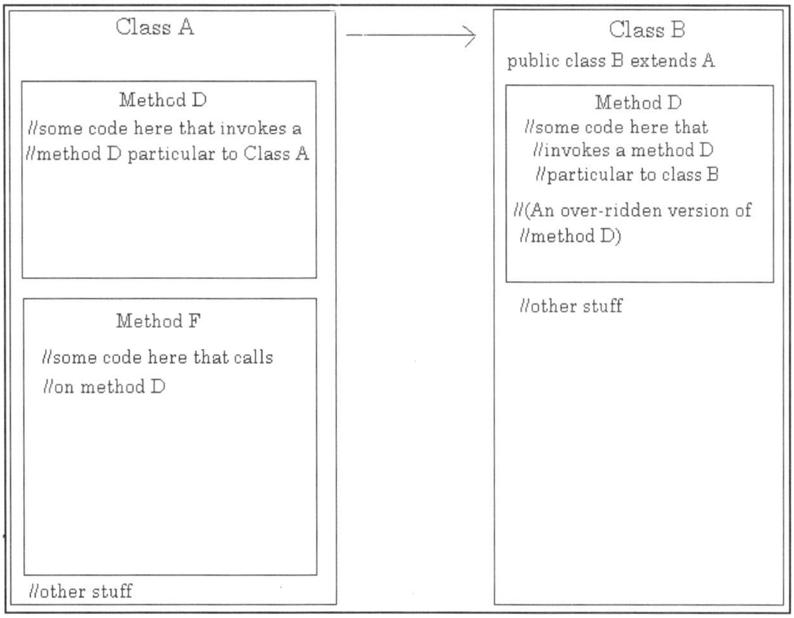

Final Attribute

When a class is given a final attribute, that class cannot be subclassed. This means that if the class ColorText.class was final, you would not be able to have subclasses called BlueText.Class and RedText.class that extend ColorText.class.

There are a number of reasons for wanting to make a class final. Making a class final prevents users from modifying the methods and variables within that class. So, if you have a class called DeleteLine, and that class has a number of methods and variables that allow users to delete lines from the screen, you may want to make the class final to prevent users from making subclasses of DeleteLine, and then modifying the deletion methods to delete more than just a line. Thus, the final attribute is somewhat like the private access attribute in that it can provide protection, and help ensure that the methods and variables you create cannot be modified. However, the final attribute does allow all of the public methods within a final class to be used if that final class is imported, whereas a private class could not be imported at all.

Making methods and variables final has the effect of preventing them from being overwritten. Thus, if you have a class Square, which contains a method Area, you may want to make Area final, so that other classes can't overwrite the formula for calculating the area of a square. The final attribute also has the beneficial effect of making the Java bytecode execute much more quickly. The point of using the final attribute is that the runtime and compiler will not have to search through the class hierarchy looking for other overwritten versions of the method or variable.

This connects to the idea of virtual methods, which was discussed earlier. For example, if you look back to the scenario from the discussion of virtual methods, you used Classes A and B, and there was a Method D, which was overridden in Class B. If Method D had been declared final in Class A, then Class B would not have been able to override it, and so when Method F called on Method D, there would only have been one to choose from.

Static Attribute

A class cannot be static. The static attribute applies only to methods and variables within a class. When a variable has the static attribute, it means that that variable can only be called on the class itself, and cannot be called on a specific instance of a class. This is probably confusing to you, as it confused me greatly at first. You use a static method or variable whenever that method or variable should remain the same across all instances of the class. In fact, the use of the attributes static and final together constitute what most programmers know as a constant. Let's look at a real example from the Java API. In the java.lang package, there is a Math class, and within the Math class there are two variables: e and PI. Figure 22.9 shows the API documentation for these variables.

The variable e has the attributes public, final, and static, and is of type double. The double type is basically for a real number with lots of decimal places. The variable is public, meaning that anyone who imports java.lang.Math can use the variable e. It is final so that the value of e cannot be overwritten. This makes sense, because you wouldn't want its value to change. It is static, because it doesn't matter which instance of the class Math you create; the value of e will always be the same.

The big difference in using a static variable is in the calling of it. You don't call a static method or variable on an instance of a class, you call it on the class itself. So, you could have the following code:

```
if (somevariable < java.lang.Math.E) {
          //some code here
}
```

If you had explicitly imported java.lang.Math, then you could have the following:

```
if (somevariable < E) {
     //some code here
}
```

Figure 22.9

The documentatiion for e and PI

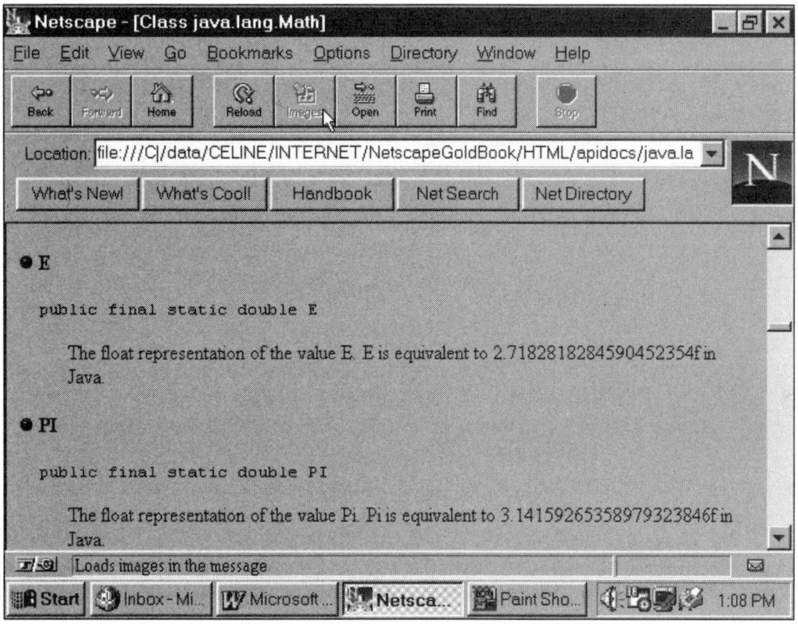

If you created an instance of the class Math, called mymath, you couldn't have the following:

```
if (somevariable < mymath.E) {
      //some code here
}
```

You cannot call a static method or variable on an instance of a class. In actual fact, there would never really be any reason to create an instance of the class Math, because all of its methods and variables are static. And you can't call an instance of a subclass of Math either, because Math is final, and cannot have any subclasses.

Abstract Attribute

The abstract attribute can be applied to both classes and class fields. However, any class which contains abstract methods or variables must itself be abstract. (This is similar to the idea that any class which has public methods or variables must itself be public.) What the abstract attribute does for a field is declare it without any details. Thus if you import a class which has an abstract variable or method, it is your responsibility to define that variable or method. You can think of an abstract class as a class which is a contract. If you import an abstract class, you promise to fill in the details and specifications for all of its abstract methods and variables, and in return the abstract class promises to give you access to all of the nonabstract data and methods which it contains. If you import an abstract class and also define its abstract methods as abstract, then you can't instantiate the class (create an instance of it to use), and so the class is useless. In other words, if you break the contract, you won't be able to instantiate a class and use its nonabstract methods or classes.

The idea behind the use of abstract classes is to create a class which contains some information and some useful methods, but which needs to be completed by the user, so that it works for each user's specific situation. Thus, if you create a class which is supposed to be able to take some kind of musical audio file, and print out to the screen an approximate musical staff showing the notes, then you might want to make the class abstract. This way you could put in a method for doing the work, but you could include an abstract method for getting the input audio file. Thus, whoever imported your class would have to define the abstract method so that it would read in the type of audio file that person was using (.ra, .wav, .au, and so forth). I have no idea if it would be possible to create such an application (maybe there is already one out there), but I've put forth the example so that you will have an idea of the purpose of an abstract class.

The idea of abstract classes is closely related to a very important Java tool which I am about to discuss: interfaces. Interfaces are very useful, and you may have already noticed mentions of interfaces in the Java API. For C++ programmers, Java interfaces allow you to get around the problem of not having multiple inheritance.

Interfaces

An interface is a way of creating a class that you can extend in addition to extending another class. That's a pretty confusing sentence! Let's look at an example. If you have a class called FlashingText.class and it extends java.applet.Applet, then it can't extend anything else. For example, if you also want it to have a whole bunch of variables and methods that are related, you couldn't just group those methods into a class and have your first class extend it in addition to java.applet.Applet. However, in addition to extending a class, your class does have the ability to implement an interface. In fact, unlike classes, you can implement multiple interfaces, not just one.

An interface is like an IOU. In fact, it's very much like an abstract class. When you implement an interface, you must provide everything the interface asks for. When you design an interface, you are basically specifying a set of services that some class must be able to provide, so that you can do something with those services later on. It's known as dynamic-binding, and it is rather a difficult concept to explain. As you grow more accustomed to using the Java API, and you start implementing some of the interfaces included, you'll gain a better understanding of what all of this means.

The classic example of an interface is java.lang.Runnable. The class java.lang.Thread implements Runnable. You've already had a quick discussion of Java's multithreading capabilities, but the following explanation can serve as a refresher.

Threads

The definition of a thread, according to the Java API, is as follows:

```
A thread is a single sequential flow of control within a process. This simply
means that while executing within a program, each thread has a beginning, a
sequence, a point of execution occurring at any time during runtime of the
thread and of course, an ending....Multithreaded programming allows a single
program to conduct concurrently running threads that perform different tasks.
```

Thus if you create an applet which imports the java.lang package, you can create a subclass of Thread, which will automatically implement the interface Runnable. You can create as many instances of your subclass of Thread as you like, and each instance will constitute a separate thread. All of these instances can run concurrently, and thus your applet can perform different tasks concurrently. What does Runnable do? It is the interface Runnable which provides the method run(). Note that run is of course an abstract method. So, when you import java.lang and you create a thread instance, you must define the method run. This will most often consist of a call to the main parts of your code.

You probably won't need to create your own interfaces until you've become a little more experienced in the use of Java. However, when the time comes, this is how you will do it:

Syntax Display: Declaring Your Own Interface

```
Form: [attributes] interface <interfacename> {
     //some abstract methods
     }
Example: public interface Runnable extends Object
```

Note that a class can implement an interface, and an interface can extend a class. Also note that an interface can have attributes exactly like a class can, and most interfaces will have the public access attribute. (An interface isn't very practical if it isn't public, because a nonpublic interface cannot be implemented.) One very important difference between an interface and a class is that an interface cannot be instantiated. In other words, you cannot create an instance of an interface, the way you can create an instance of a class.

What you'll more than likely need to do fairly soon after you start programming in Java is to implement an already existing interface, such as Runnable. Here's how.

Syntax Display: Class Declaration Using Interfaces

Form: `[attributes] class <classname> extends <superclassname> implements <interfacename>`
Example: `public class Snowball extends ToyClass implements Runnable`

In this example, the user has declared a new, public class called Snowball, which extends the class ToyClass, and which implements the interface Runnable. Thus, you can see that any class can implement a public interface (in other words; it is not only the class Thread which can implement Runnable). However, you might find that if the class java.lang.Thread is not imported into the code for Snowball.class, then the interface Runnable may not be terribly useful.

That's all I will say about interfaces. You'll get used to them after you spend some time looking at Java code. Now, I must spend a few paragraphs talking about another aspect of the Java programming language—error handling.

Handling Errors—Throwing and Catching Exceptions

When you write Java code, it is a good idea to anticipate the kinds of errors which might occur. Suppose your code tells the applet to get some pictures from a URL or a directory somewhere, just like in the Animator applet. It's a good idea to have something in your code that can handle such things as nonexistent URLs or directories.

The way to do this in Java is to use something called an *exception*. Exceptions take a form quite similar to if-else statements, except that the words are try-catch. The syntax for a try-catch statement is shown below.

Syntax Display: Try-Catch (Exception Handling Structure)

```
Form: try {
     //some code here which might throw an exception
     } catch (exceptionType name) {
     //some code here which will handle the exception
     } catch (exceptionType name) {
     //some code here to handle a different exception
     }
Example: try {
          kicker.sleep(25);
```

```
    } catch (InterruptedException e) {
system.out.println("applet interrupted");
} catch (Exception e) {
system.out.println("Some other error occurred");
}
```

In this example, there is a call to the method sleep, by the object instance kicker. This method may throw an Interrupted Exception error. In this example there isn't actually any error handling, except that the user is notified that an error occurred.

Note that for any try statement, you can have catch handling for a number of different errors. Also note that your catch may not actually correct the problem; it may just alert you or the user that an error has occurred.

Java Packages and Classes

The Java API is something which you as a Java programmer should become intimately acquainted with. No one wants to reinvent the wheel, and due to the extensive class libraries provided by the API, no one should have to. Before you begin trying to write the HelloWorld applet, or any other applet, for that matter, it's a good idea to skim through the API documentation to acquaint yourself with classes and methods that may be relevant to your code. In this section, I will take you on a quick tour through the API class libraries, so that you'll have a basic idea where to go when you want to find something specific.

java.applet

The java.applet package is the most important one to know about when you are writing an applet. This package contains only one class, the applet class. There are three interfaces that java.applet can implement: AppletContext, AppletStub, and AudioClip. The AppletContext interface deals with exchanging information between the applet and the browser. The AppletStub interface is used for implementing an applet viewer, and you aren't going to be creating any applet viewers, so you definitely don't need to worry about it. The AudioClip interface allows you to work with audio files as background to an applet. You'll concentrate on the applet class for now.

The applet class has a number of very important methods, some of which will sound familiar to you from running the Animator applet. For instance, if you remember the HTML you used for including the Animator applet in the Web page, you had a bunch of PARAM tags, which were used for entering parameter values. In the applet class there is a method called getParameter(String name), which is used to get the values from the HTML tags. You also may remember that you specified a CODEBASE (a URL or directory of where the applet code is located). The applet class contains a method called getCodeBase(), which returns the URL of the applet itself.

Other important methods in the applet class include the resize method, which calls the applet to be resized, and getAppletInfo, which returns a string containing information about the applet's author, date of creation, and so on. Finally, there are the init, start, and stop methods, which are basically abstract methods, although they are not explicitly abstract methods. What I mean is that the init, start, and stop methods included within the applet class don't really do anything; however, they can be overwritten so that they do. Thus, you can re-declare the init() method so that it resizes the applet, every time the applet needs to be initialize. That, in fact, is what you will often want to do.

You could also re-declare the stop() method, so that every time an applet is stopped, a message is printed to the viewer's screen, alerting them that the applet has stopped.

java.awt

To completely describe what the java.awt package accomplishes would take a full book. The package is so extensive that it is almost impossible even to describe what it does overall. The java.awt package contains a number of very important classes. AWT stands for Advanced Windows Toolkit, and the awt package contains methods and objects that allow Java programmers to create Windows, panels, scroll bars, buttons, menus, text areas, images, and event handling for such things as mouse clicks. There are three specific classes within the java.awt package that you will look at here: java.awt.Event, java.awt.Graphics, and java.awt.Component.

Let's look at java.awt.Graphics first. This is a class that is used very commonly in creating applets. If you look at the java.awt.Graphics page in the API documentation you'll see why. The list of methods available in this class is quite large, ranging from draw3Drect (int, int, int, int, Boolean), which draws a highlighted 3-D rectangle, to fillRoundRect (int, int, int, int, int, int), which draws a rounded rectangle and fills it with the current color. There is also a setColor(Color) method, which changes the current color to the one specified. Color, by the way is another class within the awt package, and preset colors in Java include black, blue, cyan, darkGray, gray, green, lightGray, magenta, orange, pink, red, white, and yellow.

java.awt.Event is also a very useful class to know about. This is the class which has all the event handling methods and variables. So, if you're writing an applet in which you want something specific to happen when a user clicks a mouse button, or hits a function key, then this is the class you'll need. Most of the variables in the awt.Event class are integer variables, such as MOUSE_MOVE, KEY_PRESS, and WINDOW_MOVED. These variables are valuable tools when you need to know if the end user is interacting with your applet. Some of the methods are quite handy to know as well, such as shiftDown, which returns a Boolean true if the Shift key is down, false if it is not. There are also methods for controlDown and metaDown (Meta is the Alt key on PC keyboards).

java.awt.Component is the class that controls how the applet interacts with the screen. This class implements the ImageObserver interface—an update interface which receives notification about image information as the image is constructed. Methods within this class include checkImage, which returns the status of the on-screen representation of the specified image, getBackground(), which returns the background color, and getForeground(), which returns the foreground color. There are also getFont(), paint(Graphics), repaint(), reshape(int,int,int,int), and resize(int, int). You will be using some of these methods to create a Hello World applet.

java.net

The java.net package implements three different interfaces, and contains eight different classes. The interfaces are ContentHandlerFactory, SocketImplFactory, and URLStreamHandlerFactory. The classes are ContentHandler, InetAddress, ServerSocket, Socket, SocketImpl, URL, URLConnection, and URLStreamHandler. Note that the interfaces and classes are very closely related.

The InetAddress class is important to know about. It contains methods for retrieving IP addresses given host names, for turning a URL into a string, and for getting the local host name. The ServerSocket class has methods for opening, closing, and determining current server sockets. The URL class has a constructor which allows you to create a URL given host, machine, and port names, or just a URL that is in string form. It also has methods that allow you to check the current port, protocol, and host. The sameFile method in URL class is used for comparing two URLs to determine if they reference the same remote page or object. The URLStreamHandler is an abstract class. If you extend URLStreamHandler, then you will create a subclass which knows how to handle different types of protocols (ftp://, http://, news:).

java.io

The java.io package does exactly what you would expect—it handles input and output operations. The package implements the three interfaces DataInput, DataOutput, and FilenameFilter. There are a number of different classes within the package, most of which deal with input and output streams of various types. For example, there are classes for ByteArrayInputStream, and FileOutputStream, LineNumberInputStream, and DataOutputStream. All of these different classes allow the programmer to direct different types of information in and out of the applet or application. Because applets are limited in what they can do in terms of reading and writing on the client system, you may find that java.io is not as important for writing applets as it would be for writing full applications.

java.lang

The java.lang class is where you will find many of the features which you expect to be built into a programming language. For instance, mathematical operations—such as absolute values, trigonometry functions, exponents, random numbers, and max and mins as well as mathematical constants such as π and E—can all be found in the math class of the java.lang package. The java.lang package is where you will find the thread group, allowing you to program applets to do different things concurrently. You will also find all of the regular atomic types that are familiar to programmers and have a class of their own in the java.lang package. For instance, there is a class for Integer, as well as for Float, Boolean, String, and Character. All of these classes have predefined methods and variables which are very useful to know about.

Some examples of useful methods which can be found in classes in the java.lang package are given below.

- isUpperCase(char) is a method which determines whether the specified character is an ISO-LATIN-1 uppercase character. Found in the Character class.
- endsWith(String) is a method which determines whether the current String ends with the specified suffix. Found within the String class.
- length(String) is a method which returns the length of the specified string. Found within the String class.
- out is a static variable within the System class which allows you to send output messages to the system, no matter which platform it is.
- isAlive() is a method within the thread class which returns a boolean variable telling you whether or not the current Thread is active.

These are just a few examples of the types of built-in functionality you can find in the java.lang package. You'll definitely want to read up on this package in the API documentation before you start trying to write any major applets.

java.util

The last package I will discuss here is the java.util package. This package implements the Enumeration and the Observer interfaces. The Enumeration interface specifies methods for counting sets of values. The Observer interface is used to watch and determine whether class instances need to be updated.

The classes contained in the java.util package include Date, which lets an applet manipulate dates independent of the platform on which the Java bytecode executes, and Properties, which allows you to specify properties about the Java class you are constructing. The Random class lets you create a pseudo-random number generator and the vector class lets you create growing arrays. The util package probably will be most useful to programmers after they have had some experience with Java.

Creating the Hello World Applet

The general strategy to follow when learning a new programming language is to start with the simplest possible program and to build on it. The conventional first program is Hello World. In other words, you are going to use the Java language to print out the words "Hello, World!" as an applet in your HTML page. Now this probably seems a little silly, when you could simply put "<P>Hello, World!" into your HTML and be done with it, but the idea is that you want to use the class libraries available in Java to print out the words, so that you can then use other parts of the class libraries to make the phrase do interesting things such as change color or flash.

The question of what to use to write Java code may be entering your mind right about now. I suggest a simple text editor such as Notepad or Wordpad if you are working in Windows, and if you are using a Sun System, you'll be lucky enough to use Xemacs. (Xemacs has a "Java" mode which makes editing Java code really easy because of the automatic indentation and fontification—you who work in the Windows world are not lucky enough to have such tools).

You already know from the previous discussion of the Java packages that every applet needs to import the java.applet.* package. You'll start with that. The question is, what else are you going to need to import in order to have all the tools necessary to print text on the screen? This is where it comes in handy to have Netscape Gold up and running at the same time, so that you can browse through your local copy of the API package documentation. Just open the packages.html file that was created when you downloaded and executed the JDK-apidocs.exe file. You'll see something called the Package Index, and you should see a number of links to java.applet, java.awt, and so on. All of these links will refer to documents you have locally on your hard drive, and these will come in very handy when writing Java code. Figure 22.10 shows the Package Index open next to my text editor, with our first bit of Java code showing.

You want to find something in these packages that will give us information about printing a string to the screen. You know from our discussion of packages that awt stands for Advanced Windowing Toolkit, io stands for input/

Figure 22.10

Java API is open in Netscape to the packages.html page, and my text editor is open beside it. (This is the best way to write Java code—with the reference handy!)

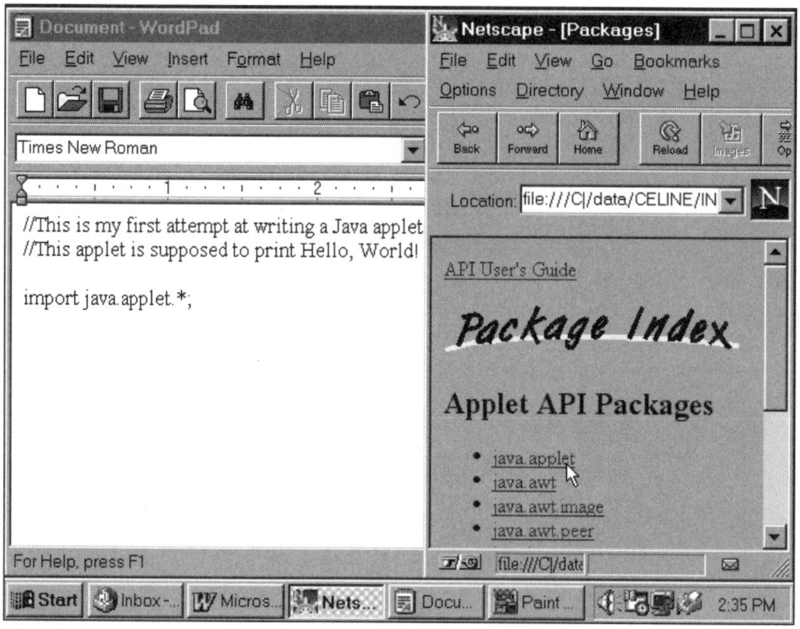

output, lang is for language, net is for Internet related objects, and util contains object utilities. Your first guess should probably be to look under java.io for information about writing to the screen. When you look at java.io, the only classes that look like they may help are BufferedOutputStream or DataOutputStream. By taking a quick look at these two classes, I determined that for a simple string such as "Hello, World!" there must be an easier way.

This is where experience is worth more than theory. I spent hours looking through the different packages, trying to find something that would write a string with ease. Experienced Java programmers get to know the packages and classes, and eventually get to the point where they only need to look at the documentation every once in awhile. However, you're not at that stage yet. After searching for hours (and a few helpful hints) I found java.awt.Graphics. This is one of the more important classes in the class libraries, and you'll get to know it quite well if you spend more time with Java.

TIP. *A confusing issue arose when I started playing with importing packages and classes, and that was with the capitalization of parts of the import statements. It turns out that the package names are not capitalized (java.applet), while the class names are (java.awt.Graphics). In the case of java.awt.Graphics, the class Graphics is in the package java.awt. It's a little confusing, but it is very important, because Java is case-sensitive.*

If you look through the java.awt.Graphics class documentation, you'll see a method called drawString. This is what you are looking for. Click on drawString, and you'll be presented with the following information on how the method is called and what parameters you need to include:

```
drawString
        public abstract void drawString(String str, int x, int y)
Draws the specified String using the current font and color. The x,y position
is the starting point of the baseline of the String.

     Parameters:
          str - the String to be drawn
          x - the x coordinate
          y - the y coordinate
```

So for our example, you would want to create an instance of the Object java.awt.Graphics; let's call our instance g, since that is the convention (I have no idea why). Then you want to operate the method drawString using the instance g which you create. You'll worry about creating the instance later. First let's figure out how to call the method.

This might look something like the following.

```
g.drawString("Hello, World!", 50, 25)
```

The g is the instance of Graphics, the drawString is the method which is defined as part of the Object java.awt.Graphics (remember that you refer to an object's method by objectinstancename.objectmethodname), and the parameters follow in the brackets. You want to write Hello, World!, so that is our first parameter, and it must be enclosed in double quotation marks. The next two parameters refer to the x and y coordinates, which give you the bottom-left corner of where the string will appear within the applet. If you call our applet in HTML using a width and height of 300 by 300, and you use 50 and 25 as the x and y coordinates for our drawString method call, then our string will end up in the very top-left corner of the applet. If our y coordinate was 0, or our x coordinate was 300, then our string wouldn't appear, because you would be specifying the bottom left corner of our string on the top or right side of our applet space.

Since you're using the Graphics object, you need to import it. So you add another import statement to our code, and you'll type in the statement you just came up with. Now our code looks like this:

```
import java.applet.*;
import java.awt.Graphics;
g.drawString("Hello World!", 50, 25);
```

Don't get too excited; you're far from done. You've imported the java.applet package, but you haven't even used it yet. There are a number of things you need to add. For instance, every applet needs to be initialized with a new class, and every applet needs the initialization method, init(), to be called.

You learned earlier that the init method should be called, and then the resize method should be called as part of the initialization process. The init method has no return value, thus it has the attribute void, and it is also a public method. Thus you should have the following line:

```
public void init() {
```

Within this method, you need to make a call to resize. This tells the compiler how much space the applet needs on the screen, and the measurement is in pixels. In our case, you are simply typing out a short phrase. You need a small rectangle of space. You don't really need to worry too much about guessing this perfectly. When I first did this, I tried 200 by 75, and found it to be too big. The resize method takes the x (horizontal) parameter first, and the y (vertical) parameter second. The values 150 and 50 seem to work fairly well. So let's add this to our init() method:

```
public void init() {
     resize(150, 50);
}
```

This initialization method should be one of the very first things in our applet, right after you declare our class. Our code now looks like this:

```
import java.applet.*;
import java.awt.Graphics;
public void init() {
          resize(150, 50);
     }

g.drawString("Hello World!", 50, 25);
```

At this point, you have imported the classes you need, you have taken care of initializing our applet with a good size, and you have a command that will draw our string, Hello, World!, onto the screen. If you look closely, or think back a page, you'll remember that you are using a variable that you haven't even declared—the g. You've imported java.awt.Graphics, and you've looked at the API to find the drawString method, but you need to declare g as an instance of Graphics. You also need some function that will cause the applet to take the drawString method, and display that method on screen. java.awt.Graphics is a subclass of java.awt.Panel, which is a subclass of java.awt.Container, which is a subclass of java.awt.Component. You can see this hierarchical structure if you look at the API, as shown in Figure 22.11.

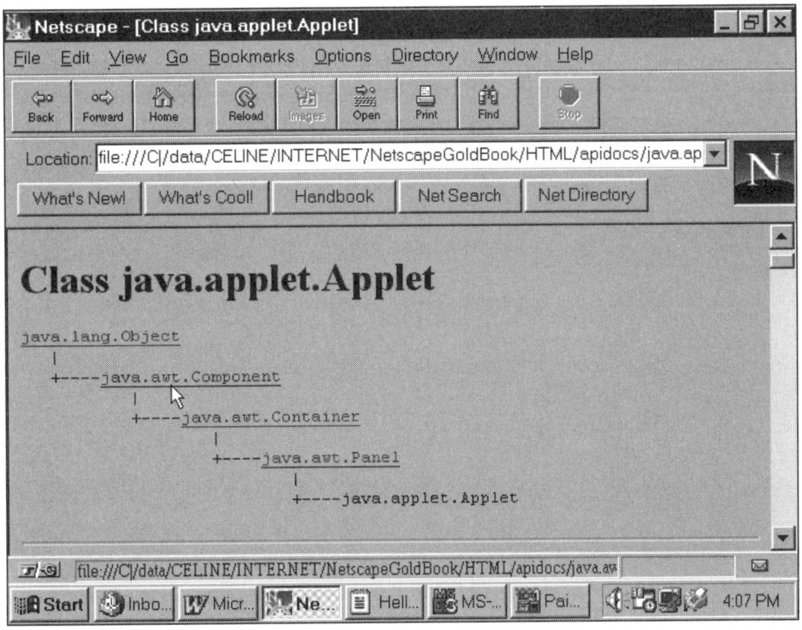

Figure 22.11

The hierarchy of inheritance for the java.applet.Applet class—the applet class extends the java.awt.Panel class, which itself extends java.awt.Container, and so on

If you click on java.awt.Component, you'll find a number of methods, which are all available to us, because Component is a public class and you imported java.awt.Graphics. In the Method Index of class Component you'll see a method called paint(Graphics). When you click on this link in Netscape Gold, you get the following information:

```
public void paint(Graphics g)
     Paints the component.
     Parameters:
          g - the specified Graphics window
```

This is exactly the method you need both to declare an instance of the class Graphics, and to tell the applet to paint to the screen the commands that follow. So, you need to incorporate our g.drawString line within this paint method.

The code will look like this:

```
public void paint(Graphics g) {
     g.drawString("Hello, World!", 50, 25);
}
```

This piece of code will cause an instance of the the class Graphics (g) to be created. Then a graphics method, drawString, is invoked, which creates the string "Hello, World!" and stores two integers as a starting point for printing out the string. The paint method, which is available to us because you imported java.applet.Applet, will cause the output of the instructions within the method to be painted to the screen, within the area of the applet.

When you put our code altogether, you have the following:

```
import java.applet.*;
import java.awt.Graphics;
public class HelloWorld extends Applet {
    public void init() {
        resize(150, 50);
    }
    public void paint(Graphics g) {
        g.drawString("Hello World!", 50, 25);
    }
}
```

Note that our two methods, init and paint, are part of the class HelloWorld. This is the structure of every applet—one class with everything inside of that class.

Your next step is to compile this code. You must first save this file as HelloWorld.java. Then you have to use the javac compiler to create a HelloWorld.class file. If your code looks exactly as above, you shouldn't get any compile errors. The next section describes how to use the javac compiler. If you do get errors compiling HelloWorld.java, then check out the common compile errors section. These are some of the errors I got while trying to get this applet to work.

Compiling Java Code

Once you have written a piece of Java code, and you think that it is pretty correct syntactically, it's time to test it out. What you want to do is compile the Java code into bytecode. A Java bytecode file is an executable which can run on any machine that has a Java interpreter. Remember that in our case, Netscape Gold is the Java interpreter. Any Java code that you write and compile into Java bytecode can run on any platform that runs Netscape Gold. This is one of Java's greatest features: You don't have to worry about making sure that our code will run on Apples as well as PCs and Sun Unix systems; you just have to compile our code into Java bytecode, and the rest is taken care of. Each individual platform then takes the Java bytecode and converts it to run on that platform's hardware. Java is not the first language which allows this to happen, but it is the first language in which platform interpretation doesn't take an excessive amount of time.

If you've set up the JDK properly, then you should be able to compile a piece of Java code no matter where it is on your hard drive. In order to compile the code you must get to a DOS prompt if you are running Windows 95 or NT. On other systems, use your regular command prompt. Find your Java file. Your Java file must have a .java extension. This may be problematic for Windows 95 users, depending on what kind of text editor you are using. If your text editor is saving your code as Name.jav, then you'll have to rename your file to Name.java manually. Once you have found your file and made sure that it has the full .java extension, you need to type the following at your prompt (make sure you are in the same directory as the .java file):

```
C:\somedirectory\> javac Classname.java
```

Substitute the name of your file for Classname. You'll have to wait a few moments, depending on the speed of your system. Now one of two things will happen. Either you'll see a whole bunch of error messages (or maybe just a few), or you'll get another command prompt. If you get a command prompt and no error messages, you should jump up and down and cheer, because your code has compiled without any errors. This will not likely happen on your first few tries, especially when you start trying to write your own Java code.

Error messages have a specific format. Each error will be reported as follows.

Syntax Display: Error Message Reporting As Seen in DOS When Compiling

```
Form:  <Classname.java>:<somenumber>: <error message>
    <Line of code in which error appears>
             ^  (pointer showing where error begins in above line)
Example:  GrowingPlant.java:8: Invalid declaration.
    g drawLine(x1, y1, x2, y2);
    ^
```

In this example, GrowingPlant.java is the name of the file which the user is attempting to compile. The number 8 refers to the line number (the eighth line down from the top of the code). "Invalid declaration" is the error message. The second line down (g drawLine(x1, y1, x2, y2);) is the actual line of code. The last line in the error report is simply a pointer, showing whereabouts in the line the error occurs. In this case the error is actually a missing period. The line is supposed to read g.drawLine(...), because g is an object instance and drawLine is a method being called on that object instance. Note that the little pointer is not actually pointing at the space where the period should be, but is pointing at the space right before it. The error location reporting is seldom exact, but it is usually pretty close to where the error occurs.

The type of error messages you'll see will vary, and some of them are quite helpful in identifying problems with your code. As you gain more experience, the error messages will become more familiar, and you'll be able to fix problems quite quickly. The following are some common error messages, with explanations as to what they mean:

```
HelloWorld.java:3: Class java.awt.graphics not found in import
import java.awt.graphics;
^
```

This is a fairly common error. java.awt.graphics is not a class. java.awt.Graphics is a class. This is where it becomes important to distinguish between packages and classes. A class is capitalized and a package is not. If you want to import a package, you could simply type *package* <package-name>; at the very top of your code. Whenever you use the keyword *import*, Java automatically looks for classes. You can also import a full package (all the classes that are related) by using wildcards: import java.awt.*;. This would import every class in the java.awt package, including the Graphics class and others.

```
HelloWorld.java:9: ';' expected.
        resize(150, 50)
            ^
```

Another common error occurs when the programmer forgets to end a code statement with a semicolon. At least the error reporting for this error is self-explanatory.

```
HelloWorld.java:9: Method resize(int, int) not found in class HelloWorld.
        resize(150, 50);
            ^
```

The error here is not obvious, because the line which needs to be modified is not the line shown. The message is telling the user that the method being called can't be found in the class HelloWorld. The method is probably located somewhere in the imported packages. There are two things to check here. First, you must determine what class you found the method resize in and make sure that you have imported that class, and second, you must make sure that your class HelloWorld extends the class in which resize can be found. In this case the user had *public class HelloWorld {* instead of what he or she should have had: *public class HelloWorld extends Applet {*.

```
HelloWorld.java:11: Class Graphics not found in type declaration.
        public void paint(Graphics g) {
             ^
```

This error is quite similar to the previous one. In this case the compiler can't find the Class graphics. The user forgot to import java.awt.Graphics.

```
HelloWorld.java:13: '}' expected.
            }
            ^
```

Forgetting a begin or end bracket is a common programming typo. The compiler keeps track of the number of begin and end brackets, and if they don't match up at the end of the code the user will receive an error as shown above.

```
HelloWorld.java:12: No method matching drawString(java.lang.String, int) found
in class java.awt.Graphics.
         g.drawString("Hello, World!", 50);
              ^
```

In this case, the compiler knows that g is an instance of the object Graphics, and is looking in the Graphics object for a method called g.drawString, with a string and an integer parameter. For some reason, it's not finding it. In this type of situation, it is best to have a look at the API documentation. The user would find out that he or she is missing a parameter; there are supposed to be two integer parameters as well as the string parameter whenever the drawString method is called. The line should actually read *g.drawString("Hello, World!", 50, 150);*.

Running Your Applet

Once your code is compiled, you'll need to create an HTML file to run the applet. Again, try a simple page like this:

```
<HTML>
<BODY>
<H1><CENTER>My First Animation applet</CENTER></H1>
<P>
<center><applet codebase="classes" code="HelloWorld.class" width=150 height=50>
</applet></center>
<BR>
<P>
</HTML>
```

Now you need to put your HelloWorld.class and your HTML file onto your Web space, making sure that HelloWorld.class is in a subdirectory called classes. Your directory structure should look something like this:

```
*somedirectory
    -Yourhtmlfile.html
```

```
*classes
    -HelloWorld.class
```

Now, go into Netscape Gold and type in the URL for the HTML page you just created. Your page should appear, and the words Hello, World! should be there in the center. If you get an error, go back to the section where you used the Animator applet, and check out the common errors that are listed there to see if they help. The most important thing is getting your directory structure working. If you don't have any Web space, you can try creating a local file structure, and then opening your HTML file locally, but this hasn't been known to work very well. It's definitely a good idea to acquire Web space!

The other option if you don't have access to Web space is to use the appletviewer which comes with the Java Developer's Kit. If you've installed the JDK correctly, then you can run the appletviewer with your local HTML pages. You need to have your HTM or HTML file in the HTML directory, and you can simply go to that directory and type appletviewer YourHTML-FILEname.htm. You must do this from the DOS prompt if you are using Windows NT or 95. The appletviewer will then open a little applet window on your screen and should play the applet for you. If there are any problems with the applet, such as thrown exceptions or run-time errors, they will appear in your DOS window. This can actually be a good way of checking to make sure your applet works. However, there are some applets that work fine when run through the appletviewer, but won't work over the Internet, so you're best to check out both cases.

A handy little debugging tool that can help you to determine exactly which parts of your code are running is to include messages in your methods. You simply type System.out.println ("Some string here"), and if that particular method does get invoked, then you'll get the message output to your system when running through the appletviewer.

Well, you've done it—you have officially written, compiled, and run your very first Java applet. Don't be disappointed because it doesn't seem to do much—you're on your way. You can now try to create some more complicated applets that involve user interaction. Unfortunately, this chapter has to stop here; it's much too long already. But by reading this chapter you've done yourself the favor of familiarizing yourself with a new and very important programming language, and even if you decide to pursue it no further, you can count yourself among those who know about Java. And you'll understand the complexity of what is going on whenever your Netscape Gold browser encounters a Java applet on the Net. This is no small accomplishment!

Applet Security

There is an entire FAQ (Frequently Asked Questions) list dealing with Java's applet security features. For a full and technical description you should really refer to that document, which can be found at http://java.sun.com/sfaq/. However, I have summarized the main points below.

Java's applet security is implemented by the applet security manager, and the high-level objectives of this manager are to prevent applets from inspecting or changing files on the client system and to prevent the applet from using network connections to circumvent file protections. If an applet is loaded through a Web browser such as Netscape Navigator or Netscape Gold, the applet is loaded using the applet class loader, which ensures that class files conform to the Java language specification.

There is one main determinant of what an applet can do, and that is whether the applet comes from a network or from the local client file system. If the applet comes off of a network, then it is very restricted in what it can do. It cannot:

- Read or write files on the client machine
- Connect to other network locations, other than the one from which it originated
- Execute other programs on the client machine

If an applet is run locally (so far this can only be done using the appletviewer—Netscape does not allow applets to run if their HTML file is loaded using the File-Open Local File command), then it can do the following:

- Read and write to files on the local machine which are specified in the access control lists
- Connect to other network locations

(continued)

The access control lists are specified in the \.hotjava\properties file. For example, if you want applets to be able to read the file "javainfo," then you would specify the following in your \.hotjava\properties file:

```
acl.read=c:\somedirectory\javainfo
```

If you allow an applet to read or write to a directory, then it can read or write to any files within that directory, as well as any files in subdirectories of that directory.

Applets loaded over the Net, as well as those loaded locally, can get information about the client machine. The information which the applets can get include the Java version number, vendor URL, operating system name and architecture, file and path separators, and line separators. The code within an applet which does this is the System.getProgerty(String key); method, where String key is java.version or java.vendor.url, and so forth.

Security features within the Java language:

- Java programs do not use pointers explicitly; instead, objects are accessed by handles. Arithmetic is not allowed on handles, preventing random access to areas of memory.
- Arrays are always bounds-checked, preventing indexing beyond the limits of the array size, and the size of an array cannot be changed.
- Strings are a class in Java, thus programmers do not have to use complex pointer manipulation to use strings.
- The compiler checks to make sure that all type casts are legal, preventing errors.
- Java provides access attributes which allows programmers to protect data and methods from tampering.

Differences between Java and C++

Integer and float sizes are not platform-dependent in Java, all integers are signed twos complement 32-bit integers, and all floats are 32-bit IEEE 754 floating-point numbers.

The Java Char type is a 16-bit type, which means that you can use characters beyond the extended ASCII set, including all of the European characters.

There are no enumerated types (enums), no typedefs, no unions, and no structs.

Java does not support multiple inheritance.

You can't explicitly touch a pointer in Java. This is what makes Java a much more secure language.

When using arrays in Java, it is not necessary to specify the size. For example, in C++ you would have

```
      int a[<size>];
In Java, this would be written:
      int[] a;
```

The only casting allowed in Java is between numeric variables and between sub- and superclasses of the same object. This means, for example, that you can't have a variable that is a Boolean take on the value of float.

- *JavaScript and Netscape Navigator Gold*
- *What Is JavaScript?*
- *What's the Difference between Java and JavaScript?*
- *Learning by Example*
- *JavaScript General Information*
- *JavaScript Error Messages*
- *JavaScript Reserved Words*

- *A Few Last Comments*

CHAPTER

23

JavaScript

IF YOU'RE CREATING A HOME PAGE JUST FOR THE FUN OF IT, YOU may not care if your page stands out above the Web's horde of sites. However if you're creating a page for the purpose of looking for employment, or for the purpose of selling goods or services, then you'll want to make sure your page takes advantage of everything Netscape Gold has to offer. JavaScript can certainly help you. A JavaScript-enhanced page can put the icing on the cake, in terms of making your page stand out and be interactive.

JavaScript and Netscape Navigator Gold

The first versions of Gold have no tools for the creation of JavaScript scripts. For now at least, you need to create your Java programs independently, then bring them into your Gold documents through the HTML Tag command on the Insert menu. In the near future, Gold is likely to possess its own set of JavaScript tools, although whether or not these will be WYSIWYG tools is unknown.

What Is JavaScript?

JavaScript is a small and very simple programming language that can be included inside HTML documents. The language looks similar to C++ in its format and syntax, but is much simpler. Of course, this means that JavaScript can't accomplish everything that a language such as C++ or Java could, but that's okay. Sometimes you're just not interested in creating an operating system, nor in developing full-featured programs.

What's the Difference between Java and JavaScript?

Java is a full-fledged programming language created by Sun Microsystems, Inc. Netscape Navigator Gold has the built-in ability to execute small programs created using the Java language. This is done while the Web page to which the Java program (known as an *applet*) is appended is loaded. Java is a fairly complex language, although certainly simpler than the language on which it is based, C++. Learning to program in Java, when you've had no other programming experience, is not an easy task.

On the other hand, learning JavaScript is not an onerous task, and although programming experience will help you, the absence of it won't put you very far behind. The JavaScript page on the Netscape site contains a small table outlining some of the major differences and similarities between Java and JavaScript. If you're interested in the subject, you can check out the site for more detailed information.

The similarities between the languages are few, but both languages are secure for networking, both use the same type of syntax (close to that of C++), and both contain an object hierarchy. The differences, however, are vast. You can read about the entire JavaScript object hierarchy in a matter of two hours, but it would take days to do the same with Java. You do not have to know about strong-type restrictions with JavaScript, and it is much easier to learn about and use the built-in functions provided by JavaScript than to do so with those provided by Java.

Learning by Example

This chapter takes on a learn-by-example methodology. You'll go through a number of different examples of including JavaScript in different Web pages, paying attention to how the language is working and interacting with the HTML. At the end of the chapter, you will find a brief description of the language itself, along with a list of keywords and some other notes.

Every example shown in this chapter can be found by pointing Gold to http://randall.uwaterloo.ca/celine/javascript/example**.htm. In other words, for the first example, the URL will be http://randall.uwaterloo.ca/celine/javascript/example1.htm. The important thing to do is to keep looking at the examples online while you're reading the book, so that you'll see exactly how the implementations work (or in some cases, don't work!).

Okay, let's get started! For the first three examples, you'll use the examples provided on the Netscape JavaScript page, although you will be altering the second one: http://home.netscape.com/comprod/products/navigator/version_2.0/script/script_info/index.HTML.

Example 1

In the name of programming tradition, your first JavaScript program will be the famous "Hello, World!" that has introduced scores of people to the vagaries of computer programming. The object of the program is to use the new language to output the words *Hello, World!* to the screen. You may be wondering why you would bother with this, especially when you could just use the <P> tag in HTML, followed by the phrase itself, to get it to show up on screen. However, this first exercise will serve a number of different purposes, such as introducing the HTML script tag.

There are two methods you can use in JavaScript for outputting text to the screen. They are built-in methods that can be called on the "document" object. The document object is simply the HTML page in which you embed the JavaScript. The methods are write() and writeln(). Write should make sense to you. Writeln() is exactly the same thing as Write, except that it places a carriage return after it writes. The parentheses after each method name indicate two things: first, that it is a method, and second, that something may be required in calling the method. This makes sense. If you want to tell the computer to write something, you have to tell it *what* to write. In our case, you want the brackets to contain "Hello, World!", including the quotation marks.

When you call a method, you have to call it on the object to which that method belongs. In this case, the write and writeln methods both belong to the document object, as do a whole bunch of other methods, such as open, close, and clear. You're just going to use the write function, and so your method call will look like this:

```
document.write("Hello, World!")
```

This is the only line of code necessary, other than the script tag. The script tag is a complementary tag, meaning that it has both opening and closing counterparts. The script tags work like this:

```
<SCRIPT LANGUAGE="JavaScript">
JavaScript here
</SCRIPT>
```

The reason that the tag is a "script" tag rather than a "JavaScript" tag is to allow Netscape the option of adding other kinds of scripts to HTML later on.

So, putting these two things together, you get the following:

```
<SCRIPT LANGUAGE="JavaScript">
document.write("Hello, World!")
</SCRIPT>
```

Of course, you have to include this in a formal HTML page, and look at it using Netscape to see what it does. A simple Web page with the "Hello, World!" script included could look like this:

```
<HTML>
<HEAD>
<SCRIPT LANGUAGE="JavaScript">
document.write("Hello, World!")
</SCRIPT>
</HEAD>
<BODY>
<P>Here's a script example.
</BODY>
</HTML>
```

You can view this example at http://randall.uwaterloo.ca/celine/javascript/example1.htm.

Note that the whole script tag is in the HEAD of the HTML document. There are a number of reasons for this, but the main one is that the head will be loaded first, before the rest of the page. This means that if users click on something in a page that invokes a JavaScript function, you can be sure that the function has already downloaded and the user will not get an error.

This has been useful but hardly very exciting, obviously, so let's go on to the second example.

Example 2

The second example on the Netscape page makes use of JavaScript's functions-building ability, and demonstrates how a function can have a parameter passed to it. Unfortunately, the example from the Netscape site passes a parameter to itself, which isn't especially interesting, so let's rewrite it so that the user inputs a value. The purpose of the function in this case is to take an input value, and output that value's square. So, if the user enters 5, you want the JavaScript to output 25.

Functions and methods are the same type of thing: They can take some input, process that input, and return some output. The only difference is that methods in JavaScript have already been defined, and only have to be called. An example is the write method. You don't need to tell the computer how to take our input string and print it out to the screen; that functionality is built in. However, sometimes you may need to do something for which there is no built-in method. When this occurs, you need to create your own method, and that is what you will call a function. In fact, function is a JavaScript keyword, and whenever you create a function, you'll need to declare it as such using the function keyword.

A function in JavaScript must be declared and defined, and then must be called when you want to use it. Functions generally have return values. In our example, you wish to build a function which returns the square of a number that the user inputs.

You are going to be using a form to get the value from the user, and so you are in effect going to be using two functions. One you use to indirectly pass the form's input to the JavaScript, and the second you use to manipulate that input and pass back out an answer. Our first function declaration looks like this:

```
function compute_square(form)
```

This statement defines a function called compute_square, which takes as input a parameter which the function will from then on refer to as form. Any values that are passed in using a call to compute_square will be referenced using the keyword "form". The reason for this will become more clear after you build the input form. In fact, you'll come back to this function in a bit; first let's look at the second function you'll need. You'll call it square(). The parameter you're going to pass in can be called whatever you like, so you'll choose number for now.

```
Function square(number)
```

The only line inside of the function will be quite simple, really. A square is just a number multiplied by itself.

```
Function square(number)
     return number * number
```

The keyword *return* is being used here. This means that if you make reference to square(somenumber) somewhere, the function will be called, and the return value will replace the reference. So, if you have a variable-named answer that you wish to use to assign the square of some number to, you could do that in the following way (assuming the number is 7):

```
answer = square(7)
```

This would call the function square(), compute the value, and store the "return" (in this case 49) in the variable answer.

Our code looks like this so far:

```
<SCRIPT LANGUAGE="JavaScript">
<!-- to hide script contents from old browsers
            function compute_square(form)
            form.square.value = square(form.number.value)
     Function square(num)
     return num * num
//end hiding contents from old browsers -->
</SCRIPT>
```

This example adds a new line, the one inside the first function. This line assumes that a form exists which has a field whose name is square, and a field whose name is number. Then the function uses the value of whatever has been input into the form.number field to call the square function. The square function returns the squared value, and that value is stored as the value in the field called square. This may seem confusing now, but that's because you haven't built a form with these fields.

Also note a new addition to our script tags. The <! .... - - > construct is used to enclose JavaScript so that old browsers which aren't familiar with the scripting language don't try to understand and interpret the script as standard HTML. You may also have noticed that the function is indented from the rest of the script and the code inside the function is indented further—this type of indenting can help to make your code more readable.

Of course, this compute_square function isn't going to do anything unless it is called. What you want to do now is build a little form which allows a user to input a value. Then that user can click on a button and the result will be output. You need a form with an input area, a submit button, and an output field. Something like the following should do nicely.

```
<FORM>
Enter a number:
<INPUT TYPE="text" NAME="number" SIZE=5 ><BR>
<INPUT TYPE="button" VALUE="Get Square of Value">
Result:
<INPUT TYPE="text" NAME="square" SIZE=15>
</FORM>
```

Now, this form looks slightly strange. It doesn't have a submit button, it doesn't have an action attribute, and it doesn't look like the input is going to go anywhere. Well, so far all three are true. You don't want the user's number to be submitted to some CGI script on some server for processing, because you have a squaring function right here on the page. Therefore, no submit or posting action is required. However, in order to use the function compute_square(form) that you created above, you need to call it. For this you are going to use another one of JavaScript's built-in tools, called an even handler. This one is called ONCLICK, and it looks like this:

```
<FORM>
Enter a number:
<INPUT TYPE="text" NAME="number" SIZE=5 ><BR>
<INPUT TYPE="button" VALUE="Get Square of Value"
ONCLICK="compute_square(this.form)">
Result:
<INPUT TYPE="text" VALUE="square" SIZE=15>
</FORM>
```

There are two important new concepts here. The first is the idea of ONCLICK and event handlers, and the second is the concept of "this." Let's discuss event handlers first. An event handler does exactly what it says: It handles events. Events can be a number of different things, but usually involve the user doing something that the computer can detect. In this case, when the user clicks on the button you created (which will have the label "Get Square of Value"), the computer detects that the button has been clicked. Thus, the ONCLICK event gets triggered, and whatever follows in the quotation marks after the ONCLICK=, gets invoked. In our case, when the user clicks the button, the compute_square function will be called.

The compute_square function will be called with the parameter *this.form*. *this* is a keyword in JavaScript that can be used to refer to the current article, be it the current HTML page, in which case you refer to this.document, or the current form, in which case you refer to this.form. Now, in our simple example there is only one input value that the form generates, so there is no need to specify any further. The this.form construct will take the values of the form and pass them into the compute_square function. In this function, the value of the form's num field is the only one passed. So, you need to reference that specific field in calling the square function. That is exactly what you do. You call the square function on form.number.value, and that function takes the value of whatever was entered in the number field of the form as its input. When the function returns the square of that value, it is assigned to form.square.value, and is therefore output to the form in the field called square.

So now, our entire HTML document will look like this:

```
     <HTML>
     <HEAD>
     <SCRIPT LANGUAGE="JavaScript">
     <!-- to hide script contents from old browsers
            function compute_square(form)
            form.square.value = square(form.number.value)
            function square(num)
            return num * num
//end hiding contents from old browsers -->
     </SCRIPT>
     </HEAD>
     <BODY>
<P>This page contains a JavaScript function for returning
the square of a number.  Please enter a number and then
click the button.
     <FORM>
     Enter a number:
     <INPUT TYPE="text" NAME="number" SIZE=3 ><BR>
<INPUT TYPE="button" VALUE="Get Square of Value"
ONCLICK="compute_square(this.form)">
     Result:
     <INPUT TYPE="text" NAME="square" SIZE=12>
     </FORM>
     </BODY>
     </HTML>
```

Now, after having gone through all this trouble, you'll be pleased to know that there is actually a much easier way to get a square of a number in JavaScript, simply by using the built-in power method, which takes a base and an exponent as its parameters. However, that would not have demonstrated the need for building your own functions. Just so you know, you can call the built-in power method like this:

```
document.write("<P>The answer to 3<sup>4</sup> is " + Math.pow(3,4))
```

or like this if 3 is stored in a variable called 'basenum' and 4 is stored in a variable called 'expnum':

```
document.write("<P>The answer to " + basenum + " to the power of " + expnum +
" is " + Math.pow(basnum,expnum))
```

You can see these two samples demonstrated on the page http://randall.uwaterloo.ca/celine/javascript/pow. You should compare the source code for this to the source code for the second example above. This source code is obviously much more simple. Note that for pow.htm, there was no need to build in a form for users to enter a number; however, that would still not make the source code as complicated as what you created above.

Example 3

The third example is actually a repeat of the second example, except that it contains some important fine-tuning. One of JavaScript's biggest uses is in the fine-tuning of HTML forms. To see why Example 2 needs some fine-tuning, go back to the page in Netscape Gold. Reload it if it was already loaded, to make sure that the fields are all clear. Now, enter a two-digit number in the input field, and press the "Get Square of Value" button. The answer will show up in the output field. Now suppose you had another number whose square you wished to calculate. If you click your mouse in the input field without actually selecting what's already there, then the numbers that are already there stay there. And if you were to inadvertently click in the field and then type in a number, the old number and your new number may get merged. What's even worse is that the combined larger number may not even be seen by the user, because the field is small, and some digits may scroll to the right, causing them to be nonvisible. Now, if you click the "Get Square of Value" button, the results may not be what you expect if the old and new numbers did get combined.

To remedy this, you're going to use another event handler. This time the event handler is called ONFOCUS. The ONFOCUS event handler is a trigger from the computer that the user has clicked the mouse or tabbed into a certain field. What you want to do is to have the input field reset to blank every time the user clicks into it, so that the above problem cannot occur. The line that needs to be changed is the form line for the input field, and I've inserted the change below:

```
<INPUT TYPE="text" NAME="number" SIZE=5 ONFOCUS="form.number.value = ''">
```

With this change added, whenever the user clicks into the number field, the script assigns a blank value (note the single quotes with nothing between them) to the value of the number field. So I made this change, saved it, and uploaded it to my server. Then I tried it out. It works fine, except that the input field blanks, and the square of the previous number still shows up in the result box. As a result, it was necessary to add another script statement to the ONFOCUS event handler. Now it looks like this:

```
<INPUT TYPE="text" NAME="number" SIZE=5 ONFOCUS="form.number.value = '',
form.square.value = ''">
```

So, when a user clicks in the input field both fields are automatically blanked. The best part is that all of this processing occurs locally, within the Web browser which loaded the page, so there isn't any processing going on across the network. You can see the fine-tuned square example on http://randall.uwaterloo.ca/celine/javascript/example3.htm.

Example 4

The fourth example is the calculation example from the Netscape JavaScript pages. The example is quite similar to Example 3 but makes use of another built-in JavaScript method for mathematics, and a few other things not yet discussed. The following is the full HTML for the page (at this point, there's no need to go through it step by step):

```
<HTML>
<HEAD>
<SCRIPT LANGUAGE="JavaScript">
<!-- to hide script contents from old browsers
function compute(form)  {
     if (confirm("Are you sure?"))
           form.result.value = eval(form.expr.value)
     else
           alert("Please come back again.")
}
//end hiding contents from old browsers -->
</SCRIPT>
</HEAD>
<BODY>
<FORM>
<P>Enter a mathematical expression:
<INPUT TYPE="text" NAME="expr" SIZE=15>
<INPUT TYPE="button" VALUE="Calculate"
ONCLICK="compute(this.form)">
<BR>
<P>Result:
<INPUT TYPE="text" NAME="result" SIZE=15>
</FORM>
</BODY>
</HTML>
```

Most of what is in this example looks a lot like the square function created earlier in Examples 2 and 3. However, there are three new things here. First, you'll notice the confirm function. The confirm function is built in to JavaScript, and basically allows you to put out a little dialog box to the user asking them a question. The confirm method automatically gives the user two choices: Yes and Cancel. So, if the user reads the question and clicks the Yes button, then the confirm method evaluates to true. Similarly, if the user reads the question and clicks the Cancel button, then the confirm method evaluates to false. In this example, when the user clicks Yes, the mathematical expression which he or she enters gets evaluated, and the answer gets stored in the result field of the form. If the user clicks Cancel in response to the confirm question, then the expression doesn't get evaluated and an alert message is given to the user.

This leads us into the issue of alert messages. An alert message is another built-in JavaScript method for allowing the HTML page to interact with the user. The alert message, however, is unlike the confirm message, in terms of offering the user any choices. When a user is given an alert message, all he or she can do is read the message and click the OK button. The alert message in this sense always returns true. You can see how these two functions work by opening http://randall.uwaterloo.ca/celine/javascript/example4.htm, and then typing in an expression and clicking Yes or Cancel in response to the confirm message. Make sure you try both.

The third new element in this example is the eval() method. The eval() method takes a string or a numeric expression and attempts to evaluate it. If it is a string such as 3 * 4, then the method turns this into the numeric expression 3*4, and evaluates. If the string is something like "three plus two," it will not be turned into a numeric expression, and the user will be given an error. The eval method is not part of the Math object, and so it is not necessary to call Math.eval(); in fact, doing so will generate an error. The eval function is what is known as a top-level function, and you can call it in any JavaScript function just by typing eval() and including what you want evaluated in the parentheses. You can put a variable name in the parentheses, as long as the variable contains a mathematical expression, or a string of a mathematical expression.

Example 5

Example 5 is a short example meant to demonstrate the use of the onMouse Over event handler. Consider the following HTML:

```
<HEAD>
<H1>My list of favorite links:</H1>
</HEAD>
```

```
<BODY>
<UL>
<LI>The <A HREF="http://www.epicurious.com/epicurious/
home.html" TARGET="top">Epicurious Home Page</A>, full of
fun and food.
<LI><A HREF="http://www2.shef.ac.uk/chemistry/web-elements/
biol/periodic-table.html" TARGET="top">Web Elements</A> (an
online interactive table of the elements).
<LI>The <A HREF="http://www.tucows.com/"
TARGET="top">TUCOWS</A> Ultimate Collection of Winsock
Software
<LI>You can also search the net using a great
<STRONG>Canadian</STRONG> search engine: <A HREF="http://
www.opentext.com/" TARGET="top">OpenText</A>.
<LI>The <A HREF="http://www.dnai.com/~sharrow/parody.html"
TARGET="top">Gallery of Advertising Parody</A>!
<LI>Being in economics, I have to link to the <A HREF="http:/
/www.etla.fi/pkm/joke.html" TARGET="top">Jokes about
Economics</A> site.
<LI>The <A HREF="http://www.brillig.com/debt_clock/"
TARGET="top">US National Debt Clock</A> site.
</UL>
</BODY>
```

It looks like a pretty basic list of links. So far, it is. However, one of the interesting possibilities available with JavaScript is the ability to change what appears in the status line of the Netscape browser. Normally, the URL of the link being pointed to is what appears in the status line. What you'll see with this example is the use of the onMouseOver event handler to give the user a little more information about the link. Here are my changes:

```
<HEAD>
<H1>My list of favorite links:</H1>
</HEAD>
<BODY>
<UL>
<LI>The <A HREF="http://www.epicurious.com/epicurious/
home.html" TARGET="top"
onMouseOver="window.status='Warning:  This site is dangerous
for your waistline!'; return true">Epicurious Home Page</A>,
full of fun and food.
<LI><A HREF="http://www2.shef.ac.uk/chemistry/web-elements/
biol/periodic-table.html" TARGET="top"
onMouseOver="window.status='Not just for science geeks!';
```

```
return true">Web Elements</A> (an online interactive table
of the elements).
<LI>The <A HREF="http://www.tucows.com/" TARGET="top"
onMouseOver="window.status='Much cool software here, but the
page is slow!'; return true">TUCOWS</A> Ultimate Collection
of Winsock Software
<LI>You can also search the net using a great
<STRONG>Canadian</STRONG> search engine: <A HREF="http://
www.opentext.com/" TARGET="top"
onMouseOver="window.status='Come on, support a Canadian
business!'; return true">OpenText</A>.
<LI>The <A HREF="http://www.dnai.com/~sharrow/parody.html"
TARGET="top"  onMouseOver="window.status='Giggles Galore';
return true">Gallery of Advertising Parody</A>!
<LI>Being in economics, I have to link to the <A HREF="http:/
/www.etla.fi/pkm/joke.html" TARGET="top"
onMouseOver="window.status='How many economists does it take
to screw in a lightbulb?'; return true">Jokes about
Economics</A> site.
<LI>The <A HREF="ks/" TARGET="top"
onMouseOver="window.status='This makes me feel better about
our Canadian debt!'; return true">US National Debt Clock</A>
site.
</UL>
</BODY>
```

Now go and check out this page at http://randall.uwaterloo.ca/celine/javascript/example5.htm. As your cursor moves over the different links, you should see the messages appearing in the status bar. Of course, displaying the status bar message is not the only thing that you can do with the onMouseOver event handler, but it's the obvious thing. You probably don't want to assign too much to the onMouseOver event handler, because some people like to move their mouse pointers all over the place and this could lead to problems.

Example 6

Example 6 is a work in progress, an attempt at using JavaScript to do something really cool. However, as it stands it won't quite work, so you'll need to dig hard into JavaScript on your own to make it function. Still, it offers a glimpse of some fascinating JavaScript features, so it's well worth working through even to this point.

Everybody has different taste in color, and colors on Web pages are pleasing to some but look terrible to others. A useful solution to this problem of diversity would be to create a form which would let users dynamically choose the colors of your pages to suit yourr tastes. Of course, the first limitation is that once an HTML page has been downloaded, you cannot use JavaScript to update any of the formatting of that page without reloading. However, it is supposed to be possible to use JavaScript to update other frames within a window.

Here the plan is to create a page with a small frame at the top and a larger frame beneath. The idea was to have the small frame contain a form through which users could choose colors for the background, text, and links. Then, when that form was submitted, the input from the form could be used to dynamically load a new page in the bottom frame with the chosen colors. The first task is to create a page that has two frames, and set the default URLs for the two frames:

```
<HTML>
<HEAD>
<TITLE>My attempt at dynamic color updating </TITLE>
</HEAD>
<FRAMESET ROWS="40%,60%">
     <FRAME SRC="http://randall.uwaterloo.ca/celine/
javascript/colorform.htm" name="top">
     <FRAME SRC=scriptintro.htm name="bottom">
</FRAMESET>
</HEAD>
</HTML>
```

This page is available as http://randall.uwaterloo.ca/celine/javascript/example6.htm . Notice that names have been given to the two frames. This will allow you to target a new document to the "bottom" frame (see Chapter 20 for details on creating targets).

The next step is to authorthe page at http://randall.uwaterloo.ca/celine/javascript/colorform.htm, which the document in Example 6 page would automatically load into the top frame. The colorform HTML page contains the form for users to choose colors. The form looks like this:

```
<FORM NAME="UserSetsColors">
Please choose colors for the following elements of this page:<BR>
<SELECT NAME="BackgroundColor">
        <OPTION>White
        <OPTION SELECTED>Aquamarine
</SELECT><BR>
<SELECT NAME="TextColor">
        <OPTION SELECTED>Black
        <OPTION>Dark Orchid
</SELECT><BR>
<SELECT NAME="LinkColor">
        <OPTION SELECTED>Violet Red
```

```
        <OPTION>Spring Green
</SELECT><BR>
<SELECT NAME="VisitedLinkColor">
        <OPTION>Thistle
        <OPTION SELECTED>Sienna
</SELECT><BR>
<INPUT TYPE="reset" VALUE="Reset Defaults">
<INPUT TYPE="button" VALUE="Submit Choices" onClick="changecolor(this.form)">
```

In the interest of brevity, many options have been omitted here; if you call up the real page you'll see about six choices per category. Note the call to the function changecolor(), which is triggered when the user clicks the submit button. And of course, it's not a real submit button, it's just a button with the label *Submit*. You have no need for a real submit button, because you don't intend for the input of this form to go to the server. Instead, the idea is to process the input using a function I've included right on the page.

Colorform.htm also contains the function which is supposed to take those color choices and then open a new document in the bottom window, with those colors. The code for the function to do this is quite long. Below you'll see only the code for the background color, and the last few lines of the function, because the code for interpreting the text, link, and vlink color is exactly the same. At this point you should note that JavaScript has a whole palette of colors that it will recognize and can display. These colors are referenced in the JavaScript color appendix at http://home.netscape.com/comprod/products/navigator/version_2.0/script/script_info/colors.HTML. Here is the abbreviated function (you can look at the whole thing if you load colorform.htm online and do a view source):

```
<SCRIPT LANGUAGE="JavaScript">
function changecolor(form) {
      if (form.BackgroundColor.value == "White") {
      newwin.document.bgColor = "white" } else  {
            if (form.BackgroundColor.value == "Aquamarine")
            newwin.document.bgColor = "aquamarine"
              if (form.BackgroundColor.value == "Yellow") {
              newwin.document.bgColor = "yellow" } else  {

if (form.BackgroundColor.value == "Magenta") {

newwin.document.bgColor = "Magenta" } else {

if (form.BackgroundColor.value == "Quartz") {

newwin.document.bgColor = "quartz" } else  {
```

```
if (form.BackgroundColor.value == "Plum") {

newwin.document.bgColor = "Plum" }

                                        }

    }

   }


    }
     if (form.TextColor.value == "Black") {
      ......
      ......
     if (form.LinkColor.value == "Violet Red") {
           ......
      ......
          if (form.VisitedLinkColor.value == "Thistle") {
           ......
           ......
openwin()
}
```

So the function basically consists of a whole bunch of nested if-else statements. Note the use of the double equal sign—this is the equality test operator (as opposed to the single equal sign, which is the assignment operator). Also note that each test expression after the *if* is surrounded by parentheses. This is a syntax requirement of JavaScript, and if you don't include those parentheses, you'll get an error.

What does this function actually do? It compares the value of the select element such as "BackgroundColor" to the options that are available. As soon as it finds a match (for example if the user had chosen plum as the BackgroundColor), then it assigns that color to newwin.document.bgColor. Of course at this point there isn't a newwin, but that's what the function openwin() is for. After all the form's input has been processed, and values have been assigned to newwin.document.bgColor, newwin.document.fgColor, and so on, then the openwin() function is called. Let's look at the openwin() function now:

```
function openwin() {
     newwin=window.open("","bottom", "toolbar=no,
     directories=no, menubar=no");
```

```
newwin.document.write("This is my new window, with my
new color settings.  What do you think?")
}
```

Window is a JavaScript object, and it has a number of methods that can be called. One of these methods is open(). The open method opens a new browser window, and it has a number of different parameters that can be set. If you visit the Netscape JavaScript pages, then you could find the following information, which outlines the window.open() parameter usage:

```
window.open("URL", "windowName", ["windowFeatures"])
URL specifies the URL to open in the new window.
windowName specifies a name for the window object being
opened.
windowFeatures is a comma-separated list of any of the
following options and values:
   toolbar[=yes|no]|[=1|Ø]
   location[=yes|no]|[=1|Ø]
   directories[=yes|no]|[=1|Ø]
   status[=yes|no]|[=1|Ø]
   menubar[=yes|no]|[=1|Ø]
   scrollbars[=yes|no]|[=1|Ø]
   resizable[=yes|no]|[=1|Ø]
   width=pixels
   height=pixels
```

You may use any subset of these options. Separate options with a comma. Do not put spaces between the options.

It turns out that if you don't specify the URL, then the window is loaded blank. This allows you to then use the document.write function on the newwin object to insert writing. In the penwin() function, the window is opened in the target frame named "bottom." Also declared is the decision not to include any toolbars, directories, or menubar. The document.write function displays the text "This is my new window, with my new color settings" in the bottom frame. If you go to http://randall.uwaterloo.ca/celine/javascript/example6.htm, then you'll see the two frames and the form. If you choose some colors and click the Submit Choices button, then you'll see that the newwin does actually appear in the bottom frame, and the text does, too. The only problem is that the colors of the frame don't change.

Example 7

Like Example 6, Example 7 is also a work in progress, and it too provides some useful JavaScript techniques. In this example, I am attempting to interface between JavaScript and a Java applet.

The Animator applet belongs to Sun, but the people at Sun have generously allowed the public to download the code and use it. This means that you can create your own little pictures and then specify those pictures as input parameters to the Animator applet, thereby creating your own custom animations. This has been done at http://randall.uwaterloo.ca/celine.htm, which you might wish to look at now. Here is the HTML source code for the part of that page that loads the Animation:

```
<B>Here's an applet that makes use of the Animator applet (I created the
graphics myself though...aren't they fabulous!) :</B>
<P>
<center><applet codebase="celine/classes" code="Animator.class" width=150
height=150>
<param name=imagesource value="celine/pics">
<param name=endimage value=3>
<param name=pause value=200>
</applet></center>
```

When you link an applet into HTML, you have to specify where the code is located (URL or relative directory), you have to specify the name of the code, and you have to specify a size for the applet. Depending on the applet, you may also have to indicate some input parameters. In the case of the Animator applet, you can see above that I have specified some parameters. First of all, I have told theapplet what directory to look in to find the images that I want animated. Second, I have specified that there are three images. Finally, I have specified that I want there to be 200 milliseconds of time between the pictures.

What I want to do with Example 7 is allow users to fill in a form and choose an animation and a speed. For this purpose I have created three different series of pictures. Actually I only created two, and for the third I'm reusing the animation from my page. So I've put the three different series of pictures into three different directories on my server. As in Example 6, I've used the idea of putting a form in a top frame, and having the output of the form create an HTML page for the bottom frame. The base page, which creates the two frames is almost identical to the one in the last example:

```
<HTML><HEAD>
<TITLE>Celine Latulipe's Example 7 Page </TITLE>
</HEAD>
<FRAMESET ROWS="40%,60%">
        <FRAME SRC="http://randall.uwaterloo.ca/celine/javascript/
animationform.htm" name="top">
```

```
        <FRAME SRC=scriptintro.htm name="bottom">
</FRAMESET>
</HEAD><BODY></BODY></HTML>
```

The form that you will find on animationform.htm looks a little different, though:

```
<FORM>
Please select an animation to view:
<SELECT NAME="animation" align=left> <OPTION>Little_Cute_Guy
<OPTION>Star_Girl<OPTION>Seasons</SELECT><BR>
Please select a speed:
<SELECT NAME="speed" align=center><OPTION>Fast<OPTION>Medium
<OPTION>Slow</SELECT><BR>
<INPUT TYPE="button" VALUE="Load New Animation" align=center
ONCLICK="LoadPage(this.form)">
</FORM>
```

Again, the form does not actually have a submit button, because I expect to process the form's input using JavaScript functions embedded right into the page. After the user selects an animation and a speed, he or she will click the "Load New Animation" button, and that will call the LoadPage(this.form) function. The LoadPage() function follows:

```
<SCRIPT LANGUAGE="JavaScript">
<!-- to hide script contents from old browsers
function LoadPage(form){
        if (form.animation.value == "Little_Cute_Guy") {
        var imagesrc = "pics" } else {
                if (form.animation.value == "Star_Girl") {
                var imagesrc = "stargirl" } else {
                                if (form.animation.value == "Seasons") {
                                var imagesrc = "seasons"}
                                                                        }
                                                                        }

        if (form.speed.value == "Fast") {
        var speed = 1 } else {
                if (form.speed.value == "Medium") {
                var speed = 2 } else {
                                if (form.speed.value == "Slow") {
                                var speed = 3 }

   }
                                        }
        LoadAnimation(imagesrc, speed)
}
```

The LoadPage function looks a lot like the changecolor() function from Example 6. This time, the function assigns the values of the variables imagesrc and speed according to what the user's input was from the form. Then, the

LoadAnimation() function is called using these variables. The LoadAnimation() function follows:

```
function LoadAnimation(imagesrc, speed) {
newwindow=window.open("","bottom", "toolbar=no, directories=no, menubar=no");
        newwindow.document.write('<HTML><HEAD><H1>My Animation</H1>
        </HEAD><BODY>')
newwindow.document.write('<center><applet codebase="/celine/classes"
code="Animator.class" width=200 height=200>')
newwindow.document.write('<param name=imagesource value="/celine/' + imagesrc
+'">');
        newwindow.document.write('<param name=endimage value=3>');
        newwindow.document.write('<param name=pause value=' + speed + '00>');
        newwindow.document.write('</applet></center>');
        newwindow.document.write('<BR>');
        newwindow.document.write('</BODY></HTML>')
}
//end hiding contents from old browsers -->
</SCRIPT>
```

This is the part that differs significantly from Example 6. In this function, I am attempting to use the string concatenation operator (+) to put together HTML tags on the fly. This is done by using the newwindow.document.write() function and writing out HTML tags. If you compare what is in the newwindow.document.write() statements in this function with the HTML from my original animation page, you can see that they are almost identical. The only difference is that in this instance, the imagesrc directory and the pause value (or the speed of animation) are both assigned dynamically, depending on the values of the variables imagesrc and speed, which are set in the LoadPage() function and passed into the LoadAnimation function as parameters.

JavaScript General Information

This section provides an overview of the JavaScript language, as well as a bunch of little helpful hints.

When you decide to start incorporating JavaScript into your HTML pages, you'll want to spend some time browsing through Netscape's JavaScript reference pages. The URL for these pages is http://home.netscape.com/comprod/products/navigator/version_2.0/script/script_info/index.HTML.

It would be a good idea to bookmark this site, because you'll probably be visiting it quite often as you become more involved with JavaScript. The site is set up with an index on the left side, and anything that you click on will appear in the larger frame on the right. A handy trick for moving through a site like this is to use your left mouse button to move backward and forward within a frame. Figure 23.1 shows what the opening page of the JavaScript reference site looks like.

Figure 23.1

Netscape's JavaScript reference pages

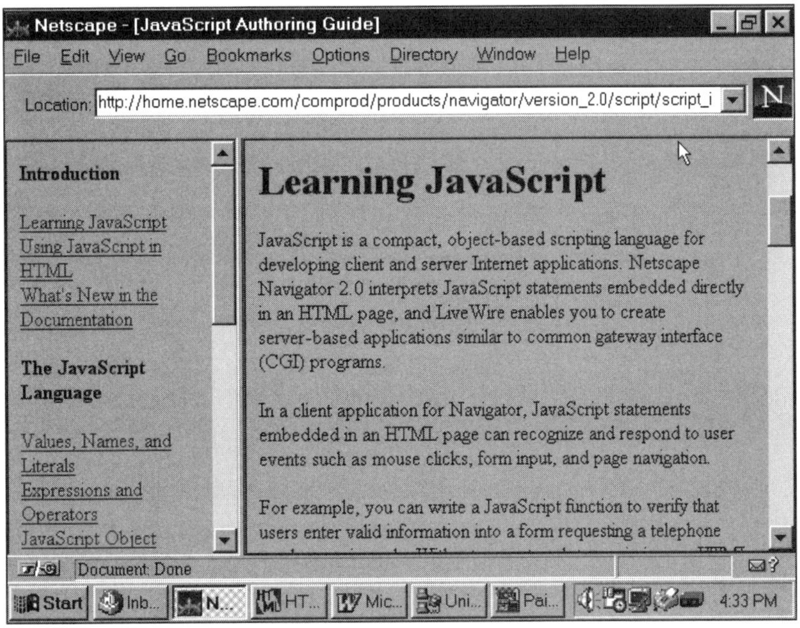

JavaScript can be incorporated into an HTML document in two ways. The first way is with the <SCRIPT> and </SCRIPT> tags, and the second way is by incorporating event handlers into other HTML tags. You've used both of these methods in the examples above, and in fact, in most cases you've combined these two methods. One common use of JavaScript is to incorporate event handlers into other HTML tags, and have these event handlers call JavaScript functions which are located in between <SCRIPT> </SCRIPT> tags. This can help to make your HTML much more readable, which is important if somebody else has to maintain it. I've already mentioned that the best way to incorporate JavaScript functions into HTML pages is to put them in the <HEAD> section of the page. The reason for this is that HTML pages are downloaded sequentially. (If the function was at the bottom of the page, but the event handler that called it was at the top of the page, an impatient user may trigger the event handler and the function before the function has even downloaded, therefore causing an error.)

Another important implication of HTML pages being downloaded sequentially is that once a page has been downloaded, JavaScript functions do not have the power to change the formatting of the page without reloading. Therefore it is not possible to update part of a page. However, the use of frames does allow updating of subdocuments, and in Example 7 (which includes Example 8), you saw how it is possible for event handlers and functions to cause changes in another frame.

Writing JavaScript functions can be challenging, especially if you've never programmed before. If this is the case, then you'll want to go over the JavaScript statements and their structures, so that you'll avoid some of the silly mistakes that result from bad syntax. A few rules of thumb:

- Always remember to put parentheses around the test expressions within an if statement.
- Always enclose all of the statements that belong to a function in begin and end brackets: { }.
- Parameters are passed into functions by value, not by reference. This means that if the value of the parameter changes within the function, the value of the parameter does not change beyond the function.
- If you want some changed value to be saved beyond the scope of the function, you must have the function return that value.
- Make sure that the number of parameters you declare your function with matches the number of parameters you call your function with.
- Remember that a function doesn't necessarily have to have any parameters. If your function doesn't have any parameters, it still must be followed by parentheses (although they will obviously be empty), because that is how Netscape can recognize that it is a function, rather than a variable or a property.
- Always alternate between using double and single quotes. JavaScript doesn't care which you use where, but you'll need to alternate when you have nested quotes, so that JavaScript knows when one type of enclosure is ending.

Variables and Literals

You can declare a variable anywhere in a JavaScript function. A variable declaration looks like this:

```
var variablename
```

At the same time as declaring a variable, you'll often want to assign a value to the variable. Assignments in JavaScript are done with an equal sign. In the following statement I declare a variable called color, and assign to it the value of the background color of the current HTML document:

```
var color = document.bgcolor
```

Then, whenever I want to refer to the background color of the current document, I can simply use the variable color. In addition to variables, JavaScript also supports the use of literals. A literal is an immediate value. A common kind of literal is a string literal. For instance, if wanted to assign the color violet to the variable color, I could do so by simply typing in violet in quotes:

```
var color = "violet"
```

Note that the string value *violet* is marked with quotations. This tells the computer that the word violet is just a word and not a variable name that the computer is supposed to recognize.

Literals can be anything: numbers, strings, Booleans, characters, and objects. A Boolean is a true or false value. JavaScript is a loosely typed language, which means that when you declare a variable you don't have to specify what type of variable you are creating. JavaScript also attempts to automatically convert your datatypes when you need to use them as different datatypes. The Netscape JavaScript pages give the following explanation:

```
JavaScript will attempt to convert an expression to the datatype of the left-
hand operand. Expressions are always evaluated from left to right, so
JavaScript applies this rule at each step in the evaluation of a complex
expression. For example, suppose you define the following variables
var astring = "7"
var anumber = 42
Then consider the following statements:
 x = astring + anumber
 y = anumber + astring
The first statement will convert anumber to a string value, because the left-
hand operand, astring, is a string.
The statement will then concatenate the two strings, so x will have a value of
"742". Conversely, the second statement will convert astring to a numeric
value, because the left-hand operand, anumber, is a number. The statement then
adds the two numbers, so y will have a value of 49.
```

This loose-typing is a feature which makes it easy for anyone new to programming, but at the same time makes it easy for everyone to make mistakes. Mistakes happen when a variable that you want to have interpreted one way gets interpreted some other way.

JavaScript Object Hierarchy

JavaScript has objects, methods, properties, and event handlers. Each separate object on an HTML page is a separate object according to JavaScript as well. If you have an HTML page that has three links, two anchors, and three forms, each form with a number of different form elements, then each of these items is a separate JavaScript object. An important note about JavaScript, which is directed to those who have not programmed in C++—whenever you need to reference an indexed element in JavaScript, such as the third form on a page, subtract 1. The reason for this is that counting starts at 0. Thus the first form on a page is referenced as document.forms[0] and the second form on a page is referenced as document.forms[1]. There are a number of objects in JavaScript which can be referenced using an index; these include forms, elements, links, frames, and anchors.

At this point you may be wondering about the difference between a method and a property, or you may have already figured it out. A method has a return value, and can take parameters. When you execute a method, something happens, or some value changes or is analyzed. A property on the other hand is more like a characteristic. Properties can be accessed and assigned. Thus, the background color of an HTML document is a property. You can access that property to find out what the color is, and you can set the color to be something different. However, nothing gets performed when you refer to an object's properties. When you refer to an object's methods, something usually happens. A good example is the window object's open method. When the open method is called, a whole bunch of things happen between Netscape and your computer, and a new Web browser window pops up.

Every different type of object can have a number of different methods, properties, and event handlers. Let's look at the example of a form. If you look at the JavaScript reference pages on the Netscape site, go to the Objects page, and click on form, then you'll see something like Figure 23.2.

The form object has five properties—action, elements, method, name, and target. These properties can be accessed in JavaScript. The elements property refers to the number of different objects that are in the form. The action and method properties are obvious. The name property is useful when you have a number of different forms in a document, because you can then name each of them and refer to them by their names. The target property is to direct the form's input to another frame or window. In the following example, I am making use of the form's element property and the modularity provided by writing one function that can be used over and over again:

```
<HEAD>
<SCRIPT language="JavaScript">
function confirmvalue(formnumber, elementnumber) {
        var elementvalue = document.forms[formnumber -
        1].elements[elementnumber - 1].value;
        if (confirm("The value of this form element is now " + elementvalue +
        ".")) {} else {
                document.forms[formnumber - 1].elements[elementnumber -
                1].value = ''
        }
}
</SCRIPT>
</HEAD>
<BODY>
```

Figure 23.2

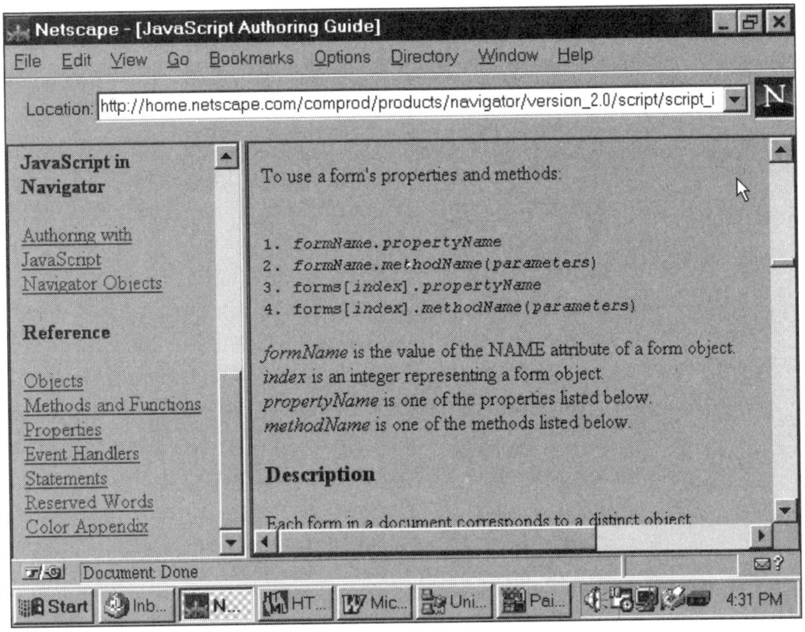

The reference for the form object in JavaScript, as seen on the Netscape JavaScript site

```
<P>Here's the first form:
<FORM>
<P>Please enter your age:<BR>
<INPUT TYPE="text" NAME="age" SIZE=15 onChange="confirmvalue('1','1')">
<P>Please enter your email address:<BR>
<INPUT TYPE="TextArea" NAME="email" SIZE=60 onChange="confirmvalue('1','2')">
</FORM>
<P>Here's the second form:
<FORM>
<P>Enter your favorite color:
<INPUT TYPE="text" NAME="favcolor" SIZE=30 onChange="confirmvalue('2','1')">
<P>Enter your second favorite color:
<INPUT TYPE="text" NAME="secfavcolor" SIZE=30 onChange="confirmvalue('2','2')">
</FORM>
<P>Thanks for participating!
</BODY>
```

What the function does for this HTML page is confirm the user's new entry every time one of the form elements' value changes. Note that the form in this case is referenced by number, because I didn't name the two different forms, and that the elements are also referenced by number; number has to be decreased, because the counting starts from 0.

The general idea of using an object's methods and properties can be summarized as follows:

- To reference an object's properties: *objectname.propertyname*
- To reference an object's methods: *objectname.methodname(<parameters>)*

In addition to methods and properties, some objects in the JavaScript Object Hierarchy also have event handlers that apply to them. For example, the form object has an onSubmit event handler, which makes sense because a form can be submitted, and that submittal is an event. (It would not make sense for a form to have an onLoad event handler, because forms are not loaded separately from HTML documents, and it would not make sense for a document to have an onSubmit event handler because HTML pages are not submitted.) Thus, as you browse through the JavaScript Object pages on the Netscape JavaScript site, you'll notice that each method, property, and event handler will apply to some objects but not others.

The JavaScript Object Hierarchy, like the rest of JavaScript, is still under development. This means that the basic structure is there, but more is being added to it. The object hierarchy I've included below only shows the objects which have been implemented as of the time of this writing. You may want to check the JavaScript pages on the Netscape site to see what else has been added and what is still on the way.

```
Window
        |
        +-- parent, frames, self, top
        |
        +-- location
        |
        +-- history
        |
        +-- document
        |
        +-- forms
        |      |
        |   form elements
        |
        +-- links
        |
        +-- anchors
```

A Web browser window is the overriding object in JavaScript. Whenever you want to refer to an object in JavaScript, you have to type out the entire hierarchy behind that object, excluding the window object. For instance, if you want to refer to the third link on a page, you can't just type link[2], you have to type document.link[2]. As you've seen from the examples you've already done, the period shows the distinction between hierarchical levels, and similar objects at the same level are referenced by number (but remember to count from 0).

So, a window can have frames, and it has a location and a history. The frames part is obvious. A window's location object is one which has properties such as host, hostname, port, and protocol. The history object is an object which contains information about the user's past URL history—the locations which the user has been to recently. The window object has a number of useful methods. These include open and close, alert, and confirm. Because these methods belong to the window object, and the window object doesn't have to be named in references, these methods can be called directly. You did this in some of the examples above when you called on the alert and confirm functions.

Of course, each window has a document. The document is the HTML page loaded into that window. A document has properties such as background and foreground colors, links, title, location, forms, and anchors. A document has methods such as open, close, writeln, and write. The document.write function is probably one which you will get a lot of use out of, and it can be particularly useful when you wish to use JavaScript to create subdocuments. You may be wondering about the document.writeln function—I already mentioned that it puts a carriage return after the string. However, this carriage return will only work if the document.writeln function happens to appear in a section of HTML which is specified with the <PRE> and </PRE> tags to signify preformatted text.

Under the document object are a number of other different objects. These include forms, links, and anchors. The forms object has the element object underneath it. As you saw in the previous example, to refer to a specific property of an object you have to type the object name, and its ancestors in the hierarchy. So, to refer to the fourth element in the third form, you have to type:

```
document.forms[3].elements[4]
```

Or, if the form was named Form1 and you knew the element was a text field named "age," you could refer to the value of the field like this:

```
document.Form1.age.value
```

The object hierarchy is quite small, compared to the object hierarchy that you will find in Java and in some other languages. However, there are quite a number of methods and properties, and some of these methods and properties apply to more than one of the objects. In the Netscape JavaScript pages you'll find that under each object is a listing of methods and properties that apply to that object. If you click on one of those methods or properties you'll get a description and a listing of all the objects to which that method or property applies, so there is a circular type of linking.

JavaScript Event Handlers

In this chapter you've already seen some examples of event handlers. You used the onClick event handler to call a function when a form was submitted, and you used the onMouseOver event handler to alter the status bar messages for some links. However, there are a number of additional event handlers, and they deserve some discussion. Event handlers are responsible for a lot of the action in JavaScript, and it is usually through event handlers that JavaScript functions are called. Sometimes event handlers don't actually point to functions, though. In the cases in which actual JavaScript statements are incorporated into the event handler it is important to remember to separate distinct statements using semicolons.

Many of the event handlers seem specific to forms and link elements; however, the onLoad and onUnload handlers are quite different. The onLoad event handler allows you to have some JavaScript code execute as soon as the current page (or frame) has finished loading. This is accomplished by including the onLoad handler in the <BODY> tag or the <FRAMESET> tag. The example that is given in the Netscape JavaScript pages is to include an alert. This might be a good way to quickly add an important message to your home page. However, I can see how it could also get very annoying if it were a page which you visited often. The syntax would be as follows:

```
<BODY bgcolor="aquamarine" onLoad="window.alert('Hey! Check out the new
Gallery link, it's cool!')">
```

The onUnLoad event handler works similarly, except that it is the first thing that is done when a user chooses a new page or attempts to close the Web browser. It also goes in either the <BODY> or <FRAMESET> tags.

Event Handlers for Select, Text, and TextArea

Select, Text, and TextArea are all form objects, and all accept input from the user. All three of these objects can take the event handlers onFocus, onBlur, and onChange. We've already discussed the onFocus event handler, and the onBlur event handler is the exact opposite. An onBlur event is triggered whenever the user leaves the element that has the onBlur handler. For example, if a form field has an onBlur event, then whenever that user focuses on that field by tabbing or clicking, the onBlur event will occur as soon as the user tabs to a different field, or clicks on something else in the document. This could be useful as a content checker if you wanted to make sure that the user had entered appropriate content into a field. You could have a function that checked to make sure the value of the field was a number, and if it wasn't you could create an alert to let the user know. The onChange event handler is triggered when the value of a form field has changed (for example, when a user selects a different option in a select menu, or when a user changes the text entered in a TextArea). Again, the obvious use of the event handler in this case is to check the validity of the new input or to confirm the user's new choice. The following is a good example of the onBlur event handler:

```
<HEAD><SCRIPT NAME="JavaScript">
        function checkdata(form, elementnum) {
                if (form.elements[elementnum].value == '') {
                                alert("You must fill in the field")
                }
        }
        </SCRIPT></HEAD>
<BODY>
<FORM>
<P>Please enter your last name:<BR>
<INPUT TYPE=TextArea NAME="lastname" SIZE=40 VALUE="You must fill in this
field" onFocus="form.lastname.value = ''" onBlur="checkdata(this.form, 0)">
<P>Please enter your email address:<BR>
<INPUT TYPE=TextArea NAME="address" SIZE=80 VALUE="You must fill in this
field" onFocus="form.address.value = ''" onBlur="checkdata(this.form, 1)">
<P>Please enter your phone number:<BR>
<INPUT TYPE=TextArea NAME="phone" SIZE=15 VALUE="optional"><BR>
<INPUT TYPE="button" VALUE="Submit" >
</FORM>
```

This example can be viewed online by loading http://randall.uwaterloo.ca/celine/javascript/onBlur.htm. The above HTML alerts the user if he or she tries to leave any important field blank. If you were trying to create an online order form for a company, this would be a great thing to do with the "Enter your credit card number:" field. You could actually take it one step further, and redirect focus to the field. In fact, let's do that with this example:

```
<HEAD><SCRIPT NAME="JavaScript">
        function checkdata(form, elementnum) {
if ((form.elements[elementnum].value == '') ||
(form.elements[elementnum].value == "You must fill in this field")) {
                                alert("You must fill in the field!");
                                form.elements[elementnum].focus();
                                form.elements[elementnum].select();
        }
}
</SCRIPT></HEAD>
<BODY>
<FORM>
<P>Please enter your last name:<BR>
```

```
<INPUT TYPE=TextArea NAME="lastname" SIZE=40 VALUE="You must fill in this
field"  onFocus="lastname.select()" onBlur="checkdata(this.form, 0)">
<P>Please enter your email address:<BR>
<INPUT TYPE=TextArea NAME="address" SIZE=80 VALUE="You must fill in this
field"  onFocus="address.select()" onBlur="checkdata(this.form, 1)">
<P>Please enter your phone number:<BR>
<INPUT TYPE=TextArea NAME="phone" SIZE=15 VALUE="optional"
onFocus="phone.select()"><BR>
<INPUT TYPE="button" VALUE="Submit" >
</FORM>
</BODY>
```

This fine-tuned example actually puts the focus back on the field the user tried to leave, and selects the field so that after the alert box is clicked away, the user knows which field he or she tried to leave. I also changed the onFocus event handler, which had blanked the field in the last example, so that it selects the field instead of blanking it. This is because in this case I'm actually checking two things: to see if the user blanked the field and to see if the user tried to leave the field without changing the "You must fill in this field" message. Of course if the user just changes one letter in that message, then the function won't be invoked. The fine-tuned version of this form can be tried at http://randall.uwaterloo.ca/celine/javascript/onBlur2.htm.

JavaScript Expressions and Operators

JavaScript uses three different types of expressions. Arithmetic expressions, such as 3*4, evaluate to a number. Logical expressions such as (x=5), evaluate to true or false. String expressions, such as "Hi!" or "1996," evaluate to a string. These expressions can be used in combination with a number of operators. The operators are almost identical to those used in the C and C++ languages. It is important to realize that JavaScript uses short-circuit evaluation, so if the expression on the right of an && or || operator actually calls a function, that function may not get called at all. The following is a brief listing of the most important operators:

Operator	Explanation
=	Assignment operator: assigns value of expression on right to variable or object on left
==	Equality test operator: returns true if value on left equals value on right, otherwise false
||	Or operator: logical or, returns true if either expression is true
!	Not operator: returns false if following expression is true, true if following expression is false

Operator	Explanation
&&	And operator: logical and returns true if both expressions are true
+, -, *, /	Standard mathematical operators
%	Modulus division (17 % 8 returns 2)
+	String concatenation operator ("Java" + "script"= "JavaScript")

In addition to the equality test shown above, JavaScript also uses the standard comparison operators:

Operator	Explanation
>	Greater than
>=	Greater than or equal
<	Less than
<=	Less than or equal
!=	Not equal

JavaScript can also handle bitwise operators; however, that is beyond the scope of what you are trying to accomplish in this chapter. If you are interested in how the bitwise operators work, your best option is to read the online reference on the Netscape site.

The incrementation and decrementation operators are also very useful, and the following table outlines their functions (assume for each example that x equals 10 to begin with).

Operator	Explanation
var++	Evaluates to variable and then increments variable by one: y = x++ ‡ y=10, x=11
++var	Increments variable and then evaluates to new value: y = ++x ‡ y=11, x=11
var--	Evaluates to variable and then decrements variable by one: y = x-- ‡ y=10, x=9
--var	Decrements variable and then evaluates to new value: y = --x ‡ y=9, x=9

The above incrementation and decrementation operators are very useful when constructing for loops, as you will see in the following section on statements.

JavaScript Statements

Within JavaScript code, there are 11 different types of statements. Some of these are essential, and others are not quite as important. Below I have outlined the purpose of each of these eleven statements, and for those which are important I have included examples and descriptions. For those that I consider to be less crucial or useful, I have simply included a pointer to the appropriate information on the Netscape JavaScript site so that if you are interested in that type of statement you have a reference for where you can get more information. Anyone who is familiar with C or C++ will need only to skim over this area, because the statement structure and syntax are virtually identical. The only difference is that not all the statements available in C and C++ are available in JavaScript.

Comments

Comments can be intermingled with JavaScript code. Any line that begins with double forward slashes designates a comment and will not be interpreted by Netscape. You can also have multiline comments by enclosing the comments in /* and */. Examples:

```
<SCRIPT LANGUAGE="JavaScript">
        function somefunction() {
                ......
                ......
        //this is a comment
        </SCRIPT>
<SCRIPT LANGUAGE="JavaScript">
        function somefunction() {
                ......
                ......
/*this is a multiline comment that can go on for as many lines as you need.
Comments are good because they make it easier for other people to understand
and maintain your code*/
        </SCRIPT>
```

Function

You've already spent a fair amount of time on functions in this chapter. The most important thing to understand is the difference between declaring a function and calling it. When a function is declared (usually in the head of the HTML), it is not executed. The function declaration is a set of code that tells Netscape what to do if and when that function is called. A function declaration can be differentiated easily from a function call because a function definition actually has the keyword "function" in front of it.

Here is the syntax for a function:

```
function functionname (<parameter_ list, separated_by_commas>) {
                coding
                coding
```

```
}
```

As discussed earlier, functions can have parameters, and you can give the parameters names, and refer to those names within the coding of the function. Parameter names, like variable names, cannot have spaces, and must begin with a character. You must always make sure that you match the number of parameters in the function declaration and the function call statement. For example, if you have a function called AreaofRectangle, which has two parameters (width, length), then when you call the AreaofRectangle, you had better make sure that you give the function two values. Note that the values you pass into a function can be literals or variables.

```
<SCRIPT LANGUAGE="JavaScript">
<!-- to hide script contents from old browsers
function AreaofRectangle(width, length) {
     <function code>
}
//end hiding contents from old browsers -->
</SCRIPT>
```

A function may or may not have a return value. That is the next type of statement you will examine.

Return

The return statement specifies a value that the function will hold after it has been called. For example, if you had a function AreaofRectangle as mentioned above, the code inside the function might contain a single return statement like this:

```
<SCRIPT LANGUAGE="JavaScript">
<!-- to hide script contents from old browsers
function AreaofRectangle(width, length) {
     return width*length;
}
//end hiding contents from old browsers -->
</SCRIPT>
```

Note that return is not like a variable. It doesn't get assigned the expression on the left with an equal sign, it just takes on that value. You can consider the function AreaofRectangle almost like a variable. Consider the following if statement (I am getting a little ahead of myself since I haven't talked about if statements yet).

```
function size() {
var side1 = 12;
var side2 = 4;
```

```
if (AreaofRectangle(side1, side2) < 100) {
      var area = 'small' } else {
      var area = 'large' }
}
```

In this example, the AreaofRectangle function is being treated almost as a variable, and this is because it has a return value. AreaofRectangle will be called with the variables side1 and side2, and these will passed into the function. The function will replace width with side1 (12), and length with side2 (4), and so the return value will be 48. Thus, the if statement will evaluate to true, because the AreaofRectangle function evaluates to 48, which is less than 100. The result in this case is that the variable area will have the string "small" assigned to it.

Finally, note that the number of open curly brackets always matches the number of closed curly brackets. If you don't match your brackets, you'll get an error.

Var

You've already seen a number of examples of the use of the var statement. Variables can be numbers, characters, strings, objects, and Booleans. A variable name can contain only common keyboard characters and numbers, and must always start with a letter. JavaScript is not case-sensitive, so if you call a variable zebra at one point and refer to it as Zebra at another point, you won't have a problem.

If-Else

The if-else statement is probably the most useful statement in any programming language. It is also known as a selection control structure. I'm not going to talk too much about it, because you've already seen several examples of it in this chapter. The structure is pretty simple:

```
if (<some expression to be tested>) {
        //some code to be executed if statement is true } else {
        //some code to be executed if statement isn't true}
```

JavaScript does not have a built-in elseif function like some other languages, so you are restricted to simple nesting if statements inside else statements to create the same effect.

For, For..In, and While

I categorize all three of these types of statements together because they are all iteration control structures. An interation control structure is a looping structure which allows a piece of coding to be reiterated over and over again. The code performs a test, and if the test passes, then the iteration takes place and the test is performed again. At some point the test will fail, and program execution will fall through to the next sequential line of code after the loop.

The most simple of these three statements is the while loop. It looks like this:

```
while (some expression to be tested for true or false) {
      //code to be executed while true
      // ''
      // ''
}
```

Every time the loop iterates, control goes back to the test expression, and at some point the test expression should evaluate to true, and control will skip down to whatever code follows this while loop.

The for loop is slightly more complicated, as it is a counting loop. A counter keeps track of how many times the loop iterates, and the loop will stop executing when the counter gets to some previously decided level. Here's the syntax for a for loop:

```
        for (variable declaration or statement; condition; update expression) {
statements
}
```

An example is the following:

```
for (var i=0; i < 10; i++)  {
        statements
}
```

In this example, the for loop is initialized with the variable counter i set to a value of 0. The loop will execute the statements continuously until the middle condition is no longer true. Thus, the statements will be executed continuously until i is no longer less than 10. The third part of the for statement specifies what happens to the variable i each time the loop iterates.In this example, i is incremented by 1 after each loop iteration. I say *after* because the incrementation is a post-incrementation operator. If it said ++i, then it would be incremented before each loop iteration. Of course, you can also decrement i, and set your test condition to be some value less than the original assigned value. It's up to you.

The third type of iteration structure is the for..in loop, which I won't bother discussing. This structure is used when you want to evaluate all the things which belong to some object or some set, and is more advanced than what this chapter is meant to present. You can get information on the for..in statement at http://home.netscape.com/comprod/products/navigator/version_2.0/script/script_info/stmts.html#for_in_statement.

Break and Continue

The break and continue statements are used within for and while loops to change the control flow. A break statement contained within the coding of a for or while loop will cause the loop to stop iteration, and cause program flow to take up at the statement following the loop. The continue statement also causes the loop iteration to stop, but the program control goes back to the top of the loop, where the test condition is.

With

The with statement, like the for..in statement, is beyond the scope of this chapter. It deals with considering object hierarchy and ownership of properties and methods, as well as the use of arrays. You can find information on the with statement at http://home.netscape.com/comprod/products/navigator/version_2.0/script/script_info/stmts.HTML.

JavaScript Error Messages

When you start incorporating JavaScript into your HTML pages, I can almost guarantee that you'll get a few errors. If you don't, you deserve a genius medal!

Because JavaScript isn't a full-blown programming language, JavaScript does not get compiled the way other programming files do. For this reason, you won't get compile errors in the usual sense of the word; you'll get what looks more like a run-time error. What I mean is that when you test out your HTML page with JavaScript coding on it, the page will more than likely load into Netscape, but then you'll be confronted by a little box in the top-left corner of Netscape telling you that you have JavaScript errors. I call this runtime because the HTML page is actually already loaded, and you can probably ignore the errors and click on links and do all the other things you normally do with a Web page. The only problem is that your JavaScript functions won't work.

There are many common causes of JavaScript errors:

- Calling methods and properties on objects to which those methods and properties don't belong
- Forgetting to use begin and end { } brackets around the inside of your functions
- Forgetting to enclose if-else expressions in parentheses
- Using variable names without declaring them first
- Passing the wrong number of parameters to a function

I could go on and on here, but I won't. What I do want to do is show you what the JavaScript error box looks like. Let's take our very first example, and use it again. Suppose I had the following embedded in an HTML page:

```
<SCRIPT LANGUAGE="JavaScript">
document.write(Hello World!)
</SCRIPT>
```

If you're quick, you may already recognize the error in this scripting. But Figure 23.3 shows the JavaScript Error Alert that will appear if you try to load a document with that script.

Figure 23.3

A JavaScript Error Alert

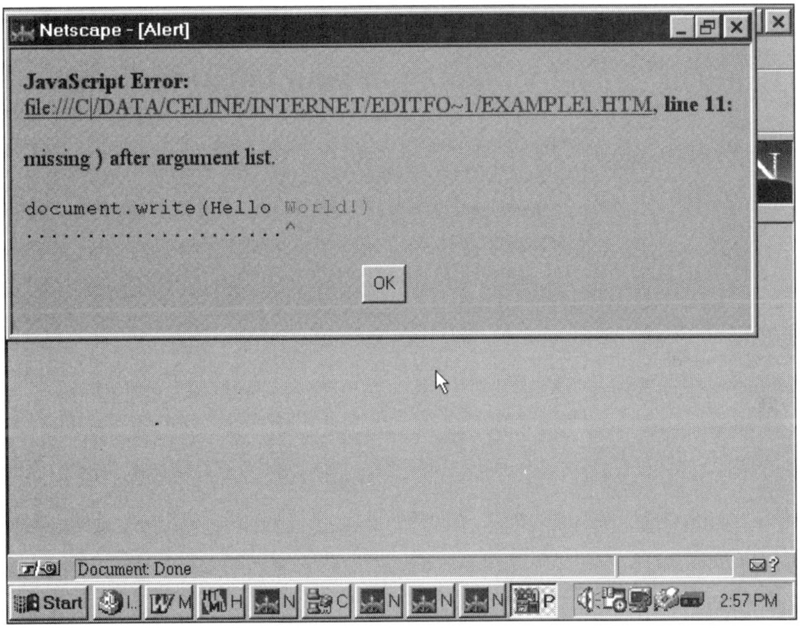

The error says "line 11: missing) after argument list," and there is a little pointer pointing at the beginning of "World." This error doesn't exactly spell out what the problem is, but with a little thinking, you should be able to figure it out. Netscape is telling you that the method document.write can only take one parameter, which must be followed by a closing bracket, and it thinks you have included two parameters. Now, you should be thinking, "But I didn't include any parameters, I want it to print out the string literal 'Hello World!'" So why is Netscape seeing parameters instead of a string literal?

Well, because you forgot to put Hello World! in quotes within the brackets. If you correct the problem like this:

```
<SCRIPT LANGUAGE="JavaScript">
document.write("Hello World!")
</SCRIPT>
```

then you can load the page, and you won't get another alert. In fact, "Hello World!" should show up right at the top of the page if you've included this script in the header.

Not all of the JavaScript alerts will be this easy to figure out (some may be even easier than this to figure out). What you will find is that the more time you spend playing with JavaScript, the more familiar the error messages will become, and hopefully they'll get easier to figure out.

JavaScript Reserved Words

The reserved words in this list cannot be used as JavaScript variable, function, method, or object names.

Some of these words are keywords used in JavaScript; others are reserved for future use.

abstract	Boolean	break	byte
case	catch	char	class
const	continue	default	do
double	else	extends	false
final	finally	float	for
function	goto	if	implements
import	in	instanceof	int
interface	long	native	new
null	package	private	protected
public	return	short	static
super	switch	synchronized	this
throw	throws	transient	true
try	var	void	while
with			

A Few Last Comments

At the time of this printing, JavaScript-generated objects would not print in Netscape. Thus, if you had the following HTML,

```
<P>Welcome to my home page!
<SCRIPT>document.write("This is my first attempt at JavaScripting")
</SCRIPT>
```

and you used Netscape's print function, then the only thing that would print would be the words "Welcome to my homepage!" This problem may have been resolved by the time this book hits the shelf, however, so you should either try printing the above page or read the JavaScript reference information on the Netscape site.

Now you know enough JavaScript to enhance a Web page, fine-tune a Web form, and perhaps create some really interesting interactive functions with Netscape. I hope this chapter has been comprehensible, and I look forward to seeing you visit my site to look at all the examples from this chapter (even if they aren't all working yet!).

■ Appendix A

■ Acquiring Netscape Navigator Gold

Netscape Navigator Gold is available from the World Wide Web or through Netscape Communications' FTP site. You can also retrieve it from a number of software download sites around the Internet.

If You Already Have a Web Browser

Users with a working Web browser such as NCSA Mosaic, Netscape Navigator, Microsoft Internet Explorer, Quarterdeck Mosaic, Emissary, WebSurfer, or MacWeb (to name only a few) can find Gold at the Netscape Communications software download site at http://home.netscape.com/comprod/mirror/index.html. From this page, you can download all versions of Netscape Navigator, and you can acquire plug-ins and helper applications as well.

To retrieve Gold, click on the Netscape Navigator link. The resulting page, called Download Netscape Navigator Software, offers a form consisting of several drop-down menus. In the Desired Product field, select Netscape Navigator Gold (the latest version). In the Operating System field, select the appropriate system you are using (note that Windows 3.1 users are distinguished from Windows 95/NT users). The Desired Language field offers a choice of languages, and the Location field lets you select download sites close to you.

When you've finished making your selections, click on the Click to Display Download Sites button. This will take you to the actual download page, where you'll see a list of download sites. Click on any one of them, and follow your browser's instructions for downloading software.

If You Don't Have a Web Browser

Users who want Gold as their first Web browser can retrieve it through the anonymous FTP process. To do so, you need to be connected to the Internet, and you need an FTP program. UNIX has an FTP program built in, as does Windows 95 and Windows NT. Macintosh users can use the popular Fetch program, and Windows 3.1 users with an existing direct Internet connection can use a packages such as Winsock FTP.

Netscape's FTP sites are growing in number constantly. As of this writing, there were 13 such sites. Their addresses are ftp1.netscape.com through ftp13.nescape.com. They all carry the same software.

To retrieve Gold through anonymous FTP, start your FTP program and choose one of Netscape's ftp addresses. Set your user name as anonymous and your password as your *full* e-mail address. When you've connected to Netscape, get a directory listing (for users of GUI FTP programs it will already be visible), and enter the most up-to-date Gold directory. Inside that directory, another set of directories will lead you to the Gold version for your operating system. When you finally get to the program directory, get a directory listing and find the Gold archive itself, which is currently called g32e201.exe (for Windows 95/NT users). Whatever it's called, perform a binary download of that file onto your hard drive. Take care that you don't perform an ASCII download; if you do, you'll waste a lot of time and it won't work anyway.

Here are the steps for a raw FTP download, using UNIX's or Windows 95/NT's FTP program. As of this writing, the only Gold version available was g32e201.exe for Windows 95/NT, so that's what you'll see here:

1. Type **ftp ftp1.netscape.com.** (In Windows 95/NT, click the Start button, then select Run, and then type in the command.)
2. At the user prompt, type **anonymous** [then press Enter].
3. At the password prompt, type your full e-mail address [press Enter].
4. At the ftp prompt, type **dir** [press Enter]. You'll see a nearly incomprehensible listing. Look for a directory that contains the word "gold." At this writing, that directory was "2.01 gold," and that's what we'll use from this point on.
5. Type **cd 2.01gold** [press Enter].
6. Type **dir** [press Enter].
7. Find the directory for your operating system. For this example, we'll use "windows."
8. Type **cd windows** [press Enter].
9. Type **dir** [press Enter].
10. Type **binary** [press Enter]. This will set the download to binary rather than ASCII status.
11. Type **get g32e201.exe** [press Enter]. This will begin the download process. Note that the program name will probably be different when you actually try it.
12. When the download is complete (the ftp prompt will reappear), type **quit** [press Enter] to get out of the FTP program.

Installing Gold

The way you install the software is entirely dependent on your operating system. Check your software manuals for doing so. For the most part, Macintosh users merely decompress the software and it automatically loads, while Windows users double-click on the .exe program they've downloaded. UNIX users have the usual installation permutations to go through.

Appendix B

Other HTML Editors

Netscape Navigator Gold is an extremely strong HTML authoring tool, but as this book has made clear throughout, its first release is decidedly underpowered. It handles basic HTML superbly, but it offers no support whatsoever for tables, forms, frames, and other advanced and more recent tools. Because of that, you're advised to check out alternative HTML editors, and when you've decided on your favorite, to attach it to Gold via the Editor Preferences dialog box.

This appendix includes only editors available on the Internet either as shareware or freeware. An increasing number of HTML editors are making their way onto the market as fully commercial offerings, and several products such as word processors are adding HTML editing capabilities. Only those available for free evaluation are included here. Even so, there's no attempt at full comprehensiveness. New versions are appearing all the time.

Many of these programs offer only a limited time in which to evaluate them, usually 30 days. Some are completely free, however. Since the status of these programs changes frequently, this appendix won't attempt to categorize them in this way.

HotDog

If you're a Windows user, you *must* try HotDog. It offers support for all HTML features, both the HTML 2 standard and the HTML proposed. It does tables, forms, frames, and much more. It's customizable, giving you the opportunity to create document templates and HTML text "boilerplates." It strips out HTML code if you wish to save HTML documents as pure text files, and it offers a wide range of additional enhancements as well. It's a text-only display, not a WYSIWYG display, but its help screens and wizards are as helpful as anything on the Net. HotDog and HotDog Professional are available from Sausage Software at http://www.sausage.com/.

Live MarkUp and Live Markup Pro

Live Markup was one of the first WYSIWYG Web editors, predating Gold's efforts by more than a year. It is available for free download only for a limited period of time. The HTML commands themselves are accessible either through toolbar icons or via pop-up menus, and the results of your choices are attractively displayed. Live Markup is usually a wee bit behind the other editors in including new HTML codes, because the WYSIWYG representation makes their implementation more difficult to program. If you like Live Markup, keep visiting the home page at http://www.mediatec.com/ to see what new features are about to be added. The program is upgraded frequently.

Web Weaver

This WYSIWYG editor offers a host of useful features, including floating lists of HTML elements, a strong WYSIWYG display, and icons for HTML 2 and HTML 3 (proposed) features. You can create your own lists of often-used HTML codes as well. The program is fast and small, and quite well designed throughout. Retrieve it from http://www.potsdam.edu/HTML_Web_Weaver/About_HTML_WW.html.

BBEdit HTML Extensions

This Macintosh editor supports a good variety of advanced tags, and is frequently updated. You can find it at http://www.uji.es/bbedit-html-extensions.html.

HTML Pro

Offering good support for advanced HTML elements, HTML Pro gives you two windows to work with. The first shows the raw HTML code, while the other displays what the page will look like in your browser. Both windows may be used for editing, with changes in one window mirrored in the other. Available at ftp://ftp.leo.org/pub/comp/platforms/macintosh/communication/tcp/www/authoring/html-pro-108.sit.

HoTMetaL and HoTMetaL Pro

HoTMetaL is one of the most powerful editors available, and one of the strangest as well. Its strength lies in its code-checking, to the extent that it will barely even let you create invalid HTML code. You can get around this, however, which you'll need to do when working with the newest code and some proprietary extensions built into Navigator. The program is fast and well designed, but it takes considerable getting used to. Freeware versions of the program can be downloaded from the SoftQuad site at http://www.sq.com/.

HTML Writer

Another fairly generic HTML editing program is the standalone HTML Writer. Though it supports the usual suite of HTML elements, including forms, it does not handle tables. The most commonly accessible HTML tags are readily available from the program's toolbar, and users may define templates so you don't have to retype common Web page layouts. But perhaps the most impressive feature of HTML Writer is its ability to drag and drop highlighted text. More information about HTML Writer is available at http://lal.cs.byu.edu/people/nosack/index.html.

8Legs Web Studio for Windows 95

A fascinating addition to the HTML editor's field, 8Legs Web Studio offers nothing less than a full Web authoring environment. It's oriented toward project development, and features some of the most unusual and yet most intelligent interface decisions of all the editors out there. It takes practice to use it well, but it's worth the time spent. The 8Legs home page is at http://www.fogsoft.com/~fogsoft/eightleg.htm.

ReVol WebWorker

ReVol WebWorker offers only a text display, but its power lies in its simplicity of design and in its inclusion of virtually every HTML possibility. An excellent choice for your Gold editor add-on, ReVol is fast and easy to use. Retrieve it from http://www.sasknet.com/~tucows/files/rwwv12a.zip.

WebThing

Another innovative design, WebThing lets you import existing documents and convert them instantly into HTML codes. It also offers a strong editing interface throughout. Available at http://id.mind.net/~lutusp/webthing.htm.

Kenn Nesbitt's WebEdit

WebEdit is an excellent HTML creation tool that offers easy start-up and strong maintenance capabilities. It shows HTML code only, but the author is continually updating it to include the latest codes. Download from http://www.nesbitt.com/.

InContext Spider

InContext got its start as a producer of the first more or less easy to use SGML editor, and Spider shows the results of refining that program over the months. It's an excellent if unusual package, and it features full support for the latest Netscape and Microsoft extensions. InContext's home page is located at http://www.incontext.ca/.

Credits

Acrobat screen courtesy of Adobe Systems, Inc.
All-in-One Search page courtesy of William D. Cross
Annette's Twice-Baked Sweet Potatoes recipe courtesy of NCSA
Annex screen courtesy of PC World Online
Applications for Windows 95 screen courtesy of Scott A. Swedorski
Atlantic Records screen courtesy of Atlantic Records Corporation
Borland screen courtesy of Borland International, Inc.
Boston Globe screen courtesy of *The Boston Globe*
Cézanne screen image courtesy of WebMuseum, Paris
CNN Interactive screens courtesy of CNN
Cocktail screen courtesy of HotWired Ventures, LLC.
CompuServe Now screen courtesy of CompuServe Information Services
Cool Site of the Day page courtesy of InfiNet
Corel CMX image screens courtesy of Corel Corporation
Designstein's Universe screen courtesy of Designstein
Discovery Channel Online screen courtesy of the Discovery Channel
Discovery On Air page courtesy of the Discovery Channel
Disney.com News courtesy of Disney
Dkim home page courtesy of D. Kim
Dr. Bob's Virtual En-psych-lopedia screen courtesy of Dr. Robert Hsiung, M.D.
Envoy image screens courtesy of Tumbleweed Software Corporation
Epicurious screens courtesy of CondéNet
Fairplay Products and Services screen courtesy of Fairplay Publications Ltd.
Formula One/NET screens courtesy of Visual Components, Inc.
Gold Rush Tool Chest home page courtesy of Netscape Communications Corporation
Hobby Club Web page template courtesy of Netscape Communications Corporation
How to Join form courtesy of HotWired Ventures, LLC.
InfiNet screen courtesy of InfiNet
Internet Shopping Network feedback page courtesy of Internet Shopping Network
James Gang screens courtesy of James Gang Advertising, Inc.
Java applets courtesy of their respective authors
Levi Strauss Company home page courtesy of Levi Strauss Company
Mario's home page courtesy of Mario van den Ancker

MarketplaceMCI form courtesy of MarketplaceMCI
Mozilla screen courtesy of Netscape Communications Corporation
NCompass Labs screen courtesy of NCompass
NCompass OLE plug-in demo game courtesy of Ncompass Labs
Neil Randall's Sole on the Web screen courtesy of Neil Randall
Netscape Navigator screens courtesy of Netscape Communications Corporation
Off-line Records screen courtesy of the Internet Underground Music Archive
Periodic Table screen courtesy of Mark Winter, Department of Chemistry, University of Sheffield, England
Qualcomm screen courtesy of Qualcomm, Inc.
RockWeb screen courtesy of Silicon Forest Media, Inc.
Silicon Graphics Products and Solutions page courtesy of Silicon Graphics
Software Publishing Corporation WebShow screens courtesy of Software Publishing Corporation
Sportszone screen courtesy of Starwave corporation and ESPN, Inc.
Star Trek Voyager welcome page courtesy of Paramount Pictures
Times Fax screen courtesy of *The New York Times*
Tubescan screen courtesy of MTV Networks
U.S. Robotics home page courtesy of U.S. Robotics
VRML site screens courtesy of their respective authors
WebMuseum screen courtesy of WebMuseum, Paris
Wienermobile screen courtesy of Oscar Mayer Foods Corporation
Yahoo! screens courtesy of Yahoo!

Index

A

B

D

E

F

G

H

I

K

L

M

N

O

T

X

Y

Z